Redeeming the Southern Family

Redeeming the Southern Family

Evangelical Women *and* Domestic Devotion *in the* Antebellum South

SCOTT STEPHAN

The University of Georgia Press | Athens and London

Paperback edition, 2011
© 2008 by the University of Georgia Press
Athens, Georgia 30602
www.ugapress.org
All rights reserved
Set in Adobe Caslon Pro by BookComp, Inc.

Printed digitally in the United States of America

The Library of Congress has cataloged the hardcover
edition of this book as follows:
Stephan, Scott, 1969–
Redeeming the southern family : evangelical women and
domestic devotion in the Antebellum South / Scott
Stephan.
ix, 304 p. ; 24 cm.
Includes bibliographical references (p. 283–293) and index.
ISBN-13: 978-0-8203-3222-2 (hardcover : alk. paper)
ISBN-10: 0-8203-3222-4 (hardcover : alk. paper)
1. Christian women—Religious life.
2. Evangelicalism—Southern States—History—19th century.
3. Southern States—Religious life and customs.
4. Southern States—Church history—19th century. I. Title.
BV4527.S7325 2008
261.8'35850820975—dc22   2008010903

Paperback ISBN-13: 978-0-8203-3980-1
     ISBN-10: 0-8203-3980-6

British Library Cataloging-in-Publication Data available

CONTENTS

Acknowledgments   vii

Introduction. From Cane Ridge to the Bible Belt: Evangelicalism, Gender, and the Southern Household in the Antebellum Era   1

CHAPTER 1
Taming the Second Great Awakening: Evangelical Identity and Worship Patterns in the Antebellum South   21

CHAPTER 2
Courting Women, Courting God: Strenuous Courtships and Holy Unions   59

CHAPTER 3
Improvising on the Ideal: Evangelical Marriages in the Antebellum South   95

CHAPTER 4
"Unto Whom Much Is Given": Childbirth, Child Rearing, and Coming of Age in the Evangelical Home   133

CHAPTER 5
Authoring the Good Death: Illness, Deathbed Narratives, and Women's Authority   183

Epilogue. "We Walk by Faith and Not by Sight": Evangelicals and the Civil War–Era South   221

Appendix. Principal Families   233

Notes   241

Bibliography   283

Index   295

ACKNOWLEDGMENTS

At times it seemed to me that this study of the life course might take my entire lifetime to complete. Fortunately, many wonderful individuals and institutions aided me along this sojourn, making the research, writing, and publication of this volume enjoyable and enriching. The ideas and energy at the core of this study originated from coursework in Steve Stowe's classes as well as research performed for two of his books. From helping me to conceptualize this study to one last pass of the epilogue, Steve has contributed immeasurably to this book. My dissertation committee and several other faculty members at Indiana University also stimulated my thinking about this project within and outside of the classroom: Wendy Gamber, Michael Grossberg, Sarah Knott, Stephen Stein, and Robert Orsi. I also benefited enormously from the informal discussions of my research and writing with staff members at the *Journal of American History*. In between article manuscripts and book reviews, the editors—including Joanne Meyerowitz, David Nord, and David Thelen—and the entire editorial staff graciously supported my research absences.

Thanks to hospitable archivists, trips to repositories across the South were always enjoyable. I single out Elizabeth Dunn at Duke University's Special Collections in Durham, North Carolina; Brian Cuthrell and Henry Fulmer at the South Caroliniana Library in Columbia, South Carolina; the staff of the Southern Historical Collection in Chapel Hill, North Carolina; James Holmberg at the Filson Historical Society in Louisville, Kentucky; the staff of the University of Kentucky's Special Collections in Lexington; Bill Sumners at the Southern Baptist Historical Library and Archives in Nashville, Tennessee; and Wayne Moore at the Tennessee State Library and Archives, also in Nashville. Because travel grants made several of those trips possible, I thank Duke University's Special Collections Women's Studies Travel Grant, the North Caroliniana Society, Indiana University's Department of History, and a Filson Fellowship from the Filson Historical Society. After I completed my dissertation, the Virginia Historical Society provided a timely Mellon Fellowship, which provided access to a treasure trove of additional manuscripts, and Frances Pollard generously shared her insights into the manuscript collections housed there.

Over many cups of coffee and many breakfasts at Bloomington's Village Deli, my good friends and fellow graduate students helped me transform a loose collection of ideas into chapter drafts. John Dichtl, Patrick Ettinger, Lynn Pohl, Paul Schadewald, and Steve Warren merit special mention because they repeatedly pushed me to clarify my ideas and my prose. As the project moved from dissertation to book manuscript, I had the great fortune of receiving feedback from a host of skilled scholars at conference panels and elsewhere, including Phillip Hamilton, Christine Heyrman, Cheryl Junk, Nelson Lankford, Janet Moore Lindman, Paul Murphy, Ami Pflugrad-Jackisch, Beth Barton Schweiger, Randy Sparks, Monica Tetzlaff, and Charles Reagan Wilson. At the *North Carolina Historical Review*, Anne Miller did a fabulous job of editing my article, "Reconsidering the Boundaries of Maternal Authority in the Evangelical Household: The Davis Family of Antebellum Murfreesboro," which appeared in the April 2006 issue and appears here as a portion of chapter 4, courtesy of the North Carolina Office of Archives and History, Historical Publications Section. The anonymous referees for the University of Georgia Press also provided valuable encouragement and critiques of the manuscript. Nancy Grayson and the entire staff of the press have also worked diligently to shepherd this manuscript through the production process. At the copyediting stage, I had the great fortune of working with Ellen Goldlust-Gingrich, who further sharpened my ideas and prose.

The most probing criticism came from my Ball State University colleague, Jim Connolly, who vetted the entire manuscript, giving me valuable direction and insight at a critical juncture. All of my colleagues have graciously supported me during my time at Ball State, but Nicole Etcheson, Carolyn Malone, Kevin Smith, Gail Terry, and Chris Thompson have been unflagging in their enthusiasm for this book. My department chairs—Dick Aquila, Bruce Geelhoed, and Dan Goffman—have also repeatedly aided this project in ways great and small. My graduate students from a colloquium on antebellum America during the fall 2007 semester demonstrated that the teacher-scholar model aids the instructor as much as the students. One graduate student in particular, Chris Werling, kindly aided me during the spring 2007 term, tracking down biographical information on most of the major families in this study. And former student James Appleby offered an insightful layperson's reading of the manuscript.

Perhaps even more than most book projects, this one has benefited from contributions from my entire family. My brothers and their spouses—Doug and Melissa Stephan and Howard and Sheila Stephan—subsidized my research visits to nearby archives by taking fabulous care of me for extended stays. My sister and brother-in-law, Ann and Bob Grilliot, provided continuous reference and genealogical support. When I needed a break, my good friends, Ryan and Jackie Cole, always welcomed me into their house. My wife, Melinda, not only counseled patience and persistence but also designed a database that greatly facilitated my writing. My sons, Isaac and Lucas, offered countless hours of fun away from the manuscript, all the while enriching my work. Finally, I thank my parents, Earl and Mary Stephan, to whom I dedicate this volume, because they taught me more about faith and family than they could possibly know. Although my father did not live to see the completion of this project, his passion for American history and education despite the fact that he never sat in a college classroom have proved a blessing indeed.

Redeeming the Southern Family

INTRODUCTION

From Cane Ridge to the Bible Belt
Evangelicalism, Gender, and the Southern Household in the Antebellum Era

After attending Cumberland Presbyterian services in the spring of 1842, Kentuckian Mary Craddock assessed her spiritual successes and failures and pondered her future:

> [The] spiritual death that reigns in my family occupies much of my thoughts and my anxiety is great, all is dark no prospects of better days before my weak vision but: I often fear that I come too far short of doing my whole duty in different stations in which I have to act, as a wife as a neighbor, as a mistress, and as a Christian, all of which are very important stations and I am convinced I should take great care in letting my light so shine that others seeing my Godly walks and good words ... glorify God.[1]

Craddock's reflections on how evangelical piety shaped her relationship with God and her family illustrate the tensions that white evangelical women experienced across the antebellum South. Her writings illustrate the psychological turmoil of a woman whose family refused to share her faith. Craddock believed that her family's failure to convert suggested that she somehow failed to relay the joys of her faith (and the punishments awaiting those without faith) or, perhaps even more troubling, that her piety possessed some fundamental flaw. And the stakes could not have been greater. Because evangelicals stressed the reunification of redeemed family members in heaven, even one unfulfilled conversion or one renunciation of belief within the family would dash the collective vision of eternal reward. As long as her family remained among the unconverted, Craddock would feel a profound spiritual disquiet.

Yet amid Craddock's deep disappointment existed a boundless optimism and determination. That optimism began with her faith and her role as her family's spiritual shepherd. According to Craddock, these labors touched every facet of her life and relationships, both public and private. She was quite simply never without spiritual purpose or meaning. By voicing her failures to lead her family to God, Craddock professed her unremitting responsibility for the safekeeping of each family member's soul. God's saving grace might be the goal, and it might arrive in her family at any time, but she would lead the charge.

Of course, not all evangelical white women faced Craddock's uphill struggle to convert her family, but as antebellum southern evangelicalism oriented itself around the family, women played an enhanced role in the nurture and discipline of piety among their kin. The challenges of managing vital but complex and uncertain rituals from conversion to death led evangelical women across the South to echo many of Craddock's attitudes: self-importance mixed with self-abnegation, agency alongside resignation, and ultimately failure and anxiety interlaced with success and optimism. And women who sought moral and religious improvement among their family members struggled to do so through example and persuasion because they lived in a society where both secular and religious leaders celebrated male authority and female submission. As these women worked from within the bounds of patriarchal authority, duty to God often put them at odds with the narrowest definitions of womanly authority offered in sermons and religious literature. In the process, as women such as Craddock sought to obtain the ideal of a harmonious family fully redeemed in heaven, they often struggled with themselves and with their family members about how to obtain that paramount goal. Women nonetheless led the charge in the churching of the South. As the number of adult evangelical adherents in the South surged from 25 percent of the population in 1776 to nearly 66 percent in 1835, women often comprised 60 to 65 percent of evangelical adherents on any given Sabbath. Women thus played a central role in both the construction and the maintenance of the Bible Belt.²

Like many southern evangelical women, Craddock embraced hardship and conflict as a means to test and strengthen an individual believer's spiritual mettle. As she wrote in her diary, "It is hard to know our selves in prosperity."³ Evangelicals—particularly women—thus turned to dramatic and often difficult events such as conversion, childbirth, and death to see God's hand in their lives. But they also turned to ordinary events—separations from loved ones, minor illnesses and accidents, daily acts of domestic devotion—to seek God's will in their lives and chart their progress toward salvation. Somewhat contradictorily, as they engaged in a desperate quest for resignation to God's will, their fundamental faith in God's personal presence forced evangelicals to search for religious meaning in the events of their daily lives. That faith also translated into an expectation and even an embrace of hardship as a means to re-create an intimacy with God and better understand God's logic in an immediate fashion. Life's challenges offered spiritual opportunity because these dramatic events, however emotionally and physically painful, closed the spiritual distance between individual believers and God.

The vernacular of spiritual affliction and resignation that flows through the personal writings of evangelicals thus requires interpretive care. First, an inverse relationship often existed between the quest for resignation and personal agency. At precisely those moments when evangelicals executed or planned to execute actions in the name of God, they most often and most loudly proclaimed resignation to God. Second, while evangelicals no doubt felt the personal and spiritual anguish about which they so often wrote, they also viewed these personal and familial crises as a time to realign their everyday lives with their eternal goals. Just as the soul-searching phase of conviction preceded salvation at conversion and often lasted days if not weeks, many evangelicals returned to life's painful chapters to reassess their lives and refine their behaviors. Rather than meaning depression and inaction, this language of affliction and resignation more typically signaled a believer's heightened curiosity and search for personal and familial transformation. These individual interpretations of events in the family and the community also created the opportunity for competing interpretations of God's designs for self and family.⁴

Through careful and even cautious use of the language of Christian resignation and through appeal to the clergy's celebration of women's superior morality and piety, evangelical women pushed to expand the boundaries of patriarchal logic and authority in their everyday lives. From cradle to grave, women borrowed the clerical ascription of their superior morality and piety to construct their role as the family's guardian of the promise of heavenly reunion. Tennessean William McCampbell, the son of a Presbyterian clergyman, advanced this concept most succinctly in a letter to his fiancée, Sue Heiskell: "Our mothers direct us to heaven while they live, then when dead again their spirits hover over us & beckon us upwards." While male and female Protestants both in the North and in the South might have shared this perspective, the language of separate spheres and the construction of the home as church had very different meanings in the two regions. Where northern women used these ascribed qualities to enhance their authority in the home and even to commence political claims through reform activities, the economic realities of slavery and agriculture in the rural South circumscribed the ability of women there to engineer significant social change. Indeed, according to Christine Leigh Heyrman, the evangelical clergy's promotion of female piety within the home possessed distinct advantages in recruiting new male members: "Identifying the home as a church appealed to southern whites because it restored moral authority to the natural family and mitigated evangelical churches' earlier, more exacting, claims on their members' loyalty and affection."[5]

Discipline and authority in the antebellum southern household would thus be returned to the traditional seat of power in the southern family—the patriarch—after a hiatus in the early nineteenth century, with only a wink and a nod in the direction of female authority still attributed to evangelicalism. While that line of logic remains largely persuasive, particularly in the prescriptive literature, as long as the clergy assigned women superior morality and piety, southern women possessed enough leverage to challenge the finer points of patriarchal authority.

Underneath women's refrain of anxiety and resignation toward their public duties existed a resolve that in most cases yielded confirmation of their personal piety as they stepped outside of their households to expand the evangelical ranks. As the nurturers of piety, evangelical women continued to play a central role in the institutional life of antebellum congregations as leaders of Bible studies, Sunday school teachers, fund-raisers, and, in the case of clergymen's wives, providers of direct aid and counsel to the members of the clergy and to the women of the congregation. Even within clerical families, clergymen largely ceded to their wives the responsibility of cultivating piety in their children, a task to which clergymen clearly assigned high priority. And while the rurality of the South undoubtedly frustrated women's efforts to gather in the same fashion as those in urbanizing areas of the North, isolation in the South also presented interpretive opportunities for women. Inclement weather, bad roads, and disease undid the best-laid plans to attend public services, creating renewed focus and opportunity for women's devotional leadership within the household. With clergymen and medical doctors often far from reach, women exercised considerable authority in the management and interpretation of medical and religious crises as they unfolded within households. As key actors in these unfolding dramas, women then possessed the authority to narrate and evaluate these high points of family faith. Custom and law may have granted dominion to men, but men may have ceded some of their authority when doing so did not jeopardize male prerogative or the fundamental social order.[6]

Of course, women's domestic devotional authority remained most firmly rooted within the household, but even here that authority possessed an ebb and flow. Spiritual stewardship of families placed women at the center of God's unfolding mysteries within households, affording women the opportunity to realize spiritual fulfillment. But that sense of self-importance carried a terrible burden when women made themselves accountable for sins within their families. A parent, sibling, or child who died unconverted, for example, caused most women to castigate themselves for failing to shepherd their loved one to God. Even a long string of spiritual triumphs could not guarantee future success because a single perceived failure jeopardized the family's most cherished hope, reunification in heaven. Women's margin of error in managing these domestic rituals always remained slim. And their expansive notion of stewardship—both interpreting God's designs for loved ones and ushering those loved ones to God—led women to both the heights of spiritual joy and the depths of spiritual anguish.[7] Yet because that stewardship brought women's faith alive and made their relationship with God more immediate, they accepted the risks along with the rewards.

While the privileges of male authority remained ensconced among southern evangelicals, it was rarely the blunt instrument outlined in prescriptive literature.[8] Because evangelical men defined their worthiness by proclaiming their genuine enthusiasm for domestic piety during courtship and marriage, they had to answer critiques of their domestic behavior.

Whether lay or clergy, evangelical men crafted many explanations to defend themselves against charges of having neglected their obligations as husbands and fathers. But their persistent defensiveness points to the protracted discussions regarding individual responsibilities within the evangelical marriage. Perhaps most importantly, evangelical men, women, and children alike proclaimed domestic piety as integral to their devotional experiences and practices. "Sunday at a hotel, and among strangers, is not like Sunday at *home*," Richard Collins wrote to his wife and children back home in Kentucky during a business trip in 1857. "I *feel* the difference; and there is nothing that so much reminds me of the dear objects of affection that cling all the closer to their mother in their father's absence, and of *you*, and of all the endearments of home, as the return of the Sabbath."[9] Southern evangelicals uniformly looked to domestic devotion as uniquely fulfilling.

More than a study of authority within the household, this volume illuminates the experiential world of southern evangelicals. Such concerns typically take a backseat in studies of the southern household or of the construction of an evangelical Confederacy in the late antebellum era, which center primarily on authority, rhetoric, and ideology. As Beth Barton Schweiger points out, studies of southern evangelicalism have typically sought to find either resistance (most often among slaves) or accommodation (most often among white southerners) to the South's political economy. But "the vast territory between accommodation and resistance," she argues, "is the space in which slave converts and women lived in the Old South. Neither evangelical women nor Christian slaves began a revolution, but this fact does not begin to tell the story of their lives."[10] The clergy legitimated patriarchal authority, and women spoke of their resignation to God's will, but as Schweiger suggests, to take those claims as the defining features of southern evangelicalism misses the point that most southern evangelicals lived well inside those polarities in their daily lives. All too often, the religious experiences and practices about which southern evangelicals wrote with such passion fail to fit neat dichotomies such as accommodation and resistance: the perverse thrill an evangelical felt when an irreligious family member met his demise at the hands of liquor; the warmth of long-separated female relatives recalling childhood services they attended together and anticipating heaven as an opportunity to rekindle that emotional and spiritual warmth; a woman's anticipation and preparation for life and death at childbirth; the vexation of a young suitor when a woman breaks off a courtship in the name of God; the joy and relief of witnessing a child convert; the anguish of creating a deathbed narrative that matched evangelical expectations even when events did not match prescription. Examining how white evangelical women's efforts to redeem their families created dynamic relationships among self, family, congregation, community, and God reveals that women found their work enriching and challenging as well as vexing. They also always found their work incomplete. They might not have shared the optimism of northern white reformers who believed that sin could be eradicated from society, but southern white women remained active and engaged in the battles against sin in their families and communities, never resigned and rarely isolated. Thus, as women struggled to redeem their families, they found their taxing work uniquely meaningful, offering historians an explanation for women's persistent domination of antebellum southern evangelical congregations in spite of the clergy's rhetorical celebrations of male authority.

To capture the ways in which antebellum southern evangelicalism oriented itself around the family and the ways in which women took control over many of the most vital domestic rituals, this book explores three levels of evangelical family life: cosmology, prescribed morality, and lived experience. The interplay of outlook, ideals, and everyday action set in motion a dynamic relationship between faith and family.

Cosmology refers to the way in which southern evangelicals ordered their world. Locating a distinctively "evangelical" outlook in the nineteenth-century South, particularly when the history of antebellum southern evangelicalism has so often been told as the co-optation of evangelical dissenters into the southern mainstream, may seem an uphill task. Yet as chapter 1 demonstrates, southern white evangelicals in the 1830s, 1840s, and 1850s continually set themselves apart from their non-evangelical neighbors and kin. Some of these actions remained publicly visible: church attendance, Sabbatarianism, and avoidance of drink and dancing. But the touchstone of evangelical identity remained the personal conversion experience. As Donald Mathews notes, evangelicalism formed a shared sensibility across denominations, including a "personal relationship with God in Christ, established through the direct action of the Holy Spirit," that culminates in spiritual rebirth through a personal conversion and results in a "life of holiness characterized by religious devotion, moral discipline, and missionary zeal." In a later essay, Mathews adds, "This surprising assurance and its complementary expressiveness offended orthodox Calvinists, traditional Episcopalians, and skeptical rationalists" but established "the dominant religious mood of the South[, which] rested nonetheless on subjective confirmation of Christian truth and personal assurance following repentance and renovation." Thus, in spite of the divergent Baptist, Methodist, and Presbyterian theological traditions, scholars continue to use words such as *mood*, *force*, and *emphasis* to demonstrate how common ground created by these values created a shared sensibility across denominations.[11]

Although much of the story that follows centers on how individual evangelicals sorted through God's designs in their lives, they naturally relied heavily on prescribed morality, particularly clerical advice received while seated in the pews or from evangelical newspapers, sermons, and religious tracts. For the most part, these writings reminded southerners of the necessity of hierarchical order in a Christian society. Sprinkling advice literature aimed at children, courting couples, parents, slaveholders, and the dying throughout the relevant chapters here underscores the clergy's faith that Christianity not only shaped individual converts' character but also led to a Christian society with Christian families as its fundamental building block. But in defining familial obligations, clergymen encountered one incongruity that frustrated their best efforts to demonstrate that a Christian family and society operated without friction or contest. In defining the respective roles of husbands and wives, clergymen conferred ultimate authority on the family patriarch yet ascribed unquestioned moral influence within the home to his wife. That ambiguity allowed women a considerable degree of latitude in shaping family relationships and mores. Of course, by acknowledging the patriarch's authority, evangelical prescription also suggested the speed with which moral power could turn to powerlessness for evangelical women. But as chapter 3 discusses, the tensions contained within the clergy's attempts to fashion clear-cut and stable roles for individual family members suggest some of the gaps within evangelical ideology that sustained fluid interpretations of moral authority.

To grasp how southerners worked through such incongruities, this analysis centers on the lived experience of evangelicals through their personal writings. "Lived religion," a cultural approach to the study of religion, stresses the "everyday thinking and doing of lay men and women" and begins to address these tensions and ambiguities. Based on many methodological traditions ranging from ritual theory to sociology to cultural anthropology, the advocates of lived religion contend that religion "comes into being in an ongoing, dynamic relationship with the realities of everyday life." Consequently, religion is not a static element in a practitioner's life but rather constitutes how people "live in, with, through, and against the religious idioms available to them in culture." In the process, little remains fixed in the lives of the faithful. As Robert Orsi emphatically reminds historians, even as individuals often subverted cultural conventions in their practice of faith, so too should historians recall "religion's complicity in sustaining structures and patterns of alienation and domination."[12] Lived religion thus opens up the possibility of taking evangelical belief seriously while seeing how everyday practice extended and limited the authority of its practitioners.

As other scholars note, evangelical laywomen spilled considerably more ink than did their husbands in reflecting on God's role in everyday life. Women not only formed the majority of congregants in evangelical denominations but also served as the hub of devotional nurture and discipline within the family. At times everyone in the household plainly acknowledged a woman's primacy as religious custodian, while at other times women operated more stealthily to exert their influence. Nevertheless, the practice and experience of domestic devotion always centered on women. Consequently, while men play vital roles throughout this volume, particularly in the chapters dedicated to courtship and marriage, evangelical women's thoughts and opinions form the core of this analysis because they dominated domestic evangelical devotion.[13]

To emphasize the commonalities of evangelical faiths in this period, however, does not imply that southern evangelicalism lacked intellectual and theological rigor or that these denominations did not retain significant theological differences.[14] Indeed, this book stresses the idea that antebellum evangelicals remained passionately committed to the experiential side of their faith as well as deeply committed to using their faith to unlock God's designs in their everyday lives. Just as southern evangelicals hoped for emotionally charged conversions and prayed fervently as individuals and families, so too did they turn to their Bibles and their clergymen for aid in grasping God's designs. In spite of evangelicals' stress on holiness, spreading the Word, and the need to define their religious commitments in contradistinction to their nonevangelical neighbors, the differences between nonevangelicals and evangelicals certainly narrowed at points in the life course. All too many southern mothers mourned the loss of their

From Cane Ridge to the Bible Belt 9

children or worried that their children were growing up too quickly. Jan Lewis, for example, forcefully concludes that in early national Virginia, "gentry and evangelical values would meld, creating for Virginians what we recognize as nineteenth-century middle-class culture."[15] Yet evangelicalism's move from the margins to the mainstream of southern society, symbolizing the social shift away from restraint and formalism and toward emotionalism and family, had costs as well as benefits: "Men and women struggled with their culture's new dilemma: Feeling was prized, yet many feelings could hurt."[16] Faith, however, helped evangelicals use those feelings to find transcendence. And while some people fell victim to the combination of self-pity and melancholy anticipated by Lewis, many more successfully transformed doubt and anxiety into spiritual renewal. This process, described by A. Gregory Schneider as "self-mortification" among early nineteenth-century Methodists in the Ohio River Valley, "began with the conversion process, but dying with Christ never ceased in this life. The dying and rising conflicts of conversion were the model for recurring skirmishes of the soul. The battle continued in one form or another until believers finally triumphed in 'happy deaths.'"[17] This process was supercharged for women, who so often claimed responsibility for managing the southern family's piety and identifying the religious import of events that affected the entire family. Consequently, women readily embraced hardship as an opportunity to reveal God's hand in their everyday lives and strip their piety of artifice.

More than capturing women's religious thinking, this volume seeks to place individual women in the relationships that mattered most to them—that is, not only with God but also with their parents, their lovers, their slaves, and their extended families. A series of family case studies demonstrates how conversion experiences shaped women's expectations for their children, how separations from extended families reshaped women's personal devotion, and how work at loved ones' deathbeds transformed women's notions of heaven. These brief biographies permit the exploration of women's devotional lives across time, across geography, and across families. This approach moves beyond the moment of individual conversion to emphasize the lifelong individual and familial pilgrimage that antebellum evangelicals used to gauge their ultimate success and failure as Christians.[18] The conversion process, which so richly captured the self-abnegation of the sinner and the self-affirmation of the saved, merely formed a starting point for a lifelong struggle for individual and family devotional fulfillment. Case studies of evangelical families also permit the examination of the development and evolution of relationships, personalities, and piety over time and over the life course, giving insight into not only the highs and lows but also the everyday quality of evangelical piety. Manuscript collections featuring documents that offer detailed religious reflections, provide viewpoints from multiple family members, and span many years form the bulk of the sources analyzed.

The families profiled here range widely across denomination and geography. In addition to mainline evangelical denominations such as the Baptists, Presbyterians, and Methodists, the sample includes families from such splinter groups as the Methodist Protestant Church and the Cumberland Presbyterian Church. The families also stretch across the South because attention to any given family almost invariably leads in many geographic directions. For example, members of the Collins and Cox families of Maysville, Kentucky, married and moved down the Ohio River Valley to Covington and Louisville. Other separations occurred as part of the quest for economic improvement: Jones Fuller and his wife, Anna, left her mother behind in North Carolina when they moved to Mobile, Alabama, where he hoped to make his fortune as a cotton broker. Similarly, Cary Whitaker left North Carolina for northern Florida in pursuit of fortunes in cotton. And many members of the clergy migrated out of professional obligation. Although some merely moved back and forth across the North Carolina–Virginia border, others pursued emerging congregations in such faraway states as Alabama, Mississippi, and Arkansas.

Using case studies sheds light on the interplay among source types—particularly between women's journals and correspondence. Journals principally provided women with an outlet for their individual sins and failures, while correspondence offered them an outlet through which to celebrate spiritual successes and to cajole family members to stay the course. Women who offered blistering accounts of their own moral and spiritual failings in their diaries often provided equally scathing criticisms of family members' piety and behavior in their correspondence. Evangelical women sought to use both media toward the same goal—shepherding their families to heaven—but did so from dramatically different angles. Women's diaries have often been the mainstay of studies of southern women's piety, while correspondence—a vital middle layer of give-and-take among family members on various counts of religiously informed ideas and ideals—has often been downplayed. Perhaps no subject here showcases the dynamic relationship between these sources and findings as Anne Davis. In her diary, she unfailingly pilloried herself and her faith, revealing, in Elizabeth Fox-Genovese's words, "a woman wracked by spiritual torment and a deep sense of unworthiness."[19] But even within her journal, Davis occasionally betrayed a sense of militancy. In one journal entry, she swung from her typical self-loathing, describing herself as the Lord's "unworthy child," to joy at numbering herself among the "militant" Methodists, noting that she "would greatly prefer death, to having my name erased from the church of my choice."[20] In her correspondence, however, she aimed directly at her children and occasionally her husband. Davis and others like her whose diaries have become part of the canon of southern social history but whose correspondence has received considerably less attention most fully illustrate the importance of establishing familial and historical context.[21] While some of the cases presented here shed new light on families and sources familiar to students of antebellum southern history (for example, the Davises, the Bumpasses, and Bethells), many others (the Douglasses and Collinses) have received little if any scholarly notice.[22]

By focusing on family and piety, this study raises questions that differ from the those addressed in typical studies of antebellum southern evangelicalism, which focus on a particular denomination or era. Such works have illuminated important differences in denominational traditions and how those practices shaped membership and member discipline. Outside of the meetinghouse, however, where evangelicals confronted the challenges of child rearing, courtship, and death, the fine points of theology and doctrine often lost much of their edge. Denominational boundaries appear to have been most sharply drawn among first-generation evangelicals, who independently chose their denominational affiliations, and among evangelicals on the southern frontier, who struggled to rebuild their denominations in sparsely settled areas. In terms of formal worship, a strong degree of cross-denominational cooperation existed because the faithful enjoyed attending services of other evangelical denominations or having ministers from other evangelical denominations make guest appearances (see chap. 1). Such friendly exchanges might raise awareness of denominational differences but were largely overshadowed by the larger, ecumenical struggle to convert the unconverted. Most of the individuals examined here were second- or third-generation evangelicals who inherited their denominational affiliations. Therefore, tracing piety through the outlines of the family tree rather than by denominational or state boundaries provides greater illumination of the dynamics of devotion. Similarly, while several scholars explore the gendered dynamics of authority within congregations using church records, particularly from church tribunals where adult members faced suspension or expulsion for ethical lapses, this study does not use those records because it centers on domestic devotion, an arena in which the patriarch largely superseded the clergyman as arbiter of propriety, religious and secular. Most importantly, with the exception of the Reverend John Poulton (see epilogue), the subjects here did not find themselves accused of misdeeds by their fellow congregants.

Despite its benefits, this approach limits the ability to address issues of class and race. Although some studies devoted to particular regions or states have examined local institutional records that offer glimpses into the lives of the South's nonliterate and nonslaveholding classes, this volume replicates the bias toward well-educated and wealthy southerners who possessed the training and leisure to write at length about their daily lives. The expanding ranks of black evangelicals, free and enslaved, therefore remain largely outside the scope of this study, although they do appear when whites' diaries and correspondence referred to slaves in matters spiritual. Not surprisingly, slaves had relatively little direct impact on white southerners' courtship and marriage but factored into southern evangelicals' thinking regarding conversion, household management, and death. But even here, when celebrating either the beginning or end of a slave's spiritual life, white evangelicals tended to note such events in a rather matter-of-fact fashion if at all, a sharp contrast to the detailed and ongoing religious ruminations afforded to white kin. Indeed, the evangelical whites who discussed their slaves' piety provide much more insight into whites' piety than into the slaves themselves. Writing to her husband, James Douglass, Frances Douglass observed that for the third time in the recent weeks a slave had discovered one of Rev. Douglass's embroidered handkerchiefs along the road and returned it to her, thus illustrating that during their separation, "he who keepeth Israel neither slumbers nor sleeps; & my husband is more tenderly cared for than even his wife could manifest."[23] Like Frances Douglass, most evangelical whites noted slaves only in the background of their correspondence and journals—individuals who offered unique challenges to managing households or who offered an index of God's providentialism but who rarely merited any detailed analysis of their faith.[24] Other scholars note the relative absence of slaves from correspondence among white slaveholders, but evangelical whites may have faced particular challenges in fitting their troublesome relationships with their slaves into their idealized notions of domestic sanctuaries on earth and in heaven."[25]

This book explores, in the formulation suggested by Cynthia Lynn Lyerly, both "what religion did *to* women" and "what religion did *for* women."[26] The first issue, which "presupposes patriarchal oppression," has constituted the traditional starting point for most studies of evangelical women in the antebellum South. The second subject, which originates from the assumption of female empowerment, has served as the starting point for most studies of evangelical women in the antebellum North. By asking both sets of questions simultaneously, as Lyerly suggests, scholars can appreciate the values and experiences that motivated women to join evangelical congregations while acknowledging the real limits of women's authority and the burdens they bore. Using these questions to craft a study of lived religion within the southern household begins a movement from a static, individualistic piety centered on conversion to a dynamic and familial struggle over the meaning and experience of faith in everyday settings that helps explain why women continued to comprise the majority of adherents in most antebellum congregations.[27]

The individualization of antebellum southern evangelicalism, coupled with its sanctification of the southern social order, has been a dominant and persuasive theme in explaining the nineteenth-century South's revivalism, racism, and patriarchy. When southern evangelicalism first received sustained scholarly attention in the 1960s and 1970s, historians attempted to establish connections among racism, parochialism, and revivalism in the construction of white evangelical institutions. In a broad-ranging critique of southern evangelicalism written during the civil rights era, Sam Hill argues that southern evangelicalism's focus on individual salvation short-circuited its ability to critique a slave society and generate social action.[28] John Boles elaborates on that theme and pinpoints its origins in the 1801 Cane Ridge revival and those that followed. Henceforward, Boles contends, "The southern Christian was taught to accept the world and try to perfect his soul." Evangelicalism created an "orthodox South, a South resistant to change and criticism in every form."[29] More recently, state-focused studies on the early national South contend that evangelicalism at best temporized the political, economic, and racial inequality that dominated the South.[30]

The scholarly emphasis on southern evangelicalism's individual salvation and exclusion of social reform has met with particular success in demonstrating how members of the clergy catered to the interests of slaveholders and patriarchs as a means of establishing ministries, constructing meetinghouses, and developing publishing and educational enterprises. Even where denominational structures remained weak, clergymen relied on patriarchs for access to their families because the clergy depended financially on attracting men of at least modest means.[31] With the professionalization of the evangelical clergy came their well-known scriptural defenses of slavery, an energized mission to the slaves aimed at reinforcing the interests of slaveholders, and ultimately the sectional division of Baptists and Methodists in 1844–45 over the issue of slaveholding clergy.[32] Finally, in stark contrast to northern evangelicalism's reform ethos, southern evangelicalism's skittish attitude toward nearly every reform movement confirmed its alignment with the South's dominant social order.[33]

Scholars of family and gender relations in the antebellum South note the ways in which southern patriarchs turned to evangelicalism to legitimize their authority over the members of their households, both white and black. As Anne Firor Scott notes in her landmark study of nineteenth-century southern women, *lord* and *master* interchangeably identified God and husband, and "any tendency on the part of any members of the system to assert themselves against the master threatened the whole, and therefore slavery itself."[34] Southern historians have developed and refined examinations of these links among patriarchy, evangelicalism, and slavery to showcase fundamental social and economic tensions between the antebellum North and South. Borrowing Catherine Clinton's terminology, Elizabeth Fox-Genovese laments the "New Englandization" of American women's history, arguing that southern women could never leverage evangelicalism's ascription of feminine piety and virtue within and beyond the home because of the "persistence in the South of the household as the dominant unit of production and reproduction." Historians thus typically emphasize the ways in which male authority in an overwhelmingly rural setting shaped family life in the antebellum South.[35]

Historians disagree, however, on evangelicalism's consequences for elite white women. Where Scott finds that some antebellum women voiced limited discontent before the Civil War, they targeted slavery rather than familial relations or religious institutions. Even though Clinton notes that southern women's "personal moral duty went hand in hand with an evangelical mission to safeguard the souls of society," those claims vanished quickly in the face of planters who "would not tolerate female temper, ... demanding compliance without complaint."[36] Jean E. Friedman concludes that southern white evangelical women not only failed to seek to reform society in the same fashion as did northern women but also "internalized" their "frustrations, anxieties, and resentments." Where Scott hears muffled discontent and Friedman sees psychological stress if not damage, Fox-Genovese identifies a struggle for Christian perfection framed against slaveholding women's larger acceptance of inequality within the family and southern society.[37] Fox-Genovese argues that diarists such as Davis "frequently turned to their journals to gain a sense of control over their lives, as well as to investigate how well they were living up to their own standards."[38] Rather than reflecting failure, according to Fox-Genovese, these journals anchored elite women in a slaveholding society, allowing them to thrive in circumscribed roles within their families and communities. That authority, however, required slaveholding women to acknowledge their divinely sanctioned inferiority to their husbands.[39]

Stephanie McCurry's study of yeomen in South Carolina's Low Country further argues that the conviction that all white men deserved unquestioned domestic authority forged a powerful bond that crossed class boundaries. As the standard-bearers of patriarchy, evangelical clergymen and their prescriptions on domestic authority played a pivotal role in McCurry's analysis. "Even modest assumptions of female moral authority," she contends, "met with unflinching opposition" from clergymen and patriarchs alike. With women's conversions frequently occurring in late adolescence, marriage only hastened the return of women's powerlessness in the domestic sphere. Similarly, any nod to superior female virtue was only a necessary step in making "the submission of the self the apotheosis of womanhood." "By the very definition of duty Christian women embraced," McCurry concludes, "they were rendered agents of their own subordination and of the sacralization of domestic dependences and masterly identity."[40] Where conflict existed in South Carolina's Low Country, it occurred largely beyond the household and exclusively among men. Historians thus couple the ideologies of patriarchy and evangelicalism to demonstrate how the two forged a South that bore little resemblance to the antebellum North. Where northern white women used evangelical piety as a means to configure their homes into sanctuaries and reform public morality, southern white women remained largely submissive in the name of their piety while living on widely scattered farms and plantations.[41]

But recent studies of the early nineteenth century and even institutional evangelicalism in the antebellum era raise new interpretive challenges by addressing what evangelicalism did *for* women, particularly in the institutional context of rapidly expanding denominations. In stark contrast to the joint emphasis on individualism and accommodation among evangelicals in the late eighteenth and early nineteenth centuries, several recent works highlight the collective vision of early evangelicalism's radically democratic message and its unflinching attack on the South's social and racial inequalities. In attempting to understand how converts became regular church members, historians such as Heyrman and Lyerly illustrate how an evangelical message centered on the equality of all believers ripped apart the social fabric of the early national South. Where authority in both the home and society of the Revolutionary-era South followed clearly delineated hierarchies of race, class, and gender, early evangelical clergymen filled their ranks with the secular order's disaffected—blacks, the middling and poor, women, and youth. Elite white men looked on with alarm as youthful adherents recounted religious dreams and visions, women and blacks exhorted others to join in, and allegiance and discipline switched from the patriarch and the family to the clergyman and the congregation. More than a mere enumeration of evangelical growth, these studies delve into the diverse ways in which evangelical ideology resonated with so many southerners, showing religion as a unique and vital force over which proponents and opponents bitterly fought.[42] For these scholars, the construction of the Bible Belt can best be understood as a successful counterculture movement. However, even those who argue that the South experienced a brief window of inclusiveness and egalitarianism in the early national era suggest that by the 1820s at the very latest, southern evangelicals had accommodated themselves and their values to the South's prevailing racial, class, and gender hierarchies.

Studies of institutional evangelicalism reveal tensions between evangelicalism's sectarian values and its place in the antebellum South. Several scholars point to evidence that many Baptist congregations granted female members limited voting privileges, particularly in the area of discipline.[43] Contrary to earlier arguments that abolitionism stunted virtually all reform efforts in the Old South, John W. Quist demonstrates that evangelicals in Tuscaloosa County, Alabama, rivaled their Washtenaw

County, Michigan, counterparts in distributing religious tracts, forming Sunday schools, and waging temperance crusades.⁴⁴ Focusing on denomination building rather than moral reform, Schweiger similarly argues that the professionalization of Virginia's Baptist and Methodist clergy paralleled such efforts among their northern counterparts. Earlier historians viewed the proslavery positions that led to the sectional split of the Baptist and Methodist denominations in the mid-1840s as the nadir of southern evangelical morality. Schweiger instead stresses that the separation forced southerners to accelerate the modernization and bureaucratization of their denominational structure.⁴⁵ Yet even as these studies of religious history have forced a rethinking of the formula of an orthodox and homogenous evangelical culture beholden to the South's political economy, the research has focused on professional and denominational sources and on the meetinghouse rather than the household.

These studies force a reconsideration of Mathews's point that southern evangelicalism contained deep tensions caused by the inherent conflicts among its egalitarian heritage, its antebellum embrace of hierarchy, and the emergent authority of women within the household.⁴⁶ Indeed, nowhere is the disjunction between prescription and practice greater than among the architects of religious patriarchy, southern clergymen, who were also the first to violate its most stringent limitations on feminine authority. Because a ministry required building and maintaining consensus, most clergymen had little choice but to draw their spouses directly into the management of their congregations, particularly to interact with the female congregants in Sunday schools, during Bible studies, and socially. And whenever money or resources required mobilization, the clergy quickly turned to female parishioners for fund-raising and support. Even women and men who labored tirelessly on behalf of their congregations celebrated domestic devotion as a uniquely fulfilling site of spirituality that held the promise they so often tied to their faith—the everlasting family. In spite of the frequency with which white evangelicals spoke of this ultimate goal, they knew that the journey would require setbacks and celebrations, conflict and consensus, and the work of a pious woman.

Mary Craddock was indeed fighting an uphill battle to convert her family to her Presbyterian faith. But to see her failure merely as a woman's individual defeat borne with Christian resignation or an illustration of southern women's powerlessness in a patriarchal culture misses the manifold ways in which evangelicalism informed Craddock's behavior and the persistent conflict within her household over individual and familial definitions of morality and piety. In this light, southern evangelicalism may have thus retained some elements of its sectarian edge, including its ability to unsettle family relations and to permit many women access to personal and public importance.

CHAPTER 1

Taming the Second Great Awakening
Evangelical Identity and Worship Patterns in the Antebellum South

Historians often point to the early republic's "anxious bench"—a row of seats prominently placed between the audience and the preachers—as the embodiment of American revivalism during the Second Great Awakening. As individual sinners moved to the anxious bench, they publicly testified to their inward, personal struggle. In the process, they often sought the assistance of the South's most socially marginal—the poor, blacks, and women—in finding a balm for their souls' anguish. To go along with the conviction of their own sinfulness, individuals hoped to obtain assurance of salvation and thus release from their personal torment. The anxious bench captures many vital themes of American Protestantism in this era: how conversions at outdoor camp meetings attended by all classes and races of southerners triggered an explosion of Protestant denominations throughout the nation and how a group of unlettered clergymen and laypeople seized this movement's democratic message and its practices. In the words of Cynthia Lynn Lyerly, "One of the enduring aspects of early Methodism"—and of other evangelical denominations of the era—was "the expansion of human agency" so that "converts from all walks of life found in the church a sense of power and control over their own destiny."[1]

As Lyerly and other scholars point out, however, those gains proved short-lived thanks to the southern evangelical clergy's shift from critics to defenders of southern culture. Though the mechanics and timing of that transformation remain murky, the clergy's embrace of slavery, combined with southern evangelicals' quest for institutional respectability in the form of the ever-expanding numbers of churches and schools, made the once-distant relationship between evangelical clergy and slaveholders increasingly cozy. Scholars chart this new antebellum trajectory in a number of ways: the rise of slave missions, theological defenses of slavery against abolitionism, denominational schisms to defend the right of slaveholding clergy, and clerical calls for womanly deference to patriarchal authority. With so much scholarly attention centered on the marriage of evangelicalism and the South's hierarchies of race and gender, the question of whether evangelicals and evangelical denominations differed in any significant way from nonevangelicals has not been adequately explored; nor has a corollary centering on evangelical practice: as the evangelical message incorporated a vociferous defense of slavery that seemingly brooked no challenges to its logic, how did clergymen exercise such stout control over their message to their white congregations? In other words, how did lay and clerical evangelicals reconcile the radical egalitarianism of the early national era with the apparent need for consensus and conformity in the antebellum era?

The South's evangelical clergy may have presented a united front in defense of slavery, but the laity and clergy rarely enjoyed such unanimity in their communities, their congregations, or their families. Evangelicals continued to base their identity—and membership—on the conversion experience. Protracted meetings and a deemphasis on the emotionalism of the conversion experience may have tamed the conversion experience since its heyday of raucous, outdoor camp meetings, but evangelical identity still hinged on a withering assessment of self. That "consuming inwardness," as Christine Leigh Heyrman describes it, transformed the individual sinner's worthlessness into a unique experience that held profound importance for sinner, congregation, and community: "Every individual triumph over sin advanced the kingdom of God, furthered the providential plan for the unfolding of human history, and cast its mite into the mounting treasury of cosmic triumph."[2]

A penetrating examination of the soul not only remained vital to the antebellum conversion process but also unleashed a lifetime quest to experience that spiritual intimacy with God anew and celebrate this process with fellow believers. The Reverend James Douglass asked his readers to grasp both the profundity of their transformation at conversion and the incompleteness of that process: "Your soul is a diamond, of infinite value, just hewn out of nature's quarry, by the grace of God; and now, during the brief and uncertain period of its deposit, in your hands, you are unceasingly to employ yourself upon it, until the polished stone shall bear upon it, indelibly engraven, the expression image of its Maker's person, and fully and faithfully reflect his glory." It would be limiting to equate antebellum evangelicalism solely with the conversion experience. However, if conversion is understood as a process that unfolded repeatedly over the course of the individual's life and relationships, pivots between self-effacement and self-importance, between spiritual anguish and spiritual ecstasy, and between spiritual decay and spiritual renewal emerge as part of the believer's larger pilgrimage toward life eternal. Indeed, moving from lessons centered on precious stones to biblical precept, Douglass asked, if Jesus "had finished his work on the earth" by the age of thirty-three, "what good work will you have finished by the same age?"[3]

The individual conversion process remained a defining element of antebellum evangelical identity, but fellow believers expected outward manifestations of the inner spirituality that led to conversion. Even everyday events forcefully confirmed God's presence and the faithful's identity as evangelicals. Whether gauging a community's level of religious activity on the Sabbath or watching who partook of alcoholic drinks at social functions, evangelicals readily monitored the level of piety among those with whom they interacted. When individuals chose to stray from God's prescriptions against a variety of vices, evangelicals eagerly anticipated the sinners' demise. The physical expiration of the alcoholic or the duelist offered powerful testimony that sins committed on earth condemned the irreligious to a miserable existence here as well as in the hereafter. Antebellum evangelicals embraced the moral lessons provided by such events within their families; believers genuinely mourned the loss of their dissolute kin but nonetheless relished the reaffirmation of their piety and evangelical lifestyle.

While evangelical identity was often constructed in opposition to secular southerners, it was also positively reaffirmed through shared devotion at the meetinghouse. Many outstanding studies of evangelicalism in the antebellum South demonstrate the clergy's intellectual rigor, dynamic organization building, and success at disciplining members, but these works rely predominantly on the professional records of the clergy. The informal channels of clergy and lay correspondence and diaries illuminate the concerns of those in power that their message (and authority) might fail to persuade on any given Sunday.[4] No one defined the community of believers more than the clergyman who led them in devotion. In addition to providing sacraments, ministers offered intellectual stimulation, moral leadership, zealousness, and pastoral care. When any of those needs went unfulfilled, the men and women of the congregation registered their criticism through both formal and informal channels. Evangelical clergymen in the antebellum South may have increasingly consolidated their authority over their congregations and reined in many of the populist elements of authority that typified evangelical practices in the early national era, but clergymen always knew that their message and their work would be critically consumed rather than passively accepted.[5]

Like the meetinghouse but with different purposes, the home served as a sanctuary for the faithful. With the growing domesticization of evangelicalism—that is, a move toward denominations consisting largely of collections of families rather than collections of unrelated individuals—the home became a vital center of spiritual fulfillment in the eyes of both clergy and laity. As Colleen McDannell summarizes in her study of antebellum domestic piety, "Each home could be an individual, privately owned, sanctified religious community."[6] Yet domestic devotion carried a particular set of challenges. Becoming an evangelical pilgrim involved acceptance of afflictions along with blessings. Indeed, evangelicals embraced trials as part of God's larger design to redirect the believer's interest from temporal matters toward matters of eternal welfare. This quest to mortify self-interest in favor of seeking God's will in daily life led evangelicals, according to A. Gregory Schneider, to look at their spiritual lives as "a series of small crucifixions" in which "momentary pain, sorrow, or suffering, would be transformed, by the grace of Christ, into lasting pleasure, joy, and comfort."[7] Like the camp meetings or the meetinghouse, the home thus held an uneasy place in the southern evangelical imagination: a site of both unique spiritual nourishment and intense devotional struggle for both the individual and the family. But those domestic devotional struggles offered new interpretive roles and challenges to women within the household. Thus, even as women were marginalized in their evangelical transformation from sects to denominations, opportunities for religious leadership often emerged within the family.

Defining Evangelical Identity through Everyday Relationships

Every journey beyond their homes or sanctuaries offered evangelicals the potential for a jarring rediscovery of the differences between themselves and nonevangelicals. Such realizations occurred most often when evangelicals encountered individuals engaged in activities deemed off-limits—drinking alcohol, dueling, gambling, dancing, or profaning the Sabbath, among others. Like their predecessors during the early republic, evangelicals' ability to label such ordinary activities forbidden enabled them "to make their rejection of the world a concrete act as well as an intellectual belief." More than merely sinful, these activities embodied "worldliness," the web of desires and behaviors on which all believers turned their backs after conversion. This persistent equation of lifestyle with religious belief meant that evangelicals daily carried their religious identity into their communities.[8]

Of course, sin and worldliness were never the exclusive domain of nonevangelicals. Indeed, evangelicals spent considerable energy attempting to exorcise a host of temptations, particularly dancing, novel reading, and anti-Sabbatarianism. Although participation in those activities quickly set evangelicals in search of forgiveness, some borderline sins, such as letter writing on the Sabbath, were increasingly deemed morally acceptable in the name of domestic devotion. Antebellum evangelicals' handling such encounters provides a window into the public and everyday dimensions of their faith. Many social behaviors still differentiated evangelicals from their irreligious neighbors, but their struggle to rationalize lesser offenses sheds light on the shifting place of discipline in evangelical denominations, away from the congregation and to the family and the individual. Evangelicals jettisoned many of the sectarian values—particularly the uneasiness toward slavery—that put them sharply at odds with the secular South in the early national era, but their belief system still created friction with their nonreligious neighbors in a myriad of ordinary ways.[9] But even as white evangelicals used their missionary endeavors to convert slaves, they exhibited uncertainty and fear toward coreligionists of color.

Eliza Leland discovered that the South Carolina community where her son lived neglected the Gospel entirely, even on Sundays: "Another sacred day in this heathen land O how my heart bleeds for this people—no gospel priviliges yet they are fully satisfied. The Sabbath a day for visiting and recreation." With few opportunities for formal worship, Leland paused to pray for the religious instruction and moral improvement of the community and her son: "I went over into the woods to suplicate for them and for my poor child whose lot is cast in this land, and for the extention of the redeemers kingdom."[10] Like many other evangelicals, Leland used the Sabbath as a barometer of a community's piety.

James Douglass took a more direct approach to improving the South's religious landscape. A two-day trip via stagecoach in 1836 created a ready-made audience for religious conversation. Disappointed at first that none of his fellow passengers shared his faith, Rev. Douglass quickly seized the opportunity to proselytize, although he steadied his nerves before launching into his efforts for fear he might be rebuked. On learning that two passengers' itineraries had been altered by the stagecoach's operator, Douglass sensed that "the Lord put them into my company, & made me their pastor for a couple of days." The passengers responded lukewarmly to Douglass's first attempt, but then the horses became frightened and crashed the coach into a tree. The driver "swore profanely" as he dislodged the coach from the brush, but Douglass saw the incident differently, as evidence of Providence, telling the driver that "he ought not to swear after such a preservation. He looked at me with surprize & laughed." Douglass dismissed the driver's response—"How little are the wicked sensible of God's Providence about them"—and continued his religious instruction of his fellow passengers after the coach resumed its journey. "It was natural to speak of our escape on [the] Sabbath; and easy to engraft such remarks upon the doctrine of Providence as I thought calculated to do good."[11] Whereas Douglass saw the passengers' escape uninjured from the accident as evidence of God's hand, those unconvinced of his logic believed that only luck had prevented them from harm.

Demonstrations of piety and moral decisions also marked evangelicals when they mingled with the world in other ways. Fearing that her son, Henry Taylor, risked "conforming" to the wishes of his friends who "have chosen the world as their portion," Frances Douglass reminded her son that he must reverse the direction of the peer pressure: "Your aim should be to do them good, by a firm & uniform endeavour to walk in wisdoms ways. You know I do not mean that you should make an exhibition of religion, but that you should never be ashamed to manifest its power over you." Douglass and other evangelical parents hoped that their children would quietly but forcefully demonstrate the power of their piety to their unconverted peers. When William McCampbell, an aspiring young Tennessee attorney, encountered several other attorneys at a reception, he publicly demonstrated his piety. Several of his peers confronted McCampbell about his temperate ways, but he replied that "if I never succeeded better at the bar than I could at a bowl of punch, . . . I might as well give up my law books at once." McCampbell succumbed to the social pressure to some degree, however, taking a glass of punch but refusing to drink from it. He enjoyed the company but could not bring himself to imbibe in the "boisterious mirth and uncouth witticisms of bachanals."[12] In a culture that so often placed a premium on shows of manly independence, young male evangelicals such as Taylor and McCampbell often had to steer a middle course of action, staying true to their religiously informed principles but also garnering approval from nonevangelicals.

Even more grievous to evangelicals than secular southerners, however, were fellow evangelicals who allowed the priorities of the secular world, especially money, to overtake religion in importance. Writing from an academy in Robertville, South Carolina, in 1821, Charlotte Verstille noted that "the inhabitants of this place . . . are very worldly minded, and even the Professors appear to think more of the rise and fall of cotton than of the rise and progress of religion." Echoing southern evangelical jeremiads against wealth that persisted from the late eighteenth century through the Civil War, Anne Davis voiced her frustration at the lack of funds raised in her husband's Raleigh, North Carolina, Methodist congregation for the missionary cause: "They are immersed in the cares of this life taking from year to year anxious thought about the decoration of their persons with costly apparel, and their houses with costly furniture, but alas, alas, for them they have failed to lay up for themselves treasure in Heaven." Even though the donations exceeded her husband's expectations, they seemed paltry to a woman who never tired of counting her heavenly blessings: "I felt today as if I could have given thousands of dollars [to] that Saviour who had done so much for me, in plucking my feet out of the mire and clay, and placing them upon a rock, a firm foundation and putting a new song in my mouth." As she witnessed membership dwindle and her pastor depart for Texas, Jane Boyd blamed the shortcomings on members and nonmembers alike who "are to prone to seek after the wealth and honor of the world, and think to lightly of a future state, and the good of others."[13]

Women, who often spearheaded special fund-raising campaigns and made up budget shortfalls through suppers and festivals, were dismayed when they discovered that their community's growing population and wealth did not result in a concomitant increase in their congregation's coffers.

Evangelicals lamented most loudly when family members turned their backs on the Gospel. Convinced of the superiority of the postconversion lifestyle, many evangelicals expressed frustration when kin failed to follow that lead. Character traits such as generosity and kindness remained inadequate testimony to an evangelical commitment. After spending a winter in Missouri, one woman described her relatives there as "especially kind to me." But, she continued, "they are gay & fond of what this world calls pleasure & with such things I am done."[14] Families in which evangelical faith failed to flourish widely demonstrate the ongoing divisiveness of piety. Very often, blood ties failed to supplant the necessity of a voluntary conversion among kin. Individual evangelicals clung tightly to the hope that their entire families—extended as well as nuclear—would reunite in heaven. When unrepentant family members dashed that hope, converted kin often took a peculiar delight in witnessing their irreligious kin suffer and expire after engaging in what evangelicals deemed sinful behavior.

Though Bertram Wyatt-Brown argues that the gap between the South's traditional honor ethic and evangelical values closed throughout the antebellum years, activities such as dueling still starkly differentiated evangelicals from nonevangelicals.[15] Few behaviors distanced the evangelical from the nonevangelical more than the consumption of alcohol. The emerging temperance movements found common cause with evangelicals, decrying the ways in which alcohol diminished self-control, squandered family income, and ultimately endangered the sanctity of the household. Although men monopolized alcohol consumption as a recreational pastime, evangelical women noted the danger such men posed to their families. When those men—even family members—fell victim to their habits, evangelicals showed little compassion for their plight. On learning that her uncle and cousin had taken up drinking, Maria Lide proclaimed her alarm and then quickly distanced herself and her evangelical sister from them. As her initial shock at the news wore off, Lide contrasted the ethereal nature of earthly riches with the eternal quality of heavenly rewards: "But a few years ago uncle Hart bid fair for a rich man but how is it changed!! how forceible does this remind us of the importance of seeking endurable riches[.] oh what is this world worth all its pleasures & with all its instruments?

how vain & fleeting!" Lide then reinforced the volitional aspect of both the secular and evangelical lifestyle. "We are p[l]aced here & permitted to choose for our selves life or death, [Our Savior] has promised 'he will cast off none that comes seeking him.'" Having separated evangelical from nonevangelical kin, Lide reaffirmed the rewards she and her sister could anticipate at the end of their earthly pilgrimage. "My dear sister how does this highten our happiness . . . at the same time call for songs of praise & gratitude to almighty God, for his distinguishing mercy to us, that we are all traveling the same road to glory, & we shall all ere long sit down with Abraham Isack or Jacob in the New Jerusalem." Word of the moral demise of their kin catapulted these two sisters into a spiritual celebration. That physical demise accompanied moral demise among alcoholics not only reified the sin of alcohol consumption in evangelicals' minds but also illustrated the real consequences of violating God's will. As Lide reminded her sister, the evangelical lifestyle required great toil, but the benefit of one day sitting beside God "is sweeter than ten thousand day[s] of pleasurable sin."[16] Even more, a lifetime of self-denial benefited the faithful on earth as well as in heaven.

When her cousin died from complications related to alcoholism in 1837, Anne Beale similarly distanced herself from him. Not content to isolate her criticism to "demon rum," Beale also acknowledged that such immoral activity resulted in an ignoble death, jeopardizing her cousin's eternal soul: "He is gone to try the realities of another world, poor fellow there was no visible change in him for the better ere he departed." In a culture brimming with descriptors for salvation, Beale mustered little optimism with her word choice. As "a warning to surviving friends" who continued to ignore religion, the experience reaffirmed Beale's preference for the family of believers over her natal family while increasing the gulf between her pre- and postconversion lives.[17] And, as in Lide's case, such events made heaven and hell more alive while creating personal intimacy with God.

Two more sensational events later that year involving her cousins illuminate the complex ways that Anne Beale used religion—and its absence—to interpret events that shaped individual and family history. "Man may appoint, but God disappoints," Beale wrote to her brother-in-law as she summed up the downfall of two more cousins. John Beale was shot and killed as a consequence of his unpaid gambling debts. After his death, Anne received a letter intended for him from another family member, Richard Beale, who asked John to travel to Washington, D.C., immediately to aid him in preparing for a duel. As the embodiment of the secular South's culture of honor, dueling was the violent antithesis of Anne Beale's evangelicalism. Evangelicals contended that the duel did not protect or enhance a man's honor; rather, they argued, reliance on violence, which all too often led to murder, "degraded" the participating men. Richard thus warned John not to mention the duel to their father or any of their female kin because "they would not allow me to act honorable." For Anne Beale, her interception of the letter not only was providential but also reaffirmed why she found evangelical faith a sufficient substitute for the nonreligious kin she denounced. "He who sticketh closer than a brother, yea, who is better to us than ten thousand brothers saw fit to place the letter in the very hands it was intended never to reach." She did not leave the matter entirely up to God, however. She handed the letter to her father, who forced Richard to withdraw the challenge and settle the disagreement through arbitration. Concluding that her cousins' wayward path would "be the fate of all those who have not been trained up in the way they should go," Anne spent the rest of her life tirelessly teaching her children to follow God.[18]

Although drinking alcohol and dueling remained strictly off-limits for evangelicals, many other activities the clergy had traditionally forbidden began to make inroads among individual evangelicals. Correspondence and diary entries from antebellum southerners relay how individuals struggled to determine the morality of activities as varied as dancing and letter writing on the Sabbath. One Delaware clergyman justified his "little dance in the woods" in 1816 as an attempt to prevent secular southerners from thinking that "religion destroyed our pleasures entirely, lest they should think it morose & unlovely." In retrospect, however, he established that although not "criminal," his actions had portrayed "a levity a thoughtless pleasure inconsistent with the serene & Heartfelt happiness the religion of Jesus inspires." In 1856, Susan Heiskell turned to William McCampbell, her suitor and the son of a Presbyterian minister, to assess the morality of a dance with another man. Although his membership in the Presbyterian Church did not allow him to dance, McCampbell declared that he had always believed dancing was "not wrong." In fact, if dancing did not contravene his parents' wishes, he would consider taking lessons. Even McCampbell's parents were "not violent in their opposition to dancing." Methodist Mary Bethell, however, recoiled at the proof of her impiety. She had not only been so caught up in a novel that she read it in one sitting but also allowed her daughter to attend a "dancing party." Wandering down such "forbidden paths," she mused, "we will surely lose the spirit of religion." Novel reading, she argued, took time away from reading the Good Book and could even lead to a loss of "all desire for reading the Bible." And dancing increased the likelihood that adolescents would "forget all their religious impressions," a catchall phrasing that suggests the frivolity of dancing and the need to keep single men and women at some distance from one another. Bethell's nearly effortless seduction by guilty pleasures confirmed the fragility of her faith, underscoring both the vast number of spiritual snares in daily life and the need for constant vigilance. As the Reverend Charles Mallary reminded children, "Dancing, for amusement, does the soul harm—it drives off serious thoughts—it hinders prayer. Serious, thoughtful people are the persons who seek and enjoy [dancing] least. Very careless people are apt to be the most fond of it."[19]

The frequency of evangelical sermons devoted solely to dancing at balls suggests that Bethell was not alone in her moral quandaries. But evangelicals from across the South noted their refusal to dance. Jones Fuller, for example, declined an invitation to a party because "parties of this kind are nothing more than private Balls." Drawing boundaries regarding dancing made a very public statement about one's commitment to evangelicalism. That message had gotten across to Sarah Fountain's acquaintances in Alabama: "There were three parties in [our] neighbourhood last week. At two of them, they danced until day-light. The folks treat us with more polit[e]ness than to invite us when they mean to dance."[20] While most uniquely evangelical practices remained confined to the home and church, dancing publicly differentiated nonevangelicals from evangelicals.

Activities related to Sabbatarianism and its place in evangelical domesticity generally proved less problematic for southern evangelicals. Unlike dancing, which could only detract from one's devotional life, Sunday activities, particularly those that contributed at least indirectly to religious life and thought, might meet with approbation among lay southerners. The pious often brushed aside qualms about the morality of letter writing on Sundays, for example. Writing about spiritual matters related to either formal or domestic devotion became a means of religious experience as well as religious expression for evangelicals. Unable to attend worship services because of a foot injury, Margaret Wallace had no doubts about the morality of letter writing on the Sabbath: "I rarely ever write letters on the Sabbath and when I do, it is to a sister or a brother, and I do not think this can be very sinful." McCampbell started a letter to Heiskell with the same query: "Sabbath evening, Nov. 2—It is not wrong to write the same things to you that would be proper to be spoken on sabbath evening, is it?"[21] McCampbell answered his rhetorical question by continuing his letter, which detailed the day's devotional exercises and experiences.

Beyond white evangelicals' efforts to parse out the appropriateness of certain behaviors, the greatest change in their outlook between the early national and antebellum eras occurred in the area of race. Scholars continue to debate just how egalitarian the early Baptist and Methodist churches were but agree that by the 1810s and 1820s, white evangelicals freely discriminated against black church members. Frances Bumpass observed at the death of an elderly white woman in 1843 that she had been "much persecuted in the early part of her Christian career, having joined the church when Meth. was unpopular here. The only minister then of that denomination, being an old Negro named Terry." A rumored slave rebellion led by Denmark Vesey in 1822 in South Carolina and Nat Turner's 1831 insurrection in Virginia in the name of religious prophecy combined with northern abolitionists' increasingly vociferous 1830s attacks on the South's "peculiar institution" to force white southern evangelicals to apply their religious ideals and practices to slavery's defense.[22] Missionary work among the slaves allowed evangelical clergymen to celebrate the twin expansions of slavery and of their denominations. Evangelicals initially faced an uphill struggle for access to slaves because many nonevangelicals deemed such an egalitarian message far too explosive for plantation slavery. Writing about her presbytery's meeting only two years after Vesey's supposed insurrection, Martha Gaston captured the fundamental tension in some of the early evangelical missions. Rev. Cunningham, who had led the Presbyterian Church's earliest efforts at missionary work among slaves, told the audience in Wilcox County, Alabama, that "if ever his cold heart was refreshed in preaching the gospel he was commanded to preach to the poor that proclaimed the liberty to the captives and the opening of the prison doors to them that are bound." Cunningham undoubtedly had in mind release from the figurative bondage of sin rather than from the literal bondage of slavery, but southern whites could no longer afford any confusion on that point. Thus, while Gaston reported that her congregation had a "small sabbath school" where "we instruct both white and black," she added that "there have been some threats made, but no attempts to disturb us."[23]

By the late antebellum period, such fears had largely dissipated, leaving evangelical denominations to applaud the number of local and regional converts acquired through slave missions. Writing to his son, the Reverend Joseph Davis gave a brief history of the Methodist Church's success on this front under the direction of Bishop William Capers. Noting that Capers had received approval from slaveholders in 1829 and that his "novel experiment was a safe and judicious one," Davis reported that the missionary activity had led to 11,500 black converts and twenty-five preachers along with the development of oral catechisms for slaves. Throughout the antebellum era, lay church members and clergy pointed to the conversion of blacks as further evidence of God's good work in their midst. Sarah Fountain, a Baptist, reported that a recent protracted meeting netted "4 persons baptized 2 white persons & 2 negros."[24] Clergymen too constantly noted when they preached to whites and blacks as they made their rounds. Even when they had some access to slaves, clergymen sought more frequent contact, including on weekdays, when such efforts might run afoul of slaveholders' desire to extract as much labor as possible.[25] To illustrate the importance the Methodist Church accorded to this missionary field and to underscore the necessity for caution to continue those gains, Davis quoted Capers's appeal to clergymen at the 1844 General Conference: "Once you have awakened the feeling that we cannot be trusted among the slaves, you have effectually destroyed us. . . . As sure as you live, there are tens of thousands, nay hundreds of thousands, whose destiny may be periled by your decision in this case. . . . O, close not this door! Shut us not from their great work which we have been so signally called of God."[26] To reach slaves, clergymen could not afford to alienate masters. In referencing Capers's dire warning, Davis reinforced the fundamental logic behind the southern Methodist split from their northern counterparts; the conference vigorously debated the propriety and constitutionality of having a slaveholder serve as a church bishop.[27]

White evangelicals thus continued to keep careful head counts on converts and potential converts, regardless of race, to confirm their missionary progress and gauge the work remaining. But even if southern evangelicals had long since made their peace with slavery, they continued to question which public and private activities separated them from nonevangelicals. The rejection of the world at the time of conversion signaled a disavowal of many temporal pleasures in exchange for the promise of life eternal. That pledge continually manifested itself in everyday interactions with nonevangelicals. Because the faithful increasingly emphasized the need for entire families to convert, many nonevangelicals experienced considerable discomfort when kin challenged their piety. Even with converted children, anxious evangelical mothers such as Anne Davis and Mary Bethell worried that a novel here or a dance there outwardly demonstrated an erosion of piety. Evangelicals set out to forge congregations of like-minded believers, people who made public statements about their identity even when they expressed their faith privately.

Clergymen and Conflict in Evangelical Congregations

Sundays were anything but a day of rest for the faithful. Weather and health permitting, evangelicals often attended individual and family prayer, two and even three formal worship services, and less formal gatherings for singing and fellowship at other church members' houses. Many evangelical southerners undoubtedly echoed Mary Brown's prayer one Sabbath morning: "Oh Lord may not this holy sabeth day pass unimproved awaken o Lord in my con[s]cience the inquiry how shall I escape if I neglect so great [a] salvation."[28]

While lay evangelicals eagerly sought out formal worship, they also made the clergymen who led them a unique focus for criticism. Laypersons depended on their clergymen for many of the most essential elements of their faith and their identity: providing sacraments, intellectual stimulation, moral leadership, and revivalist energy. Some clergy thrived in all of those aspects, but most had at least one Achilles' heel. As one Presbyterian pastor's sister remarked, "It is seldom you can find a minister that is liked by *all* his congregation." The laity rarely directly or formally challenged the clergy's authority, but men and women nevertheless voiced their disagreements to family and friends. Pastors heard the grumbling, saw parishioners nodding off in the pews, and felt the meager returns in the offering plate. Fearing such outcomes, some clergymen altered their message to meet their listeners' needs. Others let matters slip into disarray, creating embittered factions within the congregation. On one level, these conflicts illustrate the enormous clerical skills required to build and maintain congregational consensus. On a deeper level, the conflicts illustrate how individual evangelicals whom conversion had trained in the art of self-criticism freely applied that skill to others within the fold. No matter the arena, evangelical piety was always critically consumed, never passively accepted. The leader-follower relationship remained thorny.[29]

Laypersons often described the absence of clergymen as a tremendous hardship. It not only meant forgoing all-important sacraments such as baptism and the Lord's Supper but also left a congregation bereft of a leader and an intellectual spark. According to H. Edwards, Charleston, South Carolina, stood on the brink of a great revival in 1822, lacking only clergy: "We who have been accustomed to having ministers settled in every village must feel the dearth of ministers in this part of our country where the fields are whiting for the Harvest, and seem only to want Faithful Laborers in the vineyard that the blessing of his Holy Spirit might be poured upon every Heart."[30]

If South Carolina was a field ready for harvest in 1822, the young states of Alabama and Mississippi and the Arkansas Territory must have seemed like deserts. Ecstatic that her husband had dispensed with the notion of moving from North Carolina to Arkansas, Mary Bethell reaffirmed the wisdom of his decision, arguing that Arkansas "is not the place to raise up children, it is not friendly to piety." Martha Gaston, however, observed that even Alabama had an evangelical oasis or two. Gaston's family had relocated to Dallas County seeking fertile soil for growing crops and saving souls, and she found that part of Alabama "much more improved than where my brothers live. They have as respectable neighbourhood here as you have in carolina. They have got preaching here, which was an inducement to me for to come up here. It has refreshed me greatly since I came up here, to here the sweet sound of the gospel." Eliza Heiskell sought to draw her sister, Nancy Lincoln, and her husband to Knoxville, Tennessee, where they "would have the advantage of a good school and good preaching—two great blessings that we never know the worth of but by the want of them."[31] If forced to relocate away from their kin, women in particular lobbied their husbands to migrate to communities with established congregations.

When good preaching was hard to find, evangelicals journeyed far and wide in search of it. With no services nearby in 1844, Mary Boyd often traveled sixteen miles to attend Presbyterian services. Evangelicals used to improvising services without clergy, especially those on the frontier, counseled kin who had to endure the same deprivation. On learning that the minister had left his cousin's South Carolina congregation, J. M. C. Boyd proffered experienced advice: "I can sympathize with you in having lost your preacher. It is the greatest loss almost that you could sustain. And I would advise you to get another by all means. If however it be impossible to get a minister keep up your monthly meeting by all means it will be of great benefit to you." The lack of a clergyman's leadership endangered a congregation's existence.[32]

Thus, despite evangelical individualism, a talented minister was the lifeblood of a congregation. "I must have preaching, I cannot live happy without it," admitted Boyd. One sermon fully rejuvenated an ill and weary Mary Bethell. Appropriately for her, the origin of the sermon was the Scripture lesson, "Be not weary in well doing, for in due season ye shall reap, if ye faint not." Barely able to make the journey to the meetinghouse, Bethell heard the sermon and became "strengthened in body and soul." This "blessing" on her soul left her "determined to go *on* and try to be faithful unto death." Two years later, the first sermon by a newly appointed Methodist minister so impressed Bethell that she predicted remarkable revivals taking place when camp meeting season started. For Mary Hort, a sermon on John 18:11 that highlighted humanity's light sufferings relative to Jesus served as a clarion call to work harder at being a Christian or face divine wrath: "I own that I have not duly submitted—not improved—I have looked for consolation elsewhere than to God. I have not known Christian tempers under trials, not acted out the convictions given at the time. What have I to expect. Shall I provoke the Lord to more wrath. Is this a time to trifle with sacred things."[33] Successful clergymen thus knew how to issue intellectual and emotional challenges that mobilized their congregations.

In addition to sermons, the clergy's leadership of the Lord's Supper and revivals stirred their flocks' spirituality. Communion offered McCampbell the opportunity to push aside all secular matters: "And oh! how unworthy I felt to partake of [the sacrament] after mixing in the pursuit of worldly objects until the mind is almost wholly taken up by them to the exclusion of Heavenly objects. It is indeed a hard task for me to act the part of a christian—my ambitious notions, the difficulties that beset me on every side, together with my own exceedingly wicked heart, urge me to become more worldly minded every day." A rewarding communion occurred for Frances Bumpass when "the Spirit made intercession." For Anne Davis, the Lord's Supper was truly a preview of heaven, a congregation of the sainted joined in worship: "It may be for ought I know the last time I am to enjoy these privileges, until I join the general assembly of the church of the first born in Heaven, where I shall drink of the new wine of the kingdom, and enjoy a perpetual love feast in the immediate presence of my Lord." The ritual gave Davis great confidence in her eternal fate.[34]

Camp meeting revivals, like the Lord's Supper, were vital to spiritual renewal among the faithful and continued to infuse new blood into the congregation. Mid-nineteenth-century outdoor meetings may have seemed tame compared to the raucous and massive revivals of earlier decades, but they retained elements of their more radical predecessors. As Ellen Eslinger and others stress, antebellum camp meetings provided much more structure for worshippers than did early nineteenth-century gatherings: guidebooks illustrated the layout of living quarters and worship sites; gender and racial segregation occurred; and a schedule of worship services appeared prior to the meeting. Even with heightened organization, ordinary rules and expectations became more pliable as part of a successful quest to shake newcomers and members alike from their everyday routines and cares. At an 1838 meeting, Anne Davis recorded how "the fire of Divine love was first shed forth in the preachers tent, it rushed from heart to heart until each one in the tent were powerfully blessed." The chaos of one revival left Sarah Fountain bewildered. Despite her gratitude for the large number of individuals "turning from their sins," she confessed to her sister that "there was so much confusion that I could not enjoy it much, nearly every person were standing on the benches so that I could neither see or hear much that was going on." Even as some antebellum southern evangelicals seemed taken aback by the disruptive qualities of revivals, evangelicals—Methodists in particular—continued to embrace those disruptive qualities as an opportunity to awaken piety in their communities.[35]

Events at revivals occasionally took clergymen by surprise. Even Presbyterian protracted meetings, the most conservative revival format, remained unpredictable and occasionally cut across the grain of southern hierarchies of power. During one such meeting in Staunton, Virginia, James Douglass noted that most of those nearing conversion were young, but among the class of converts was an eighty-year-old man and an old "French quack." In spite of his jaundiced view of particular inhabitants of the anxious bench, Rev. Douglass rushed to count them among his fold: "Thanks be to God all may come to this fountain and *Drink* and *Drink* and Drink again and still are dry—all classes of persons are invited to this *great* salvation from the *Prince* to the beggar." But the real coup at the revival occurred three days later. A female member eager to see her husband convert employed two tactics to battle his ongoing hostility toward religion. After having a friend speak with him about his spiritual state, she petitioned the ministers for his conversion. The first indications that she had achieved her desired ends occurred at their home: unable to sleep and feeling "wretchedly," he sought an explanation from his wife. "The spirit of God is operating upon your heart," she answered. After proclaiming himself "the greatest sinner in the world" and enduring a sleepless night of prayer and introspection, the husband appeared at the meeting the next day as an eager convert. Douglass reported that the meeting at Staunton yielded an additional fifty new members, acknowledging that many of the most valued conversions started with seeds sown at home.[36]

Even when ordinary revivals failed to produce large numbers of converts, they allowed existing members to renew the commitment to their church that started during conversion. After another uneventful meeting, Anne Davis inventoried her spiritual state: "Although I do not feel as much quickened and revived as was my privilege to have been[,] yet Glory to God, I do feel that my prospect is blooming and bright for a seat at God's right hand, when the trials of mortality cease; if I know my heart I went to that campmeeting expecting to meet with my Saviour, and I was not disappointed. The Father and the Son manifested themselves unto me in great Glory, thereby comforting and rejoicing my heart."[37] For Frances Bumpass, the soul-searching of revivals called forth religious obligations left unfulfilled: "At the first [revival] I was much revived & towards the close enjoyed the comforts of the Spirit & determined to spend more time in secret & the study of the scripture. [F]or sometime I went on my way rejoicing, & was not conscious of any backsliding, until the second revival commenced some months after & then I found much of my comfort gone, so that I was not prepared to rejoice in the Lord." But the hope for renewal at revivals persisted. Putting an exclamation point on his anticipation of an upcoming camp meeting, George Whitaker wrote to his parents of his thirst for a "nip" of revival culture: "I am like a grog drinker in this respect, when the time for camp meetings come on I wish to go." No matter how common or idealized, revivals demanded tremendous amounts of time and discipline from evangelicals. Maria Lide blamed her delinquent correspondence with relatives in South Carolina on a recent flurry of meetings in Alabama: "I have been going to church day and night for the last 17 days.... [W]e had prayer meeting at 10 oclock ... preaching at 11; we would get home about 3 oclock PM and stay until early candle light when we would go back again and get home about 11 oclock."[38] Antebellum camp and protracted meetings occurred on a smaller scale than their early-republic predecessors, but evangelicals continued to look to such gatherings as something more than merely a means for recruitment; these meetings rekindled personal piety among the faithful and set them out as a community of believers apart from secular southerners.

Evangelical identity still frequently cut across denominational lines. Although evangelicals largely remained loyal to their families' denominations, they still looked to other denominations for a dose of spiritual renewal or for a harbinger of revivals that might be just over the horizon. Early nineteenth-century revivals had been large enough that they often required the labor of more clergy than one denomination could supply. Furthermore, revivals were seen as shared events among the community of believers. Those qualities of revivals persisted into the antebellum era. While Baptist Mary Lide noted that she traveled thirteen miles and pitched a tent at a Methodist church in anticipation of a revival in Alabama, Kentucky's Samuel Haycraft, also a Baptist, participated in a Methodist revival "with some spiritual advantage," followed by a revival at his home church, where his "spiritual strength [was] renewed." Even when direct cooperation among clergy did not exist, both lay members and clergy closely watched neighboring denominations for signs of an impending revival that might jump across denominational lines. The Reverend Sidney Bumpass, a Methodist, took great delight in learning that four young women from the neighboring Presbyterian congregation had come forward to profess religion in early 1841. Revivals soon engulfed North Carolina, and the number of converts in his church exceeded seventy-five, confirming Bumpass's hunch about the propitious nature of the activities in the Presbyterian congregation.[39]

Especially in the rural South, many evangelicals simply had to make do with services at evangelical denominations other than their own. In Alabama, which had few clergymen, hearing ministers from a variety of evangelical denominations was the norm. Sarah Fountain recorded one such adventure: "We went to the Presbyterian church last Sunday with the expectation of hearing a baptist preach, (a Mr. Tolbert who is said to be quite a smart preacher) but were disappointed, we however heard a very good sermon by a Methodist (a Mr. Freeman) who frequently preaches at that church." It is unclear how many individuals may have been enticed to cross denominational lines through the practice of guest sermons, but hosting ministers must have been aware of the risk. The Presbyterian McCampbell praised the preaching ability of one Methodist minister: "If he preached about here a good many of us would join the Methodist[s]." For

Maria Lide, the solution was to convert the clergy. After attending several days of Episcopal meetings during the denomination's state convention in Alabama, Lide, a Baptist, informed her niece that she had been "a zealous Episcopalean for the last three or four days." Although she found the Episcopalian rituals "tiresome," Lide was nonetheless captivated by the preaching. One minister in particular, she wrote, "is too good to be an Episcopalean": "he ought to be a baptist." Laypersons occasionally crossed denominational lines. One woman in Savannah, Georgia, shifted attendance from a Methodist to a Presbyterian church to shorten her commute through the sweltering summer heat. Consequently, she attended church on Tuesday evenings, three times on Sunday, and other days as events at the church merited.[40]

When white evangelicals looked beyond their own denominations for inspiration, they at times found it in observations of black piety. Yet white evangelicals' pleasure at the sight of slaves practicing Christianity remained mingled with anxiety and uncertainty. No matter how hard white evangelicals worked to make evangelicalism's message safe for their southern slaves, it remained a volatile subject because of its appeal across race and class, particularly in light of the growing linkage of evangelicalism and abolitionism in the North. Mary Lide casually noted that she had heard a "good sermon" from "Mr Stephens (a colored man from Chesterfield)" during revival season, while Frances Bumpass recorded the piety of black congregants.[41] Charlotte Verstille found "thirty white and a hundred black members of the Baptist church" in Robertville, South Carolina, while Eliza Leland felt both anxiety and joy when she and two female friends attended an otherwise all-black Baptist service: "We heard a good sermon from Old Lanco—it was a strange event to me."[42]

But racial fissures remained just below the surface. On more than one occasion, Rev. Bumpass noted his work with the black faithful. In April 1842, he used the occasion of a free black man's lynching by more than one hundred whites, "principally of the very lowest classes of the people," to observe that "satan has now begun to work in good earnest." The mob, calling itself the Raleigh Regulators, claimed that the man, Lansford Lane, had violated a recently passed statute and could not remain in the state. However, Bumpass sympathized with the free man's efforts to purchase his wife and children and clearly viewed the mob with alarm, not only for its injustice but also because the group's ill will portended the end of his congregation's recent efforts to raise money for Sunday schools and other charitable endeavors. Bumpass also worked the gallows, occasionally interviewing blacks about their faith on the eve of their execution. In one instance, Bumpass seemed uneasy about the verdict, writing that "George had accidentally killed a white man, in self-defense who attempted to beat him with a hoe." Bumpass chose to focus on what he could control, authenticating the conversion of the condemned and administering baptism, wondering, "How would a Baptist minister have managed this case?"[43]

Race and community fear among whites took on a much more vivid and personal tone when rumors of a slave insurrection circulated in the Bumpasses' community. These rumors, combined with the Bumpasses' proximity to the site of Nat Turner's rebellion and Rev. Bumpass's frequent absences from home for ministerial work, created nothing short of sheer panic for his wife, Frances, who wrote that she "dwell[ed] too much on an imaginary sense of murder—fear to sleep—when slumbering often start to dread." Thereafter, her ability to sleep became a testament to her faith. Two days later she reflected, "My fears about slave insurrection have almost vanished—sleep soundly. I feared more than others. Help me I pray, to watch & be ready for death."[44] For the next three months, Frances Bumpass revisited the difficulties of slave management and pondered whether the family would migrate to the North, a move that never occurred.

White congregants rarely sustained the harmony and depth of interest produced by the revival season. The absence of revivals or poor attendance at them sent evangelical ministers into another mode of leadership, jeremiads against the impiety and worldliness of their congregations. When revivals in North Carolina failed to produce the clergy's desired results in 1855, the Reverend William Wills of the Methodist Protestant Church used his denomination's newspaper to decry the ways in which his members desecrated the Sabbath and virtually ignored their obligations to prayer and class meetings. "The House of God on that day is too much neglected, or if attended there is too much of the *form* without the *power* of Godliness, and too often not even the form is evidenced." Too many members participated in "sinful conversation" at church, while still others arrived late for services. Worse yet, when camp meetings did occur, "their usefulness is destroyed by the parade and show" of lavish carriages and dress. Practices central to the growth and integrity of the Methodist tradition, such as the class meeting, which required small groups of believers to meet regularly to discuss the state of their souls, had fallen into disuse. In addition to fellowship, these meetings allowed members to police one another's behavior. Now Wills commonly heard members complain about this institution: "Oh! I don't like class meetings, I cant bear to be interrogated, it is too much like the Roman Confessional." Wills came close to admitting defeat at the hands of his parishioners: "It cannot be denied that Class Meetings are losing much of their former popularity, and in this free land, public sentiment will influence if not control them." Still, he argued, "all experience shows" that class meetings "are most valuable aids to the Christian." Wills saved his final salvo for the ministry itself. Citing the clergy's lukewarm commitment to meeting with families and holding class meetings to improve devotional habits, Wills highlighted the danger posed by clergymen who failed to pay attention to grassroots worship: "The Watch misleads an individual, the town Clock a whole community."[45] Wills thus underscored lay expectations that the clergy provide intellectual leadership and revivalist fervor in the household, the meetinghouse, and the community.

As William Wills's son, Richard, discovered in his congregation, that pastoral ideal did not always work in practice. Clergymen had to adapt their messages to meet the congregation's needs and sustain interest, a challenging compromise for a young, second-generation clergyman. Richard Wills sought direction from his father: "I do not know but feeling is frequently produced by appealing to something other than religious principles—too frequently by speaking of friends, distresses &c. . . . It appears to me that such preaching is not the proper kind. If the love of Christ and such things as that can not move us what can. Paul preached Christ. Am I not correct pa in this sentiment?" But the wandering minds of lay members during sermons must have convinced Wills to retreat from preaching sermons of "the proper kind" on many occasions. William McCampbell, for example, spent the better part of a two-hour church service thinking about the measurements of the house he was constructing and how much material would be required to finish the job. He left church knowing more about building his home in the Tennessee mountains than he did about building a mansion in heaven: "After preaching I could tell with much more certainty that it would take 450 feet of weatherboarding, 320 feet of flooring &c, to build a kitchen of the dimentions we needed, than I could tell from Mr Smith's sermon how the mourning should be comforted." The harder ministers pushed their congregations, the more they risked alienating them. After listening to a ninety-minute Presbyterian sermon, McCampbell again conveyed his frustration to his fiancée: "Mr Hood is going to try to preach us all to death when he does get a lick at us—only preaches once a month & he thinks he must give us a good one when he is at it."[46] Even the son of a Presbyterian minister such as McCampbell could grow weary of the clergyman's Sunday message.

Learning to command the attention of an audience from a pulpit was not easy, particularly when most of the congregation had seen a variety of preachers and preaching styles as a consequence of pastoral turnover and visits to neighboring churches. Worshippers arrived at the meetinghouse with high expectations and critical minds. After hearing her new Presbyterian pastor in St. Charles, Missouri, preach for the first time, Mary Gray took little pity when reporting his abilities: "The sermon was a poor thing from a young clergyman only 23 years old, light in his manner, full of gesture, which has no meaning[.] [M]ight have served, as Saml Johnson says, 'to track a dog down' it was so unconnected no one could gather after him." George Whitaker, another youthful clergyman, noted the chasm between writing and delivering a good sermon: "I can select many [Scriptural passages] that I can write a sermon from, but when I get up before a congregation it seems that I lose half my ideas, but I hope that will wear off soon; if I will act my part and trust in the Lord as I wish to."[47] Like acting, preaching required rehearsal and timed delivery to meet the lofty expectations of the listeners.

Often preaching between 100 and 250 sermons per year, even veteran ministers inevitably had some flat deliveries.[48] The problem for the clergy, according to Frances Jane Bestor, the daughter of a Baptist preacher, was that a minister was sometimes only as good as his last sermon—or at least the last pass of the offering plate. Her father had arranged for a visiting clergyman to deliver the missionary sermon to his congregation. After a strong start, the visiting pastor "became embaressed or bewildered," most likely because of men who surrendered their seats to female latecomers. The nonplussed pastor sat down to regain his composure, but his sermon never got back on track. "The congregations seemed to feel much for him, but their sympathies availed but little on such an occasion. A collection was taken, for Missionary purposes, but the sum was small."[49]

Clergymen learned quickly that financial success relied heavily on female congregants' willingness to pitch in. Women routinely gathered to raise much-needed funds for their congregations in both rural and urban southern churches. The women of the Maysville Presbyterian Church held strawberry and raspberry dinners, raising several hundred dollars to renovate their church. The church's pastor proceeded with his plans to improve the building only after he had made sure of female members' willingness to engage in fund-raising. Equally important, however, was the fact that the call for the fund-raiser originated from the pastor.[50] Maria Lide reported her participation in a choral event aimed at raising funds for a bell for her Baptist meetinghouse in Alabama. Though poor weather kept attendance down and only fifty dollars was raised, many parishioners demanded that a second concert be held and anticipated raising enough money for the church bell.[51] Sarah Lowry Pollard of King and Queen County, Virginia, reported that the women in her congregation had cleared one hundred thirty dollars at their annual missionary fund-raisers, while one minister's wife lamented that constant sewing for a church fund-raiser had given her intense headaches.[52] Women's fund-raisers could also assume a partisan quality integral to the survival of their denominations. In the wake of the Presbyterian schism of 1837, women eagerly joined the fray, in which New School clergymen such as Charles G. Finney pushed the Presbyterian Church farther and farther from its Calvinist roots, which emphasized God's mysteriousness and the world's sinfulness through doctrines such as predestination, original sin, and limited atonement, and toward an Arminian perspective that emphasized the believer's free will and optimistically hinted at the potential for individual perfectibility. Writing from near St. Louis, Mary Gray informed Frances Douglass that the women of her congregation had taken sewing orders for shirts and slippers from the men of the congregation in an effort to "build a Church, or help to build for the Orthodox Presbyterians." In spite of her deteriorating eyesight and insufficient patterns, Gray pledged her labors to the Old School cause.[53] The patterns of female fund-raising across the South remain to be charted, but these examples illustrate that women played significant roles when congregations found themselves in financial need.

The clergy's dependence on laymen's and laywomen's involvement and financial assistance put pressure on all pastors, especially those who lacked the charisma and talent necessary to gain devoted flocks. Ann Thomas wrote to her daughter that the Methodist preacher on her circuit demonstrated great personal piety but failed to inspire a following: "We have only one preacher on the circuit he seems to be a pious man but the congregation dont seem to take much interest in his preaching." For Thomas, the preacher's powerlessness in the pulpit boded ill for her community of Louisburg, North Carolina. His inability to generate a revival left the church helpless to combat a recent rash of social balls and the arrival of the circus. Other women skipped church altogether when they knew that a poor country preacher would be in the pulpit. Mary Hort saw the "excellent truth" and "application" of a sermon delivered from Job 23:31 but thought the text "ill-delivered." Unable to attend evening services because of rain, Hort appeared to profit more from devotional reading than formal worship. Ministers at one Presbyterian church in Tennessee came and went as if through a revolving door: one minister had deceived the congregation but delivered great sermons, while another had impeccable character but no charisma. If forced to choose, Hu Brown preferred the former to the latter; "I think I would prefer hearing Mr. Gallaher the year round and being cheated by a trick or pretence now and then, to sitting from sabbath to sabbath under the ministrations of a humdrum preacher that can not present religion in any form that is enticing, that can produce no effect whatever." Brown looked enviously toward the Presbyterian congregation at Rogersville in hopes of procuring the services of Rev. Macklin, who Brown thought had "been raised religiously, among a pious people and if can but remember and repeat the feeling prayers of his old father, he will be very interesting and well worth employing. Besides he is a man of warm sensibility . . . and will awaken his congregation." Whether the clergyman was appointed, as in the Methodist Episcopal tradition, or called by a congregation, as in the Baptist and Presbyterian traditions, the faithful prized his ability to inspire. When he failed to do so, laypeople questioned his skill as a minister and registered their disapproval through nonattendance, decreased giving, and spiritual lassitude.[54]

Even when clergymen mustered enough inspiration, passion, and polish, many in the audience still craved intellectual challenge. By the mid-nineteenth century, generational divides within the clergy started to appear. Whereas most early nineteenth-century Baptists had scorned an educated clergy and indeed even favored a nonprofessional clergy whose primary source of financial support was farming rather than the ministry, many mid-nineteenth-century Baptists desired clergymen who were both educated and inspired. At an association meeting in Alabama, Bestor, the daughter of a clergyman, discounted another pastor's abilities: "After tea we went to church, a Mr. Witt, Baptist Minister preached & realy we were not repaid for our dusty ride. He is an uneducated man, & has not a strong mind. Father ex[h]orted after he sat down & made the subject much more clear than Mr. Witt has left it." Bestor's critique demonstrates that an increasing number of southerners thought spiritual inspiration could occur only when passion joined intelligence in the speaker's message.[55]

Lay critiques of the clergy most often focused on delivery and style in the pulpit, but theological disagreements were not off-limits. Hu Brown agreed with his minister that "Christ has tasted death for every man and all would be saved if they would comply with the terms of the gospel" but balked at the preacher's claim that "God had done all he could for the salvation of mankind": "I have always felt unwilling thus to limit the power of the Almighty." Although he remained deferential in his disagreement, concluding that "ministers have studied the subject and ought to know," he nevertheless remained unpersuaded. For Frances Douglass, the Presbyterian Church's divisive 1836 General Assembly afforded an opportunity to impart a moral lesson even as she pronounced her opinion on the debate. After lamenting the assembly's "contentious spirit," she encouraged her son "to pray against Finneys decision": "An opinion hastily formed, without due examination & then adhered to, because it has been exposed as an opinion, is folly, & leads to blindness of mind & hardness to heart." Douglass did not possess a vote in the theological debate between Old School and New School Presbyterians, but she certainly thought she could influence its outcome.[56] In antebellum America's democratic culture, many laywomen and laymen certainly felt comfortable weighing in on theological matters great and small.

Although men controlled the levers of ecclesiastical authority in southern evangelical churches, women made their voices heard through informal networks of family and friends. In both the meetinghouse and the home, women pursued authority through informal channels when formal avenues remained closed. With evangelical membership increasingly overlapping with family ties, many women had ready access to male kin in positions of church authority. In one case, three sisters plunged themselves into an ugly dispute among the elders, deacons, and the minister of the Presbyterian church of Maysville, Kentucky. Their knowledge of the minister and congregation, their belief that they played a role in the dispute, and even their ability to ostracize the minister's wife suggest that women had greater access to informal power in southern congregations than historians have imagined.

When Rev. William T. McElroy, the pastor of Maysville's Presbyterian church, used the pulpit to blast the elders and deacons for withholding his salary and then poisoning his reputation with the entire congregation, sisters Lizzie Cox and Fanny Brodrick defended the officials in a letter to a third sister, Mary Collins, in Covington, Kentucky. As she penned her fourteen-page letter, Cox surely knew that Mary's husband, Richard Collins, would learn its contents. Richard's father, Lewis Collins, was one of the elders at the center of the Maysville controversy, had ties to many of the founding families of Maysville's Presbyterian church, and had previously served as publisher of one of the town's leading newspapers, the *Maysville Eagle*. Richard had strong connections at his Presbyterian church in Covington and throughout the denomination in the Ohio River Valley.

Aware of the multiple audiences for whom she was writing, Cox struggled about whether her letter constituted a private or public religious document. She worried that the elders' humility might cause them inadequately to defend themselves, so she sought to aid their cause: "A delegation of elders will attend [the presbytery] to see that everything is done *discreetly*, and in *order* in this matter, but I know they are all too modest to speak such things of themselves." Consulting with Brodrick, Cox decided that the letter should serve as testimony to the presbytery and the church elders: "Sister Fanny suggests that I should write all this as expressive of her feelings as well as mine, and to give you the privilege to communicate whatever portion you thought best . . . as we esteem it a duty we owe our elders, and ourselves. I would not object so far as I am concerned to their reading every word of this." But by the time Cox had finished writing, the sisters had changed their minds: "Sister Fanny thinks I have mentioned some things which I should have left out . . . so you must exercise judgment and I *beg* of you not to let any one see this, as no one can understand my manner of expressing myself as well as you."⁵⁷

Cox had reason to show confidence in submitting the letter as evidence of the laity's perspective on the matter. She had a good command of church affairs and theology. When McElroy charged the elders with failing to visit him often enough at his home, Cox countered by pointing out that the pastor had not visited her father's house over the previous four months, "excepting upon two occasions and then to borrow, neither time even sitting down." Transcending the social dimensions of McElroy's ministerial labors and drawing on a vast number of Presbyterian books and Presbyterian ministers, Cox directly questioned McElroy's orthodoxy, arguing that many of his sermons contained "not the least iota of Scripture from the beginning to end." She further critiqued his preaching as unnecessarily threatening: "He makes the strongest denunciation of the Bible apply to Christians." Cox contrasted McElroy, "who would *drive* men to duties they have no heart for," with an ideal pastor, who should "seek to *win* souls to Christ." "Let a minister gain the affection of his people and he can exert a great influence in making them active and zealous."[58]

A few days later, Brodrick wrote to Mary Collins, echoing Cox's critique and distinguishing his preaching abilities from his other pastoral duties: "I have always endeavored to discharge my duties to him as *my Pastor*, the offense I have given is not liking him as a preacher . . . and it has been a real trouble to me that I have not been able to profit by his preaching."[59] The incident apparently ended McElroy's tenure in Maysville, with the elders and deacons escaping punishment by the presbytery. The controversy had ominous overtones for the congregation, however: the Civil War would further divide the northern Kentucky congregation, hindering its ability to raise the funds necessary to attract rising and established stars from the ranks of the Presbyterian clergy. In a culture that valued hierarchies of race, class, and gender and in denominations where white men held absolute ecclesiastical authority, many voices went unheard in the meetinghouse. But the lack of formal authority, particularly on the part of white women, failed to silence their critical pens and tongues.[60]

A common foe did not always create a united struggle in the evangelical South. Indeed, clergymen repeatedly discovered that they provided a unique focus for congregational criticism. On one hand, the clergy embodied the most fundamental hopes of evangelicals—that they might transform the religious landscape of the South by inspiring the faithful and converting the faithless. Evangelicalism's growing institutional footprint across the South in the form of churches, educational institutions, missions, and publishing ventures pointed to success on that front. On the other hand, the laity always critically consumed the clergy's message and behavior, often creating friction between a clergyman and his congregation. Although such grumblings were often confined to private diaries or correspondence, members of the clergy anticipated criticism and occasionally redirected their message to avoid conflict. Just as often, the clergy demanded greater evidence of parishioners' piety. On occasion, as in Maysville, clergymen and lay leaders clashed, bringing much of the congregation, including women, into the fray. Regardless of whether the clergy or the laity had the upper hand in such disputes, the members of the congregation voiced their displeasure. With strife invading even the meetinghouse, evangelicals sought to turn their homes into sanctuaries filled with unsullied piety, free from the distractions that occurred in the larger community of believers.

The Discipline of Domestic Devotion

Like formal worship, domestic devotion contained dual, often conflicting, expectations and experiences. Antebellum evangelicals idealized their homes as a haven from the world and a doorway to heaven, a site privileged above all others for its confirmation of evangelical identity. Most evangelical mothers instilled devotional habits in their children at home long before they entered the church sanctuary. And the quest for life eternal concluded with the deathbed, nearly always witnessed by family at home. Thus, evangelicals believed that the most difficult passages of faith—such as the quest to convert children and the death of loved ones—would take place within the home. Evangelicals viewed afflictions as a precondition for piety, a means to eliminate sin and worldliness from their households. To prepare themselves for those eventualities, evangelicals combed their Bibles, prayed regularly, and expressed their faith collectively as families. Men as well as women celebrated the unique spiritual dividends that occurred during domestic worship.

Clergymen worked in tandem with their parishioners to construct the home as a site of profound spiritual opportunity. According to evangelical clergymen, the quality of domestic worship and training dictated the fate not only of the individual, family, and congregation but also of the community and nation. The evangelical clergy therefore prescribed family devotion, the wellspring of the South's social order, as a duty and obligation for all believers. In 1837, the Presbyterian Reverend Rufus Bailey pinned all of his hopes for society on the pious home: "The Gospel has made our families what they are. O, that they might become all, which the Gospel required, the sanctuary of every virtue, the fountains of love, the headspring of those streams which enrich the land and bless the world." Writing ten years later, the bishop of the Methodist Episcopal Church, South, James O. Andrew, echoed Bailey's metaphor, proclaiming that the "domestic circle . . . is the fountain which must be sweetened, that the streams may be pure." Many newlyweds, Andrew argued, prayed individually but neglected joint devotion, thus falling into one of the devil's snares. Therefore, he directed, newlyweds should pray together at the family altar, Bible in hand. Once established, family worship should grow with the family and become part of the daily routine: "Having taken up family worship, never neglect it. Let neither your weariness at night, nor your haste in the morning, nor the presence of strangers, nor your supposed want of gifts, be pleaded in justification of such neglect."[61] More than merely endorsing family worship, clergymen marveled at its potential to transform the entire southern landscape by swelling the evangelical ranks as converted parents passed along their faith to their offspring.

Ideally, worship at home complemented worship in the meetinghouse, but the home often served as the center of devotional exercises out of necessity. Transportation troubles ranked as a major obstacle to church attendance. Lame horses or roads made impassable by rainstorms frequently scuttled plans to attend worship services. Women in the later stages of pregnancy and anyone battling the pervasive illnesses of the Old South stayed at home rather than venturing out to church. Even with ideal weather and health, many southern evangelicals lived in rural locations where services occurred only once or twice a month because of the insufficient number of pastors. And many congregations went several weeks without pastors after the incumbents died or transferred to different congregations. While the exchange of pulpits and pews offset some of these challenges, this range of obstacles often rendered church attendance sporadic.

However, more than mere necessity led evangelical southerners to proclaim the centrality of domestic devotion. Even clergymen felt spiritually hampered by the absence of family on Sundays. Stopped overnight in Baltimore, Rev. Douglass lamented the lack of familiar surroundings: "At this Hotel, there is no Sabbath. . . . How necessary is christian society, & family worship to our comfort! Had I wings, like a dove, how delightful it would be to alight in your quiet, & I hope, consecrated retreat! I hope there is a blessing in it this evening."[62] His wife, Frances, had so much faith in the power of domestic worship that she used it as an opportunity to proselytize among young women when they paid social visits, writing to her son, "I like to have [callers] come & stay all night because then they can be twice present at our family exercises."[63] When the Civil War interfered with the Wills family's collective worship, Richard Wills asked his parents to lift up their prayers in chorus at the same time, one o'clock, "before the same 'blood bought mercy seat,'" "with the blessed assurance that our prayers will be heard."[64] No matter how great the challenge, antebellum evangelicals worked to maintain family devotion because here evangelicals claimed that they experienced their greatest devotional rewards and their greatest devotional tests.

While family devotion in the home ranked among devout evangelicals' chief delights, the home also served as the principal site of struggle for individual believers. All evangelicals anticipated hardships in life, and many embraced these opportunities to better understand themselves and God's will, as Mary Craddock articulated when she wrote, "It is hard to know our selves in prosperity." Craddock found her family's failure to convert a constant test and source of turmoil. Nevertheless, "nothing but trials will prove of what we are. I have seen more of the corruptions of my own heart since I have been so sorely tried than ever I did. I had thought I had given the world up. But how I was mistaken the love of the world is still in me." Although she confessed that her "heavy trials" had caused her to "murmur," she also found them enriching because they "forced [her] to seek closer communion with God."65 Like most evangelicals, Craddock believed that blessings could be appreciated only in light of afflictions. Consequently, she and others frequently voiced both apprehension and optimism regarding their domestic afflictions—fear that their faith might not stand the test, hope that their faith would be renewed and enriched.

To capture the vicissitudes of the evangelical journey, believers likened their struggle to that of a pilgrim or a soldier. Even when celebrating spiritual victories, evangelicals closely examined the meaning of such events and acknowledged the contingency of outcomes in matters both great and small. After safely delivering a baby boy, Mary Bethell wrote,

> The Lord did certainly bless me, I will praise him for his goodness to me in times of trouble[.] [E]very trouble seemed to work for my spiritual good, it teaches us that this is not our resting place, we are pilgrims, traveling to a better country, to a home in our Fathers house in heaven[.] [E]very trial our Heavenly Father sends, cuts the cords that bind us to earth, and then we set our affections on things above which are lasting and permanent, and then we look to God for consolation. Whom the Lord loveth he chasteneth and scourgeth every son whom he receiveth, if we be without chastisement we are bastards and not sons.

Writing to her sister, B. E. Verstille used a militaristic metaphor: "We have engaged in a good cause and must expect to meet with trials and difficulties on the way, if we be christians it is through much tribulation we must enter the kingdom of Heaven, let us then my Dear Sister prove good

Soldiers of Jesus Christ." Similarly, Mary Hort took to heart a sermon in which the pastor reminded his listeners, "with such enemies and always on the alert—we need all our armour."[66]

A useful affliction realigned the believer's priorities so that God and devotion retook precedence over everyday concerns and sins. Evangelicals thus prepared for all contingencies and outcomes during their sojourns on earth. "Who can tell what this year may bring forth?" queried Mary Davis Brown on the first day of 1858. "Who knows whether it is to lead us over a comparitive smooth and beaten high way or over a rough and thorny path?"[67] Faithfulness demanded vigilance and preparedness for the next bend in the road.

While evangelicals anticipated suffering in life and spoke of resignation in the face of inevitable trials, they consistently struggled to understand the meaning of setbacks in terms of personal and family piety. When evangelicals scrutinized themselves and those around them to see where they stood on the path to salvation, they used the homeliest of terms to proclaim their resignation to God's will and reinforce their dependence on God. "I have had some peace and comfort of late," wrote Mary Bethell, "it is my daily prayer that I may be resigned to his will in everything." During much gloomier times, Bethell struggled mightily to decipher God's purpose in the afflictions cast upon herself and her family: "I felt sad last night, I got up out [of] my bed and wrestled in prayer with God to help me. This text of scripture flashed into my mind. 'And shall not God avenge his own elect which cry day and night unto him I tell you that he will avenge them speedily,' so I shall hold on to that promise and wait on God for deliverance."[68] As Bethell and other evangelicals sorted through the blessings and afflictions in their lives, they steadfastly proclaimed that God would never deliver burdens that the faithful could not bear (or, phrased positively, that they would have sufficient grace to withstand any trial) and that all events served some higher purpose.

In many ways, the trials of the conversion process that yielded salvation mimicked the lifetime of "skirmishes of the soul" that evangelicals expected would persist until heavenly rewards could be claimed.[69] Throughout their lives, some evangelicals wavered in these two convictions under severe distress, but few rejected them altogether. Though they employed the language of resignation to demonstrate their obedience to God, antebellum evangelicals relentlessly assessed and reassessed the meaning of events that touched themselves and their families. Indeed, the wife of

Bishop John Early of Virginia, E. B. Early, counseled her daughter to seek "spiritual advancement" through "daily self denial, and taking up some cross" during personal prayers. Early viewed every day as an arduous contest between good and evil that served as a rehearsal for the individual believer's day of judgment:

> It is only by retiring from the busy scenes without, and looking patiently into the inner chambers of the heart, that we can ascertain our true condition. This we shall be compelled to do in our last hours—whether we will or not. Then let us come to the task *now*, while we have the power to correct what is wrong; and through grace to strengthen, what is right. I know by experience that the heart is much opposed to the work, and much more so in our great adversary the Devil—who knows too well that this is one of the most efficient weapons a soul can use, to vanquish, & retain the victory over our every fear. I know my child, and you will find it so, that the flesh will shrink, and cry for release—but it is only by crucifying the flesh, with its affections, & lusts that we shall be prepared for heaven. May the spirit of truth enable us to serve him in sincerity & forthrightness all the days of our lives.

Much like intellectual advancement, Early reminded her daughter, "spiritual advancement" would require daily attention and discipline. Indeed, the devil had an abundance of weapons, so she should always place religious education ahead of secular education.[70] To advance religiously thus required unremitting examination and a willingness to practice self-denial and experience suffering—in short, evangelicals faced a lifetime of spiritual struggle.

Because events ranging from the mundane to the miraculous could be saturated with meaning, antebellum evangelicals eagerly read the Bible and prayed in an effort to discern God's signposts in their lifelong sojourn. With faith in the Bible's authority serving as a cornerstone of evangelical beliefs, reading the Good Book individually and collectively as a family not only provided pilgrims with a map but also demonstrated devotional discipline. Reading the Bible and prayer made staying on the narrow path to redemption all the easier because both practices offered the believer opportunities to interpret more clearly God's designs for their lives.

With deafness in one ear preventing her from hearing sermons, Mary Bethell found "much pleasure in reading my Bible, 'tis a lamp unto my feet, and a light unto my path." Eugenia Leland cited the same scriptural passage, Psalms 119:105, and then provided specific directions to her children: "Take the Bible, God's blessed word for your guide and not only through the slippery paths of youth but through the temptations of manhood and womanhood and when you are old." Baptist Lucy Gwathmey reminded her children that although human frailty might prevent her from providing perfect instruction, "let the pattern marked out for you in the Bible be your guide, and strive to the utmost to follow that, let others say and do as they will." With the Bible as a map for daily behavior, according to Leland, Christians would accrue benefits on earth as well as in heaven. "True faith," she wrote, will "make a man happier in this present life, even amidst trials and self denying services than any other man can be made by all the pomp, pleasure, wealth, power and honour which the world can bestow on him."[71]

Reading the Bible provided Samuel Haycraft with tangible proof of his religiosity while marking progress in his personal pilgrimage toward heaven. Indeed, the Kentucky Baptist commenced charting his religious reading after losing a vote for a clerkship in 1851, when he pondered whether his defeat stemmed from God as "punishment for neglecting the Bible & duties enjoined by it." The more than five years he spent reading the Bible in its entirety left Haycraft wondering whether its lessons had taken root in his life. "In that period how many have died, what scenes have transpired in the world[,] how many temptations I have endured & submitted to—much in strife for office and no little in politics all of which is vanity." Each time he reached the last page of the Book of Revelation, Haycraft continued to wonder aloud whether God would permit him to live long enough to return to those pages once more. By 1861, Haycraft had joined a Bible-reading group and trimmed his reading time for the entire Bible down to thirteen months, holding out hope that God's "holy precepts take deep root in me and be as seed sown in good ground."[72] Haycraft's experience suggests that reading the Bible gave evangelicals the sense that they remained in tune with God's purpose as they marked time in their march toward heaven.

But the Bible was more than a moral map or even a yardstick for measuring one's spiritual progress; it was, in Mary Gray's words, "the Book of life," an invaluable resource in times of doubt or crisis. The Bible provided Frances Bumpass with a spiritual spark, a means to reignite her piety, sometimes producing peace, at other times generating energy. Feeling a "void within," Bumpass turned to her Bible during domestic devotions.

Although she at first found it difficult to confine my mind," she "soon found the word of God food for my soul," generating a "sweet peace." Amid "darkness" and "doubts," Bumpass prayed that she might profit from studying Scripture and "grow wise unto salvation. O! for light from above to illuminate my dark mind." Mary Bethell battled loneliness when her married daughter migrated to Arkansas. Feeling "deserted" and "stripped of every pleasure," Bethell turned to her Bible for immediate relief. "There are many sweet and precious promises in the Bible, to us, they come to me now like ministering angels to comfort me in my distress."[73] In times of crisis and doubt, evangelicals well versed in the Bible set out to discover that their pain had some higher purpose.

Prayer too demonstrated devotional discipline while offering instruction and nurture. As one evangelical pastor succinctly put it, private prayer kept the devout "spiritually minded" and in "communion with God" while permitting the faithful to "ask God's direction in *all* things."[74] Communing with God included both confessing sin and searching for solace in times of grief. All evangelical parents pointed to prayer as the surest means through which their children could keep their journeys to heaven on course.

Evangelicals emphasized the necessity of routine prayer to underscore their dependence on God and to create the first line of defense against sin encroaching on their spiritual journey. When Eugenia Leland wrote about the mechanics of prayer, she highlighted both aspects: "Have a set time for special prayer, independent of morning and evening prayer, at which time you should read a Psalm or some other portion of the scripture, medi[t]ate a few moments, at the same time invoking the aid of his Holy Spirit that you may meditate and pray aright." After cultivating the proper attitude for prayer, she instructed her children, they should call "to mind the sins you have commit[t]ed then pray for strength to be enabled to resist them, to watch against them as well as for grace to permit you to go through the remainder of the day bearing it's hourly trials with the patience of true devoted Christians." Leland bore witness to the power of routine prayer, relaying how it had readied her for all of God's dispensations. It had enabled her to grasp God's purpose in the face of events both miraculous (her two sons' survival when a feeding trough fell on them) and terrible (the deaths of four of her children). Leland set out to prepare her children for the blessings and afflictions that awaited them.[75]

Because individual prayer was conducted privately—"in the closet," to use the term most familiar to antebellum ears—much of the best evidence of its practice resides in correspondence from parents to children who had recently left home for school. Parental direction on devotion targeted maintenance of everyday habits. When Richard Collins left his family's home in Maysville, Kentucky, for Centre College, a Presbyterian school in Danville, Kentucky, his father sent fifteen rules of conduct to be repeated aloud weekly and followed daily. Five of the fifteen rules dealt directly with the practice of religion, including the first: "Offer secret devotion to the Giver of all Good, immediately upon rising, in my room, and also be present at family worship."[76] The frequent lack of privacy and familiar environment, however, created anxiety for young men and women attempting to maintain their domestic habits. Arguing that just such a lack of privacy might compromise the integrity of his private prayers, William McCampbell illuminated what many evangelicals treasured most in their domestic devotion:

> It is so unpleasant to be with one whom you do not know—whose religious training has perhaps been entirely different, & who, perhaps, has no religious scruples at all. I love to be so situated that I can kneel down morning & night or offer up my feeble devotions, & feel, if there be any one present that they too sympathize with me, & join with me in my devotions. 'tis in my own private room by myself, or with a confidential friend, that I feel like offering up my prayers to Almighty God.—The prayers that are offered in public, are too often framed to please the ear of those who hear; but when one is away from the gaze of others, out of the hearing of all but God himself, 'tis then the feelings of the heart are poured fourth, 'tis then there is not [hypocrisy] in prayer—Or there is less danger of its being hypocritical.[77]

Private devotion allowed great openness between pilgrim and shepherd. That honesty offered spiritual nourishment for McCampbell and most other evangelicals who extolled the unique virtues of domestic devotion.

Although evangelicals frequently assessed their daily and weekly progress on their pilgrimage toward heaven, most also took more reflective breaks—often on New Year's Day or on their birthdays—to make annual assessments. Unlike their daily ruminations, these reflections had the added advantage of hindsight, revealing how short-term experiences and long-term expectations joined together in the evangelical imagination. In one typical reflection, Mary Bethell assessed her relationship with God and how everyday events and hardships fit into God's larger plan for her:

The Lord has spared me to see another year, goodness and mercy have followed me all the days of my life. . . . I will now renew my covenant with my God. I am determined to deny myself, take up my cross daily and follow Christ, if the Lord will bless me and mine. . . . The Lord has been with me the past year, I think I have grown in grace, I am pressing forward in the path to Heaven. I enjoy religion 'tis my meat and drink to do the will of God, he has heard and answered my prayer. All things work for my spiritual good. I have my temptations and trials and sorrows and cares, I expect to have them as long as I live, but I know that God's grace is sufficient for me. I have always found it so. The Lord has been with me in every trouble and comforted and blessed me and brought me out of many troubles, therefore I will continue to look to him with strong confidence and faith, he is my best friend.[78]

Samuel Haycraft worried that he was making little headway in his spiritual journey. On his fifty-eighth birthday, Haycraft wrote of his fears that he had accomplished little good, though he had lived longer than most people of his day: "If it was possible to sum up his mercy, the amount of good and evil I have done morally speaking in this world how fearful would be the preponderance be in favor of the latter." While writing in her diary on the last day of 1855, Mary Davis Brown's thoughts of those who had died over the past year set her mind on eternity: "This closes another of the fleeting time theire has been many an aking head sick heart and broken spirit since this year came in and many a one gone to theire long home to give an account of theire stewardship only think of the bodies that lies moulding in the dirt and be admonished. . . . [T]hink of the vanity of earthly things and of the shortness of life Oh think of eternity and be wise."[79] In the evangelical worldview, nearly everything in life had spiritual purpose. Life's setbacks, no matter how painful, played an essential role in validating faith. As the cycle of crisis, doubt, and relief repeated itself throughout evangelicals' lifetimes, their faith strengthened. Though evangelicals often spoke of resignation to God's will, a necessary precondition to maintaining orthodoxy, they continually sought to make their interpretations fit the larger narrative of their spiritual pilgrimage.

Individual believers' attempts to scrutinize everything and everyone for evidence of God's designs generated both stability and instability among southern evangelicals. The faithful took comfort in the belief that God had a plan for them and readily intervened in human affairs to execute that plan. While conversion may have reframed believers' purpose and meaning during their lifetimes, they also readily acknowledged that assurances of salvation never foreclosed hardship. Evangelicals also depended on their clergymen for intellectual and devotional leadership and guidance. When the rural South's religious landscape offered sparse opportunities for spiritual renewal, evangelicals even attended meetings of other denominations and listened to black preachers as part of the quest to understand God's role in everyday life. Evangelical expectations may have called for grudging acceptance of life's tribulations, but believers continually sought answers. Conversion thus connected southern evangelicals with individual destiny, pious kin, and the larger community of evangelical believers.

As historians of the antebellum South note, the orientation of evangelical identity and worship toward the individual and the otherworldly created a religious sensibility resistant to social change. Yet destabilizing forces remained embedded within southern evangelical identity and worship. Nothing proved more disruptive than the persistent emphasis on individual believers' authority to make personal interpretations of God's designs on earth. Even in an era when evangelicalism embraced family piety, individual men and women freely disassociated themselves from kin who had remained unwilling or unable to maintain evangelical standards of morality and belief. Clergymen too, constantly struggling with individual authority, occasionally adapted their messages and practices to popular demand rather than rigidly enforcing orthodoxy. With domestic devotion assuming increasing importance, many of God's greatest rewards and challenges—those events in life that demanded closest scrutiny—now originated from within the home. The forces of stability and instability within southern evangelicalism—the tension between self-abnegation and self-promotion in the conversion process and the tension between resignation and interpretation in the pilgrim's outlook—thus kept matters related to faith and family particularly alive and unpredictable within the antebellum evangelical family. Although evangelical clergymen increasingly circumscribed the formal authority of women in the meetinghouse, they increasingly acknowledged women's devotional leadership within the home.

CHAPTER 2

Courting Women, Courting God
Strenuous Courtships and Holy Unions

Unlike other points in the life course, where women often pushed the bounds of their influence beyond the narrow limits suggested in advice literature, single women discovered that clergy and kin alike sanctioned women's authority in courtship. A strenuous courtship offered single women the only assurance that they might achieve a harmonious and companionate ideal in marriage where "mutual respect and romantic love" between husband and wife would lead to the conversion and heavenly reunification of the entire family in heaven.[1] After marriage, women in unhappy or even abusive relationships had few avenues for public redress—divorce or even support from clergymen or fellow congregants remained elusive. The best safeguards for women's happiness remained extended courtships that tested suitors' patience, faith, and affection. This process unfolded on two fronts: at church and at home, where couples found themselves under the ever-watchful eyes of others; and through correspondence, where men and women set out to overcome suspicion and ritual and forge genuine bonds of love. Faith and God remained at the center of this process. With a collective vision of heaven and growing concern about the passage of faith from one generation to the next, evangelicals desperately wanted to ensure that piety spread throughout the family tree. The distrust and testing inherent in courtships allowed evangelical families simultaneously to assess suitors' character and piety and their depth of feeling. Even a presumably safe match with an impeccably pious man did not prevent a woman from using her faith to frustrate her suitor's rush to marriage. She might call off the courtship altogether after prayerful reconsideration of the match, or she might mention that her filial obligations to an aging parent prevented her from seriously entertaining courtship. Men may have initiated courtships, but as they progressed, women often took control. Pious men gauged their potential for success in courtship on women's willingness to share their feelings and imagine a future together, a process that inevitably included discussion of faith and family.

Evangelical values thus placed a sharper edge on many of the characteristics that historians have traditionally identified with courtship patterns in the antebellum South: circumspection and even alienation between men and women in the courtship process, continued involvement of family members in courtship decisions, and the challenge of discovering personal fulfillment against such a ritual-laden backdrop. These courtship characteristics, particularly among the planter class, contrast sharply with northern courtship patterns in this era, in which couples had privacy from parents, engaged in a quest for mutual self-discovery, and ultimately made falling in love a precondition for marriage.[2] While these authors point to the numerous hurdles that northern couples encountered—particularly the vulnerabilities that candor in courtship created for men and women alike—such works orient courtship around individualism and affection to a much greater degree than do most historians of the antebellum South. Indeed, Karen Lystra contends that "romantic love contributed to the displacement of God by the lover as the central symbol of ultimate significance." Moreover, she contends, nineteenth-century middle-class Americans "were making deities of each other in the new theology of romantic love."[3] Southern evangelicals would have insisted that their courtships and marriages retained much greater room for God and piety but like their northern counterparts would have aspired to construct companionate marriages. But the means of southern courtships—particularly limiting courtship to public settings and including family opinion in the courtship process—diverged strikingly from emerging northern patterns in this era.

Although nonevangelicals and evangelicals used many of the same means of courtship, evangelicals differed greatly from their secular counterparts in their desired ends. First, evangelicals believed that spouses dramatically shaped individuals' odds of obtaining evangelicalism's greatest promise, that of life eternal. Second, evangelical men and women imagined their journey to heaven commencing at their own doorstep. To court outside of one's denomination or beyond the evangelical fold altogether jeopardized the collective satisfaction of sharing piety within the household. In short, evangelical faith mattered enormously in courtship decisions because it forced men and women to assess their choice in light of eternal judgment, not merely happiness in the foreseeable future. Faith inspired some evangelical southerners to marry pious individuals from lower social classes, even when family members protested. In spite of her brother's objections, Maria Lide married Josiah Pauncy, whom she described as "a pious man, but poor." Piety could thus trump class in the calculus of courtship decisions, a move few nonevangelical white southerners dared to consider.[4]

In addition to imagining how courtship decisions would uniquely shape their future happiness, evangelicals experienced variations in the courtship ritual itself that differed noticeably from their nonevangelical peers. First, wariness and even alienation between young men and women ran deeper among evangelicals than nonevangelicals. When evangelical parents warned their children—especially daughters—of the dangers of courtship, the risks transcended family reputation to envelop sin and its eternal consequences. Second, women who courted clergymen had to gauge their ability to shoulder the informal but burdensome public and private obligations of a minister's wife in addition to women's traditional roles of child rearing and domestic management. Third, many southern women felt torn between their desire (and expectation) to marry and establish their own families and the sacrosanct duties to aid and comfort their parents. A sense of religious duty heightened the stakes, but women often found the answer to their dilemma through prayer. Suitors found God's involvement in their courtship both an asset and an obstacle—an asset when women used prayer to alleviate their concerns regarding their filial duties, and a nonnegotiable obstacle when prayer justified a woman's desire to end a relationship. Fourth, unlike their nonevangelical counterparts, evangelical men used the vocabulary of domesticity to appeal to the women they courted. When contrasted with their secular peers, who privileged control, dominance, and individual honor in both courtship and marriage, evangelical men neared a feminized version of both. Many evangelical men undoubtedly sought some of the same material ends through marriage as their nonreligious peers—maintaining or enhancing their economic standing, for example—but evangelical men stressed the future possibilities of marriage over the immediate risks to a family's established reputation.[5] Secular men of honor, conversely, placed their future fulfillment in their own hands—specifically, in their ability to enhance their public image among other elite men. Marriage provided evangelical men with the means to unlock the possibilities of faith, requiring them to intertwine personal fulfillment with home and companionship. In courtship, the introduction of domestic concerns allowed men to downplay self-interest's inherent role in courtship and to foreground their expectation of mutual fulfillment in religiously legitimized language.

The evangelical emphasis on domesticity also underscores how the stakes of courtship differed for men and women. Women often felt torn by self-interest, family interest, and duty to God in courtship, whereas men experienced a singleness of purpose. Once engaged, women also ruminated on the daunting challenges of repeated pregnancies, child rearing, and household management. Quite simply, single men typically had much more to gain from marriage in the worldly terms of authority, affection, and fulfillment.[6] Creating one's own domicile marked an evangelical man's rise to independence and unquestioned manhood. To accomplish those ends, evangelical men exploited the feminized language of domesticity. When a woman joined her suitor in describing and defining their joint domestic expectations for the future, both parties knew that they were well on their way to marriage. Ultimately, while the evangelical courtship process paralleled many of the processes of elite southerners, their professed goal of a companionate marriage more closely resembled northern, middle-class aspirations. But as southern evangelicals sorted through these courtship challenges in their correspondence, they set uniquely evangelical expectations and principles into motion.

Keeping the Opposite Sex at Arm's Length

Faith provided evangelical men and women with ample justification for keeping the opposite sex at arm's length. Beyond the experience of sex-segregated education in the academy and the Sunday school, both young men and young women found religious and intellectual rationales to keep their distance. Of the myriad adolescent endeavors that threatened a young woman's eternal salvation, none posed a greater risk than courtship. Though spiritual and emotional fulfillment through marriage inspired courtship, older evangelical women counseled young women that courtship itself offered far more opportunities for danger than for fulfillment. This dark vision of courtship, which fused evangelicalism's emphasis on the eternal consequences of daily decisions with the mutual suspicion between young men and women that characterized the South, contrasts sharply with that presented by historians of courtship in the antebellum North, who stress mutuality and the quest for self-discovery throughout the courtship process. Indeed, according to southern evangelical women, courtship enhanced the need for a young woman's religious armor, because young women could count on men to be filled with carnal and treacherous designs. Given that southern women married younger (typically around age twenty) than their northern counterparts (twenty-two or twenty-three), such advice may have seemed all the more essential for young southern women.[7] Indeed, southern men had the benefits of greater age, experience, and education than the women they courted.[8] Evangelical men such as William Wills felt less trepidation about courtship than about marriage itself. Men whose real-world experiences had repeatedly challenged the clergy's declarations of matrimonial harmony and bliss might question the utility of marriage altogether.

The Reverend James O. Andrew, bishop of the Methodist Episcopal Church, South, explained that evangelicalism enhanced marriage while aiding couples in accomplishing evangelicalism's ultimate ends: "Let me say to both, seek, by all proper means, to promote each other's happiness; and especially remember that the great object of your union is to help each other to heaven." As Andrew acknowledged, however, getting to heaven required much more than affection and romantic fulfillment. The path to a harmonious and pious marriage, he argued, required close scrutiny of a prospective mate's character in the courtship process. In addition to warning men and women of the dangers of using courtship and marriage as the means to either material gain or the fulfillment of novel-inspired romance, Andrew cautioned that any prospective spouse should be thoroughly examined for evidence of sobriety, piety, industriousness, and love of family. Noting the dreadful and permanent consequences of selecting an impious or ill-suited mate, Rev. Andrew implicitly recognized that these ideal qualities, while simply stated, often proved difficult to discern during courtship. He advised evangelical men that the evangelical wife "is to be a sort of presiding divinity at thy family board, and her countenance the mirror in which must be reflected the faithful image of thy domestic bliss or wo." Women also should proceed cautiously to the altar, Andrew believed: "Deliberate well before you bind yourself with cords which you can never loose, and which may become more galling than the chains of the galley slave."[9] With temporal and eternal happiness inextricably tied to the choice of a mate and the formation of a new family, evangelicals entered into courtship suspicious and wary, seeking to find their way through the rituals to unlock their lovers' Christian character.

Adult women used faith to educate younger women about the conflicting interests of men and women in courtship. One evangelical woman's frank directive underscored the foreboding attitude many families took toward courtship, a passageway that was at once inevitable and perilous. Writing in 1817, C. A. Hill offered an unvarnished treatment of sex and faith to a female relation, Sarah Thomas, a teacher. Hill opened gently, empathizing with Thomas as she faced one of life's most important crossroads: "I assure you my heart is enlarged towards you. I view you on the pinacle of an awful precipice; such is the situation of all females, as well as males, just immerging into life." Hill then became more blunt, advising Thomas about the particular perils young women faced: "Peculiarly delicate is the crisis, and one false step forever blasts the fame of a female. Not quite so with the other sex—Let me then impress on your mind, what the prudence and sagacity of a fond mother has no doubt labored to inculcate, the utmost caution and circumspection in all you do or say." A woman's pure and pious reputation was not only essential to her family but also fragile, liable to ruin merely by rumor. Because men lacked womanly restraint, women had to police their own behavior and thoughts as well as those of the men in their lives. "Altho the soul of man is not invunorable to the distress of a female, yet malevolence is so predominant in the human heart, that in all, it displays the devouring jaws of a mighty Malestrom, ready on every touch to destroy the vessel that per chance may be cast into the whirlpool—Such is the human heart, which omniscience has disclosed to be desperately wicked." In a society where single women from the middle and upper classes were expected to be chaperoned by male relations when in public, nonevangelical southern women no doubt heard similar refrains. While members of both groups certainly feared irreparable damage to their families' reputations if single women demonstrated excessive familiarity with the opposite sex, evangelical women had the added burden of facing eternal damnation if they faltered.[10]

Having thus set the stage for danger and conflict, Hill instructed Thomas to use her piety to cautiously and warily engage the opposite sex. Against these dangers, Hill rhetorically asked, "How necessary to be continually armed? And how can this be done better, than by acquiring the harmless innocence of the dove and sublility of the serpent?" Hill thus suggested that fire must be met with fire in courtship. Innocence might be the preferred course of action, but effective if stealthy means could justify the ends. Making certain that her allusions to biblical embodiments of purity and cunning did not obscure her larger point, Hill hammered home her argument with a popular reference to Ephesians: "This only can be acquired by putting on the whole armour of God."[11] The military metaphor aptly captured women's defensive posture in courtship (men, after all, initiated relationships) while emphasizing the strength of women's position. A woman need not be defenseless, Hill argued, but she did need to know who posed a threat and when to prepare for battle.

Hill legitimized and exaggerated the social gulf between the sexes. The impregnability of armor evoked both the physical and psychological space that should separate the sexes. A woman who took off her armor was vulnerable; conversely, however, women could also improve their defenses. Refinement of morals and intellect would greatly aid Thomas's watchfulness and decision making. Hill reminded her young relative to seek "useful knowledge . . . to mature your mind and protect your deportment," and above all to avoid "the delusive charms of fashionable amusements." Hill warned Thomas to recollect St. Paul's directive that "while you are teaching others, you may not require yourself to be taught." Again, the prevalence of sin everywhere, especially in matters related to sexuality, necessitated deep mistrust of others and nonstop self-circumspection. Familiarity in a relationship with a man, let alone flights of emotion, propelled young women (and their families) toward a whirlpool that could cause irreversible damage. Seeking to promote Thomas's ties to her faith and family, both of which Hill believed would significantly check sexuality, the older woman hoped to sustain a steady and open exchange of letters. "Write me, as often as you can—consult me on any difficulties in your pursuit. In whatever I am able, I will always with pleasure, give you any instruction."[12] As confidante, Hill hoped to respond to Thomas's courtship concerns with a level of openness and sincerity that exceeded that of a mother. Hill's letter indicates that religious women entered the courtship arena with trepidation, if not anxiety, about the intentions of any suitor, regardless of appearances or even faith.

Rather than distrusting women in courtship, William Wills questioned whether marriage—even a pious marriage—would lead to emotional and spiritual fulfillment. As he compared his life experiences with his observations of married couples, Wills noticed a disjuncture between the harmonious, ideal marriage outlined by clergy and the way in which married couples actually lived. The twenty-four-year-old Wills thus wrote to his close friend and mentor, Spencer Cotten, to ascertain whether marriage to a woman could lead to a level of spiritual and emotional fulfillment unavailable to single men. Wills pondered the advantages of celibacy less in the interest of spiritual purity or authority and more out of a desire for his own brand of domestic tranquility. Visiting a friend whom he identified only as the "Old Bachelor," Wills pronounced the superiority of single life based on the order prevalent in the man's home: "The beautiful clean yard, fine trees, good paling with painted gates. [H]ouse in good order, sideboard & bureau shining, carpeted floor in one room, another so handsomely waxed that I have to be very careful how I walk." Wills contrasted this scene with that at the home of the average married couple, striking blows at domesticity's exaggerated virtues in evangelical prescriptive literature: "No scolding wife with blowsy, dishevelled hair blustering among the servants: No bawling, crying children to distract the mind, but all calm, serene and placid as a lovely summer's eve." Decrying domesticity as a sham, Wills argued that the grimy reality of managing a household overcame even the best married women. A woman who one day gracefully carried all the charms of womanhood would the next day wear a greasy apron, neglect her hair, and let "dirty rags and disarranged furniture fill the room." Possibly seeking to distance himself from an earlier era of Methodism that celebrated the celibate itinerant, Wills closed his letter by adding that he was not a "misanthrope" who took no interest in women. Rather, his travels had taught him that single women lost much of their charm when burdened by the duties of managing households. He therefore imagined himself following in the bachelor's footsteps, living a "life of single blessedness." Although Wills's letter is playful and perhaps exaggerated at times, the fact that he shared these thoughts with the same man to whom he looked for straight answers on the Methodist Protestant Church's doctrine suggests a serious undertone to Wills's musings on bachelorhood.[13]

As Wills surely anticipated, Cotten replied that marriage not only held many blessings for men but also constituted virtually a Christian duty. Although the "Old Bachelor" likely possessed many qualities worth emulating, Cotten insisted, celibacy was not one of them, because "man was not born or intended to live alone." Regardless of the gulf between ideal and practice, Cotten argued, marriage was a divinely sanctioned institution from which another duty, child rearing, would emerge. Cotten also advised Wills to court while he still had the "advantage of youth" because "young men can marry to more advantage than old ones." Indeed, Cotten thought Wills's peripatetic ways an advantage in the courtship process, increasing the odds that he might meet a "good girl" who "will be willing to join her faith with yours."[14] In an era when men feared that they might not find a good match if they had no serious prospects as they reached their twenties, Wills had reached the point where he needed to make hard decisions about marriage.[15]

Although prescriptive literature spoke of marriage as natural, inevitable, beneficial, and even desirable, many evangelical men and women remained wary of courtship. Both men and women knew that they had a large gulf to cross to achieve the trust, openness, and love promoted by evangelical prescriptive literature. The courtship process further complicated matters. Its familial dimensions combined with its conventions to make the discovery of genuine feeling and emotion all the more difficult to discern.

The Dynamics of Evangelical Courtship

In nonevangelical courtships, young men had to persuade women and their kin that marriage would benefit both the individuals and the families involved. For evangelical men, God presented a third variable to consider. In the cases of Anne Beale, Rosannah Davisson, Frances Bestor, and Anna Thomas, women leaned on God to make a final determination in their decision to marry. Although Davisson's courtship with Methodist clergyman John Poulton did not hinge as fully as the other three on God's immediate role in the relationship, the situation forcefully illustrates women's inability to voice affection or even to discuss personal piety until after an engagement had been concluded. Bestor and Beale felt that God's approval of their union negated the disapproval of family members, while Anna Thomas found justification for breaking off her relationship with Jones Fuller after submitting the matter to God. Women's ability to move between self-interest and divine direction during courtship gave them an unusual degree of authority. Women's authority also shifted during the courtship process, from an initial position of reactivity to suitors' overtures to a position of control in the latter stages of the courtship.[16] Although this shift in authority typifies southern courtships generally, evangelical women based their personal authority in their personal piety, an evasive source of authority for family and suitors alike.

Similarly, the tension between women and their families during courtship resembles conflict in nonevangelical families but with added religious overtones. When torn between their desire to marry and a sense of obligation to care for elderly parents, evangelical women confronted obligations to God as well as parents. As Bishop Andrew reminded Methodists, the commandment to "honour thy father and thy mother" demanded filial obedience and respect for a lifetime—not just childhood. "Your duty," Andrew advised evangelical children of all ages, requires "you to see that [your parents'] evening of life is rendered as pleasant and cheerful and comfortable as you can render it."[17] In practice this duty fell most heavily on southern women, especially single women, who added the care of parents to their list of domestic chores.[18] Single women therefore often had to make wrenching decisions about whether to retain the sanctified role of filial child or fulfill the sanctified role of helpmate. Two women, Frances Bestor and Anna Thomas, decided to leave their parents' side but did so with trepidation because they knew that marriage meant relocation far away. That lingering guilt, combined with the evangelical expectation that life always contained trials alongside blessings, led many women to hold onto a bit of gloom even as they optimistically anticipated marriage.

When Anne Beale's family resisted her decision to marry Methodist minister Joseph Davis, she sought and discovered religious legitimation for her decision. Under normal circumstances, this courtship and marriage would not have been problematical, but after the death of Martha Beale Davis, Anne's sister and Joseph Davis's first wife, Anne had moved into Davis's home to care for his son.[19] Playing the part of surrogate mother to Robert Davis, Anne Beale thought marriage to his father a natural progression. Some members of her family, however, saw the transition from in-laws to lovers as unnatural and discomforting. That unease forced Anne to reexamine her decision and circumvent their disapproval. Prayer and devotional introspection convinced Anne that her courtship and marriage had God's approval.

Anne Beale felt an aura of inevitability surrounding the sequence of events that led her to assume her sister's role in Rev. Davis's life. Robert Davis was only three months old when his mother died in 1835. When Anne assumed the duties of raising the child, she thought it fulfillment of a dream she had had well before her sister's death. The dream, which she did not recount on paper until nearly twenty years later, lasted three nights and had been relayed to several people—including Martha and Joseph Davis: "I thought I saw my sister dying, and I was called to her bedside, in a room I had never been in before; when she called the nurse to bring her infant son to her; and then asked me if I would take him, I answered, 'I would,' she then looked at me with solemnity, and said, well bring him up in the nurture, and admonitions of the Lord." When Anne next saw the baby in person, after her sister's death, the room was the same as in her dream, and she "took the child as from the hand of God, always feeling my responsibility." Anne had daily reinforcement of her sacrosanct maternal duty every time little Robert called her "My mama." Although the dream apparently had not foretold her marriage to her sister's widower, Anne saw their union as a logical extension of her role as the rightful religious steward of her sister's son, a shift from surrogate mother to mother, from sisterly helpmate to spousal helpmate.[20]

How Anne Beale and Joseph Davis crossed the line from kin relations to lovers remains a mystery, but they apparently did not commence an intimate relationship until approximately five months before their marriage, which occurred three years after her sister's death. Before their courtship, Anne signed her letters to Joseph, "Your sincere friend" or "Your sister in Christ," but she signed later letters with the trademark of courtship, "Yours affectionately." In January 1838, Anne instructed Joseph to earmark correspondence that was meant solely for her perusal: "I omited saying to you when we parted, that your letters to me, were considered as it were, public property, accordingly when ever one arrives, every one of the family must have a reading for themselves, or else they dont think they have heard from you." If Joseph marked his personal letters, Anne could avoid subjecting her "feelings to a severe test."[21]

Anne Beale and Joseph Davis apparently succeeded in concealing the new state of their relationship from friends and family because word of their engagement shocked many. Beale described her sister, Emily, as "greatly distressed and mortified" by the engagement. Although Anne never spelled out the reasons for her family's disapproval, the critiques were based on uncertainty about how the couple had reversed the proper order of courtship, marriage, and parenthood. Because Beale and Davis had courted in private, behind the shroud of domesticity, kin were left to wonder how the romantic relationship had formed. Nonetheless, Beale wished Davis to observe all of courtship's customs, insisting that he seek her father's consent and the opinions of her sister and her brother, although their approval was not "absolutely necessary."[22]

The negative reaction of some kin displeased but failed to dissuade Beale from following through with the marriage. Despite lamenting, "Oh me, how unfortunate am I, to give so much uneasiness and dissatisfaction to those I dearly love," Anne forged ahead, laying claim to a higher basis of authority: God "orders all things for the best, and I think it has been with due reference to His will, and a single eye to his Glory, that I have consented to take the step I have taken."[23] Writing those lines to the clergyman she was about to marry only enhanced Anne's sense of propriety and piety.

In fact, the controversy fit neatly into her evangelical worldview. Her actions—raising her sister's child in the faith (as foretold by a remarkable dream) and then marrying a minister—gave her a great feeling of religious righteousness. Yet she felt unfairly maligned by some kin, and she advised her fiancé on how to heal the rift. She viewed this family spat as yet another of life's tests for the faithful. More than familial crises that could be defused through faith, such challenges gave evangelical pilgrims opportunities to profess their dependency on God and seek renewed spiritual intimacy. "Through the strength of Grace Divine, I am still supported, and nothing less than this could have enabled me to bear up under my manifold trials, amidst all, the Lord has comforted, supported, and cheered me by the prospect of immortality, and eternal life beyond the grave."[24] Her faith had more than stood the test. She had persuaded herself of the justness of her cause and emerged with her faith reinvigorated.

The courtships of Rosannah Davisson, Frances Bestor, and Anna Thomas were more typical: lovers showed wariness toward one another and sought to work through the conventions of courtship to establish an emotional bond. Like Beale, these women struggled to garner complete family approval, but Davisson, Bestor, and Thomas did so in a much more public fashion. The personal and familial dimensions of courtship worked simultaneously as evangelical faith shaped emotion and choice in courtship.

With more than one hundred miles separating them, John Poulton, a

Methodist minister in Petersburg, Virginia, and Rosannah (Rose) Davisson, the daughter of a prominent physician in Warrenton, Virginia, relied on correspondence to sustain their intimacy during their courtship in 1857–58. Few of Poulton's courtship letters survive, but Davisson's letters often respond to his queries and therefore offer insight into his thoughts and expectations. As was typical in courtships of this era, Poulton was much more eager than Davisson was to advance their relationship to engagement and marriage. Indeed, Poulton's clerical mentor, the Reverend William Fulton, mocked a letter from his understudy: "Let me read: 'If I remain thus alone 2 years longer, I shall die so.' What! Only two years? And then, if not in that time, never!" Fulton wanted to talk seriously with Poulton before he exchanged the "life of single blessedness" for marriage and "certain cares, and uncertain comforts," but Poulton sought the companionship, connections to female parishioners, and household mastery that marriage would provide.[25]

Davisson repeatedly reminded Poulton that his professions of love far outpaced hers in terms of eloquence and passion. In a typical compliment, Davisson wrote, "I like the 'sermonlike' manner in which your letter was written. and also the cheerfulness of it. I almost felt that you had been talking to me." She acknowledged often that her letters offered a "poor return" and that she labored to find the words to convey the depth of her feelings. At times, she blamed her pen and imagination. At other times, she justified and defended her reticence as the product of womanly restraint: "I cannot help thinking you are mistaken in thinking me so 'extremely cautious' or that there was any lack of confidence on my part. I would much rather you should think me too cautious than not enough so." On another occasion, she wrote, "But I must not compliment you in even a 'disguised' manner. You do not know how much some parts of your letter made me feel. I felt like 'weeping' particularly where you allude to the future, your own feelings, and I may say almost fears, with regard to yourself, and if I could only write and express myself with as much satisfaction as I can converse, it would be very gratifying to me, but when I see you I will tell you all I think and feel about it. I have never been disturbed by a doubt, or fear, that you will not do all in your power to render me happy. I feel no fears. I know your feelings for me too well, and know you will be just what I think you, are." As she alternately defended and bemoaned her inarticulate writing, she apologized in advance for any misunderstanding but promised to clarify any concerns at their next meeting. Davisson's letters at times seem encrypted, as she relied on Poulton to fill in the gaps with shared knowledge or better yet to visit in person to sort matters out. After their engagement, Davisson wrote more openly, despite the risk of betraying her true feelings, an action that might harm the relationship.[26]

With her feelings largely absent from her letters, a good deal of Davisson's writing centered on the rhythms of the courtship correspondence itself, as she alternated between the reward of a newly arrived letter and worries about Poulton's health during an unexpected silence. Like many southern evangelical women during courtship, Davisson discussed a lingering depression that had no identifiable source. "This evening do not feel very cheerful, and yet there is no particular reason why I should not feel so, and if my letter is not cheerful, you will know that it is owing to my feelings." She hinted that her mood might stem from her separation from Poulton and acknowledged that the feeling, like some contagion, could spread to her suitor when he opened her response. Several scholars argue that these dramatic emotional swings among elite young women in the final stages of courtship may have resulted from women becoming aware of the impending transition from the relatively carefree world of adolescence to the impending challenges of pregnancy, child rearing, and the other cares involved in maintaining a household.[27] In Davisson's case, the murky origins of her melancholy must have kept Poulton guessing, further encouraging his visits and letters.

But Davisson also implicitly acknowledged throughout their courtship that she was auditioning for the rigorous role of a minister's wife. In contrast to her rather bland reporting of events in her household and community, her reports on church life seem vivid and casual. "Mr Haynes has gone home ill," she lamented. "No doubt he would have had a large congregation if he had been here, many were disappointed in not hearing him who had never heard him. He is more popular as a minister in the pulpit, but I think Mr Crown is more popular with the members. I think I like him better than Mr. Haynes." She no doubt learned to critique clergymen, including distinguishing their pastoral talents from their preaching skills, from her mother, who offered Poulton some friendly advice regarding his congregation: "I am afraid you will have a church debt on your hands, if you are extravagant in your notion about your new church, don't have it too fine & costly." Although Elizabeth Davisson momentarily questioned whether she had overstepped the boundaries of ladylike behavior, she clarified the purpose of her insight: "Excuse this plain talk. I am not giving advice, only making a suggestion."[28] Still too early in their courtship for Poulton and Rose Davisson to discuss their personal piety in depth, she nevertheless offered insights on her clergymen and congregation, thereby validating her ability to take the pulse of a congregation, a vital skill for a minister's wife.

However, Davisson's continued reticence to discuss her feelings for Poulton deeply disquieted him. On one occasion, Poulton attempted to pull Davisson out of her shell by asking her whether she would still consider marrying him if he faced certain death in matter of days or weeks. She mustered only an equivocating response that further shrouded her feelings: "This is a very serious question, and one I have never thought much about, while my feelings now prompt me to say 'yes,' judgement might dictate differently, but do not think this anything positive, it is a very painful subject to me, separated as we are, and when I see you I will talk more freely, if you wish it." She then threw the whole muddled discussion back at him, asking, "Can you not tell me your reasons for asking me? . . . Please do not think strangely of me for not answering your question unhesitatingly, but I cannot answer it to my own satisfaction, on account of its importance." No doubt aware that her answer was not what Poulton had hoped, she meekly concluded, "You know my feelings—and that I want to do just exactly what would be right, under those circumstances."[29] If Poulton had hoped to elicit a simple profession of love, Davisson was clearly not ready to offer it.

Four months later, after Davisson and Poulton had become engaged, Poulton had the indelicate task of asking for a postponement of their wedding date, an action that he feared would alienate Davisson and her immediate family. Although she approved the delay, she echoed the attitudes of many courting southern women when she noted her annoyance at family members and others who gossiped about the status of their courtship. Davisson also discovered that some of her female friends and relations pulled back from her as she prepared to enter marriage. In addition to one persistent suitor who followed the courtship a little too closely for the liking of either Davisson or Poulton, Poulton anxiously feared that his postponement of their wedding had created friction with his future father-in-law. Quick to clarify matters, Davisson explained that she had not passed along her father's love in recent letters merely because he had not been present during their composition and that the absence of such greeting did not signal any change in her father's feelings toward him.[30]

The couple survived these difficulties, and as their June 1858 wedding approached, Davisson's correspondence warmed considerably in tone and insight, signaling that she was prepared to imagine their future together and share her emotions more freely. Shortly after their engagement, she reflected on Poulton's recent visit to her family's parlor: "This little room is hallowed by fond remembrances, I often sit here at the sweet hour of twilight, for then *particularly* do I feel that our spirits hold communion." That new sense of spiritual and emotional intimacy revealed itself in many ways after their engagement. In the early months of their courtship, Poulton loaned Davisson religious writings by other clergymen, and she reported on events at her congregation; in the latter stages, however, she spoke more openly about her personal devotion. After noting that her father was attending church during revival season, Davisson observed, "I almost think sometimes we never are to have a revival again. I try to pray for it, but my faith is so weak." The future bride and groom also began an intellectual exchange, with Poulton sending Davisson copies of his sermon outlines and Davisson suggesting sermon topics. About the time of her engagement, Davisson observed the sixth anniversary of her conversion, remarking that she hoped to continue to "grow in grace" but knew that her spiritual pilgrimage would now have to continue within her marriage. In addition to emerging discussions of their personal and shared piety, the couple's postengagement correspondence featured a new intimacy and honesty, as is evidenced by Davisson's use of "Frank," her pet name for Poulton, and her shift from signing letters "fondly and with affections true" to using "yours till death."[31]

At the age of twenty-five, Frances Bestor professed deep suspicion toward intimacy and marriage. When J. G. Robertson, a widower with two children, suddenly removed those reservations, she felt torn between her newfound interest in marriage and her responsibility for her father's health and home. As the daughter of an Alabama Baptist minister, she knew that the entire community would second-guess whatever decision she made. She too doubted herself, wondering whether she could simultaneously take on the role of wife and mother. Although she ultimately married her suitor, the relationship took many twists and turns as Frances sorted through her preparedness for commitments freighted with so much importance.

Like many southern women who postponed marriage, Bestor was surprised when at last she found herself in love's grip: "A change has come, the spirit of my dreams & I who have been 'loves whip,' who have ridiculed love sick swains & married life have been caught napping & to my great astonishment I have been aroused by the startling fact that my heart ... is now won by a widower with two children." Like most southern courtships, Robertson and Bestor's commenced in a public setting, among folks who were familiar with another. On a trip to Gainesville, Alabama, in April 1854, Bestor first encountered Robertson at a tea party, likely attended by members of the local Baptist church. Robertson apparently showed an interest in Bestor at that initial meeting, but Bestor "payed very little attention" to him because "all eyes were gazing" and she "felt no particular interest."[32] Robertson's flattering attention must have made Bestor acutely aware of the public stage on which her courtship would appear. Older than most unmarried southern women, the daughter of a minister, and tirelessly engaged in events at her church, Bestor surely felt the gaze of many curious onlookers. No doubt aware that southerners looked on older, single women with some suspicion and that most single women had difficulty in finding the financial means to maintain their independence, Bestor likely felt some pressure to find a suitable match. But as a widower with children, Robertson faced even greater pressure: most women would have hesitated before taking on the double challenge of forging intimacy with a husband while managing children.

A few months later, Robertson visited Bestor at her father's home, when he "evidently intend[ed] I should see what his *thoughts* were," she recalled. The rapid pace of the courtship forced Bestor to consider both the responsibilities that marriage to Robertson would bring and her existing responsibilities to her father. If she followed the courtship through to marriage, she would simultaneously fill not one but two sacrosanct roles, but her "new station," as she delicately put it, would carry dramatically increased expectations. Moreover, she had difficulty justifying her departure from her widowed father's side: "My seperating from him & our family will be a great *struggle*, but ... I have asked assistance from my Heavenly Father & *have received* a degree of *comfort* I had scarcely expected." Bestor feared that others might not be so generous in their interpretations of her actions, however: "I have tried to do my duty as a Daughter & a sister," regardless of what the "hard hearted world" may think. The intellectual and emotional tumult involved in courtship caused Bestor great discomfort: "My brain whirled, my heart fluttered, & I could scarcely see." In the face of such a wrenching choice, Bestor chose to break off the relationship with her suitor: "My proud & hauty spirit said: away with such weakness &

under this influence of distraction (I may say). I wrote him a letter stating I did not love him."[33] Like many antebellum women, she chose not an outright rejection but an opportunity to put the relationship on hold and test the depth and sincerity of her suitor's feelings.

Robertson responded by pursuing her with increased vigor, forcing Bestor to seek divine counsel regarding the best course. He "soon returned after the reception of my note, & insisted I should retract what I had said, I was much moved, but still did not believe that, I would make him happy, & I disclosed the fact to him he was willing to bear with my weaknesses & could not think as I did. Alas! human nature how frail she is?" His tenacity in spite of her constant misgivings about her ability to become a wife and mother reached its culmination on the way to church one Sunday when Robertson turned to Bestor and simply said, "Come share my cottage." Even though his "strait forward course" had won her over, Bestor remained unprepared to concede as much to her suitor: "My heart could resist no longer & he discovered the dearest secret of my heart, still I attempted to conceal it. . . . [H]e left town again without an answer." She again turned to God for counsel: "On bended knee I appealed to my Heavenly Father to decide for me if I loved [Robertson] sufficiently to perform the part I must act in accepting his hand, I felt assured he could make me happy but the doubt was still in my mind that I would not be what he expected."[34] The elevation of marriage and motherhood to a divine calling must have given women pause as they pondered whether they could realize such an ideal. Bestor found the reassurance she sought, bolstered by her experience rearing her siblings after her mother's death and by Robertson's persistence, and she agreed to the union.

In spite of their impending nuptials, Bestor continued to have difficulty communicating freely with Robertson and to worry about her future happiness. With the engagement announced, Bestor declared that the "struggle was over," creating a moment of opportunity for the two lovers to begin to confide in one another and break through the trappings of courtship conventions. Robertson asked that his fiancée "talk freely & openly to him & feel that our spirits were *kindred*," but Bestor retained her fears about honesty and love. She hesitated to confess her disappointment at the limited time they shared together: "My heart was sad, but 'we are taught in this cold world to smother each feeling which is most dear' & altho' my thoughts often reverted to him I dare not let any one know it." She also saw herself as helpless prey caught in a spider's web: "My—friend wove a Webb around me which I hope may never be broken, but by cherishing that affection which both of us possess for each other, we may glide through lifes stormy way and be a support to each other until that gloomy & dreadful day when one of us shall be taken away by that destroyer death."[35] Such a metaphor captured both Robertson's aggressive pursuit and the evangelical worldview, in which believers prepared for the valleys in their earthly sojourn even as they celebrated its peaks, always with an eye toward death and ultimate judgment. Bestor remained suspicious of love and affection, fearing that dependency on anything other than God might bring about heartache.

Anne Beale struggled to persuade her family of the propriety of her marriage, Rose Davisson struggled to articulate her feelings for John Poulton, and Frances Bestor struggled between her loyalties to her father and her interest in courtship. Jones Fuller confronted all three challenges in his courtship with Anna Thomas. First, Fuller confronted family members unwilling to part with their widowed elderly mother's primary companion and caregiver. Second, perhaps as an outgrowth of the first condition, Thomas vacillated in her affections to Fuller throughout the courtship. Even after receiving her brothers' reluctant approval to marry, Thomas broke off the relationship, proclaiming God's support of her decision. Third, amid the personal and family confusion in the courtship, Anna's mother, Ann Thomas, appropriated the voice of a patriarch, charging her future son-in-law with solemn obligations to care for her daughter. The Fuller-Thomas courtship concluded on a traditional note: the evangelical man accepted a parent's charge in his own idiom, acknowledging his accountability to God for his wife's care while confirming his mastery over his wife. Thus, the couple wrestled not only with the approval of family members but also with their faith and God's authority. Piety thus could frustrate as well as reinforce the authority of individuals and families throughout the courtship process.

When Jones Fuller approached Anna Thomas about marriage, Anna dutifully turned to her older brothers, Gabriel Thomas and W. George Thomas, for permission to marry because her father was deceased. The approval process proved thorny because distance prevented all of the principals from interacting with one another face-to-face. Although he was from the Louisburg, North Carolina, area, where Anna Thomas resided, Fuller lived in Mobile, Alabama, during their entire courtship. Gabriel Thomas lived in Petersburg, Virginia, and George Thomas lived in Tarboro, North

Carolina, and neither man had ever met Fuller. Both brothers played the part of surrogate patriarch and commenced investigations into Fuller's character.

Writing from Virginia, Gabriel Thomas offered cool approval of Fuller while emphasizing that his sister should proceed cautiously and thoughtfully. Moreover, Gabriel applauded Anna's willingness to adhere to his opinion as an acknowledgment of the laws of humankind and God: "I advise that spirit of submission with which you have submitted to the better opinion of your Senior and Counsellors—and be assured Anna that such a spirit will not pass unnoticed or unforgotten by man and will be recorded to your credit, in the annals of Eternity." As long as she continued to practice "prudence[,] discression[,] and submission," he wrote, "all will be well with you." Lacking personal knowledge of Fuller, Gabriel Thomas's strongest reservation stemmed from Fuller's profession, cotton broker, which Thomas unflatteringly likened to gambling: brokers "often invest all they are worth (and more, too) in speculations entirely dependant upon *Contingencies*, and they are men too who are fond of risking their all up the *turn of a card*." But a letter from an acquaintance of Fuller's, combined with Ann Thomas's sanction of the union, persuaded Gabriel Thomas to tender his tentative approval in the belief that his sister "cant do better." Nonetheless, Gabriel urged Anna to move forward cautiously, prayerfully, and with an eye toward the eternal ramifications of her decision. Sounding more like Bishop Andrew than a brother, Gabriel underscored his emotional distance from his sister with formal advice: "View the whole ground—ponder well your footsteps—commune with your own heart—be sure that you love him and that too from right principles—be not carried away with feeling for a desire for a change of life, nor from the anticipations of the short lived pleasures of receiving the congratulations of friends as a bride. Act upon principle and from motives high and holy." Discharging himself from any further role in the matter, he concluded, "I am done—yours is the responsibility."[36]

George Thomas was even less forthcoming, withholding complete approval of the union and wounding Fuller's feelings in the process. Merely contemplating the matter of his sister's marriage and removal, he wrote, "draws so powerfully upon all the tenderest feelings of my heart that I hardly am willing to approach it." Although he conceded that Anna, "if suitably married . . . will be happier," he had hoped that his sister would not marry during his mother's lifetime. Thomas refused to grant full approval on the grounds that he was not personally acquainted with Fuller. Thomas also declined to check Fuller's references, arguing that the opinion of strangers would carry no weight and that only the opinions of family members mattered: "What you think together with the corroborating opinions of my dear brothers & sisters can but have some—yes great influence on my mind, and I would be, and am, more influenced by it than the opinions of an hundred uninterested witnesses." Thomas finally gave tepid approval based on the opinions of his mother and sister: "Altho it almost makes my very heart bleed to say so . . . I give my consent."[37]

Having gained her brothers' permission to marry Anna Thomas, Fuller turned his attention to the challenges of courtship correspondence directly with her. As in the courtships of Bestor and Davisson, the pronouncement of affections remained lopsided throughout Fuller and Thomas's courtship: the future groom crammed his letters with reassurances of devotion, affection, and mutuality, while the bride-to-be remained aloof and reserved. Fuller always took the lead (and the risk) in an attempt to break through the conventions of the courtship ritual to share more openly his emotions and thoughts. In one of her more strongly worded affirmations of her affection for Fuller, Thomas wrote near Christmas 1845, "Absence, instead of alienating and lessening my regard for you, has served only, to *increase it*." Most of the time, however, Fuller had to content himself with vague claims of affection. When the topic of marriage cropped up in the same letter, Thomas enshrouded her feelings with a double negative. After "much reflection" on the issue of marriage, she wrote, "no unfavourable change has come over the spirit of *my* feelings." Fuller, by contrast, gushed with affection, dedication, and confidence: "I have read and reread your letter repeatedly and I am unable my *Dearest* Anna to convey to you the *pleasure* it has given. . . . I can only repeat to you my Dearest Anna the assurance (which I do with all my heart) that it *shall* ever be my constant study through life to promote your comfort and happiness to the utmost *extent* of my power. Oh that I could see you *this* day and repeat to you in Person the *love* that this throbbing heart of mine feels for you."[38] Fuller clung to Thomas's half-hearted pledges of interest, but his correspondence failed to push the relationship beyond the most formal bounds of convention and custom.

In an effort to energize their courtship while forcing Thomas to confess her true feelings, Fuller proposed. The usually reserved Thomas responded forthrightly: "I do not love you sufficiently to marry you." But she gave him no further reason, leaving him to wonder whether he had made some courtship misstep, whether she had decided that she could not leave her mother, or whether some other motive lay behind her decision. Moreover, she foreclosed debate on the matter by claiming that she had had the benefit of divine counsel. Following her brother's advice and retiring to her "closet" to seek heavenly advice and scrutiny, Thomas submitted the marriage proposal "to an 'all wise God,' hoping and believing I shall be guided aright." But Fuller too had petitioned God and had received his endorsement of their marriage. Thomas had an answer: "You remarked yesterday you confidently believed, we would be married, that you felt you had the sanction of high Heaven, if that be the case, I hope, and believe too, that after I have tried and tested my feelings longer, I shall be led to act in a way that will conduce to your happiness and mine." She pledged that she had only his best interests at heart: "I have been prompted by the purest motives, none other than the regard I have for your feelings" and manifested her newfound disinterest by signing the letter, "Respectfully, Anna L. Thomas," a dramatic departure from her earlier closing, "I am *yours*."[39] Much like Frances Bestor, Thomas felt pulled in opposite directions by her family and her suitor, and she refused to proceed further until she knew the depth of Fuller's interest and commitment.

Fuller ultimately resurrected the relationship, although his answer to Thomas has not been preserved. A month passed during which Fuller received no letters from Thomas, causing him to write of his unease, disappointment, and anxiety. She finally resumed writing in early February 1846, but she remained unable to transcend her tone of withdrawal and reticence: "Your letters are fraught with so much affection, and devoted *love*—I fear you will conclude that I am of a cold temperament, in consequence of the reservedness, I deem it prudent to use." At times, Thomas seems to have delighted in keeping their relationship in the limbo of courtship, where she retained authority and affection: "Although my mind is thus fluctuating, there seems to be an enchantment thrown around me, that I cannot yet, get my consent to discard you. I hope you will bear with these little inconsistencies, should you deem them such, and make allowances for my tardiness in deciding this important matter." She closed her letter coyly, "May you be *always happy* is the sincere wish of one who entertains for you feelings of more than *ordinary regard*."[40]

By March, Thomas finally seemed to be inching toward marriage, and Fuller attempted to end his ordeal by closing in on the specifics of their marriage ceremony. Thomas's response contained only more ambiguity. Persistent yet ever respectful of Thomas's authority, Fuller could only gently chide her reserve while offering reassurance and affection in return. "Altho your letter today is not altogether as explicit as I would have liked I was so *glad* to hear from you that it has given me *great* pleasure. It is possible I may have expected too much." Fuller continued to push for closure by suggesting a date for the wedding and establishing a honeymoon itinerary. The move worked, finally gaining Thomas's consent. In late March, she wrote, his marriage proposal received "the approving smile" of both her mother and "our Heavenly Father." Yet much like Bestor, Thomas still doubted whether marriage would bring her happiness: "While I regard the *future* as having in store for me many *bright realities*," she wrote, "I can but feel some anxiety, and even pain when I reflect, that the ship I am about to take is for life, and will involve either my happiness or misery." Fuller empathized: "Under the circumstances deep solicitude for the future is to be expected." He sought to transform her moment of loss and doubt into an affirmation of their mutual affection, claiming that her departure from her mother's side reflected her profound love for him.[41]

Facing the imminent loss of her daughter to marriage, Ann Thomas challenged Fuller to love and adore her daughter, thereby satisfying both a mother's wish and God's mandate. Ann Thomas had been Fuller's chief ally during her daughter's courtship, but with the impending marriage, she sought to do everything in her power to protect her daughter's future interests. Likening the loss of her daughter to Fuller's home in Alabama to "taking the last lamb from the fold," Ann Thomas simultaneously asserted her profound maternal grief and directed her daughter's fate to God's superintendence. She now resigned herself to her daughter's departure because the "King of Heaven" created "the first matrimonial compact [to] solomnise the nuptial." If she had to bow to divine will, she pointedly reminded Fuller, he had do so, too. "The parties who do enter a conjugal state, are bound under pain of divine displeasure to keep their plighted vows of fidelity and affections, with a tenacity as uncompromising as the love of life, and sincere and sacred as the increase of devotion." She sought a direct and personal acknowledgment from Fuller of scope and authority of God's laws. While praising Fuller for his character and promise as a husband to her daughter, Ann Thomas warned him not to violate her maternal trust: "Did I not think that your arm was nerved, to sustain, and keep sacred the charge about to be committed to you—with a bosom glowing with all the refined sensibilities of ardent affection—this tremulous *hand* would refuse to hold the *pen* that dictates these lines." Finally, acknowledging her own powerlessness and uncertainty at this new crossroads in her life, Ann Thomas reiterated her faith in God's guiding Providence. Praying that God's "ministering angels, may direct and rule in wisdom, the future events that are, concealed from our view," Ann recalled the Scripture's words that "the hairs of our head are numbered."[42] The same lesson that symbolized trust in Providence also reinforced the bridegroom's accountability to God for all of his behavior and particularly for his future deeds.

George Thomas's reluctance to offer a full endorsement had irked Fuller, and in addition to laying down ground rules and expectations for Fuller's custodial care of her daughter, Ann Thomas played family peacemaker, attempting to reassure Fuller of his warm welcome into the Thomas family circle. Attempting to cast her son's position as a reflection on himself rather than on Fuller, Ann Thomas explained, "George has always given evidence of [the] highest principles of honour and deep sense of propriety, I have thought he has raised the standard a little too high for very many to reach." In addition to repairing the damaged relationship between Fuller and George Thomas, Ann Thomas thus challenged her future son-in-law to excel in his new role as husband, reminding him of the family's high expectations—and making the point that a protective older brother would be watching to ensure the welfare of "the pet of the whole family." The language of evangelicalism thus gave Ann Thomas the authoritative voice she needed to play the part of patriarch, approving her daughter's marriage and establishing expectations for Fuller's conduct as a husband. Although motivated by both love and duty and amply able to execute her responsibilities, Ann Thomas found the patriarchal role uncomfortable: "This is a liberty I have never before taken with a gentleman before the marriage is consummated. It may need an apology—I can only offer—the intensity of feeling, and deep solicitude which I cant find language of sufficient tone to express."[43] Despite her awkwardness, however, she forcefully used her faith and family to remind Fuller that the Thomas family's blessings remained contingent and that both God and family would hold him accountable.

Fuller responded with gratitude and reverence, acknowledging the external authority of both kin and God. Communicating his keen sensitivity to the "severe trial" that surrendering her daughter represented for Ann

Thomas, Fuller addressed the religious duties that devolved on him after "receiving from you so *precious* a charge":

> I trust I am fully sensible of the obligations that I am about to take upon myself in the marriage vow which I hope to do in the fear of God whose Divine sanction I often upon my knees implored and believe I recd before I took the first step in the matter, and my prayer is daily that our Heavenly Father would order all things as shall be well pleasing in His sight. I have full confidence in the superintending care of Providence over our every step, and should our Heavenly Father withdraw His goodness from us for a moment how dreadful would be the consequence.

Proclaiming his dependency on God's guidance in all matters and particularly in marriage, Fuller acknowledged that his authority did not go unbridled. Yet Fuller simultaneously claimed divine sanction for his newfound domestic authority. Omitting any reference to the bumps along the courtship road, Fuller wanted others to view Anna Thomas's decision to marry him as evidence of his godliness, thereby legitimizing his authority over his wife after their marriage. Fuller continued to acknowledge his filial obedience to his future mother-in-law, however distant she might be, and attempted to assuage her grief by telling her that he hoped that she would consider herself as having gained a son rather than having lost a daughter.[44]

All of these courtships reached neat conclusions that belied the messy realities they typified. Evangelical men discovered firsthand that women exercised authority throughout courtship. Once men had initiated the process, they had little ability to dictate the pace at which it progressed, and faith made the outcome all the more unpredictable, with the potential either to frustrate or to advance a courtship. Moreover, women feared that with the end of a courtship would come the demise of their authority in the relationship. Knowing that concern, many evangelical men sought to reassure their lovers regarding a bright future of unmitigated mutuality in which husbands would delight in the emotional and devotional pleasures of their wives.

Women's "Hieroglyphical Pen," Domesticated Men, and Matrimony

When evangelical men courted women, they initiated conversations about feelings and emotion, but they did so through the idiom of domesticity. Unlike their nonevangelical peers, who focused on the present—the courtship itself—evangelical men used the vocabulary of domesticity to open up discussions about the couple's future. While men of honor occasionally demonstrated some emotion during courtship to provide evidence of the genuineness of their feelings, they shied away from lengthy discussions of the domestic future for fear that such talk might tarnish masculine notions of future public importance. Men of honor believed that true satisfaction derived from public importance, a status an individual man had to achieve on his own and other honorable men had to confirm. Women and children within the household could not enhance a man's honor; they could only damage it.[45] While southern evangelical men no doubt looked to matrimony as confirmation of their mastery and a step toward fulfilling their public ambitions, they also viewed the home as the privileged site of personal and devotional fulfillment, at least on par with the importance and satisfaction they placed on their public pursuits. In fact, many evangelical men believed that their lovers' piety would enhance their own, creating a domestic sanctuary for rearing children. Evangelical men often used the expectation of domestic piety and fulfillment to convince their lovers that mutual interests superseded self-interest in their relationship. When women joined their suitors in conversations about their domestic future together, both parties knew that the relationship had taken a dramatic turn toward marriage.

In his 1856–57 courtship of Sue Heiskell, William McCampbell found talk of domesticity vital to sustaining their relationship. Slow to marry because he needed time to finish his legal education and launch his career in eastern Tennessee, McCampbell found that his linkage of piety, domesticity, and affection kept their relationship energized. Even in an unusually open and informal courtship such as this one, McCampbell frequently referred to Heiskell's "hieroglyphical pen," a phrase that elegantly captured the mysteriousness of her heart and mind during their courtship.[46] Using the language of domesticity, McCampbell hoped to forge common ground in the courtship so that the meaning embedded in his lover's correspondence might be more readily comprehensible.

Like most successful suitors, McCampbell persevered through rejection in his advances toward Susan Heiskell. A friend of Heiskell's brothers, McCampbell had spent considerable time at her home prior to their courtship. As he attempted to cross the threshold from family friend to suitor, however, Sue Heiskell closed the door on his amorous overtures. After "having fathomed the depths of my soul," Heiskell wrote to McCampbell in 1856, "I have no heart to give in return for yours." She apologized if her actions had unintentionally indicated any interest beyond friendship. But she did not foreclose the possibility of future visits: "Altho' your sentiment is not reciprocated, I will be pleased to see you whenever you may favor me with a call."[47]

McCampbell's persistence soon paid dividends, but the authority in the relationship remained with Heiskell. Only six months after her initial rebuff, Heiskell actively participated in the exchange of courtship letters. The correspondence held added weight in their relationship since their geographic separation enabled them to see one another only occasionally. Unable to read Heiskell's attitude in person, McCampbell scrutinized the meaning of every word. A missed exchange of letters necessitated deep concern.

> Never in my life have I been more sadly disappointed than I was Saturday when the mail came . . . and I did not receive one of those "winged messengers" that are wont to visit me once a week, bearing on their pinions news to gladden the heart—breathing forth from every fold of their hi[e]roglyphical drapery the unfeigned yearning of affection—that deep pure, unchangeable affection which has its source only in woman's heart. And when no letter came, it made me think surely some one is going to come instead of sending the traces of her thoughts, her heart yearnings on paper. But so it was, no letter came, and no body, and what is more astonishing than any thing else, I lived over it!

Careful to flatter Heiskell with his dependence on her correspondence rather than to blame her for a missing letter, McCampbell delicately pressed for greater reassurance in the form of more frequent correspondence. By refusing to jump to any hasty conclusions, William parlayed his legal training into a flattering acknowledgment of her authority in the relationship: "I am with you, and hope I may ever remain so, as the laws of England are with their King they assert that he can do no wrong."[48]

Even when one of the worst possible courtship scenarios befell the couple—one of their letters fell into the possession of a third party—McCampbell transformed the mishap into a celebration of his lover's virtues. Dismayed that a mail call did not include a letter from Heiskell, McCampbell soon heard an "immoderate fit of laughter" from another Rogersville man, who confessed, "Upon my honor I have read one of your letters through." Knowing that the misdelivery of the letter would mortify

Heiskell, McCampbell used the opportunity to extol the sophistication of her writing: "It is very gratifying to me that all your letters are so entirely devoid of the ordinare, childish foolerie of similar correspondence, that if any of them should by accident fall into the hands of those to whom they do not belong, they contain nothing that will not manifest your good sense—nothing that will not prove them to be the effusions of a mind whose womanly development towers above the sickly childishness of school girl love letters." Indeed, she could seemingly do no wrong. "Your style of letter writing—it pleases me very much—fills my eye perfectly, as almost every thing you do, does." Heiskell's correspondence, McCampbell argued, embodied her virtues: maturity, femininity, intelligence, and groundedness. He believed that she had mastered the conventions of letter writing, both hewing to his expectations and shaping the medium to her expressive needs. Because many of their face-to-face meetings were spent in the presence of family and friends, their correspondence often served as the most open form of communication between the two lovers.[49]

Evangelicalism increasingly crept into their courtship under the rubric of domesticity. McCampbell yearned to share time with Heiskell, not only because he enjoyed her company but also because he believed her piety improved his. Traveling on horseback on a beautiful autumn Sabbath, he confided that "amongst others," he felt "far out of the path of Christian duty." The antidote, he argued, was spending more time with her: "There is no place where I can keep Sunday better than in your parlor & in the company of your ladyship." He also hoped that the dose of domesticity he imbibed during his weekend visits with her would improve his faith and character. As a dress rehearsal for marriage, weekend excursions to Heiskell's home recharged McCampbell's piety and morality in ways that nothing else could. The "pure unselfish attachment" of her affection toward him checked the encroachment of a sinful world on his soul.[50]

As they anticipated marriage, however, their fears of failing to attain those ideals emerged. When a pious man with whom they were acquainted died, McCampbell ruminated on the challenge of steadfastly maintaining a Christian temperament amid everyday frustrations and pettiness. The deceased man set such a sterling example of Christian patience and virtue that McCampbell felt obligated to observe the growing gulf between his piety and that of Christians whom he admired. He told Heiskell that "there is no reason in the world why you and I should not be as good as he," before turning to deceased exemplars of faith from their families to bring home his point: "You have a mother in the grave. . . . [T]here never was better woman, and I have a father—whose life-time and talents—has been devoted to doing good. Yet for all teaching I have had, often gloomy doubts rise in my mind, and especially have they lately. When I get down on my knees to pray to my God, my heart seems not to be in what I say—seems to be filled with worldliness, & even *revenge*."[51] The longer McCampbell delayed marriage to meet his aspirations in law, the more unfit he felt to fulfill his aspirations as a husband. Domesticity, he hoped, would provide the necessary intellectual and moral shelter he needed to sustain his piety.

Heiskell's concerns veered in the opposite direction. Rather than seeing marriage and piety as mutually reinforcing, she feared that marriage might interfere with her piety. The intense love and loyalty required of a successful marriage, she thought, might diminish her ability to commit herself fully to God. Answering her query, McCampbell contended that affectionate relationships between Christians were consonant with the Gospel and therefore did not diminish piety:

> You ask me if I think "there is any true love to God unless we love him more than all the world beside, and love to do our duty because He has commanded us so to do." Now Sue, I know you must love God supremely, yet I think there is a marked difference in the love we have for God and for our own friends. The latter may seem sometimes seen to be much more intense than the former, yet both exist. The one has for its object a spirit that pervades every place and everything; the other has tangible, ocular objects, that affect not only the mind—the soul, but affect the senses—are perceptible to our bodily senses. We cannot judge so well from the appearant strength of our love for the Creator and things of time & sense, whether the love of the Creator is true or not, as we can when they conflict. If our earthly affections are consistent, with, and follow after our duties to our Maker, they are not wrong.[52]

Indeed, William contended, human relationships acted as a barometer, warning individuals that they were drifting away from a path consonant with God's will. McCampbell saw marriage, piety, and domesticity symbiotically growing over the course of his shared future with Heiskell.

Even late in their courtship, however, McCampbell struggled to get Heiskell to respond openly to his straight talk on marriage. He sought reassurance that she shared his views of the future: "I cannot see the time yet when we should have our vows consummated, yet I want you to sit down and write to me your feelings fully and freely—Sometime before I left Rogersville I wrote you my own feelings without asking you for yours." Although he had visited her home since the exchange of letters, the lack of privacy there precluded the discussion of marriage anywhere but on paper. McCampbell pressed Heiskell to be more forthcoming in her opinions on concluding their courtship with marriage: "I only wish you to write to me on the subject without reserve—say just what you think and feel, and all you think. I have done so to you."[53]

In late 1857, she finally consented to marry him, and he moved on to trying to secure her father's approval. In writing to T. H. Heiskell, McCampbell had not only had to acknowledge the man's success as a father (and the filial respect he merited) but also had to pledge to act as a benevolent Christian patriarch. Stating his awareness of the "great sacrifice" that the loss of Sue would mean to the Heiskell household, McCampbell showered Heiskell with praise for having raised a "tender delicate flower": "The winds have not been allowed to blow unduly upon her, nor the sun too intense heat to scorch her, and she has no doubt been a well spring of joy to your parental heart in your household." Again drawing from nature, McCampbell announced his fiancée's desire to leave her father's household to start her own family under the careful watch of her husband-to-be: "Yet she has calmly and with due affection said, that, with your consent, she is willing to leave her pleasant, her delightful home and meet the current of lifes fortune and misfortune with me." Tracing the plodding character of their courtship, McCampbell offered reassurances regarding the certainty of his and Sue's emotions for one another before closing with liberal doses of deference and promises of filial respect: "And if you feel that [you] can consent to these our plans and wishes, we will ever be proud to render you the reverence, respect and obedience due from affectionate children."[54]

The courtship hit full stride in the three months between the engagement and the wedding, when McCampbell freely ruminated on the domestic happiness and fulfillment both lovers would experience upon marriage. Because of their lengthy courtship, he argued, their marriage would be surer and therefore more companionate: "I am not sorry that we have been so long acquainted before our marriage is to take place. By this means we have been enabled to see more of each other than lovers usually do—we know each other better than some do after years of married life— We now can lean on each other with the confidence of [an] old & well tried friend." That familiarity, however, had not diminished his romantic notions. Quoting Sir Thomas More, McCampbell reminded Heiskell of their future happiness fusing together the crucial elements of the domestic ideal—mutuality, piety, love, and domesticity.

> The pure, open, prosperous love,
> That, pledged on earth & sealed above,
> Grows in the worlds approving eyes,
> In friendships smiles & home's caress,
> Collecting all the hearts sweet ties
> Into one knot of happiness.

Realization of that domestic ideal could not come soon enough for McCampbell, who believed "that two loving hearts suffer much from being separated as ours have been, & their happiness can only be complete when united indissolubly." McCampbell revealed his eagerness both to end the suspense of courtship and to experience the benefits of marriage in his frustration over the rumors swirling around the timing of their wedding. To his "very great surprise," he reported to Heiskell prior to their marriage, "we had been married some three weeks—Will Wallace says I have been married three or four times during that time." The upbeat McCampbell brushed aside the rumor, writing that he hoped "they can tell such a tale truthfully three weeks hence."[55]

Evangelicalism often reified the barrier between the sexes. Because domesticity conflated marriage, faith, and home, however, it gave evangelical men a unique means to attempt to close that gendered divide. Domesticity allowed men to express their self-interests in the language of mutual interests and enabled men and women to imagine an idealized future as they worked through (and past) the difficulties inherent in a courtship process that involved distance and even distrust. Evangelical suitors could take little comfort in the courtship routine until they had engaged their lovers in conversations that had both narrower and broader contours than earlier exchanges had possessed—narrow in the sense of specifics surrounding the timing and nature of their wedding, broad in the sense that both lovers claimed a shared vision of the benefits of domesticity.

The relationship between William Wills and Anna Whitaker demonstrates the power of domesticity in evangelical courtship. Having overcome his earlier qualms regarding the institution of marriage, Wills eagerly intertwined piety and domesticity in his courtship correspondence. The man who had previously belittled the equation of domesticity with intellectual and spiritual fulfillment now wrote to his lover that marriage and domestic piety offered the only means to true happiness. Nevertheless, he also occasionally telegraphed his self-interests: "Soon by the will of God," he wrote to Whitaker, "I shall be enabled to call her 'mine.' Sweet Word! mine! yes, mine till time shall end with one or both of us."[56] Even as he wrapped his correspondence in the language of affection, Wills commented on marriage as conquest.

As the wedding day neared, Wills set about elaborating on the blessings of domesticity he and Whitaker would share after marriage, when they were no longer lovers testing the bounds of their relationship but rather helpmeets. The give-and-take of courtship would immediately yield to his notion of a companionate marriage as their vows would occasion the collapse of all physical, emotional, and spiritual hurdles between them: "The barrier which now intercepts will be broken down; the restraint imposed by prudence will be removed." They would no longer need to test one another, to assume a public front, or to fear family interference after they became "one in interest, one in affection, one in hope, and one in love," he rhapsodized. At the core of that newfound mutuality in all phases of married life would be the regular practice of faith together within their home: "O Anna, how will our joys be heightened and purified, for us to worship together at the same shrine: to sing the hymns of Zion together: to bow our knees together to the same Holy God; and in mutual, fervent prayers to ask His blessings on our heads." Domestic worship would do more than enhance their individual piety and sanctify their home; it would efface virtually all differences of opinion between the newlyweds, drawing them forward to eternity. "In one word," Wills wrote, faith "will enable us to live together; it will enable us to think *together* here; it will enable us to act *together* here; it will enable us to walk *together* here; and it will enable us to be more firmly united and together, drink from the fountains of eternal bliss, where parting will be no more." But even during these moments of unbounded optimism preceding his marriage, Wills realized that his sentimentalized notion of faith and family strained the bounds of credibility, and he concluded his letter, "I fear I am giving too great a loose to my fervid imagination, and must try and restrain myself."[57] Perhaps reflecting on the intellectual ground he had trod in his shift from celebrating bachelorhood to marriage, Wills feared appearing naive in promoting such a fantasy of marital domesticity to his fiancée.

When Anna and William Wills's son, Richard, courted seriously some twenty-six years after his father, he too appealed to the benefits of domesticity to justify his marriage. Logic that might have convinced lovers did not always convince fathers, however. Long after discarding his romantic notions of domesticity, William Wills worried more about his son's professional future in the ministry than about his personal happiness. Now the patriarch of a family in eastern North Carolina and a leading authority in the Methodist Protestant denomination, William Wills informed his son that personal ambitions for domestic fulfillment needed to wait until after he had obtained a firmer footing in the church.

Like his father, Richard Wills remained ambivalent about marriage in his midtwenties. Citing the confusion generated by the commencement of hostilities at Fort Sumter and his self-proclaimed selectivity in courtship, Richard wrote to his brother in April 1861 that "it would not surprise me if it were to be years yet before I become satisfied" regarding marriage. In one breath, Richard left the matter in God's hands, downplaying his agency in his search for a mate: "If Providence sees fit, he may open the way, and when the way appears to be open there perhaps I shall walk in it." In his next breath, however, Richard took the matter into his own hands, quickly reviewing the eligibility of a couple of women. He concluded ambivalently, "If I am ever ready, I may come across some one that will suit & whom I will suit, or my notions in reference to some whom I now know may change."[58] Caught between the self-interest of courtship and deference to an all-powerful God, evangelicals often spoke of courtship as a matter that easily slipped in and out of an individual's control.

Only three months later, Richard Wills used domesticity to introduce the topic of marriage at the end of a letter to his father: "I tell you there is no place like home any way. This thing of being where one can do a good deal as one pleases." Richard continued somewhat vaguely, "Don't you reckon I had better get married too, and live at the Parsonage (provided there is one) so I can work some and thus take exercise, and have my food to suit me? I think right seriously about it sometimes." He reassured his father that he would "not want to get married until you are willing to it," but, he cautioned, "don't be too long getting willing." Richard quickly closed the issue while warning his father that it would not go away: "Enough of this *at present*."[59]

In September, Richard Wills returned to the issue with new urgency. Directly addressing the subject, he sought to convey his thoughtfulness and respect for the opinion of his father and his family: "I have thought a good deal about the matter which concerns me, and in fact all of us; viz. of changing my condition." He devoted the balance of the letter to demonstrating to his father that logic and sagacity, not love and passion, lay behind this consideration of marriage. At this point, he clearly had a woman in mind, although he did not divulge her name:

> As to the lady herself, I really can't tell at present that I can do any better. I may find one more intelligent, but then piety is lacking, & even were she pious her habits might not suit me: I may find one that could endure the hardships of an itinerant life better, & may be better acquainted with domestic economy, but then Something else to be considered does not suit me, &c. &c. but to find one in whom piety, intelligence natural & acquired, proper age, amiability, good family and other things are combined in a greater degree, and then one whom I can love seems to me is not such an easy task.

Wills's description fit the profile for a minister's wife, the perfect complement to the pious Wills clan, and the ideal religious and moral steward for Richard's anticipated household. However, Richard reminded his father that the woman retained authority in the matter and that any conclusion to the courtship remained in the distant future: "If she should say 'no,' 'the cake will be dough.'" Wills then closed with a nod to patriarchal authority, urging his father "to write immediately . . . and just give me your views in full, and any advise, counsel, direction which you may see fit." But he also posed a challenge, warning his father that in the absence of an airtight case for delaying marriage, he would ask for the woman's hand.[60]

William Wills rose to his son's challenge. The only argument in favor of marriage that he could muster was his son's age, twenty-five. On the other side of the ledger, however, William Wills had a number of concerns, all of them centering on Richard's ministerial career rather than on the war. William Wills feared that some in the pastorate might doubt his son's motives and questioned the economic feasibility of marriage. Although the days of enforced celibacy had ended, the Methodist system depended on the local church or circuit to support the pastor and his wife. Only four Methodist Protestant circuits in North Carolina had the means necessary to support married pastors, and Wills feared that his son might jeopardize his future employment by marrying too early. He also resurrected the traditional evangelical argument that marriage interfered with piety. He was arguing not that his son should remain celibate but rather that he should defer marriage until his ministerial training had been completed and his career was off the ground: "For a preacher to burden himself before he has character or experience is doing injustice to himself & to the Church. You might not be amenable to this charge, and yet I would say to not consummate it before your fourth year." William Wills left the matter in his son's hands, asking him only to pray for guidance from God: "In all thy ways acknowledge Him and He shall direct thy paths."[61]

Although Richard Wills heeded his father's advice, delaying his marriage to Anna Norman for at least two more years, his attempt to garner his father's approval for marriage based on domestic concerns reveals the limits of that appeal when tested against the informal authority of family to shape courtship outcomes. William Wills may have left his son as the final arbiter of his marital fate ("Your own happiness is most intimately involved; your own choice and your own judgment must exercise a controlling or determining influence"), but the decision was never that simple.[62] If Richard Wills had ignored the friendly advice and professional warnings in his father's letter, he would have jeopardized both his own and his family's reputation. From his experience a quarter century earlier, William Wills knew all about the passion that young men experienced when courtships turned serious, but he also knew that those desires had to be held in check for the benefit of Richard's professional ambitions.

When evangelical men and women courted, they felt the full force of expectations shaped by their faith, but they also found ways to improvise on those strictures.[63] Where evangelicals' obsession with sin and its inherent role in courtship enlarged distrust between men and women, men used the language of religious domesticity to close that distance in the courtship process. Forced to begin by broaching the topic of domesticity, a man knew that his amorous appeals constituted only banter until his lover joined him in a conversation about their domestic future together. Where young women often felt torn between religious obligations to family and a desire to marry, they also found that prayer might aid them in resolving their dilemma. Commanded to honor and obey their parents, evangelical men circumvented that limitation through appeals to God and family. Thus, both convention and improvisation point to the uniquely religious overtones of evangelical courtship. When set against the evangelical expectation that marriage and family profoundly shaped both spiritual pleasures during their lifetime and the odds of obtaining life eternal, evangelical courtships differed markedly from nonevangelical courtships in spite of the fact that many of the processes appear similar.

Evangelical women thus found the cautiousness of courtship advice literature beneficial to their pursuit of suitable mates. But that strenuous process also left engaged couples seeking ways to put their mutual suspicions behind them and realize the unity that they had professed during courtship. Courtship may have marked the zenith of a woman's authority, but her entry into marriage did not signal the end of her ability to use evangelical language and values to make claims on her husband and family both to achieve a companionate marital ideal and to vouchsafe the entire family for God. Indeed, the tension between expectation and reality fueled as much conflict as mutuality in the evangelical marriage.

CHAPTER 3

Improvising on the Ideal
Evangelical Marriages in the Antebellum South

As evangelical couples passed from the turbulence of courtship to the anticipation of engagement, most individuals claimed to experience unparalleled emotional fulfillment. Susan Heiskell, who had been prone to bouts of the blues during her courtship with William McCampbell, turned awestruck at the joy she found after their engagement, asking him, "Were you ever so delighted as to grow dizzy, I have been so often, and to you I am indebted oftenst for that exstatic pleasure." Not to be outdone, McCampbell continued to shower her with hyperbolic claims of affection:

> Oh! how much I would like to see you this evening & hear the accents of your voice. I can see you at all times in my imagination, but, to have you here *propria persona* would give me unbounded joy almost. Yet tho' you are far away in person yet you are here in thought. Your spirit is here with me in my office. 'Tis more pleasing to me to know this—to know that wherever I am and whatever I am doing, that your good wishes & prayers are with me than it would be to have all the gold of California.

Below their optimism ran an undercurrent of concern that they might not experience the emotional and spiritual fulfillment they anticipated that marriage would bring or, worse yet, that their relationship might deteriorate over time. "I hope my visions of happiness are not too bright to be realized," McCampbell wrote to Heiskell. As their wedding drew closer, he could not let go of his fears that their marriage would contain more disharmony than harmony: "I see married folks get clashing often—this we will not, we cannot."[1] McCampbell's mixture of hopes and fears captures the dual impulses of antebellum evangelical marriages. Like new converts, newly married couples rejoiced in their personal transformations and established lofty goals for their new station in life. And while they anticipated challenges throughout their lives, bride and groom alike found that evangelical ideals provided a rich vocabulary for debating how best to accomplish individual and collective goals in marriage.

As southern evangelicals attempted to reconcile their ideals of mutual affection with the realities of everyday life, they encountered a dilemma that cropped up repeatedly in the period's prescriptive literature: the clergy ascribed wives with superior piety and virtue yet vested husbands with final authority. A mother had the obligation to instruct and correct her children's behavior, but those obligations had no corollary in her capacity as a wife. According to the advice literature, a wife should merely model pious behavior for her husband.

Perhaps nowhere was the gap between ideal and reality greater than among married clergymen. While clergymen publicly celebrated patriarchal authority in the pulpit and in their published writings, they knew from firsthand experience that the success of their households and their ministries hinged on the promotion of their wives' authority within and beyond the household. Clergymen relied on their wives to help build and maintain consensus within their congregations, including visiting female parishioners, organizing and leading fund-raisers and prayer meetings, and monitoring church gossip. With women and children comprising the majority of most congregations, clergymen's wives played an indispensable role as their husbands' pastoral eyes and ears. Most clergymen traveled regularly as part of their ministerial labors, and during these absences, their wives kept them abreast of activities within both the household and the congregation.

Women contemplating marriage to clergymen knew from a lifetime of observation the crucial role they would be assuming and voiced considerable trepidation at the new public responsibilities marriage would bring. Despite expressing anxiety and resignation early in their marriages, these women transitioned into their new public roles, finding them richly rewarding. As chapter 5 will show, Anne Davis used her position to receive pay within her husband's ministry, while the widowed Frances Douglass and Frances Bumpass refused to cede their public authority (and their husbands' legacy) to other clergymen. However, they often felt frustrated by their husbands' failure to honor their courtship pledges to contribute substantial time and affection to child rearing and marriage. As clergymen traveled across the South to professional meetings, guest pulpits, and seminaries, they continued to proclaim their love of family, home, and domestic piety, but they also announced that their professional obligations to denomination and God trumped the personal desire to remain at home.

In lay marriages too, women and men used evangelical ideas and values to debate responsibilities and roles within marriage. Historians have reached no consensus about whether church tribunals, which set out to discipline members for actions that ranged from drunkenness to spousal abuse, merely reaffirmed male domination or afforded female members some protection from the harshest elements of patriarchal authority. But an examination of more ordinary tensions within evangelical marriages—that is, those that did not require external mediation—demonstrates that men could exercise their religiously sanctioned right to dismiss critiques from their wives but that layman and clergyman alike took these charges seriously and felt compelled to address them.[2] Some men, however, continued to dismiss evangelicalism's call to conversion, forcing their pious wives to question the quality of their own piety if their domestic and public worship habits could not inspire their husbands to pronounce their faith.

The finding that evangelical values could both reinforce and undermine patriarchal authority in marriage points both to the problematic place of women's authority in the southern household and to the transformation of women's place in southern evangelicalism. In addition to the prescriptive gap between womanly piety and male authority, Lynn Lyerly insightfully notes that pious women faced an inherent contradiction: "A proper mother was strong, influential, and authoritative, while a proper wife was submissive and subservient."[3] Southern evangelicalism's reversal on the seat of authority between 1800 and 1830—from the congregation of fellow believers to the family (and by extension the family's patriarch)—further complicated authority within the household. Sitting on the margins of southern society in the early nineteenth century, the evangelical clergy directly challenged patriarchal authority and demanded that the female church members renounce their secular, natal families as a precondition for acceptance into their church families.[4] By the 1830s, the antebellum clergy had shifted their message to celebrate the family and by extension to restore patriarchal authority within the household, but undercurrents of evangelicalism's sectarian past may have existed below this sea change in rhetoric.[5]

The tension within evangelicalism's recent past, coupled with its ambiguous mixing of womanly piety and male authority, suggests that evangelicals may have shared many values and goals but that religious values also framed strong disagreements. Scholars of marriage in the antebellum South have long debated whether southern marriages were companionate or competitive, affectionate or distant, often referencing marriages in the antebellum North. Even amid disagreements, scholars of southern marriage typically stress harmony over disharmony.[6] In contrast, Steven M. Stowe's analysis of elite marriages uncovers evidence of ongoing strain among southern couples as they simultaneously celebrated intimacy and power within the household.[7] Though his research centers on honor—largely as a secular ethic—rather than evangelicalism, he offers a crucial insight: a shared outlook on marital relationships never foreclosed conflict, particularly in a society with sharply gendered roles within marriage.

Evangelicals also used the idiom of their faith to prize love, passion, and mutuality in their marriage, especially in the latter days of courtship. Yet the clergy's ongoing sanction of the privilege of patriarchal authority—and their condemnation of the henpecking wife—problematized those ideals. At one extreme, the ideal of mutuality enabled clergymen to encourage their wives to participate actively in the ministry. At the other extreme, husbands resisted and resented their wives' repeated attempts to convert them to evangelical piety. At both extremes and in between, women criticized their husbands for failing to contribute fully to their households' sanctity. While men could use their prescribed authority to repel charges of moral deficiency, they nonetheless felt compelled to respond to these religiously informed accusations, an avenue of protest closed to nonevangelical women. Unlike the public records maintained by church tribunals, which yielded brief but clear-cut verdicts, personal letters and diaries illuminate a range of experiences closer to the everyday relations that southern evangelicals faced. In spite of religious and legal prescription that ensconced male authority and female submission in the name of family harmony and order, women could still lay claim to affection and labor in the name of piety. These marital relations fell beyond the congregation's purview, but they nevertheless underscore the fact that evangelical values keenly informed everyday relationships among believers.

Defining the Holy Union

Written by evangelical clergymen, prescriptive literature on marital relations appeared regularly in sermons, tract literature, and denominational newspapers, forming an important baseline for newlyweds' expectations. Across denominational affiliation and locale emerged two common themes in this literature. First, as men interacted with the world beyond the household, women were expected to cultivate a home that served as a spiritual haven for their weary husbands and their innocent children. Second, although commentators equated manhood with strength and worldly acumen and womanhood with virtue and domesticity, final authority unequivocally resided with the husband when the two clashed in the home. Moreover, clergymen argued, such divisions simply reflected God's plan. But in attempting to explain the precise workings of womanly virtue and manly authority within the southern household, both members of the clergy and evangelical southerners struggled to reconcile the two positions.[8]

Functional evangelical homes, clergymen argued, never experienced contests of wills because conscientious husbands and dutiful wives intuitively knew their proper and complementary roles. Pious wives should acknowledge their husbands' patriarchal authority and exhibit love for their mate second only to their love for God. Bishop James O. Andrew of the Methodist Episcopal Church, South captured the theme well when he advised women, "Let your husband see, let him feel, that next to God, he is enthroned in your heart. Let him have the proof of this in your looks, your words, the neatness of your person, and the arrangement of your household matters." Evangelical women thus faced a daunting challenge, remaining both submissive to their husbands and accountable for the upkeep of the home as a haven for the entire family. Clergymen found their precedent in the Book of Proverbs, which described pious, trustworthy, benevolent, wise, and diligent wives as "far more precious than jewels."[9]

Evangelical clergymen from across the South and across denominations repeated the assumption that observation and education enabled married evangelicals to understand how each gender complemented the other. The Reverend Rufus Bailey, a Presbyterian, published a series of sermons subtitled "Domestic Duties Illustrated and Enforced in Eight Discourses," in which he declared, "How happy the family where love reigns, and controls all the actions, where all bitterness is put away, and each is happy in his sphere, in mutual forbearance, quietness and peace." Similarly, Rev. Andrew counseled that if a man treated his wife as "friend," "counsellor," and "comforter," she would "feel that she is respected as well as loved by her husband." And while all humans might be fallen creatures, Andrew reminded men in particular to practice the maxim to "*bear* and *forbear.*" Bailey even made the case that women held the balance of authority in marital relationships. Love, he argued, was the vehicle of womanly authority: "The Gospel, in its practical influence, is found to elevate the sexes to a happy equality, while one is clothed with power, and the other rules by the impressive force of purity and truth. Indeed, this relation of power, woman by her weakness, always holds the balance." He continued,

> Her power is in her weakness. Unadorned,
> She shows in native grace adorned the most.
> Rules, when she modestly declines to rule,
> And in submission, conquers us by love.[10]

Thus, in the model evangelical household these clergymen envisioned, all members knew their roles, creating frictionless relationships that did not require the flexing of authority.

Much like their northern counterparts, southern evangelical clergymen stressed women's superior piety and virtue, particularly within the household. Working from the injunction in Colossians 3:19, Bailey directed husbands to "love your wives, and be not bitter against them." His portrait of the ideal Christian marriage revealed the complementary roles envisioned for each partner: "The wife, therefore, is entitled to the love of her husband in her station as a companion, counselor and friend; not as an animal furnished to administer to his pleasures, but as an angel of mercy sent to aid his counsels and to exert a kindly influence on his destinies." As the Reverend E. P. Rogers of the First Presbyterian Church of Augusta, Georgia, addressed the graduating class of the Washington Female Seminary in 1849, he discussed the natural progression that the women in his audience would make from young scholars to young brides. All of women's natural attributes honed by seminary training, including benevolence, affection, and piety, were properly exercised in the domestic sphere, where the wife was "the queen of the little world of home." Not a bit part consigned to the periphery of southern culture, women's role was vital to the training of society's future leaders—coming generations of manly heroes. Women also wielded influence through their part in fashioning a companionate marriage: "The cherished companion and friend of her husband, not a plaything, not merely one in whose society he may spend his leisure hours, but his other and dearer self, whose judgements and counsel he seeks in all matters seriously affecting his interest, and whose constant and devoted affection is the day-star of his existence." Furthermore, women ruled the domestic sphere with "the sceptre of Love," the "most potent which is wielded on earth."[11]

Rogers's rhetoric of womanly supremacy in the domestic sphere also described the limits of feminine authority, however. Because women should serve as models rather than enforcers of morality and piety within the southern household, Rogers acknowledged that evangelical women might pass nearly unnoticed in their indispensable roles to family and society. Even if humankind failed to acknowledge fully their sacrifices, God would reward faithful women heartily on judgment day. Until that time, Rogers told the young women in his audience, they should cast aside any lingering youthful desires to indulge in "gaiety, frivolity, and dissipation" or risk a "miserable, remorseful eternity." If, however, they became loyal and pious wives, they would "be an ornament and a blessing to their native land," shining "as one of the brightest stars, in an eternal Heaven."[12] Because his audience comprised only women, Rogers neglected to spell out the duties and expectations of evangelical men in marriage, leaving many ambiguities regarding where marital authority rested. How could a woman simultaneously rule the domestic empire as queen yet go unnoticed?

In exchange for manly protection from material want and worldly corruption, clergymen argued, wives owed husbands unquestioned obedience. The starting point for all clerical directives regarding women's marital obligations was the scriptural injunction in Colossians, "Submit yourselves unto your own husbands, as it is fit in the Lord." But hierarchy also presented itself as the natural order of things. A husband, Bailey contended, "is fitted for the duties of his station by his superior strength, by the adaptation of his powers to command, by the peculiar form and sphere of service assigned him, by his peculiar facilities for public enterprise, by a masculine conformation of body and of mind, and by an instinct, which, through the whole animal creation, prompts the one sex to assume authority, and the other to yield to submission." Through a blend of physical strength, worldly acumen, and most fundamentally God's design, men had the right, wisdom, and authority to demand obedience from their wives. Bailey warned men against the dangers of "angry reply" and "fretful temper," twin evils of everyday interaction that threatened to rob husbands of the "tender ties and sympathies, which once controlled [their] passions and regulated [their] domestic intercourse." Bailey acknowledged that the "tyrant," the man who exploited evangelical precept to rule his household "with severity," faced bleak prospects at the bar of divine judgment.[13] Feminine piety and love clearly could face an uphill struggle in an evangelical marriage.

Acknowledging the possibility of a tyrannical husband forced Rev. Bailey to address strategies that would enable virtuous but powerless wives to cope with husbands who abused their authority. This dilemma required Bailey to assert wives' moral and spiritual independence from their husbands: "The wife ... must not submit to the husband in sin. She must neither aid, abet, nor countenance him in any sin." But although the wife might recoil at her husband's sinful behavior, even voicing her "decided dissent" and "uncompromising resistance," she had only extremely limited means through which to change his behavior: "She must employ her powers of persuasion, her moral influence, her breath of prayer, her gentle admonitions," Bailey argued, to reform her husband's character. When womanly virtue clashed with manly authority, clergymen pronounced authority the victor every time. "She may not be required on any subject to render a slavish submission. The light, which she has, may be revealed, and her conflicting views compared with his. But, then, she will not usurp authority. She will persuade, and compel by an influence so gentle that there will seem to be the absence of all authority or irksome constraint." What if the husband became the domestic tyrant that Bailey had earlier described? The course of action for the pious wife remained the same: "There are indeed some husbands who are beyond control; men whose souls seem to be brutalized by long habits of cruelty or crime. ... But even such cases, the most desperate, have been greatly meliorated, if not entirely reformed, by the judicious and powerful influence of a devoted wife."[14] The clergy held inexhaustible faith in the power of feminine example and patience, even in the face of brutality. If nothing else, a woman who tolerated abuse courted Christian sacrifice, reinforcing her faith even as she waged a losing battle.

Marriage demanded limitless results from women who possessed limited authority. Andrew directed women to exercise patience with their husbands lest they become alienated: "Does he return home from contact with corrupt men and adverse fortune, his brow clouded with disquiet, and a look of trouble and ill-humour? Be sure you meet him with a sunny countenance. Let love be in your looks, and in the sweet and gentle tones of your voice. Wait a little, and he will soon be himself again." Andrew thus provided evangelical men with a means to excuse virtually all of their behavior. The final burden of a happy marriage rested on the evangelical wife. With enough feminine domesticity, any husband's worldly cares would disappear. Bailey's confidence that a woman's "soft answer turneth away wrath" led him to conclude that a wife's far-reaching influence would prove that "the family is very much what the wife chooses to make it."[15] By implication, any wife who failed to temper her husband's wrath possessed insufficient piety.

Under almost no circumstances, however, was a woman to overstep the bounds of her authority. Indeed, the prescriptive literature authored by men placed greater emphasis on the dangers of dominant wives than of tyrannical husbands. Bishop Andrew put the issue most starkly when he directed his discourse to those women who mistakenly believed that husbands had a reciprocal duty to obey their wives: "This class of wives are generally fond of displaying their superiority in intellect, taste, and judgment, over those who are by God's appointment constituted their governors. Such a wife, especially if she be given to extravagance and fashion, is a sad drawback upon the pocket and peace of any poor fellow who happens to be her subject. God pity him, he has a sorry time in this world, however he may fare in the next."[16] These women, Andrew continued, not only overstepped their proper marital roles but also frequently transgressed many other basic tenets of evangelical dogma.

Aware of the clerical scorn heaped on women who assumed too much authority in the home, some women surely entered marriage with trepidation. The situation constituted a reversal from the authority that women often exercised during courtship. After marital vows had been exchanged, however, legal and religious recourse was virtually nonexistent, regardless of a husband's actions.[17] And as some evangelical wives discovered, clerical advice on the topics of impious and ill-tempered husbands often backfired. Years of playing the part of the stalwart, pious wife often failed to improve a husband's piety or character while embittering his wife.

But the ascription of piety and morality to women in idealized marriages also created elasticity in the application of those ideals to relationships. It allowed women to offer tempered criticism of their husbands' fulfill-

Improvising on the Ideal 103

ment of domestic duties. It also offered the potential to enlarge women's roles within marriage. Particularly in the case of clerical marriages, feminine piety and virtue enabled an expansive definition of wives' roles in their husbands' ministries. But even in nonclerical marriages, evangelical women used the moral and spiritual authority vested in them, however minimal, to establish a surprising degree of authority within a narrowly defined patriarchal marriage.

Prescription versus Practice: The Case of Clerical Marriages

Although the clergy frequently offered marital advice from the pulpit and in the press, the gap between the prescribed ideals and practice in the Old South was perhaps widest among married clergymen. Clergymen and their wives often keenly experienced their dependence on one another for success in their gendered realms of work—clergymen in their public calling to sustain and enlarge their congregations, and women in their private calling to rear pious and virtuous children. While clergymen occupied high-profile positions of respect in their communities, the success of their ministerial enterprises hinged on their ability to build and maintain congregational consensus. With women comprising the majority of most congregations, clergymen found pious and gregarious wives an indispensable part of their ministries. Women who married clergymen engaged in a whole range of duties to support their husbands, including visiting female parishioners, monitoring church gossip, interacting with the wives of other clergymen, reporting on services during their husbands' absences, and organizing and leading fund-raisers, prayer meetings, and Sunday school classes.

In all four of the clerical marriages examined here—those between Frances and Sidney Bumpass, Anne and Joseph Davis, Frances and James Douglass, and Anna and William Wills—marriage transformed the private and public roles of husband and wife. Whatever their religious denomination, women who accepted the role of minister's wife often did so with tremendous trepidation. Some questioned the orthodoxy and depth of their personal piety, while all questioned their preparedness for such a public role. They knew from the congregations they attended that clergymen's wives assumed various auxiliary duties. Most clergymen's wives were resigned to these tasks, but Frances Bumpass and Frances Douglass ultimately came to value their public visibility and authority and only grudgingly released it. Here in particular, the language of self-abnegation often translated into deeds of self-promotion. The language that consecrated the family and domestic worship also cut both ways for clergymen of various evangelical denominations, as the elevated nature of their vocation provided a unique justification for their absences from home at the same time that their promotion of the home as a sanctified enclave provided their spouses with powerful critiques of those absences.

Women who married clergymen worried about whether their private piety would match their husbands' expectations after marriage, whether they would be able to cultivate a perfected level of piety at the individual, family, and public levels. With the formality of courtship behind them, would the new bride let down her guard and reveal her spiritual shortcomings in her everyday interactions with her husband? If prescriptive literature endowed women with superior piety in lay households, how did that play out in households where the patriarch was also a clergyman? And how would women largely unfamiliar with public responsibilities succeed in roles for which they seemingly had little training but which figured so prominently in their husbands' success? Given the enormity of each of these challenges individually, let alone in concert, these women not surprisingly felt a powerful mix of apprehension and opportunity. Consequently, they initially discounted their ability to contribute in any significant way to their husbands' ministerial labors, hoping only to avoid detracting from their professional success. Soon, however, and often at the urging of their husbands, these women gained confidence in both their domestic and public piety, playing a central role in their husbands' ministry.[18]

After marrying clergymen, some of these women imagined their husbands scrutinizing their domestic piety for its depth, constancy, and orthodoxy. For Frances Douglass, marriage to a Presbyterian clergyman created a unique opportunity to view her piety in a new, more transparent way. In a religious culture that prized self-awareness of sin as the pathway to salvation, Frances hoped that her husband's deep piety and intimate familiarity with her might yield a candid review of her devotional shortcomings. During one of James Douglass's absences, Frances requested that he "do me a kindness by writing me a criticism on my whole conduct during the last year, as a help to self knowledge; you might point out many faults which self love have hid from my eyes." She continued,

> Truly my cup has been made to run over with the blessings of the Lord. But, on my part there has been much, very much, that was hateful &

abominable in his eyes; so much that I would not, I think, live it over again, even if I might have the priviledge of improving. I have no assurance that I would do better, & I think I would not be put back one year from that glorious possession, upon which I hope to enter through the perfect righteousness of my great high priest, where, I shall no more offend.

Her self-deprecation echoes the Calvinistic emphasis on humanity's depravity. Yet as she concluded with some optimism regarding her eternal fate, Frances still sought approval from her husband: "Tell me my kind friend is this presumptuous. I am persuaded that it is only through faith in the word of God that I feel thus." Openly sharing thoughts on personal piety required Frances to exercise some circumspection to ensure that she did not overstep the bounds of religious orthodoxy. Still viewing James equally as a pastor and a husband, Frances struggled to balance marital openness with Presbyterian orthodoxy.[19] Indeed, her effort to emphasize her humility and orthodoxy early in their marriage verged on self-loathing. Over time, however, such candid reflections on personal piety began to run both ways in the Douglass marriage, with James confessing his personal religious failings.

While Frances hoped to deepen her personal piety, she worried that she might hinder her husband's ministerial efforts. After witnessing a female friend's health decline precipitously, Frances pondered what would happen if she had been the victim of such a sudden onset of illness: "The idea of being burdensome to you in your ministry, is now the appalling thought that makes me recoil from such a state." Yet even as she minimized her potential to contribute to James's ministry, Frances acknowledged her husband's faith in providential wisdom: "You will say the lord could make a sick wife a blessing."[20] Over time, Frances gained much greater confidence in both her personal piety and her contributions to her husband's ministry.

Even women who felt a greater degree of comfort and confidence in their marriages to clergymen often doubted their potential to contribute to their husbands' ministries in any meaningful way. Indeed, women most often couched their potential contributions in negative terms. Like Frances Douglass, they sought to avoid hindering their husbands' clerical duties. For example, while celebrating her marriage to Sidney Bumpass, Frances Bumpass recorded persistent doubts about her role in his ministry. On their first anniversary, Frances relished the success of her marriage: "The Lord has truly blessed me with a husband, pious, affectionate and &

every way suitable for me. When reflecting on his goodness to me in this as well as other things, I am sometimes led to ask, why such an unworthy creature is so highly blessed?" However, her informal apprenticeship in her public role as a minister's wife had proceeded more unevenly than her transition to married life at home. She feared that her fascination with her husband and his piety had impeded his execution of ministerial duties: "I must hinder my husband less by talking to him & learning about him, lest I become troublesome."[21]

As a minister's wife, Frances Bumpass found herself in the spotlight. One woman confronted Frances about her silence at a love feast at her husband's new Methodist congregation in Pittsboro, North Carolina. The Methodist love feast required individual believers to testify about their personal piety to fellow believers with the hope that each believer's testimony would stimulate the group's religious passion, thereby placing tremendous pressure on the clergyman's young wife: "A lady told me that I had set a bad example at love feast. That the people here looked to their minister's wife, to set an example in all things." The laywomen demanded leadership. Frances, who was in her early twenties and was eleven years younger than her husband, must have felt quite inadequate for such a role. As the wife of a Methodist minister, however, the challenge of speaking publicly would not go away. Following a tradition established by the denomination's first bishop, Francis Asbury, Methodist clergymen remained some of the most peripatetic professionals in the Old South, with the Methodist bishop controlling ministerial appointments on a biannual basis. As soon as a minister and his wife established networks of parishioner support, they were often transplanted to another church and community. Visiting thus remained an integral part of a woman's duties as a minister's wife. Indeed, later in her marriage, Frances Bumpass worried that her sojourns with female parishioners had become so routine that she had lost sight of their loftier purposes: "I think too little about glorifying God & too much about self-interest, on pleasing womankind in my visits."[22] Previously uncertain about what role if any she might play in her husband's ministry, Frances Bumpass now concerned herself with locating the ideal blend of socializing and Christian fellowship.

Like Frances Bumpass, Presbyterian Frances Douglass quickly adapted to her public role. With her husband's frequent absences from their church in Fayetteville, North Carolina, she often served as the eyes and ears of his ministry, faithfully reporting both good and bad news about their congregation. In May 1835, she delighted in telling her husband of an impending revival of religion in both the congregation and the adjacent boys' academy. Just as clergymen searched their congregations and communities for public manifestations of personal conversions, so too did the women of the congregation and the community. In this case, the boys, once unruly and lighthearted, now "walk[ed] in a slow and quiet pace & [spoke] as if they feared the sound of their voices would offend a present deity." Frances Douglass added that one of her husband's colleagues had lamented his absence during such an auspicious time. As Frances sensed the waning of the revival spirit among the boys, she called into question the ministerial judgment of her husband's peers. Nonstop sermonizing, she thought, had allowed "weariness . . . to take the place of feeling."[23] At other times, Frances Douglass stood in her husband's stead as congregational peacemaker. When talk of colonization of African Americans in Fayetteville generated "great dissatisfaction of our coloured members," Frances attempted to diffuse the situation by telling the proponents of colonization to cease their activities among the congregation's members. Her efforts were to no avail—three members refused communion at the next service over the matter—but she had chosen to step into the fray. Likewise, after attending services at a nearby Methodist church, Frances informed her husband of the strained relations between the town's Presbyterian and Methodist congregations, which emerged partly from theological differences and partly from her personal affront when the Methodist minister's wife's failed to recognize her. Frances ultimately concluded, however, that "the great Head of the church owns & blesses [Methodist] efforts to do good in his name, & shall we gainsay the doings of the Lord."[24] Zestfully reporting on congregational matters both great and small, women such as Frances Douglass found an important niche in their husbands' ministries. Although this phenomenon emerges most prominently in correspondence when clergymen left town, women surely performed the same task—particularly among the women of the congregation—when their husbands were in the pulpits. With the passage of time, Frances Douglass turned her critical gaze from herself to others, yielding valuable information to a clergyman seeking to maintain consensus among his congregants.

Anne Davis and Frances Bumpass contributed more directly to their husbands' efforts to generate both converts and income. As chapter 4 discusses in more detail, Davis ran the boarding operations at the Wesleyan Female College, an academy that her husband managed in Murfreesboro,

North Carolina, for much of the 1850s. The income generated by the girls who boarded there provided an important supplement to Joseph Davis's annual income. Providing physical, intellectual, and spiritual care for sixty to ninety girls was no small feat. Anne Davis spoke of them as her own children—youths whose souls were extremely vulnerable to the opportunities of salvation and the temptations of sin. Her efforts not only benefited her family but also contributed to the fortunes of the Methodist Episcopal Church, South when she nearly single-handedly brought fourteen converts and four mourners from the academy into the church in 1856–57.

Frances Bumpass taught classes at her husband's academy in North Carolina. When transferred to the Pittsboro, North Carolina, circuit, the couple decided to restart a defunct Methodist school for girls. Even as both Frances and Sidney Bumpass pointed to Frances's teaching responsibilities as a providential blessing from God, they viewed the event from different perspectives. For Rev. Bumpass, the school represented income at an underfunded appointment and a check on the growth of the Episcopal Church's educational endeavors in the Pittsboro area. Frances Bumpass likely shared those concerns but relished the opportunity to educate young Methodist girls in Latin: "Thus am I enabled to be useful to others, while I am benefitting myself. May the Lord aid me & enable me faithfully & prudently to perform what I have undertaken."[25] Her efforts apparently succeeded: Sidney soon sought to have Frances teach an entire day, not just a half day, and to add to her repertoire additional topics such as sacred history.

Ministers' wives thus possessed substantial informal power, often finding intellectual and spiritual fulfillment on a personal level as they helped their families make ends meet. At the same time, however, the peripatetic nature of clerical work created ongoing conflict between clergymen and their wives. In one such skirmish, James Douglass sheepishly asked his wife if she would mind if he absented himself from his planned meeting with his in-laws because of the need for him to minister to ill parishioners during an outbreak of scarlet fever.[26] "Yes dear husband," she fired back, "I am very very much disappointed that you do not come down," wanting her family and friends to affirm her new husband's virtues. Although Frances believed that her husband had "acted conscientiously in this matter" and "entirely acquiesce[d]" with his absence, he continued to offer apologies and explanations.[27]

The demands of the ministry often generated strife between clergymen and their wives regarding the proper balance between professional and domestic obligations. Just as many women actively shared in their husbands' ministries, so too did many women want their husbands to participate actively in the domestic sphere. Yet the travel demands of the ministry—including the exchange of pulpits among ministers, the joint efforts of clergy at revival and protracted meetings, and all manner of local, regional, and national administrative meetings—necessitated frequent absences from home. Many women painfully learned the limits of reciprocity between clergymen's public and private work. Women who married clergymen might be drawn into their husbands' ministries in inventive ways, but clergymen often offered professional justifications for their separation from their homes and families. First, they argued, the hardship of temporary separations opened the door to probing self-examination. When done regularly, such introspection offered Christians an opportunity to reassess the individual pilgrimage to heaven and resulted in the believer's renewed confidence in God's ability to provide for the faithful. Second, clergymen reminded their wives, they had a manly obligation to provide for the material welfare of their families. And third, ministers argued, their labors on behalf of humankind would have lasting and even eternal importance, while the hardships of their families were but temporary. At times genuine, at other times merely convenient, these responses highlight the constant tension clergymen felt between their careers and the domestic ideals they espoused. Because they married evangelical women, evangelical clergymen had spouses who empathized with the church's larger mission of converting the unconverted. Unlike their secular peers, whose claims to "imperative duty" and paternal sacrifice often fell on deaf ears, clergymen had a professional purpose that resonated with their spouses.[28] Yet in spite of this seemingly taut defense of their absences, as long as clergymen publicly professed the sanctity of the household, they also gave their spouses a means, however limited, to criticize those absences.

Even before he joined the Methodist Protestant clergy, William Wills attempted to illustrate the utility of his wife's newfound faith during his unwelcome absences. Anna Wills's first pregnancy dashed her hopes of traveling with her husband on business, but William turned the situation into another opportunity. With sufficient faith in God, he argued, came the resources necessary to cope with any of life's challenges, including loneliness and mounting domestic burdens: "Let us not forget that the Good God above is our friend, and let us not fail to ask His Assisting grace in all things. Oh! He is near you my precious wife tho' your husband is not, and He will not fail to succour you if you ask of him." Like many evangelical men, William deflected his wife's criticism with piety. If Anna had sufficient faith in God, she would find solace and not sorrow in his absences. It also displaced responsibility for outcomes from William to God. Through the example of his life and devotion, William attempted to demonstrate that faith could provide profound peacefulness, writing that a "high degree of resignation came over me at the happy reflection, that you were under the guardianship and parental care of One, who protects His children whether on the peaceful shore, or on the stormy sea."[29]

In addition to arguing that God served as the faithful's shield against adversity, Joseph Davis encouraged his wife, Anne, to see their separations as purposeful afflictions filled with lessons for the devout. As in a good sermon, Davis reinforced his point with Scripture. Quoting from the Book of Matthew, Davis argued that although painful, their separation allowed each spouse to perform essential duties and satisfy a higher purpose: "Let us submit our necks patiently in the easy yoke of Christ for it is enough for the servant that he be as his Master and the disciple as his Lord." Anne must have grumbled about their separations both in person and in correspondence, for Joseph revisited the lesson. Two years later, for example, he turned to Job to illustrate the virtue of spiritual mettle: "I trust, my love, you have been comforted and sustained by the all-sufficient grace of God during the long absence of your husband, and that this seeming evil is made to operate as substantial good. You are not now to be informed that many of the christian graces, and those the most lovely in the sight of God, are brought to earliest maturity by the influence of circumstances very painful to flesh and blood."[30] Given the necessity and inevitability of his absences, Joseph encouraged his wife to embrace her disappointment, channeling the pain of their separations into spiritual introspection and renewal. Her continued complaints might indicate a lack of faith in God's sufficiency.

But Rev. Davis knew that faith alone would not succor his wife. He acknowledged that she always "suffers so much when I am away" and conceded his own selfishness in repeatedly imposing "upon her self sacrificing spirit." When their son became old enough to afford his mother some measure of comfort and companionship, Joseph cautioned the boy not to underestimate his mother's sensitivity: "We men, owing to the sternness of our nature, are not prepared always to appreciate the extreme sensitiveness

Improvising on the Ideal III

of woman's heart, and hence we often inflict pain, where it is our purpose to administer relief and comfort."³¹ The son could help to prevent his mother's daily burdens (including separation from her husband) from jeopardizing her physical and emotional health. While Davis wanted his wife to know that some emotional discomfort could be spiritually beneficial, he also feared that excessive anxiety might be counterproductive.

When all other arguments failed, some evangelical men insisted that they had contemplated sacrificing their professional calling for the sake of their families. Writing from Randolph County, North Carolina, William Wills described to his wife, Anna, the problems he encountered in his ministry: "These preachers up here, many of them will not do. One has had a fight, one has neglected his circuit and all is confusion, and one has not only neglected, but did worse than that and his circuit is distressed." Matters only got worse when Wills attended national meetings, where he endured testy exchanges between his northern and southern colleagues. In 1850, William told Anna that he was "getting very very tired of my honors, and some times I feel much in the humor of backing out." He contemplated leaving the ministry but concluded that "this will not do; especially were I to do so, it would derange the whole affair. Preachers are so scarce that to take one to fill my place would leave a vacuum not to be filled." When frustrated by the vicissitudes of his ministerial labors, William turned his attention to spiritual victories closer to home: "I can but believe that in Eternity I shall see at least sons who will ascribe their salvation to my feeble efforts. It is that [that] encourages me onward."³² While similar challenges accompanied proselytizing in the household and in the community, William sought to reassure Anna that her domain provided him with fewer burdens and far more numerous pleasures.

Joseph Davis also ruminated on the possibility of quitting the ministry to find greater balance between his professional and family lives: "Sometimes I have serious thoughts about the propriety of changing my present relations," he wrote to Anne, "and gladly would I do it, if I did not fear the displeasure of God. I imagine to myself sometimes a quiet & permanent home, myself engaged in the instruction of our dear children and a few select ones besides, and yourself present she in the sunlight of your loveliness to enliven and sweeten the scene." Joseph considered the possibility of blending his career and family into an occupation that would be both financially and spiritually profitable, but his calling remained too important to limit himself and his ministerial labors to the domestic sphere: leaving the ministry might "be pleasing to flesh, but not to the wisdom of God."[33] Although Anne and Joseph Davis ultimately found a way to work side by side managing the operations of the Wesleyan Female College, Anne still complained that her husband was absent from home far too often for her liking.

Although clergymen invoked their faith and their sacrifices to demonstrate their sense of self-importance and to justify their absences from home, these justifications often resonated with their spouses. Women reported that they indeed found solace through their faith during separations from their husbands. And evangelical women celebrated when their husbands reported recent harvests of souls for congregations far and wide. Even the physical hardships of travel renewed couples' collective devotion. Harrowing tales of stagecoach accidents and serious illnesses while on the road affirmed God's authority and goodness in evangelicals' everyday lives. Finally, clergymen voiced an abiding interest in their families, continuing to write of their longing for the companionship and piety available exclusively within the family circle even after years of traveling. Domestic piety remained a vital component of religious practice for clergymen.

During recurring bouts of anxiety, often ignited by her husband's absence, Anne Davis's piety contained her deepest fears for her family. With her husband away from home on Christmas Eve, Anne lamented the march of time and her growing sense of isolation.

> The approach of Christmas was wont in days of yore to produce a pleasing excitement of feeling; when I was in the midst of near and dear kindred; beneath my paternal roof; but now the scene has changed; early associations are broken up; friend after friend has departed; and us, who remain are widely separated; encompassed each, with a little family of our own; but so it is, and so it must be, whilst time lasts; in a few more years, not one of our former joyful happy family circle will be in existence; we must depart to make room for our children.

Her foreboding thoughts retained a spiritual silver lining beyond her belief that the pious in her family circle would share in her heavenly pilgrimage. Her faith eased some of her greatest apprehensions over her husband's welfare, affording her some measure of relief: "My gracious master for the sake of Jesus, I beseech thee at this time to take from me all that would disturb my peace of mind; and while my beloved is necessarily away, may all uneasiness on his account be banished from my mind, and may I from

Improvising on the Ideal 113

past experience be constrained, to trust thee for all things." Through self-abnegation and faith in God came reassurance. "I am always lonely when separated from him; Oh my blessed Master be pleased to bless him, and protect him whilst away, and in Thy own good time bring back in peace and safety to gladden the heart and lighten the cares of thy weak and dependent handmaid."[34] Though she couched her thoughts in the language of resignation and weakness, Anne realized some comfort from the knowledge that God controlled the events involving herself and her family.

Anne Davis's willingness to part with her husband's companionship also stemmed from her deep-seated confidence in the purpose of her husband's ministry. To that end, she took Christian solace in the belief that her sacrifice benefited countless North Carolinians: "I humbly pray that my beloved husband's labours may be greatly blessed unto his dear people, and that there may be a much great ingathering in to the fold of Christ of precious, immortal souls, such as shall be eternally saved than in any past year." The unique nature of his profession was the only justification for the privations of his company: "My husband goes at the bidding of Thy church and by the special order of Thy providence, were it not so I could not let him depart."[35]

But Joseph Davis's execution of his professional duties often put him directly in harm's way, a reality toward which Anne Davis held an ambiguous attitude. Rev. Davis's travels and continuous preaching brought him physical discomfort and thereby demonstrated the depths of his Christian conviction. Those same activities also raised the specter of a premature death, a frightening prospect for his wife:

> It is really a scene of laborous toil for him, my very heart faints and desponds within me when I think of his suffering, the arduous duties he is called to pass through in prosecuting his Master's work, and yet up to this time, I have never heard him utter a single murmer or complaint, but cheerfully when the time arrives for him to leave, does he mount his horse, and travel through rain, hail, snow, never loitering behind the time on account of severe or inclement weather but always punctual to the hour; if there were no other state of being no reward in store for him when done with these trials on earth, I should think that his was a sad lot indeed; but it somewhat reconciles me to his toils when nothing else can that if faithful unto death, he will then lay down the cross, and wear a crown.

Rev. Davis's faithful and uncomplaining execution of his professional duties outwardly manifested the steadfastness of faith that inspired both congregation and kin. The thought of Joseph's role as a visible saint—even a Christlike martyr—only "somewhat" reconciled Anne to his ministerial toils. Therefore, she prayed to God that her husband's usefulness to the ministry might spare his life for the sake of church and family: "May he be faithful to every trust reposed in him, may his precious life be spared to the church, and to his children, for greater usefulness for many years to come; and may I be a help-meet for him in every sense of the word, and may our children be blessed and may they rise up in the day of the Lord and call us their parents blessed, so prays thy servant for Christs sake."[36]

Anne Davis's worst fears were nearly realized. While attending the Methodist Episcopal Church, South's general conference in St. Louis, Missouri, Joseph Davis contracted a serious case of cholera, causing his wife to reflect on the connections among faith, health, and Christian fellowship: "Although I could not see him and be with him to nurse [him] in his affliction . . . God our blessed adorable master watched over him for good, raised up friends, kind friends to nurse him, and saw best to restore him so far to health, as to make home a week sooner than I expected him."[37] This episode reaffirmed her faith in God and the brotherhood of believers, but Anne knew that her husband might not be spared the next time such a crisis arose.

When Frances Douglass contemplated her husband's welfare, she too vacillated between her confidence in God's superintendence and her morbid fears of the risks attendant with travel. Widowed in a previous marriage, Frances yearned to hear from her husband regularly during his absences. When James Douglass journeyed from home in January 1834, Frances worried more than ever about her husband's welfare: "I have just read your letter & do feel sincerely thankful that your health has not suffered very materially in consequence of the exposure to cold & fatigue. I have had many gloomy forebodings but hope that he who ordereth the steps of his saints, will watch over my dear Husband & restore him again to my presence." Yet her faith in God's "omniscient eye"—her belief that "not a hair can fall to the ground without his Father" knowing—typically allayed her anxiety. During one of James's absences, Frances found comfort in an acknowledgment of her powerlessness and the power of God to care for her husband: "I feel too a calm reliance upon one covenant Father,

Improvising on the Ideal 115

that he will do all the good you need. He can give rest & sleep without my aid, & without him, all that I could do, would not insure it."[38]

While evangelicals expended considerable energy preparing for physical suffering, nothing infused more life into a believer's spirituality than an escape from a perilous event. Knowing that Frances would read of a stagecoach accident in the vicinity of his travels, James Douglass wrote quickly to relieve her fears: "You will have noticed a stage accident happening. . . . The driver nearly killed. A passenger's back broken &c I passed that same bridge, probably *not 6 hours before*. Why was it not our stage, and *my* back?" Although his health had been preserved, Rev. Douglass embraced the opportunity to explain how he would have interpreted the events had they not turned out so happily: "I do thank my God that it was not me. Yet if it had been, I sh[oul]d have been submissive, I hope, for *He* could make a broken back a blessing." Like evangelical women, James Douglass proclaimed a thoroughgoing faith in God's omniscience and authority regardless of the outcome of events.[39] He also interwove resignation with examination in the daily quest to find God's visible hand at work.

In spite of couples' best efforts to manage separation through their correspondence and their mutual faith, obligations to family and church might still collide. In the Wills family, for example, when William reported a slew of conversions in Randolph County, North Carolina, in 1850, Anna balked at the physical toll his ministerial exertions claimed: "Take care of yourself dont preach too often[.] you know I dont say any thing as long as it does not injure you." Her husband's ministerial obligations tested the bounds of Anna's willingness to sacrifice his company—and his management of their cotton crop. When ministerial obligations jeopardized the breadwinner's health, his growing family faced threats of financial distress. William could only reassure Anna that his maladies—hoarseness in particular—reflected his hard labors in the ministerial field but posed no serious risk to his health.[40]

Although Anna Wills rarely complained but generally provided matter-of-fact reports about the burdens she bore, she made sure that her husband knew that both he and his labor were sorely missed during his absences. Her gloomiest letter on domestic burdens started with the caveat to her husband, "I can't write very cheering today. . . . I have to be quite a Dr. this week" as a result of various injuries and illnesses among members of their household. She ended in an upbeat fashion, however, noting that "the wheat is heading" and the oats "are pretty." But frustration with slave labor always lurked just below the surface. In August 1850, Anna lamented that although the conditions for harvesting their wheat crop were ideal, their slaves had been called to work on the local roads. Later in the year, after hearing of Joseph Wills's reappointment to the presidency of North Carolina's Methodist Protestant Church, Anna Wills's brother wrote to her that he "was sorry to hear that" the reverend "thought it necessary" to accept the position. Lawrence Whitaker also offered to assist his sister in managing the Wills slaves if her husband decided not to hire an overseer. Anna Wills surely identified with her father, Cary Whitaker, who had left North Carolina in the mid-1830s to pursue greater riches growing cotton in Florida, when he shared with her that the burdens of managing slaves and growing cotton left him confessing that "I am far too remiss in the discharge of my Christian duties; but I hope, by Divine aid, to grow in grace and in holiness, and finally, be enabled to work out my soul's salvation with fear and trembling which is of more importance than the wealth of the worlds."[41] As Anna Wills dealt with her domestic headaches—some of them, such as tending to ill kin, traditionally associated with women's duties and others, such as managing slaves, traditionally associated with men's duties—she certainly looked to William for assistance whenever he could stay at home.

William Wills's correspondence consistently evokes his longing to partake of home life generally and of Anna's companionship in particular:

> Often when riding the dreary road, I feel sorrowful and sad, but soon I am lost in contemplation and the sweet and cheerful countenance of my wife presents itself to my imagination; I again hear the voice that is sweeter than music to my soul and again do I say in the presence of the partner of my sorrows and sharer of my joys ... grant Merciful Father, that thy servant, after wandering through a strangers land may again return to the bosom of his wife and meet those smiles that have so often been his solace and his joy!

Writing letters assumed religious overtones for William as he sought a spiritual connection with his wife. After reaching Camden, South Carolina, William wrote to Anna, "I have reached this place in safety, health, and peace, and now set down to hold sweet communion with the dearest wife of my earthly affections." As in courtship, correspondence remained the lifeblood of marital relationships. When unreliable mail delivery misdirected a letter Anna had sent to William's temporary residence, he took

Improvising on the Ideal 117

solace in their shared faith: "When fear or gloom enter my mind in consequence of not hearing from you, I endeavor to banish them by thinking it owing to a derangement of the mails and by a resort to my Heavenly Fathers Throne." The anxiety and relief that transpired during their separations and subsequent reunions reinforced William's need to fix their sights on the permanent rewards of piety: "We part in time, with sorrow, yet anticipating the hour of meeting again; and so sooner or later death will separate us, but blessed be Jesus! if Christians, we look forward beyond that point to the one when we shall meet in the realms of unsullied felicity, and meet to part no more."[42] Wills also left little room for sustained criticism of his absences by appealing to the faith he shared with his wife and the intimacy and sustenance that redounded from it.

As both Anne Davis's domestic responsibilities and Joseph Davis's ministerial demands grew more burdensome, the couple found religious meaning in the stress of their separations and their respective duties. During one trip, Joseph commented, "Absence from you is more painful to me than ever, and I feel an increasing concern for you under the heavy responsibilities that fall on you in my absence." But Joseph resisted his yearning for home life, regardless of the victories and defeats he experienced in his ministerial labors: "Yes my dearest love we are *one*, indissolubly *one*. My devotion to you can know no abatement but I trust will increase with advancing years and received its endless consummation in Heaven in the society of the blessed ones whom we have known and loved on earth." At times, the burdens of the here overshadowed the rewards of the hereafter, but clergymen and their wives used evangelicalism's language of duty and devotion to sift through their respective roles. Like William Wills, Joseph Davis showed more interest in hearing about the happenings of his home than in reporting on the demands of the ministry. Professional cares often prevailed over family cares when the two collided, but unlike many of their nonreligious peers, who managed cotton crops, politicked in legislatures, or spent time drinking or hunting with other men, these ministers retained an abiding interest in the affairs of home and family.[43]

Nowhere does this sense of mutuality emerge more forcefully than when a clergyman turned to his wife for spiritual guidance and direction. According to James Douglass, his wife, Frances, and their shared domestic piety held the only opportunity for him to awaken from his spiritual lethargy. During the weeklong journey from Pittsburgh to his North Carolina home, James ruminated on the relationship between his public and private devotional practices. As his public performances and declarations of piety grew, he felt, his personal piety decayed, and he saw his wife as leading the way out of this spiritual phoniness: "I do seem to myself to have less religion, & a great deal less, than I had years ago. And, what is most of all, I seem incapable of fixing upon any course that would, probably, restore me." The slip in piety was most prominent in his "secret walk with God," and in fact, his "humanity" and "genuine philanthropy" had improved since his marriage. However, "since I began to love you, as my wife, I have seemed to myself to decline in public engagedness and usefulness. What is the fact? I am perfectly sure that you are not the cause, nor the occasion I believe, of my real decline." James Douglass wrote to his wife "without reserve" in his search for the restoration of his piety.[44]

Douglass had already attempted to deepen his piety through individualized devotion: "I have read, planned, resolved, prayed, examined, and acted enough to have made an angel of me, and yet I seem to myself less like an angel than I was years ago." He had approached those earlier attempts with a Job-like perseverance: "I like to go through with a thing which I undertake; but if the thing have no end I get tired of repetition. I am sure to give it up." Here, however, Frances entered his daily devotional life: "Now, in regard to settled religious duties, can you not keep me to them? In order to [do] this you must be with me every night. We must not be separated. Ordinarily, if we cannot both go, we must both stay. As to myself, perhaps every thing, perhaps my salvation depends on it." He hoped that her stronger resolve would reinforce his flagging piety, as she would "supply my defects by bringing into our holy partnership, my sweet friend & helper, qualities which I have not." James Douglass couched his alarm as an awareness of what he might do, not what he had already done: "I have often said that we are, any of us, capable of committing any sin whatever, if tempted, and left." As proof, James cited recent news that a Charleston minister had engaged in an adulterous affair with a member of his church.[45]

James Douglass directly asked his wife to help him improve himself: "And hereafter, if I forget these remarks, as I will, and in levity or obstinacy am proposing to act contrary to them, I give you leave, my dear guardian, to show me this letter." James entrusted this responsibility to his wife rather than his colleagues because, he believed, they would mistakenly argue that he had matured as a Christian, that his acute sensitivity to sin in his life was a natural byproduct of "a keener vision, & a tenderer

Improvising on the Ideal 119

conscience." But Douglass thought that such "certainly is not true." He was eager to return home and begin his self-prescribed spiritual exercises.[46] Although Frances Douglass had entered her marriage concerned that she might present a liability to her husband's ministry, he now looked to her to salvage his personal faith and his public ministry.

Marital Discord and Evangelicalism among the Laity

Just as many of the women who married clergymen ably exploited the evangelical emphasis on women's superior piety and virtue, many men exploited the antebellum South's secular and sacred emphasis on patriarchal authority within the bounds of marriage. For many married couples, debates over piety itself widened the emotional gap between husband and wife. Pressed by their clergymen to convert their irreligious husbands, evangelical women sought to do so through prayer, patience, and example. When these subtle means failed to accomplish the desired transformation, women often despaired, believing that such results indicated the inadequacies of their own piety, jeopardized the transfer of piety to their children, and foreclosed hope on one of antebellum evangelicalism's most cherished promises, the heavenly reunion of faithful kin.

Even evangelical couples with deep senses of shared piety often sniped at one another with religiously inflected critiques. Evangelical husbands found themselves vulnerable to criticisms of their behavior, particularly when professional work interfered with domestic expectations and family responsibilities. But the ultimate authority vested in men by evangelicalism made such attacks difficult to sustain. Nonetheless, the fact that evangelical men felt compelled to respond illustrates evangelical rhetoric's power to critique as well as reinforce authority. In evangelical marriages, faith allowed criticism to flow in both directions between spouses.

In writing to her niece, Nancy Lincoln relayed her incessant efforts to interest her husband in her evangelical piety. With revivals erupting around their Knoxville, Tennessee, home in 1852, Lincoln hoped that the fervor might finally awaken her husband's spirituality. One male relation who had converted during the revival relayed his "great happiness and wondered that he had not been religious before and thankful that he had been enabled to see that error of his way and turn from it and to worship the true and living God." Thinking that her husband's conversion might soon follow, Nancy Lincoln turned up the pressure by mentioning her anxiety regarding his piety and by incorporating him into her domestic and public devotional practices. She soon discovered that she had overplayed her hand. Her husband disliked her proselytizing, and Lincoln "quit and did not ask him to hear me or to go to church with me." His rebuff did not conclude her efforts, however: Lincoln and other female relatives began praying for his conversion. She wrote, "Sarah can pray for him that will not annoy because he need not know it and that would be my advise to her let her go on discharge her duty and pray for the effectual fervent prayer of the righteous availeth much and we can all unite in praying for him and I hope that he will before very long see the necessity of preparing for another and a better world." This conflict brings to light the subterranean and collective search for domestic faith. Her example also illuminates the stakes of the struggle. Men could simply dismiss their wives' nagging.[47]

Mary Craddock, an evangelical in Louisville, Kentucky, experienced a lifetime of anguish because she failed to convert her husband, children, and neighbors. When Craddock attached herself to the Cumberland Presbyterian Church in 1825 at the age of twenty-three, she vowed in her diary "to convince to the world that there is a reality in religion."[48] Craddock tenaciously performed that enormous obligation throughout her life, but because her family failed to share her piety, Craddock's faith isolated her from them, generating tremendous bitterness on both sides.

Craddock's diary entries convey both the challenges of domestic piety and the scope of duties that evangelical women imagined for themselves. After an 1842 camp meeting reinvigorated her spirituality, Craddock realized that her piety had created a gap between her and the rest of her family: the "spiritual death that reigns in my family occupies much of my thoughts and my anxiety is great, all is dark no prospects of better days before my weak vision but I must resign all to discharge my duty." Her burdens as a spiritual steward included not only her nuclear family but also her slaves and her neighbors: "I often fear that I come too far short of doing my whole duty in different stations in which I have to act, as a wife as a neighbor, as a mistress, and as a Christian, all of which are very important stations." Craddock measured the success of her spiritual stewardship by outcomes more than intentions, even among her slaves. Merely catechizing among her slaves was never enough; she sought validation through conversions and earnest piety: "My large household has laid near my heart: I humbled and beseeched my heavenly father to allow to make his dwelling in this house: my servants are sickening and dying and many without religion: I feel my station is too responsible for me to be at ease: I feel awful when I

Improvising on the Ideal 121

reflect about the many souls that is entrusted to My Care!" Her anxiety peaked the following year, when the sale of a slave "who I felt from *circumstances my* duty to take care of as long as he lived" caused her to dread that the sale would "*mar my happiness* as long *as I live.*" She feared that her sense of hopeless distress had caused her to near the precipice of "sin against Jehovah" because she continued to "weep and mourn, as one that had none to comfort, none to help."[49] Now, thanks to her duties as a slaveholder, not only had her "temporal" concerns encroached on her "spiritual concerns," but she had also called into question the quality of her piety.

But much as in the case of women married to clergymen, that sense of shortcoming yielded not to resignation but rather to a redoubling of efforts to demonstrate the joy that evangelical faith brought to daily life.[50] Just as the prescriptive literature detailed, Craddock sought to persuade the irreligious in her midst of the benefits of religion through example rather than confrontation. Even as she professed her uncertainty amid the enormity of her challenges, Craddock felt compelled by God to forge ahead in her struggles.

Craddock's decision to follow the norms of domestic proselytizing—quietly demonstrating piety and praying for the conversion of loved ones—failed to generate the desired results. In 1846, Craddock recorded, "For the last 3 months I have been unusually drawn out in praying for the conversion of my family. my husband especially, and my neighbors has lain on my mind with more wait than usual and I have prayed and implored almighty God for their conversion every day: and often with strong cries and tears." Eight years later, her family remained intransigent regarding faith. But just when she felt tempted to "give up praying for my husband and family, thinking I can doo nothing," Craddock reflected on the parable of the widow and the unjust judge in Luke 18:1–8, in which Jesus relays the success of a woman who tirelessly appeals her cause to a profane judge. Recounting the virtue of the widow's tenacity, Jesus said, "And shall not God avenge his own elect, which cry day and night unto him, though he bear long with them? I tell you that he will avenge them speedily." Rejuvenated in her faith, Craddock resolved "to doo some good either in instructing some child, or some wayward individual in the ways of God." It was not the last time she turned to that parable for solace and more importantly renewal in her effort to change the spiritual condition of those around her. In 1856 she again recalled the parable, leading her to reflect on the ebb and flow of her struggle with domestic impiety: "When

I would begin to despond and begin also as peter did to sink I would rally and inquire of me in the language of the sweet songs of Israel why art thou cast down."[51]

By that time, however, years of rejection had finally sapped Craddock's patience, forcing her to concede that she had failed in her domestic proselytizing efforts. Finally relinquishing her hope that her husband and family would adopt her faith, Craddock left her appeal at the bar of divine justice. She prayed that all of those who refused to convert would be put into "open shame" and ultimately forced to reside in that "kingdom set for others."[52] Realizing that she would never fulfill the evangelical ideal of a heavenly family reunion, Craddock reasoned that isolation in heaven was preferable to a collective journey to hell.

Craddock's painful experience illustrates the difficult position occupied by many women in the Old South. Clergy expected women to use Christian example and private prayer to convert loved ones who felt indifferent or even hostile toward evangelicalism, but a failure to do so constituted one of the greatest setbacks of women's lives. They might turn inward, doubting the quality of their own piety as a testament of their faith, or they might turn outward, as Craddock did, lashing out against their unconverted kin. But their unfulfilled quests rarely garnered them any outside sympathy, especially from clergymen. Indeed, the prescriptive literature squarely blamed Craddock for her family's failure to convert, while she suffered tremendously because she had little or no hope of either seeing her family in heaven or validating her abilities as a domestic proselytizer. She eventually found solace in her own salvation, but in a religious culture that prized family conversion and celebrated the promise of a shared heavenly reward, such a victory must have seemed Pyrrhic indeed.

In addition to the intense clashes between evangelicals and nonevangelicals within the same family, conflict emerged within lay households where everyone shared the same faith. Much in the same way that clergymen and their wives sparred over the proper balance between domestic and public household responsibilities, lay evangelicals also used religiously informed language and values to debate everyday actions and responsibilities. Though these discussions were less devastating than those between believers and nonbelievers—these families could take some solace in a shared heavenly reward where conflict would eventually cease—such disputes nonetheless contained acrimony created by strongly held notions of right and wrong. Shared faith did not necessarily translate into a shared outlook. Indeed, the vocabulary of faith might well ratchet up dissent within the evangelical household.

Not far up the Ohio River from Mary Craddock, a Presbyterian couple in Maysville, Kentucky, used religiously informed expectations and language to challenge one another in their marriage. Troubled finances lay at the heart of the marital squabbles between Mary and Richard Collins. Although Richard Collins had been trained as an attorney, he preferred risky business investments to the practice of law. With repeated business failures keeping Richard away from home and threatening his family's economic welfare, Mary criticized his absences as a dereliction of paternal and domestic duties. Richard countered with religiously inflected defenses that made it difficult for Mary to quarrel with him. If Richard's investments succeeded, he claimed to be fulfilling his manly obligation to provide for the welfare (financial, educational, and spiritual) of his children; if he failed, God merely wished to keep Richard's love of material gain in check. After repeated bankruptcies and the constant threat of migration, Mary renewed her charges that Richard's actions endangered their growing family's welfare.[53] Feeling the sting of her charges, Richard lashed out at Mary, criticizing her abilities as a mother in an attack designed to hit her where it hurt most. Even as they clashed, piety continued to inform their relationship. Mary Collins's faith connected her more firmly than ever to female kin, who applauded her tenacious resourcefulness in the face of family crisis. Richard Collins's faith allowed him to vindicate himself as a parent even as he jeopardized his family's well-being.

Despite their conflicts, Richard and Mary Collins strove to uphold a companionate ideal of marriage and family. While away from home, letter writing served as "a sort of substitute for our Sabbath evening conversations, too great a privilege and too sweet a duty to be omitted unless positively unavoidable," Richard Collins wrote, describing writing as a form of "sweet sign-language." During his trips, Richard craved letters from his wife detailing family matters. One "short" but "sweet" letter from Mary "told me of *home* & our little ones—& that was what I wanted to know." Moreover, during private prayer, "I never forget you & our dear little ones when I approach a throne of grace."[54]

Because the ideals of home and Sabbath were so interwoven for Richard Collins, he frequently lamented the flatness of his devotional experience when travel prevented him from worshipping with his family. Visiting a diverse range of evangelical churches during his trips stimulated him intellectually but left his devotional experience incomplete. During a lengthy 1857 trip, Richard spelled out the necessity of family worship as a complement to formal worship: "If I could only spend my Sabbath with my family, I should not so miss them in my protracted absence, and so often desire to hear from them." But his absences could overwhelm him emotionally, as when he tearfully recounted reading one of Mary's letters: "Swimming in tears," Richard confessed that "they may not be *manly*, but they are *honest* tears, and as I wipe them away I feel all the better that they have flowed so freely." The moment caused Richard to give thanks "to God for his mercy and his loving-kindness" in blessing the Collins family "with such health and so many comforts." He even gave thanks for his ability to show emotion because "I am sure that no one can have a very bad heart, if it only wells up with sympathy as mine does frequently."[55] The distance created by Richard's business travels forced the young couple to put down on paper thoughts and emotions that many evangelical couples shared privately: the home was as integral as the meetinghouse in fulfilling spiritual needs. Correspondence allowed both Richard and Mary the opportunity to re-create their most cherished devotional experience, family worship.

But for the Collinses, conflict churned beneath that ideal. Starting with a stone extraction company shortly after their marriage in 1846, Richard demonstrated his knack for betting on bad investments. At first, Mary deferred to her husband's judgments, financial and otherwise. Even as she complained about his absences, she acquiesced to his need to leave home to attend to his business affairs, reconciling this tension in an 1850 letter: "Let me know in your next letter when you will return. Suspense is unpleasant, there is not a hint in your letter as to your return. I could not but wish to day that it might certainly be before next Sabbath. I have not been out today and have felt as lonely as the children would permit—without Husband, Mother, Church, or Pastor. But I won't ask you to come back till your duty is done."[56] But as his absences grew longer, his family grew larger, and his financial blunders continued, Mary used faith as a means of critiquing his behavior. Richard thus discovered that the home's sanctity was a double-edged sword for his business pursuits. Like his clerical counterparts, Richard Collins described the deprivation of family and domesticity as a spiritual and devotional hardship. He thus convinced his wife of the depth and sincerity of his disappointment even as he justified his absences as his manly duty to provide for the material welfare of his family. In using that rationale, however, he opened himself to serious critiques from his wife. Richard's absences, coupled with his poor investments, threatened to undermine the Eden he had constructed in his imagination.

As they weathered their first financial crisis in 1850, Richard urged Mary to remain patient and submissive, first to God and then to her husband. Faced with bankruptcy, he urged Mary to "join me in prayer for divine guidance & assistance. May God strengthen our hearts, and resign us perfectly to his will." He further rationalized his financial failure and minimized his role in creating it by contending that "God may be thus afflicting me to leave me the blessing of contentment, and to check me thus strongly lest I sink my Christian hope in the love of sordid gain. *His* will be done." He hoped their shared devotion and perseverance ultimately would enhance their faith and their marriage and lead to greater wealth: "God *will* answer prayer & bring relief in some shape. . . . [T]here's 'a good time coming, wife—wait a little longer.'"[57] Richard Collins took the lead in interpreting God's designs for the family's fortunes.

But unwilling to wait for either an explanation from Richard or the gradual unfolding of providential design, Mary demanded immediate and full disclosure of her husband's financial dealings. No matter how much Richard attempted to couch the financial crisis as his alone, Mary knew that it directly affected the entire family. Mary wanted all of the details and promised that she could bear the news, however painful. "Be candid let me know all. I can hear it. I could bear the *worst* cheerfully, were it not for the distress it would bring on our parents. Act cooly, act with judgement and if *possible* act *silently*." Moreover, Mary wanted a say in their future. While Richard discussed moving as far away as Chicago as a financial cure-all, she held up the positives of moving to a closer locale where he would have financial opportunity and she would have continued access to family: "Now let me make a suggestion," she wrote, "how would it do to open a land agency and law office in Louisville that is a place you do like and a growing business place." She quickly diluted her authority in the decision by adding, "I feel too weak too ignorant to advise [you] but have all confidence in my husband and know that he will act for the best." But her final piece of advice required Richard to acknowledge an authority greater than himself: "Seek all the light you can and look for guidance and direction from above."[58]

Richard soon found himself relying on his wife for financial advice, although he continued to expect her to support blindly his judgment and decisions. That put Mary in a bind. He needed her to manage and report on his accounts during his absences, but he also wanted her unquestioningly to support his financial decisions on the basis that he alone possessed the authority to make them. Richard came to rely so heavily on his wife because his father no longer trusted the soundness of Richard's business schemes, leaving Richard no one else to turn to. As the manager of Richard's correspondence during his trips, Mary now possessed solid knowledge of their financial status. Considering yet another move, he requested Mary's input: "Tell me fully the light in which you regard my movements about St. Louis. I say *freely* because you *know* that in many things you are my *only* adviser and in some things have been (I do not mean it in a sacrilegious sense) '*my guardian angel*.'" Like virtually all of Richard's attempts to relocate Mary farther from her family, this one resulted in her opposition. In the absence of her support, Richard returned to divine sanction for approval. As he neared purchase of the *St. Louis Presbyterian* in 1857, Richard focused on God's role in this momentous decision: "I hope I am not self-deceived in the belief that [the] finger of God is pointing me to that peculiar field of labor and of usefulness—where I can be vastly more useful, and I hope better contented and happier, than at Maysville." Even after his plans to purchase the newspaper fell through a week later, Richard continued to overlap his will with God's, writing that at times he thought that he would "take my family [to St. Louis], and trust Providence to open up the right kind of employment. But 'God helps those who help themselves' is an idea that is developed in the Bible, although I cannot now recall the language as it is in the Holy Scriptures."[59] As was often the case in his life, Richard Collins pledged to share the glory of success with God; when he failed, as all too often happened, he gladly shared the burden.

Because Richard shared information about his business ventures with Mary, he opened himself up to further criticism as she brushed off his attempts to diminish his accountability for his investment strategies and by extension for the spiritual, emotional, and financial welfare of their family. When Mary insisted that he settle down at home and substitute the steadier income of a legal practice for his business schemes, he replied that doing so would compromise his honor as a public man: "I am anxious—*you only* know *how* anxious!—to get into business again, and get *settled*, with my little family and their *wealth of love* around me. But I have a great deal of pride about me, and do not wish to live a *very* quiet, because *too useless*, a life." Richard, the son of a prominent Maysville magistrate, never let go of his ambition to exceed or match his father's success while receiving the approbation of other prominent men. Yet knowing evangelicalism's strictures against seeking money and influence, he attempted to downplay his avarice and ego. Trying to strike that balance, he wrote, "I wish to feel that I have sound influence and can exert it for decided *good*. I am unwilling to be a word cypher in the world, but wish to be a *positive* character, while I do not seek to be very prominent before the world. My heart naturally shrinks from notoriety." Richard concluded his letter by warning his wife of his persistent financial doubts but simultaneously encouraging her with his characteristic blend of personal and divine authority over future outcomes. "'Have faith, and struggle on!' is my motto, and I hope I have put my trust in God and resigned myself to Him."[60]

Richard deflected criticism of greed and self-interest by emphasizing his sacrifice of domestic piety and emotional fulfillment as a consequence of his frequent separations from his family. Early in his travels, he contrasted the cutthroat world of business with the sacredness and warmth of family correspondence: "I am engrossed with business to that extent that almost unfits me for that sweet communion with you which I ordinarily enjoy when I write to you." Richard claimed that separation from home and family deprived him of spiritual sustenance: "This is a hard life to live, my Mary—so constantly away from home & all its endearments! I feel it, I assure you—I feel that I am making large sacrifices, for the sake of my children."[61] But in spite of his best efforts to claim that he suffered more than his family during his business travels, Mary never stopped challenging his claims, as his ongoing need to justify his absences illustrates.

Richard Collins's persistent financial failures made him highly defensive, particularly toward his wife. After still more financial blunders, Richard lashed out in 1864, questioning Mary's competency as his financial assistant: "You will take up a page of paper in telling me about trifling matters, but neglect to tell me anything about important matters." Mary in turn complained about his grumbling and fault finding, and he responded with praise when she provided him with fuller and sharper accounts of business activities at home. Richard also disparaged Mary's competency in the home, surely a much more damaging indictment than his critiques of her business acumen. On one occasion, he ordered Mary to "learn to *fold* your letters in 3 folds, instead of 3 & a *fraction*," harping on his dislike of "*slovenliness* in *anything*." Taking another direct shot at his wife, Richard complained about his daughters' letters, which he described as "far too *carelessly* written. Make them write again, & copy until they get them *neat* and *correct*."[62]

The exchange of criticism became particularly heated when Richard directly accused Mary of putting herself and her social interests before the welfare of their children. Richard wrote with great concern that Mary's involvement in an 1864 Presbyterian Church fair "could not have been accomplished except at some *unreasonable* sacrifice—in loss of sleep, neglect of children, postponement or neglect of other duties, or trifling with health by too-long-continued exertion and labor!" Spelling out the dangers, Richard observed that "two ladies, among the most active & efficient at the recent Sanitary Fair at New York, have gone to the grave—victims of mistaken duty!" Mary, however, believed that Richard's neglect of their home and family posed a far greater threat to their family's future. Richard parried with the argument that his quest to attain financial security for his family amounted to a religious sacrifice on behalf of his family. "My exposure in a holier cause—'providing for my household,' and educating & preparing them for long lives of usefulness—keep you restless and anxious; and I hope will soon be safely over; that I may come home & stay—to help guard my wife's health and life from the horrors and dangers of this new disease, 'Fairs on the brain!'"[63] With each spouse charging that the other had neglected custodial roles in favor of personal interest, Mary and Richard accused one another of undercutting their home's sanctity.

Richard's father was not the only member of his family suspicious of Richard's business acumen. In one letter outlining new investments in Chicago, Richard told Mary not to show the letter to his sister, Ellen Blatterman, who "so often blames me for my [business] plans & movements." In fact, Richard's sisters showed much greater concern for Mary and the children than for Richard, casting his wife as a Christian heroine. Learning of Richard and Mary's 1860 bankruptcy, Blatterman complemented her sister-in-law's Christian poise: "Your dear letters, so full of fortitude and cheerful self denial are a constant source of wonder and pleasure to me; wonder, when I think of the trials through which you must pass and pleasure when I know and feel that my poor brother has so true and affectionate a help meet in his wife." Richard's other sister, Kate Collins, wrote to Mary that her strength during such an affliction both confirmed her faithfulness and her position in the Collins family: "You are so comforted and supported under this great trouble by faith and trust in One who 'tempereth the wind to the shorn lamb.' We all sympathize you know

Improvising on the Ideal 129

how deeply, Sister Mary, with you and Brother. Like Ruth of old, we can say 'your troubles are our troubles, your joys and happiness ours.' You do indeed feel as a daughter Sister Mary to Father and Mother."[64] Despite Mary's private criticism of her husband's financial and family decision making, her sisters-in-law saw only Christian fortitude and resignation regarding temporal crises.

At the same time, Mary's sister, Fanny Brodrick, struggled to come to terms with the Collins family's latest setback. After learning of Richard's bankruptcy, Brodrick underscored her frustration with the distance that separated her and her sister: "Since we had had to be separated I have tried to be submissive and feel that it is right, God only has enabled me to feel so, but when I know you are in trouble I am rebellious still and I feel that any other affliction I have can hardly be compared to this." Brodrick pleaded with Mary to "be as confiding as if we were together and that will do me good and I may in return lighten your care a little." Brodrick worried that this latest bankruptcy would require the Collinses to relocate even farther away, and she wondered how Mary's children would handle the adversity and humiliation, hoping that their understanding of the crisis would be framed by faith:

> This may be one thing that will work greatly to the advantage of your children though it may seem the greatest part of their affliction now. What a comfort it is to feel that all events are controlled by One who is kinder than an earthly parent (and who can measure this love) and who would therefore spare us any pain that was not necessary for us to bear, if, we can only realize this as we should how much better we would be prepared for whatever is ordered for us in this life.[65]

Frustratingly unable to help her sister and her family, Brodrick prayed that the financial crisis might eventually yield spiritual dividends. Like most evangelicals, Fanny believed that trials were inevitable but that God calibrated them to the particular needs and limits of the individual pilgrim.

Many women lacked the evangelical tools of critique that Mary Collins possessed because their husbands did not convert. Women such as Nancy Lincoln and Mary Craddock discovered the devastating results of high expectations and limited means. Although Lincoln and Craddock demonstrated remarkable perseverance in their efforts to proselytize in their household, they ultimately failed. And while Craddock felt an incredible emotional chasm in her marriage and family, she retained a strong sense of righteousness in her faith and allowed her husband and children to fend for their own eternal welfare.

Evangelicals struggled to reach the harmonious marital ideals imagined in the waning days of courtship. The contradictory impulses in the ideal evangelical marriage—intimacy, affection, and spiritual equality as well as submissiveness, authority, and hierarchy—created a wide interpretive lens for southern evangelical couples. With southern clergymen ascribing virtue and piety to women and authority to men, most marriages involved latent conflict, while others moved on to outright hostility. The sharpest disturbances clearly emerged where husbands and wives did not share the same faith, thereby denying the evangelical mistress validation as the religious steward for her family, the hope of transformed relationships within the household, and ultimately the reunion of the family circle in heaven.

But even in the best of marriages, evangelical ideals and rhetoric informed and shaped quotidian conflict. That conflict emerged in a variety of ways, but all shared women's expectations that their husbands would aid and enhance the spirituality of the domestic sanctuary through their presence and piety—not surprisingly, since evangelical men put forth such expectations during courtship. Such ideals went largely unfulfilled as a result of career obligations or of husbands' outright refusal to share in evangelical piety. When those disappointments and conflicts emerged, women used their piety to challenge their husbands' physical and devotional absence from the home, even when such absences were caused by ministerial obligations. These challenges simultaneously demonstrate evangelical faith's unique ability to place demands on patriarchal authority—even if those demands were conservatively aimed to force the patriarch back home—as well as the persistence of the male prerogative to fend off such claims. Nonetheless, a shared faith gave women a language with which to question and prod their husbands, and most evangelical men felt compelled to respond to these challenges. And, as in the case of the Collins family, shared piety among female kin could sustain critiques of patriarchal decision making and could forge bonds of support among the family's far-flung women.

A shared faith did not translate into the clergy's prescribed vision of an idyllic Christian home where men gently exercised authority and women exuded piety for all to emulate. Indeed, the architects of patriarchal privilege, the southern evangelical clergy, created the greatest disconnect between ideal and reality by relying heavily on their wives to manage and maintain consensus in their pastorate. Although the women who married pastors initially found such challenges daunting, they quickly learned how to create and manage their informal channels of authority. Laywomen too learned how to translate their authority over domestic piety—in such areas as childbirth, child rearing, and conversion—into informal public channels such as Sunday school teaching and church fund-raisers.

CHAPTER 4

"Unto Whom Much Is Given"
Childbirth, Child Rearing, and Coming of Age in the Evangelical Home

In spite of her heavy burdens as the matron to more than sixty young women boarding at the Wesleyan Female College in Murfreesboro, North Carolina, Anne Davis found time to write to her oldest son, Robert, away at college and far from her supervision, to warn of the new threats to his immortal soul. Indeed, she reminded him that evangelical southerners believed that "moral, upright young men, are the very ones the wicked beset more stealthily, & cautiously, & often more successfully bring over to their vices." In addition to prescribing regular doses of prayer and Bible reading, Davis clung to the hope that the moral and spiritual lessons learned in an evangelical home would not be lost as her son made his way to manhood: "You have had the advantage of me, in that, you have started for the kingdom of Glory, so much younger, your habits of sin are not so inveterate as mine were. You have also been blessed with religious instruction, and knew much more of the things that belong to our eternal peace at 5 years of age than I did at 20." Nevertheless, Anne Davis feared that Robert might squander all of the spiritual advantages that she and her husband, Joseph, a

Methodist clergyman, had worked so diligently to bequeath to their children. Virginia Baptist Lucy Gwathmey, who reminded her children as they entered into adulthood, "Unto whom much is given . . . will much be required," would have shared Davis's concerns.[1]

Despite the significance of domestic piety in the lives of antebellum southern evangelicals, it never foreclosed criticism within the family. Indeed, as both Anne Davis and Lucy Gwathmey suggest, inheritance of an evangelical identity only heightened maternal expectations for exemplary piety. Clergymen and laypeople alike spoke of the home as a sanctuary, but evangelical beliefs inspired conflict as well as consensus within the family. Thus, even as evangelical women became less and less visible at camp meetings and in other public settings, their work deepened and even broadened as they set out to nurture and discipline the piety of those they loved. Women soon discovered, however, that their new interpretive roles in family piety carried considerable risk.[2]

Scholars of the antebellum South have long questioned the application of an emerging northern, middle-class model of womanhood that stressed women's superior morality and piety alongside the need for womanly submission and domesticity. Because northern women ultimately turned many of the claims of superior morality and piety into calls for political and public reform, many scholars of southern history have stressed that only the more limiting claims of the "cult of domesticity"—womanly submission and domesticity—apply in the context of the South's ongoing commitment to patriarchal authority. To uncouple religious and moral values from northern women's growing political activity, scholars of the southern household have stressed its fundamental differences from its northern counterpart: southern patriarchs' continued dominance of labor and relationships within the household, in contrast to northern, middle-class men who increasingly worked outside of the home; the existence of slavery, which required men to simultaneously establish "white women's inferiority (in terms of gender) and their superiority (in terms of race)"; and a rural landscape that prevented the mobilization of grassroots women's reform movements on par with those in the urbanizing North.[3] But the gap between prescription and practice often varied widely. Although antebellum southern evangelical men retained authority in the public and private spheres, because they prized domesticity, they honored women's contributions to the construction of the home as sanctuary and even countenanced occasional migration into the public sphere as long as those actions did not threaten male prerogative or the social order.⁴ Prescriptive literature by southern evangelicals simultaneously celebrated womanly stewardship and manly authority within the household, but women could still cross from the private to the public sphere in the name of faith and family.

Like their northern counterparts, southern women looked to motherhood as the foundation of their domestic authority. Elite women in both regions merged motherhood, domesticity, and child rearing into a "sacred profession," as Sally McMillen so aptly puts it. Unlike their northern counterparts, however, southern women found their work circumscribed by patriarchal authority and never possessed the opportunity to sentimentalize their homes into idealized sanctuaries.⁵ Because the southern household typically remained a site of labor and economic production and because of southern white women's frequent pregnancies, large families, and often slave management responsibilities, such women did not have the luxury of idealizing their households into worry-free sites of purity and piety.

Childbirth offered one of the sternest tests of individual piety any southerner could envision: it both offered evangelical women the opportunity to bring disciples into the world and confirm their maternal stewardship and imperiled the life of mother and child. Antebellum southern women typically married at a younger age and had larger families than their northern counterparts, giving birth nearly every two years during their childbearing years.⁶ Faced with the possibility of death at each delivery, women preparing for childbirth often sought—and found—a closer dependence on and relationship with God. After safely delivering their children into the world, women thanked God by dedicating those children to a lifetime of discipleship, optimistically imagining that this process would reshape the South's moral and spiritual landscape. Underneath the confidence of a mother's religious stewardship lurked strikingly dark fears, however. In fulfilling their religious duties to rear their children in the ways of faith, many evangelical mothers worried that they might love their children too much, forcing God to transform the child into a cherub to remind the devout mother that nothing on earth—not even a child—should become an idol. A common fear reserved for women, this reasoning found currency as an explanation for the deaths of infants while forcing all religious mothers to seek the proper balance between their duty to love God and their duty to love their children.

Child rearing confirmed and extended women's moral authority beyond the home. Like the era's advice writers, who simultaneously stressed the dominant role of environment in shaping a child's character and a woman's superior piety and morality within the household, southern evangelical women eagerly assumed the lead in teaching their children the narrow path to life eternal. The frequency with which clergymen and fathers celebrated maternal success at this work led many southern women to train the children of strangers at the Sunday schools and academies popping up across the South. Anne Davis's seemingly meek language to appraise her integral work during a revival at her husband's academy while he was absent demonstrates how women often used the language of self-abnegation to proselytize beyond the household. Even as women's public roles increased, their domestic authority eroded as their sons came of age. Women retained full authority in the rearing of their daughters as they neared adolescence, but fathers increasingly stepped in to take over parenting duties for their sons. Although mothers inculcated values such as piety, discipline, and obedience in their young children regardless of sex, fathers showed greater involvement in the development of adolescent sons' assertiveness and other skills necessary to succeed in the world beyond the home.

As children approached adulthood, many evangelical mothers proved unwilling to let go. Although most parents had undergone halting and inexact conversion experiences in their own early adult years, they fully expected their children to have immediate and clear-cut conversion experiences at very young ages—as young as ten and twelve. Even when their children converted, many mothers found the victory hollow. Mothers attempted to reassert their children's dependence by emphasizing the infinite number of snares set for pious youth. When children failed or encountered challenges, evangelical mothers took the outcome as a vindication of their children's ongoing moral dependence. Fathers, however, showed much greater confidence in their sons' ability to make moral judgments and less concern regarding the moral pitfalls awaiting adolescents. Indeed, implicitly acknowledging the perils of dependence and weakness in a slave society, evangelical fathers urged their sons to demonstrate mastery and independence.[7] Mothers viewed their children as mirrors of piety, while fathers hoped that their sons would transform maternal nurture into manly independence.

These informal channels of domestic and public authority were often short lived and full of their own disappointments, but they suggest ways in which the practice of evangelical piety in the antebellum South gave women a sense of calling that required tireless vigilance. Evangelical women, who frequently turned inward the ideals and rhetoric of their faith, readily turned those values outward to cajole and critique family members into living more pious and virtuous lives. Even in the Davis, Douglass, Bestor, and McCampbell households, mothers assumed the central role in raising their children in the faith.

The Blessings and Perils of Maternal Affection at Childbirth

Childbirth dramatically initiated and reinforced women's claim to moral and spiritual authority within the household. Evangelical women hoped that their physical and emotional fortitude during childbirth would serve as testimony to their piety, enriching faith among the entire family circle. Unlike other afflictions, such as accidents or illnesses, which arose without warning, women could emotionally and spiritually prepare for childbirth several months in advance. Women feared not only dying but also divine judgment, while they embraced the trial of childbirth as an opportunity to forge a more intimate relationship with God. Mothers quickly pledged their children to God's service and promised God that they would spare no effort to produce more disciples. On many levels, women thus gained a deep sense of self-importance in shaping and reshaping the entire family's faith during the period surrounding childbirth.

But a cruel possibility lurked underneath the surface of women's spiritual authority in the period surrounding childbirth. Mothers claimed and received great praise for bearing and nurturing children who survived the physical and spiritual perils of childhood, but the same mothers often faced criticism—much of it self-imposed—when failure on those counts occurred. Especially when children died, mothers often heard or even told themselves that the tragedy had occurred because they had loved their children too much. In effect, a jealous and omnipotent God removed children from their mothers' presence to remind them of the supremacy of divine relationships over terrestrial ones. Motherhood thus promised southern evangelical women countless blessings and a unique sense of individual importance. But moral and spiritual stewardship also carried heavy burdens. When a physically and spiritually dependent child died or failed to convert, evangelical mothers indicted their personal faith.

Young evangelical couples prepared for parenthood and its responsibilities soon after marriage. Shortly after he wedded Anna Whitaker, William Wills conveyed the mix of apprehension and enthusiasm that filled his thoughts on the topic of parenthood:

> You know with what contemplation as well as anxiety I look forward to the time when God may be pleased to make you a mother, and both of us parents; and should that ever be the case, let *us* find the proper faith in which to walk, and then more safely may we teach our offspring the way that leads to Glory and to God. This is a strait and narrow road that shines brighter and brighter unto the perfect days; and O thou high and Holy one! direct thine erring creatures here, that guided by that heavenly lights, we may safely tread the path of life and find ourselves conveyed at last up to the throne of God.

Wills's comments touched on many of the deepest wishes and fears of evangelical parents, who saw parenthood as a natural, worthy, and particularly fulfilling station. To be complete, the Christian pilgrimage of the individual and the married couple required parenthood. But parenthood also posed unique challenges to faith. Wills worried not only that his wife's health would be imperiled but also that both he and Anna would fail to overcome the many obstacles that lay in the path of raising pious children.[8]

While fathers had the luxury to ruminate over their future as parents, mothers concentrated on the immediate concerns of pregnancy and the physical and spiritual health of their newborn children. Much as evangelical individuals and communities spent weeks preparing for revivals, women had several months to prepare for the challenges of childbirth. And when the later stages of pregnancy confined women to their homes, they spent much of their time addressing their familial hopes and fears through prayer and Scripture. Because the physical risks of childbirth did not decrease with additional births, this cycle of preparation unfolded again and again. Each childbirth, as the peculiar domain of women, forged deep spiritual bonds among mother, child, and God. And when women became grandmothers, they often relived their own spiritual passage through the childbirth process.

With one of every twenty-five southern women dying from complications related to childbirth in 1850 and married southern white women pregnant every two years until menopause, each pregnancy sharpened a woman's awareness of her mortality and raised immediate concerns regarding her readiness for divine judgment.[9] Hope mingled with those fears, however, as women prayed that successful deliverance from the trial of childbirth would confirm their faith and their stewardship role in their families. Frances Bumpass discreetly referred to childbirth as the "approaching critical period" with "its sufferings and its dangers" and hoped that she would "be prepared for the event, whatever it may be. What if death should come! Am I prepared? Do not doubts arise? O Lord wilt thou guide aright." Anne Davis was even more explicit about childbirth as a solemn spiritual trial:

> I have for months past looked forward to the time of my confinement, with gloom and doubts, and fears, lest at that time my Master may call me from time to an awful eternity. I am now in daily expectation of that time of eternity, but as our extremity is often God's opportunity, I think I can say this morning with resignation "O my God let thy will and not mine be done, and if I die Oh grant that it may be unto the Lord, and if I live, Oh grant that I may be more wholly devoted to the Lord than I ever yet have been, be pleased to bless the fruit of my womb also, and accept it even now, as an offering devoted unto thee; O do thou for Christ's sake prepare me for any and every event of thy Providence respecting me and mine, and Thine shall be all the glory in a world without end. amen."

In the evangelical imagination, the "extremity" of childbirth, like other illnesses and afflictions, exceeded the limits of human control and therefore held the potential to make tangible and transparent the often hidden and abstract relationship between faithful follower and God. In echoing the Apostle Paul's claim that weakness from infirmity deepened faith because "when I am weak, then am I strong," Frances Bumpass embraced childbirth as an opportunity to enrich her intimacy with God.[10]

Evangelical mothers routinely commenced their spiritual stewardship over their children when they consecrated their newborns to God. Mothers prayed that their dedication would insulate their babies from the dangers of a sinful world and form a spiritual link between mother and child in case the mother did not survive the birth. This pledge took place directly between mother and God, unmediated by the husband. Having dedicated the "fruit of my womb . . . unto thee," in an earlier pregnancy, Anne Davis subsequently became even more selective in her pronoun choice: "Do thou be pleased to bless the loved fruit of my womb; and . . . accept it as another offering from me; entirely unto thee." Similarly, Mary Brown used the first person to record the dedication of her newborn son to God: "I dedacate this infant Lord[—]take it fore thy own[. O]n the soul of this dear child draw thine holy image and keep it forever from the pollutions of this wicked wourld." She did not introduce her husband into the narrative until she mentioned the child's upbringing: "Give me and it[s] Father grace to set it a constant good example and may we bring it up in the nurture and admonition of the Lord."[11] Just as women had played the lead role in the child's birth, they anticipated playing the lead role in the child's nurture in the ways of faith.

When evangelical women recorded their passage through childbirth, they often emphasized God's agency over the men and women who assisted in the delivery. Recalling her child's birth one week after it occurred, Mary Brown mentioned only herself, her child, and God. Mary Bethell listed those present for the birth of her daughter but reserved her greatest praise for the divine presence she felt that night: "I was safely and speedily delivered, and done well. The Lord was with me to bless. Glory! and honor! to his excellent name, I feel like praising him with joyful lips."[12] A successful childbirth provided evangelical women with one of the most spiritually sublime moments of their life. Even through the physical, emotional, and spiritual challenges of childbirth, women did not resign themselves to God's hand. Rather, they saw their faith at work: their prayers had been answered, their physical afflictions had ceased with their faith renewed, they had brought a new disciple into the world, and they started to plot the next stage in the family's pilgrimage.

The mother's role as moral steward reverberated beyond the mother-newborn relationship to encompass the entire family circle. On learning that his daughter had safely given birth, the Reverend James Douglass envisioned her heightened piety as a spiritual current that would envelop his grandchild and son-in-law: "God grant that this my first grand child may be dedicated to God—may she be an ornament to her sex—and donated to God—Enable the Mother to train her in the paths of piety and peace—may religion be the chief concern of all their lives. . . . [M]ay the parents and all the children be a united family on earth that will not be disunited in Heaven." Likewise, witnessing her granddaughter's birth reignited Mary Bethell's faith in much the same way that childbirth had revitalized her faith earlier in life, inspiring her to renew her "covenant . . . to love and serve [God] long as I live." The deepened devotion of childbirth commenced with mother and child and radiated out to the entire family.[13]

Scholars have often charted the ongoing role of womanly expertise and comfort in the birthing chamber even as antebellum physicians set out to take charge of childbirth in the name of professionalization; however, much less well known is the process by which evangelical women reassured evangelical mothers-to-be of God's presence and protection. Sarah Fountain overcame her anxiety about her cousin's fate at childbirth by remembering that she "had the same kind Protector as ever, and many kind friends and neighbours." Unable to attend her daughter's childbirth during the Civil War, Mary Bethell described the separation as a "great trial" but "committed her into the hands of God." On learning of the good health of both her daughter and grandchild, Bethell rejoiced and renewed her faith: "I feel so thankful to God for blessing my dear daughter. I had faith to believe she would do well, the Lord heard and answered my prayer, glory and honor to his name. I will praise him with joyful lips." In her jubilation, Bethell proclaimed, "If I had a thousand souls I would give them all to God. Oh it is good to trust in God."[14] Much like the deathbed, the challenges of childbirth interwove more tightly than ever faith and family. Even when physically separated, evangelicals looked to God's superintendence as a source of solace.

Deliverance from the trials associated with childbirth led many evangelical mothers to think of ways to repay God for blessings already bestowed. Mothers such as Anne Davis looked beyond the immediate concerns of her pregnancy to envision the eternal glory that her child would bring forth for the Davis family and the kingdom of God: "O blessed Lord, May he or she (if spared) be a burning and shining light in thy Church militant, and afterward, in Heaven a light to go and move out forever." Mary Bethell and Anne Davis hoped that God would direct their infant sons to the ministry. Davis prayed to God to "make the dear boy . . . a useful and devoted Christian minister, one who shall have the honour of turning many from the error of sin, to the service of the only true God." Acknowledging God's supremacy in dictating future events, Davis also placed herself in the script of her children's future. From within the household, she envisioned her maternal influence on her son one day improving the religious landscape of the South. Such lofty expectations at birth reminded evangelical mothers how much work awaited them and presaged mother-child conflict later in life if pledges failed to fulfill expectations for piety at the individual, family, and community levels.[15]

Although the unique spiritual bond between mother and newborn cast the mother as the devotional center of the family circle, it also created unique maternal burdens. The responsibility for cultivating immortal souls weighed heavily on many evangelical mothers because clergymen and mothers alike held limitless expectations for a mother's faith and because failure carried eternal consequences. Even though Anne Beale had become the surrogate mother to her nine younger siblings when her mother died, she evinced little confidence in child rearing when her brother-in-law asked her to raise his child after the death of her sister: "Oh how incompetent and unfit I feel myself, to discharge faithfully my duty to the dear little fellow, and were I to trust to my own strength, judgment, &c, &c. I should request you to place him in better hands; but my dear brother, [I] look to the Lord for help; I look to Him alone for guidance, and direction, in bringing him up in His nurture and admonition." Anna Fuller's excitement halted abruptly when she assessed the readiness of her faith to prepare her for parenthood: "When I look at my precious babe and see him so healthy and thriving, I much deplore my ingratitude and often make new resolve to live more as a Christian should than I do. I daily pray for aid from on high for of myself I know I can do nothing."[16] Evangelical motherhood occasioned both the promise of supreme fulfillment and the perils of dire consequences. Now more than ever, evangelical mothers scrutinized their every action to assess its wider impact.

As childbirth deepened women's relationship with God, faith in God's omnipotence led many evangelical women to see themselves as most clearly able to discern God's designs for their families. Such a position proved perilous, as evangelical mothers took both the blame and the credit for all physical and spiritual endeavors. Even more importantly, evangelical mothers in particular felt compelled to pry open God's logic in meting out both punishment and reward, placing themselves at the beginning, middle, and end of that explanation. In her diary, Anne Davis recorded side-by-side misgivings regarding her faith and the recent illnesses of her family members, especially her infant son's life-and-death struggle with "bilious fever." Despite her gratitude that "our dear little prattler was restored to our embrace, as one almost from the dead" by God's "Almighty helping hand," Davis continued to question her own faith, writing "I sometimes awfully fear that I have, instead of advancing in the Divine life, retrograded."[17] Her musings suggest the emotional burdens that could accrue when stewardship created spiritual accountability for the entire family.

Children's deaths caused other women more directly to link their personal faith with God. Elizabeth Early, whose husband was Methodist bishop John Early, sought to explain God's logic to her daughter after the death of her young son: "Our Father loved him too tenderly to permit him to tread the thorny paths of this sin stricken earth & ere his spotless spirit had been touched by the fatal plague—it was translated to bloom in eternal purity in the immediate presence of his Father & God." Elizabeth Early stressed God's mercy and the promise that her daughter one day would be reunited with her child. Until that time, Elizabeth argued, her daughter could not indulge in her grief but instead needed to redouble her attention to her two surviving children and her own spirituality, because "you need great wisdom & grace to curtail what is superfluous, to suppress whatever is wrong & train & give direction to whatever is good." Writing in her diary after a difficult pregnancy, Mary Bethell less ambiguously read the purpose of her afflictions, which included a bout of measles during the final stages of pregnancy as well as a household of sick children and slaves and her husband's absence. Because everyone survived, she saw the events as demonstrating God's mercy and blessing, but during her darkest moments, she had entertained doubts: "In my distress I cried unto the Lord, it seemed that his face was hid from me, had not comfort from on high." "It was a little comfort to me," she continued, "to know that the Lord['s] eyes were on me." In the throes of feverish dreams, she "felt that I had been unfaithful, had served God at too great a distance. I did not know that my sins were all forgiven, doubts and fears, perplexed [me.] I prayed fervently to God, that if he would raise me up again to health, that I would read my bible more diligently, and frequently, and I would seek for a witness of the Spirit, to feel and know that I was a child of God." As she continued her narrative, she reported that God had answered her prayers, jointly restoring her health and her faith. Proclaiming "I am the Lord's and he is mine," she pledged to express her renewed faith by being "*instrumental* in the conversion of sinners."[18]

While Early's reassuring advice and Bethell's pilgrimage narrative ultimately reaffirmed and refined their faith, other mothers feared that excessive affection toward children might tempt God to remove the infants from their earthly families. This fear created a terrible dilemma for evangelical mothers: loving a child provided unique emotional and spiritual happiness while fulfilling an essential duty of evangelical parenting, yet too much affection violated the pledge to privilege love for and the relationship with God above all others. Women frequently warned one another about the danger inherent in making idols of their children, and all struggled to locate the proper balance between the two impulses, as Ruby Gillett warned her sister-in-law:

> I doubt not but he is a lovely child, and you probably may see no defect in him, it is certainly your duty to love him, and to watch over him with all the tenderness of a Parent, but my dear Sister is it not possible that you may love him too much? that you may make him an idol in your heart. [T]his you cannot suppose would be right, no, my sister your child is the gift of God he has lent him to you for a season[,] how long we know not, but that he must sooner or later return to God wh[ich] gave him is certain, and oh that you may be enabled by the grace of God to discharge every duty towards him that whenever he may be called to leave this world you may be prepared to give him up feeling that you have done all for him that you could do.

No one had an easy formula for finding the right balance between affection and distance in relation to their children. Cary Harrison cautioned her friend, Mary Collins, not to place her affections too heavily on her child, particularly in light of her father's recent death. Harrison reminded her old schoolmate to love her daughter "as though she was but lent. Remember the instability of all things earthly." Harrison celebrated the health of her nine-month-old son, acknowledging the difficulty of following her own advice: "I often fear he is too much the idol of our hearts."[19] In an era in which both evangelical and nonevangelical social commentators stressed the irreplaceable influence of maternal piety and affection in shaping a child's character, uncertainty and anxiety over the exact threshold between maternal love and idolatry loomed with each child.

When Ann Thomas warned her niece, Ann R. Sexton, against excessive affection toward her children, Sexton deflected the warning by claiming that she had long ago absorbed the lesson and carefully distinguished between acceptable and unacceptable levels of maternal affection: "I have been taught by *sad experience* that we should not worship our Children or any thing we have on this earth, our Children you know are bone of our bone & flesh of our flesh, and it would appear inhuman not to love them as we do our own lives; but still I know that God has given them to us, and can take them away at *his* pleasure, therefore I pray that the *Lords will, may be my will*. He knows what is best for us."[20] By voicing her awareness of and concern regarding the potential problem, Thomas tactfully reaffirmed God's omnipotence over all events while carving out a justification for maternal tenderness.

Other women had less success in striking a balance between the doting and the distant mother. When scarlet fever ravaged North Carolinians in 1843, Anne Davis turned to God to safeguard her children. Faced with the possibility of having little time to prepare either herself or her children for death, she began to imagine their angelic fate, seemingly distancing herself from them. "The disease has been particularly fatal to children, and I often view my little ones as already inhabitants of another world," she confided in her diary. As if to reassure herself, Davis then deployed a litany of scriptural justifications for leaning so heavily on God in her time of trial: "We are not our own, but we are bought with a price, and that price the precious blood of the adorable Saviour of mankind, our children are only loaned unto us; they belong to God alone, and when He sees best to demand them of us, O that we may be enabled to resign them with cheerfulness; well knowing that He does, and can do, far better for them than we can even ask or think." Davis's professed resignation to divine will soon faced a test as her two-week-old daughter succumbed to the fever. Of that time, Davis wrote, "I really felt that the hand of the Lord rested heavily upon me, while at the same time I ackno[w]ledged that I deserved it all, and much more in view of my former unfaithfulnes and ingratitude to the author of all my mercies and favours." Several months later, Davis thought she comprehended God's purpose: "Never before were afflictions so truly sanctified to the welfare of my soul as these. Since I have been raised up unto my former health and strength I seem to be in a new state of existence.... I realize a constant sense of the Presence and favour of God." Aware of the lesson and renewed in her faith, Davis vowed no longer to dwell on the past: "I am endeavouring by my daily conduct and practice to forget as it were the things that are behind and to press forward unto the mark and prize of our high calling as it is in christ Jesus."[21]

In the wake of the tragic death of a child, grieving mothers often could not find Ann Thomas's nuance or Anne Davis's ability to foreclose further scrutiny of past events. Instead of serving as a buffer to grief, the popular admonition against excessive maternal affection could become twisted into a causal explanation for children's deaths. Struggling to find God's purpose in her son's death, one South Carolina woman wrote, "A jealous God has lain the little Idol low in the dust." Like many evangelical women, she understood the loss as a lesson from God to emphasize heavenly objects over earthly ones. That point, often implied or alluded to, was explicated in a letter from Priscilla Taylor to her old friend, Mary Collins: Taylor believed "that we had our affections too much centered upon our Darling Clara, for the silken cord that will sometimes en twine itself too closely round those we love has been as it were unduly broken, not however to remain suspended but to be fastened at the feet of Jesus to entice our earthly wayward hearts, more firmly and constantly there." Because her daughter had professed her faith on her deathbed, Taylor confidently described Clara's death as a "triumphant departure." But the event and the explanation forced Taylor to reexamine her relationship with God: "It is hard to feel that the dealings of a merciful and kind Providence are right and just and good, and that 'he does all things well,' but I pray that I may humbly submit to his holy will."[22] A child's death represented much more than an emotional loss; it also indicted a mother's spiritual stewardship because she had knowingly crossed the well-known if ambiguous threshold between maternal duty and maternal indulgence.

The vocabulary of affection and affliction so thoroughly infused female evangelical discussions of childhood death that it even cropped up in correspondence between strangers. Shortly after Edward Collins's death, his mother, Mary Collins, donated her deceased son's jacket to the missionary cause of the Presbyterian Church. When Juliette Dorland, the wife of a Presbyterian clergyman in Ohio, received the jacket on behalf of her son, she found a note pinned to the lapel. Mary Collins had penned a description of Edward, and the bonds of faith and maternal affection quickly closed the distance between the two women. Dorland wrote back to Collins, opening, "Although a perfect stranger to you I feel freedom in addressing you, through the reception of a little cloak worn by your dear little boy." Dorland then inquired about the tragedy's effect on Collins's faith: "I hope that severe affliction has been blessed to you, and has proved to be one of those golden links in that chain which is to draw your affections heavenward."[23] On one hand, Dorland's inquiry seems more invasive than consoling. On the other hand, it suggests both Dorland's confidence in discussing others' piety, likely because of her role as a minister's wife, and the pervasiveness of the language of affliction in evangelical discourse. Particularly given the passage of time, Dorland probably thought she could safely probe the tragedy's effect on Collins's personal piety.

Because the death of a child naturally generated intense grief and because the bereaved felt that the event constituted a profound lesson from

God, evangelicals used the anniversaries of children's deaths to reflect on faith and the level of piety within the family circle. The correspondence between Lizzie Cox and her sister, Mary Collins, regarding Edward Collins's death points to the tenacity of affliction in the faith of the surviving kin. Two years after Edward's death, Cox reassured Collins of her son's place in heaven. But Cox hoped to turn her sister's lingering grief into an opportunity to rekindle faith among the survivors: "'No affliction for the present is joyous but grievous, but afterward it worketh the more peaceable fruits of righteousness to them which are exercised thereby.' Surely such thoughts should urge us to greater diligence and activity in our Christian life that *we* too may be prepared to enter that 'rest' where the 'wicked cease from troubling and the weary are at rest.'"[24] More than in most afflictions, God's purpose in the death of a child remained shrouded in mystery. Because of that mystery and evangelicals' quest for spiritual intimacy with God, they revisited those afflictions annually to scrutinize their effect on devotion to God and family. Women thus hoped to transform their personal loss into cosmic purpose.

Childbirth thus posed enormous challenges for southern women. When tragedy struck and an infant was lost, women felt devastated spiritually as well as emotionally. Women whose children survived through early childhood described childbirth as one of the most spiritually fulfilling events in their lives. Their escape from such a physically perilous experience combined with their direct delivery of a new disciple to God provided women with a unique sense of intimacy with God. It also empowered women, unequivocally reinforcing their moral and spiritual authority within the household. Mothers now worked ceaselessly to see that their children made their own promises to God.

Child Rearing

Imagining the manifold challenges to a child's faith between infancy and coming of age, mothers early impressed on their children the benefits of piety and the penalties of irreverence. Eugenia Leland noted the narrow window of opportunity that childhood's innocence created for the evangelical message to take root, beseeching her four small children "to pray earnestly for the Holy Spirit to be given you while your hearts are tender and open to its gentle influences." Later stages of life did not foreclose the opportunity to adopt faith, but evangelicals and nonevangelicals alike stressed childhood as the formative phase of life for an individual's character. Conversion deferred also meant the passage of important crossroads in life and the ever-present specter of death without the shield of religion.[25] And, most importantly, as parental success became equated with producing pious offspring, evangelical parents sought early reassurances that their children were securely on the path to eternal salvation.

Mothers held a dominant position in the inculcation of morals and piety in their children. Evangelical mothers created and maintained southern homes as sanctuaries. Mothers relished their position as their children's moral and religious stewards. Indeed, women's pivotal role in inculcating religious values within the home allowed them to press their domestic role into more public arenas such as the Sunday school classroom and seminaries for young women. Just as women advanced their influence outside of the home, they quickly discovered the erosion of their influence within the home. Mothers remained firmly in command of their daughters' training for a future in the domestic arena, but their husbands began to exercise greater influence in preparing their sons for futures beyond the home. Men continued to encourage their sons to demonstrate filial obedience, industriousness, and piety but increasingly hoped that they would also demonstrate assertiveness and independence, qualities deemed essential to success in the wider world. Even more, because evangelical fathers viewed this transition to manhood as a process, full of miscues and mistakes, they tolerated failure. An untested faith was an unproven and domestic faith. Southern evangelical women no doubt shared the concerns of other antebellum women that a young republic required all of the virtue, selflessness, and piety that could be cultivated among its young men.[26] But southern evangelical women limned those concerns with uniquely religious concerns, imagining life as a perpetual struggle between good and evil. More than character and education were required to know right from wrong. A man's misstep would also surely reprove a mother's personal piety and imperil her deepest wish that her work result in the redemption of the entire family. An emphasis on environment shortly after childbirth may have allowed women to rhapsodize about their sons' limitless potential to transform the South's landscape, but as their children came of age, many evangelical mothers feared that the South's environment might overwhelm even the firmest Christian character. As fathers groomed their sons for manhood, however, they pulled their male offspring farther and farther from the mother's orbit of influence and generated conflict within the household.

Deep theological and ecclesiastical divisions may have separated evangelical denominations, but clergy of all stripes agreed that women possessed a type of nurturing piety that made them indispensable in the indoctrination of future generations of evangelicals. As Presbyterian clergyman Daniel Baker wrote in *An Affectionate Address to Father*, "Whilst it is the special duty of the mother to instruct, it is the special duty of the father to restrain." Another Presbyterian, the Reverend T. V. Moore of Richmond, Virginia, used a nature metaphor to illustrate the complementarity of men and women: "The attributes of man's nature stretch out their strong and rugged roots toward earth . . . whilst those of woman lift up their graceful stems and unfold their fragrant foliage to the sky." He further argued that men possessed superior ability in "logic," whereas women possessed superior ability in "intuitional powers," precisely those sensibilities where "religion makes its strongest appeal." Moore added that women's "superior religiousness" appeared most prominently at the cradle and the grave, giving piety the best opportunity to bloom in this life and the next among men in the household. That antebellum dichotomy of separate spheres—women's superior piety vested in the household and men's superior authority vested in the public arena—has caused scholars to question whether antebellum women exerted much public influence over politics or religion, particularly in the rural South. While southern women felt the limitations of this formula more keenly than northern women did, it did not foreclose women's public influence, however limited and circumscribed, even in the South. Calling for a Sunday school in every Baptist church, noted clergyman Basil Manly looked to women to lead that work as they applied to the meetinghouse their unique skills developed in the home: "Sunday school affords a noble and appropriate sphere for the activity of pious ladies, and that in the very thing for which God has especially fitted them, the training of the young. They can attend to this with more of affection, and simplicity, and patience, and therefore, of effectiveness, than ordinarily falls to the lot of the other sex." In addition, he observed, women comprised nearly two-thirds of his denomination's membership.[27]

But amid their proclamations of women's superior piety and morality, clergymen did not overlook women's weaknesses, demonstrating that men and women required one another to complement their virtues and minimize their defects. Nevertheless, clergymen continued to lay the blame for parental failure and neglect largely at the feet of evangelical mothers. Moore, for example, noted that a woman who did not convert to Christianity failed to fulfill "the destiny of her nature, and lends her example to endorse those depreciations of her nature." Without piety to check a woman's character, she would become vain, evidencing a keen interest in balls, theater, and socializing that would lead to "indolence" and immorality and ultimately "the irreligion of woman [and] the immorality of man." Even as he urged fathers to play a more integral role in the discipline and development of their sons, Baker's choice of Scripture placed greater accountability on women's shoulders: "'A wise son,' says Solomon, 'maketh a glad father, but a foolish son is the heaviness of his mother.' When children turn out well, the parents feel richly rewarded; but when the reverse, then comes affliction which enters the very soul."[28] Although both parents sought the conversion of their children as parental validation, a check against bad behavior, and insurance for the eternal soul, the clergy suggested that women's character was especially well suited to this work. As a consequence, clergymen both expounded on women's perceived shortcomings and made each woman squarely responsible for the piety of all within her household.

Practice echoed prescription loudly on this point as antebellum southerners repeatedly proclaimed that women constituted the primary architects of a domestic sanctuary. Even the children of clergymen pointed to mothers' essential and unique role rearing pious children. As her mother's health deteriorated, Frances Bestor pondered her future alone with her father, an Alabama Baptist minister. More than an emotional void, her mother's death jeopardized piety among her siblings: "Children without a Mother, are truely to be pitied, thrown upon the kindness of this hardened world no loving voice such as a mother's, ever sounds in their ear, to correct their little troubles, & above all to direct their thoughts to Holy things. I know we have one of the kindest, most indulgent Fathers, yet a child to be 'trained up in the way he should go' should have both parents." Similarly, William McCampbell, a clergyman's son, articulated how the unique bond of affection between mother and child shaped a child's piety: "A mother can feel for her children when no other can, their affection is truer, purer & more undying than anything else earthly." This affection transported piety between mother and child and in the process directed emotions outward. Maternal affection, McCampbell wrote, "'tis more akin to heaven than earth, 'tis the link that binds heaven to earth that turns our thoughts, our love thither." Outward emotional and intellectual links, he continued, forged an eternal link among mother, son, and

God: "Our mothers direct us to heaven while they live, then when dead again their spirits hover over us & beckon us upwards."[29] Many evangelical mothers took this admonition to heart, working single-mindedly to ensure their children's salvation.

Always on edge about faith taking root in their children's impressionable minds, evangelical parents seized every available opportunity to introduce and reinforce religion in the home. Anne Davis prayed to God that her children's supple minds might absorb the religious training she imparted: "Make them obedient and teachable, so that Thy blessed word of truths may sink into their tender minds and hearts, and from thence spring up into eternal life." Other evangelical parents attempted to recreate the experience of the meetinghouse in their homes. Richard Collins, who traveled frequently on business, attempted to direct his wife's efforts at domestic religious training from afar: "Gather the little ones together *every day*, and sing with them, as well as read and pray with them. In teaching them to *sing* together, you imperceptibly increase their *love* for each other—and I am sure they cannot love each other *too much*!" Methodist clergyman Joseph Davis chose to model his children's domestic religious training after Methodist class meetings, a popular practice among late eighteenth- and early nineteenth-century Methodists in which small groups of laypersons, usually segregated by gender and race, openly discussed recent triumphs and failures in their personal piety: "I have thought recently that we might increase the profits and pleasure of our social circle," Davis wrote to his wife, Anne, "by having an hour or so devoted specially to conversation with our children, each evening during twilight; Not in the form of lecture but in the full interchange of thought and sentiment in which the children should be the chief speakers. The subjects to be of a cheerful character, seasoned with a due measure of spirituality."[30] Davis hoped to avoid the tedium of sermonizing and engage his children in open dialogue with fellow family members and God. Imagining both home and church as refuges from sin, evangelicals envisioned the transfer of teaching techniques from one sanctuary to the other.

The responsibility for cultivating faith in their children weighed most heavily on mothers. Maternal duty, Anne Davis wrote in her diary, required her to be not only devotional exemplar but also guardian of her children's eternal souls: "May us their parents, and me especially not fail to improve every opportunity we have in impressing upon their young hearts sound principles of morality, virtue, and religion." Davis saw instilling her faith in her children not as an abstract duty but rather as a responsibility demanding immediate attention with dire and tangible consequences, and she believed "that it is my most imperative duty to set before them the best example I possibly can, such a one as I will delight to reflect upon, on a dying bed; such a one as will tell favourably upon all their future lives; and such a one as will not condemn me, when we stand face to face at the judgment bar." After all of the Davis children converted at early ages, Rev. Davis congratulated his wife on fulfilling her maternal duties: "My children are endeavouring . . . under the counsel and example of their pious mother, to secure the interest of their immortal souls." He acknowledged her "affectionate solicitude" toward their children's upbringing and prayed that God's "spirit of wisdom and faith and patience" would sustain her labors.[31]

Because a pious mother remained necessary but not sufficient to ensure the family's redemption, evangelical parents turned to children's literature to reinforce domestic lessons. Decreasing the emphasis on innate depravity that had prevailed in earlier works, authors of antebellum advice literature set out to show that children were capable of good and evil, putting a sharper edge on the necessity of their moral and religious instruction. Such advice literature aimed at children stressed concrete example over precept with the goal of instilling such Christian values as "virtue, self-control, charity, and a willingness to put the wishes of others above one's own." Conversely, these works commonly denounced selfishness and ambition. But this literature also sought to charge "mundane objects" within the household with a "profound spiritual significance" to validate the promises of spiritual transformation. In *Daniel Baker's Talk to Little Children*, the Presbyterian clergyman first set out to explain the concept of a soul. While the little boy in his anecdote thought it "a little round thing like a hickory nut," according to Baker, a little girl offered a better response: "It is my think!" Comparing the soul and body to a watch that keeps ticking even after it is removed from its case, Baker informed children of their prospects for heavenly reward (and the terrors of eternal damnation) while instructing them about how to cultivate everyday habits that would encourage the former. Baker offered few surprises with his advice on how boys became "jewels" rather than "plagues" and how girls became "roses" rather than "thorns"—practicing piety through prayer and attendance at Sunday school, obeying their parents, telling the truth, avoiding passion, reading religious literature, and donating money to missionary work. He directed boys to avoid marble playing and swearing and suggested that they substitute the phrase "Pot-hooks, and Hangers!" when tempted to curse. Like other commentators, Baker eagerly appealed to death to illustrate just how close the paths to redemption and destruction remained and the dire consequences that awaited even children. When a bullying older sister pushed her younger sister into a shallow stream during his missionary work in Galveston, Texas, he recalled how the younger girl's wet clothes led to fever and then death.[32]

In a similar fashion, Baptist clergyman Charles Mallary, who published children's advice literature under the pen name Uncle Charles, set out to create a casual familiarity with his youthful audience, but he did not shy away from bluntly spelling out the perils that awaited a child's every decision. Mallary announced in his preface that while his stories "may in some degree innocently amuse, they may at the same time be the channel of spiritual good to some immortal souls." Despite the volume's warm, casual, and conversational tone, Mallary quickly shifted to the topic of death in childhood, reflecting on the many children "now sleeping in the grave" with whom he had shared his stories over the previous twenty years. By dwelling on the "shortness of life," he hoped to "bring our minds into a serious frame, and prepare us all . . . for a blessing" and disabuse the young of the idea that they could put off attending to matters of the soul. He too spoke endlessly of the snares set for unsuspecting children and parents and the need therefore to construct a Christian home and attend church so that a diligent mind and soul would create "worthy children who are anxious to improve their minds and hearts and grow up ornaments to society, and blessing to their fellow-men." The alternative, he lamented, would be "lazy and idle boys who do not care for their own improvement and usefulness, nor for the happiness of any body else."[33]

Evangelicals sought to instill self-discipline so that their children might one day guard their own souls. When Anne Davis reflected on her marital and parental goals, she wrote, "I will endeavour to use patience and forbearance towards my son, and correct him in a spirit of mildness for every offence, of which he may be guilty." Clergymen and mothers alike repeatedly stressed the need for calm correction within the household. The loss of parental self-discipline would undo all other means of instruction and might send children into open rebellion against their parents. That ideal eluded France Bumpass after the failure of her efforts to curtail her one-year-old daughter's "peevishness," "fretful[ness]," and "temper." Even though she believed her daughter's behavior had roots in a physical ailment, she nonetheless expected the infant to demonstrate self-control and viewed her behavior as willful disobedience: "She cries for what she wants, & shows much temper sometimes. I have whippted her severly for a child of her age, this week—but little seems to be effected." Later in the spring, when her husband, the Reverend Sidney Bumpass, returned home from his travels, Frances Bumpass gladly turned parenting responsibilities over to him. But the results were the same. "Mr. B has twice corrected her & she had long cries. I like for him to manage her now he is at home—Yet how it grieves me to hear her cry thus! It draws tears from my eyes. Lord our help must come from thee. Without thy grace we cannot train her right. O! for wisdom, wilt thou grant unto our daughter now & even more the gentle & controlling influences of thy Spirit."[34]

More distressing than her failure to correct their child's behavior was Frances Bumpass's loss of self-control. The ideal of measured parental correction remained elusive three months later, when Bumpass wrote, "I perceive that I must now learn her that our will [is] to be her law, for the longer I defer this lesson, the greater difficulty I may have to encounter." Evangelical parents believed that the young mind was more open to lessons of devotion as well as to lessons of authority. The Bumpasses' use of force also speaks to the high-stakes struggle of evangelical parenting—parents employed all necessary means to keep their children on the narrow path to moral purity and eternal salvation.[35]

Evangelical men and women showered their young children with nurture as well as punishment and advice. When Richard Collins wrote to his youngest children, he emphasized that they should obey their mother, exercise kindness toward their siblings, and pray that their parents would instruct them in the ways of godliness and obedience. Collins concluded his admonitions by asking the little ones to "kiss your Mother and Sisters and Brother *twice* apiece for *me*, and to be *good* children until I get home." Having other family members express his affection in absentia was a favorite tactic of Collins's. On another occasion, he placed the impetus on his wife "to kiss our little ones for me, from Edward *up*, at least *three* times each, and let them kiss *you* for me just as often. What a kissing scene . . . I have plotted—and the father away a thousand miles from it all!" At home, Mary Collins rewarded her children for good behavior by allowing them to sleep in her bed during her husband's prolonged absences.[36]

Although evangelical parents hoped to train all children to be pious, watchful, and diligent, the training of boys and girls started to diverge as adolescence neared. For boys, the universal traits of evangelical children were tempered with the expectation of an active public life in adulthood. Taken under their father's wing as they approached adolescence, boys learned to negotiate the public world. Fathers encouraged sons to demonstrate command and refinement while showing ease among others. For girls, amiability and piety with an eye toward pleasing others remained the core values. Boys were directed toward increasing expressions of their autonomy, while girls were taught to demonstrate their capacity to comfort others.[37] In spite of the emphasis on sex-segregated tutelage, however, all acknowledged the necessity and unique influence of a mother's piety over the entire domestic circle.

Events surrounding childbirth served as a portent of the differences boys and girls would face when they came of age. Prior to his birth, Sidney Bumpass's father had had a "singular dream" that foretold Sidney's name and his future as a "professional character." Although he did not know whether dreams influenced the future, Bumpass confidently concluded "that they often influence our conduct." As a consequence of his faith in the sagacity of his dream, Bumpass's father had invested in a solid education for his son, which opened the door for Sidney to enter the ministry. And, like most children, the progeny of preachers often mimicked their father's occupational role. The Reverend Joseph Davis's oldest son, for example, imitated his father by standing atop a trunk and delivering short sermons to other members of the household. Anne Davis reported that her son defended his father's reputation against playful barbs from his grandfather, writing to Joseph, "Whenever he hears any person speak of you as he thinks derogatory, he is incensed and will say in a sharp tone of voice, you must not talk about my farder so, I tell you."[38]

One of the chief parenting challenges that evangelicals confronted was exercising the right blend of authority and permissiveness with adolescent boys. The proper combination, evangelicals believed, would yield men of great piety who also engaged in the South's larger public life. As sons matured and parents lost the ability to shield them from the world and its depravity, evangelical parents sought to interweave real-world savvy with the traditional lessons of obedience associated with piety. Some men felt that they alone could fully grasp the delicacy of that challenge and that they alone possessed the ability to transmit that training to the next generation of evangelical men.

Writing to his sons, Richard Collins, whose father was a newspaper editor and Presbyterian church elder, offered directives that touched on the traditional virtues associated with obedience. He instructed his thirteen-year-old son to read his Bible regularly, study diligently, and respect his siblings. Like Davis, Collins's correspondence with his children bolstered his wife's domestic authority during his prolonged absences: "Resolve that you will promptly and cheerfully obey your parents, and never grudgingly and whiningly do what they tell you." More specifically, he insisted that his son make himself "useful" to his "Mother and those at home and be always kind and gentle and uncomplaining." Collins also encouraged the boy to protect the interests of his younger siblings, to "regard *yourself* as their protector, and always be ready to do them a service."[39] No longer solely responsible for governing his own behavior, his son should now begin to aid the development of his siblings' character.

Richard Collins believed that leadership qualities in boys should be encouraged at home when they were young so that they could later succeed in the larger world. In 1857, he told his wife, "I wish you to keep a very close watch over the dispositions of our little boys. They are head-strong and self-willed. I wish they were even more so." He clarified, "What I ask is that we may have grace and firmness and wisdom to train them up aright, that they may grow to be useful citizens and pillars in the Church." Boys needed assertiveness to compete vigorously for positions of public importance.[40]

Peers Collins, Richard's younger brother, accompanied him on some of his travels, thereby affording him an opportunity to use his parenting skills even while away from home. Richard placed great importance on both the timing of the trip and his role in preparing Peers, a "noble-hearted brother . . . with far fewer weaknesses than boys of his age generally have," for manhood. Richard eagerly embraced the opportunity "to mould [Peers's] character and tastes, and *fix* his habits permanently." A successful effort would require the cooperation of the entire family: "Tell Kate and sister and brother George and Father to write to him *frequently*, and affectionately and *encouragingly* (*never* in a *fault-finding* spirit, for he rebels instantly against any thing of that sort)." If the family members avoided criticism, Richard hoped, his brother would show less self-doubt and circumspection. Yet he continued to hold high hopes for their mother's influence on Peers's character: "Tell *Mother* to add a little *postscript*. . . .

for a *postscript* from *her* will do more to influence him for good than *four pages* each from *all* the others." To prepare his brother for adulthood as a Christian and as a public man, Richard Collins yoked the unique powers of motherly encouragement with manly advice suited to a life beyond the home.[41]

Parents struggled to determine the speed with which to develop worldly acumen in their sons, but daughters received their apprenticeship in domesticity from a very young age. The idealized qualities of an evangelical womanhood included efficiency within the home, sterling piety and virtue, restraint in dealing with those beyond the family circle, and respect for authority. When Kentuckian Samuel Haycraft's daughter died at thirty-three, he penned a memorial to her in his diary that highlighted the southern definition of womanly virtue: "For more than 20 years she was an uncomplaining child of affliction she was prudent, sensible was very retiring with strangers wise in counsel and was anxious to do good. Her life was a mixture of affliction, devotion & submission."[42] In sum, she never allowed her concerns to transcend the bounds of home or family, except perhaps for her Baptist faith, which he surely credited for her ability to endure suffering with fortitude.

For evangelical girls, maintaining a virtuous reputation in both the family and the community was paramount. When his daughter, Anna, left home, Cary Whitaker demanded that she maintain a reputation beyond reproof: "I wish you to be discreet in your conduct; never act such as to give the least room for censure; the best legacy a girl can have is a pure and spotless reputation; it is what I would prefer my daughter should have to all the wealth all the accomplishment and the beauty in the world. . . . I hope never to hear any thing from you but what is praiseworthy." His daughter apparently offered similar advice to her children: thirty years later, her son, Richard Wills, employed biblical imagery to guide his younger sister, Mary, in developing a character consonant with the constructs of Christian womanhood: "Above all things be a *good* girl & try to do right. . . . Don't get mad & pout; that is not pretty. Try to cultivate a sweet trumpet. Overcome every thing of an opposite character. Pray to the Lord to help you and to help you to do right about every thing. Be sure to be kind to all the little children."[43] Although Whitaker focused on community approbation while Wills focused on character development, both pieces of advice illustrate the scrutiny of character that young evangelical girls experienced from all corners as they came of age. Unlike boys, who needed to begin to show competitiveness and gregariousness, girls needed to continue to show self-discipline and meekness toward strangers.

Parents and adult kin universally admonished young women to cooperate with siblings and exercise diligence in studies, especially those related to religion. Richard Collins told his daughters that to be "*good girls*," they should "learn their lessons well, . . . practice their music faithfully," and "visit Grandma's frequently." Evangelical kin hoped that early lessons in domesticity, diligence, and learning would carry over to adulthood. Many evangelical families hoped that the growing number of academies for young women would enforce lessons of domesticity and piety. Perhaps fearing that his sister would take a greater interest in socializing than studying, Richard Wills urged Mary Wills to seize the opportunity that education afforded her: "A great many persons there may be, who trifle their time away at school, & afterwards regret that they did not improve more. Try then to study hard and learn all you can."[44]

Of course not all girls hewed to the evangelical ideal for adolescents. While entertaining guests with two young daughters at her Fayetteville, North Carolina, home, Frances Douglass contrasted the two girls' personalities. One girl, Mary, possessed "the rudiments of fine character": she was "calm & quiet, of domestick habits & in a remarkable degree obedient to her mothers wishes." But Sarah was "gay thoughtless, [and] fond of company." Douglass found the girl convivial but proclaimed that "without the restraint of Religion she would run into many excesses."[45] Religion thus shaped children's personalities by reinforcing good behavior and checking misbehavior. Because such seemingly innocuous traits as inattentiveness or sociability suggested deeper character flaws, evangelical mothers felt compelled to scrutinize their children's behavior and piety in tandem.

As women's reputation for virtue and more importantly their talent for cultivating evangelical souls increased, so too did the possibility that women might use their skills to train children other than their own to follow God. Although they typically couched such ideas in modest language and domestic ideals to assuage any concern that they had overstepped their fundamentally domestic duties or privileged assertion over restraint, women nonetheless proselytized in a wide range of venues. Mary Bethell assumed care for five orphans from the Torian family. As they matured and left her home, she assessed her parenting in spiritual terms, the same calculus she used with her own children: "I hope I have done my duty to them. I tryed to lead them in the way to Heaven, I have talked to them about Jesus Christ as the Saviour of the orphan, and I have prayed for their conversion. I pray to God that his blessing may rest upon them, that all of them may be stars in the crown of rejoicing in Eternity." Two years later, when Bethell learned of the death of Tony Torian, she again reflected on her parenting of the orphans: "I gave him religious instruction with the other children. Tony was about 11 years old when he professed. I hope he is in heaven. I pray for all the children . . . that God may make them happy Christians."[46] Faith thus could transcend blood ties, in this case forging a sense of fictive kinship. The responsibilities and rewards of raising these children did not end with conversion or even coming of age but figured into her calculation of souls won or lost for the cause of Christianity. Like many southern evangelical women, Bethell's desire to proselytize, which sprung from women's exalted position in spiritual matters, often had the unintended consequence of expanding the umbrella of domesticity.

Women's comfort level with proselytizing decreased the farther they moved away from their own homes, but their discomfort failed to stymie their efforts. Sunday school teaching, for example, offered an ideal arena for transferring the skills of domestic religious training into the congregation. The opportunity to instruct young girls both thrilled and awed women, but if the responsibility for domestic religious training was taxing, then instruction of neighbors' daughters at the meetinghouse nearly overwhelmed women's sense of duty. On learning that she would be instructing five young girls in her church's Sunday school, Maria Lide wrote to her cousin that she "almost tremble[d]" when thinking of the "responsible station I have assumed." But she overcame her fears through her "very great desire to do something that shall redound to [the] glory of God." With the weight of the new responsibility still hanging over her, she expected to find the new station a "pleasing employment." And, as Sunday schools took root across the South, women's enthusiasm for this new institution—and their ability to use it to reshape the southern religious landscape—seemed almost boundless. One resident of East Tennessee, Eliza Heiskell, communicated that optimism to her sister: "We have a Sunday School attached in our neighborhood. [I]t is a real infantile concern, but as very small babies sometimes make very large women I am in hope if we are industrious we will make it grow at least to a respectable country school." Because her sister had taught in a Sunday school, Heiskell welcomed "any hints that you may think usefull." After visiting a poor woman with a sickly infant,

Mary Craddock was so inspired to start a Sunday school at her church that she refused to return home until several children had pledged to attend. Even when she bemoaned that only 20 percent of the children in her immediate neighborhood attended the Sunday school, she observed that most of the children "have no other opportunity to get religious instruction." And the bonds that formed between pupil and teacher sometimes paralleled those between parent and child. When one of her students left her community, Eugenia Leland lamented that she would never see the girl on earth but hoped to meet her in heaven because she was "one of Christ's little ones."[47]

New opportunities for religious instruction such as the antebellum Sunday school classroom muddied the boundaries between public and private proselytizing. Unlike the early nineteenth-century female religious "virtuosos" described by Christine Leigh Heyrman, who deliberately stepped onto the public stage to proselytize among strangers at outdoor camp meetings, evangelical women in the antebellum South did not actively seek opportunities to provide religious instruction to adults. Rather, antebellum women limited their proselytizing beyond the home to children and adolescents. In that way, women confirmed the exceptional piety ascribed to them by clergymen while answering the call to improve the dire state of religious affairs in the South. Such public proselytizing largely has gone overlooked because women in the antebellum South typically downplayed their responsibility for the outcome. Indeed, no less than Methodist bishop James O. Andrew observed the intersection of womanly self-abnegation and public service in his written eulogy for his wife, Ann Amelia Andrew: "She never made any very loud noise about her religion. In fact she seemed to be always deeply impressed with a sense of her unworthiness." "Yet," he continued, "she was not melancholy; but went cheerfully on in the path of duty, *doing* all she could, and in those hours when sunk in deepest self-abasement, clinging closely to God's promise, and saying continually '*the Lord is my helper.*' She was always active in doing good—in promoting Sabb. Schools, in visiting the sick, and in relieving as far as possible the necessities of the poor."[48] Southern men and women repeatedly yoked womanly humility and domesticity with Christian mission and purpose beyond the household.

A close examination at a revival sparked by Anne Davis illustrates how evangelical women bent the restrictive ideals of domestic piety to apply them broadly to their families and communities. Anne and her husband, the Reverend Joseph Davis, moved from Virginia to North Carolina in the mid-1850s so that he could take the helm of the Wesleyan Female College in Murfreesboro. Anne's consistent success at domestic conversion contrasted sharply with the more public fortunes of the area's Methodist clergy, and the fall and winter of 1855 seemed inauspicious times for the spread of Methodism in northeastern North Carolina. When a nearby revival netted only two converts and four mourners (people in a transitional state between sinner and convert, experiencing distress regarding the state of their souls but still unable to claim reconciliation with God) in spite of stirring preaching and exhorting, Anne lamented to her son, Wilbur, "Our Zion is in a very languishing state." Moreover, the Chowan Baptist Female Institute had possessed a monopoly on female education in the area for seven years prior to the founding of the Wesleyan Female College. Any ecumenical spirit among Murfreesboro's evangelical denominations broke down as the Baptists and Methodists competed to make their respective academies succeed. While both schools set out to provide young women with training in the liberal arts ranging from composition to science, the fighting for income and souls turned so vicious that Anne Davis accused Chowan's leadership of spreading a rumor that a case of scarlet fever had erupted at Wesleyan.[49]

Yet despite these challenges, only eight months after the school's founding, a dramatic revival, managed by Anne Davis, emerged at Wesleyan Female College. In December 1855, with Rev. Davis away at the Methodist Conference meeting in Richmond, Virginia, Anne had little choice but to see that the young women under her charge successfully transferred the anxiety over the state of their souls into a fruitful conversion experience. The manager of the school's boarding operations, Anne took a maternal attitude toward the sixty-two resident girls, and she shepherded fourteen girls to the status of convert and another four to the status of mourner. In spite of her doubts and anxieties about her ability to guide her children through conversion, she embraced this opportunity to transfer domestic child-rearing skills beyond the family. That nearly 30 percent of the girls who boarded at the academy underwent spiritual transformation testifies to Davis's managerial acumen, no matter how sheepishly she credited herself.[50]

As important as the revival itself is how Anne Davis chose to describe and record the events that unfolded around it. Although she periodically acknowledged her role in the revival's success, she most often downplayed her agency. To legitimize the spirituality of young girls in a patriarchal culture, Davis had to convince her husband (and others) not only that the students' enthusiasm was genuine but also that she had channeled that fervor into orthodox belief. That process entailed a description of events that included much more self-abnegation than self-promotion. Davis's drive to legitimate her efforts also points to the relationship of correspondence and diaries in the spiritual lives of southerners. That she fails to mention such a spiritual triumph in her diary but discusses it freely in her letters suggests that women often turned to journals in times of spiritual crisis when they possessed enough time to record their thoughts. Because the events of the revival unfolded so rapidly, demanded so much of her time, and required external validation, Anne chose instead to write letters to her husband and sons seeking advice and reporting on the academy's progress.[51]

Anne Davis's moral authority over her own children merged with her role as boardinghouse matron. She reflected on her moral and spiritual responsibilities to the girls under her charge, dedicating herself to treating the students as her own children: "Oh! God . . . may I be enabled by thy assisting grace to go in and out before these dear young ladies, who have immortal souls to save, in that way and manner as will influence them to follow Christ, to take Him for their portion now in the bloom of youth, ere the evil time comes. And may I be enabled to give such advice and counsel to them in all cases as Thou O God will be best pleased with." Indeed, Davis's role as the academy's "assistant principal in charge of student life" allowed her to mediate most aspects of each student's life, particularly their access to young men in the community. Stretching the bounds of domestic female influence, Davis sought to secure the eternal fate of girls whose souls were particularly open to both the temptation of sin and the promise of salvation. That move was made all the more seamless for her by the fact that one of Davis's daughters, Olin, was among the converts. Rev. Davis glowed not only at the prospect that the revival could spread but also in the news of his daughter's conversion.[52]

Typical of nineteenth-century revivalism, the revival at the Wesleyan Female College started rather uneventfully amid ongoing concerns for the state of the college, Methodism, and evangelicalism broadly in the area. To quiet the din of "idle laughing & talking" among the female boarders on a Sunday night, an instructor, Miss White, proposed reading aloud a chapter from Anne Davis's copy of *Voices of the Dead* (1852) by John Cumming. White's summary of the book, "that the sound of every word we uttered would never cease through the endless eyes of eternity," piqued the young girls' interest. After hearing the first chapter, the students quietly and solemnly retired to their rooms for the night.[53]

In retelling the events that initiated the revival, Davis deliberately portrayed herself as the reluctant protagonist. After everyone had retired for the night, she was awakened by two girls who told her that one student was "under serious conviction, and had arisen from bed, and kneeled to weep & pray for mercy." Davis wrote to her son, Robert, that she did not investigate further because she did not feel well, and she apparently doubted the authenticity of the girl's claims. When she arose in the morning, Davis pulled the girl aside and began "instructing her as well as I could." As soon as classes concluded on Monday afternoon, several girls retired to the room of the girl under conviction to "sing, and exhort her, and encourage her." The girls then sent for Davis, "saying they had a glorious meeting." One girl claimed to have been converted, while several others declared themselves mourners. Thrown off balance by the initial scope and intensity of the spiritual fervor among the girls, Davis sought advice from others. Whenever she dispersed the girls in one room, urging them to return to their normal routines, another meeting erupted in a different room. She then asked some of the male teachers for advice: "We scarcely knew what to do, all our ministers are at conference, and Messiers Carr & Williams, think best, not to make a public meeting of it but merely allow them to hold their meetings, among themselves every afternoon." But the gatherings had become raucous: "There were . . . about 30 or 40 [girls] in the room," Davis wrote to her husband, "some shouting, some crying aloud for mercy, while others were exhorting." Davis found such a level of religious enthusiasm awesome: "What are we to do? I dont know what to do, fearing either to encourage or discourage this work. I talked to them when up there a few moments since as calmly as I could, and told them not to give away too much to excitement, and that if it was a genuine work of the Holy Spirit, God would carry it on." Even as she took the middle road, she wrote to her husband, "I wish you were here." But she also genuinely feared that events would spiral out of control. "Please write if you cant come, and instruct me how to act."[54]

A week later, Anne Davis had the situation firmly under control. Eleven-hour religious meetings now took place under her close direction. In addition to instructing and praying with the converts, she and a female teacher were doing all "the audible praying," thereby "allay[ing] all violent excitement." Before listing the fourteen girls who had been "reclaimed and converted," she directly addressed her agency in the revival: "Behold what God has wrought, without human aid, or at least the weakest of His instruments."[55] With the harvest now in sight, even the humble Davis took partial credit.

Davis's shift from awestruck observer to poised revivalist points to her deft use of evangelical language to pay heed to social and theological conventions. Too much emphasis on the role of anyone (other than the Holy Spirit) during the initial phase of the revival might bring additional scrutiny and theological dismissal to an event that lacked clerical sanction. Even in religiously sponsored academies such as the Wesleyan Female College, where the religious environment combined with the age and gender of the pupils produced cycles of conversion, clergymen and male educators typically served as the principal exhorters and counselors. After many years of marriage to a clergyman, Anne Davis knew that emphasis on the sequence of events that pushed her into a leadership role would only affirm the Holy Spirit's pull on the girls' souls. For the revival to succeed, however, Davis also had to demonstrate that the girls' spiritual vigor had been directed toward orthodox piety. Her wealth of domestic conversion experience—as the wife of a minister surrounded by converts and conversion narratives and as a mother and surrogate mother who had already ushered three children through conversion—provided Davis with a deep knowledge of the conversion process. Where possible, she could claim at least partial credit as an exhorter, but credibility required that she ultimately assume the role of passive observer and reporter. Her correspondence reveals the tension between the two roles.[56]

Anne Davis's postrevival letters contradict her meek claims of agency and purpose, revealing her thrill and optimism. For example, Davis boasted to her son, Robert, that "one of the converts is Miss Anderson, whose father's greatest, and only objection to sending his daughter here, was, the fear of her becoming a christian. O! that it may be the means of the conversion of her father & mother." Much as Anne's youthful conversion had a domino effect within her family, leading to the conversion of some of her younger siblings and eventually her father, she hoped that a similar process would unfold in the Anderson family.[57] She clearly knew that clergymen and parental example were not the only means of spreading the Gospel.

By describing the girls' behavior before and after the revival, Davis located another subtle means through which to take partial credit for the changes wrought by the revival: "After Mr. Davis left for conference, the irreligious among the girls, were rather noisy and inclined to throw off restraint. But you would be astonished to see how calm and subdued every one seems to be and what a blessed influence is felt by all." Wilbur Davis confirmed his mother's assessment: "The revival has been of great service to the students, indeed its fruits are manifest in the change for the better in the conduct & recitations of its subjects, and of all. They have now some fine students. Among them are some who, last session were remarkable only for wildness and neglect of studies." The shift from insolent adolescents to obedient Christians provided Davis with immediate and tangible confirmation of conversion's rewards. As soon as the spotlight shifted to her role in the events, however, Davis's depiction of herself again switched from that of moral steward and exemplar to that of reluctant leader: "How good, and how gracious is our God, and how condescending in thus using such weak instrumentalities in the advancement of His cause."[58]

This small revival illustrates how remnants of evangelicalism's sectarian past survived into the antebellum era. Some disobedient acts among the students, which would have ordinarily merited punishment, suddenly became permissible. "When the bell rang for study," Anne Davis reported to her son, "I went up and told them to repair to their several rooms, which they did at once, but ere the bell was rang for bed hour, Miss Thackston, came down to tell me that they had assembled in another room, to encourage and instruct one who was in an agony of distress."[59] Davis relinquished her normal role as disciplinarian as long as the religious fervor did not spill beyond the walls of the academy. And her hope that the spark of faith could generate a firestorm of converts illustrates evangelicals' continued confidence in the ability of their faith to subvert the patriarchal dissemination of ideas and values.

That Joseph Davis surely claimed formal credit for the eighteen girls who experienced spiritual transformations during his absence also points to the limits of Anne Davis's authority. And some combination of factors beyond the immediate control of the Davis family contributed to the conditions that often presaged revivals, including a rivalry with the Baptist academy in town, unease over the community's state of piety, and the young women themselves, who reflected the southern age and sex cohort most likely to convert. But those involved in the informal revival at Wesleyan Female College as well as Murfreesboro's larger evangelical community must have known that Anne Davis had been instrumental in dramatically quickening the state of Zion there. And at least two more revivals would occur at the academy before the Davises' departure in 1859. The revivals certainly did not harm the Wesleyan Female College, as enrollment surged to 133 students in 1859, well ahead of enrollment at the Chowan Baptist Female Institute.[60]

The scope of Anne Davis's involvement with a revival exceeded the common experience of southern women, but it typified the process and language of domesticity that women used to extend their influence beyond the household. Women openly demonstrated their moral authority over children within the home but delicately applied that authority outside. Nonetheless, under the rhetoric of resignation to religious duty, women made dramatic inroads in the ranks of the unconverted. Yet even as women discovered ways to extend their domestic authority, as children came of age, mothers' domestic authority eroded. Women's previously uncontested authority over the development and education of young children became increasingly embattled.

Conversion and Coming of Age

Conversion marked a crossroads not only in believers' relation to God but also in the mother-child relationship. On one hand, mothers felt that their children's conversion marked the fulfillment of the pledge at childbirth to rear a pious disciple for God. On the other hand, many mothers struggled to let their children manage their own moral and spiritual development despite the belief that sin and temptation, so prevalent during adolescent years, outmatched young people's powers of resistance, even when those youth had converted.[61]

During the 1840s and 1850s, many parents who implored their children to convert at an early age had taken a more circuitous route to conversion. Like the young women at the Wesleyan Female College, these evangelicals experienced the classic stages of spiritual rebirth: preconversion life (that is, life as sinners, outside of the evangelical fold); a period of conviction or mourning; and then conversion (when the helpless sinner "threw himself on God's mercy and in that moment was made acceptable to Him"). As Rodger M. Payne notes, despite its formulaic nature, the conversion process allowed ample narrative room for individual improvisation. Indeed, as individuals authored extended accounts of spiritual rebirth, they necessarily inserted more and more of themselves into a narrative structure designed to negate the importance of the individual. A generational split often emerges among individual conversion narratives. Whereas early nineteenth-century evangelical converts, especially first-generation converts, experienced a prolonged and uneven conversion process, second-generation converts were much more likely to collapse that process into weeks instead of months or years.[62]

When parents recalled their struggles through the conversion process, they noted that their families had played a limited role. Many adults recorded their conversion experiences as lengthy on-again, off-again affairs. Religious impressions occasionally commenced as early as age eleven or twelve, but formal conversion often did not occur until much later. Although a meeting at Leesburgh "had an effect on" Mary Bethell, she "resisted the spirit, and would not yield to my impressions." She blamed her pride for the missed opportunity and claimed that she knew immediately when "the spirit" left her. She converted five years later, but even then her faith was "weake" and she "did not bring forth fruit" as a Christian for several more years. Anne Davis, who first learned the concept of resurrection from a slave at the age of nine, did not fully engage evangelicalism until the age of seventeen, when she struggled with her poor health and the death of her sister. Still another deeply devout adult evangelical, Frances Bumpass, recalled that years of turmoil commenced when she spoke "of release & relief" to another young convert. While the girl mentioned Bumpass's imminent spiritual change to others, Bumpass remembered that the "next morn [when] I awoke my comfort had fled." "For years," she continued, "I thus lived rather seeking than professing the graces of the Spirit."[63]

Men too acknowledged the time lag between an awareness of salvation and their conversion. Although Samuel Henderson Jr. listed a camp meeting in Spring Hill, Tennessee, as the moment when he "became fully convinced of the reality of Religion," he chose to date his conversion nearly two years earlier. Deep in meditation in his father's field, Henderson had vowed not to leave until he was "released." Sidney Bumpass also enjoyed the benefits of a pious mother, but the influence of impious boys in his neighborhood impeded his progress toward conversion. Although the timeline of his conversion narrative is somewhat unclear, the sequence of events—including the arrival of a pious teacher, Sunday school instruction, and new friends who shared his fear of God—suggests that at least several months elapsed before his conversion. William Wills, who had twice before "resolved and broke the resolution of seeking religion," finally made headway during a third attempt at the age of twenty-one. Even then the change was not instantaneous, spanning several months and many spiritual undulations.⁶⁴

Of course many antebellum southerners experienced sudden and dramatic transformations in their spiritual condition in the 1810s and 1820s, most famously as a product of camp meetings. As Frances Bumpass struggled to obtain "comfort from above," she noted "generally at home hope prevailed, with others at class or revivals fears prevailed when I heard their confidence expressed." William Wills, who enjoyed sharing his faith with other new converts, also proclaimed that "great doubts arise in my mind respecting my own state" when "I look at the experience of others [and] the instantaneous change which they profess to have undergone." Elder W. W. Hill of the Methodist Protestant Church attempted to quell Wills's doubts by assuring him that the conversion moment often ranged from "a flash of lightning amidst the horrors of surrounding darkness" to the dawn of morning "after the chills and shadows of a long and dreary night." Hill likened the latter experience to a traveler who at daybreak remained uncertain whether the twilight represented day or night "until he finds himself surrounded with lovely day, and cheered and strengthened with the sun shine of Heaven. [P]erhaps he can never mark the moment when the day dawned and the shadows fled away, still he is sure he must have been borne, because he injoys the delights of existence."⁶⁵ All would-be converts sought sudden and dramatic conversions, but such clear-cut markers could remain elusive.

These qualified conversion experiences, however, did not prevent evangelical parents from pressuring their children to proclaim themselves converted at early ages. Conversion itself retained many familiar features as a profoundly personal and spiritual experience with conviction and release but increasingly became fundamentally a family concern—especially a mother's. Conversion still reflected personal piety, but its structure, meaning, and purpose were shaped through family devotion. Most new converts came to a denomination through the influence of family members rather than through a gathering of strangers at a camp or protracted meeting. And when evangelical families celebrated children's conversions, they considered the individual testimony to the family's collective devotion and the promise of eternal reunion in heaven, where pious kin would reunite. Youthful would-be converts received little respite from the pressure to convert.

Mothers silently recorded in their diaries their deepest fears for their unconverted children and their deepest wishes for a sudden change in their hearts. Until her son converted, Anne Davis sought comfort from God: "O bless my precious boy and soon, very soon, make him Thine own devoted follower, succour him when tempted, comfort him when cast down, aid him in his studies and influence him in all his ways. I now faithfully commend him to Thy care and keeping." Eliza Leland repeatedly beseeched God for more time so that her children might yet absorb her faith: "Oh that the Lord would in tender Mercy bring them to the foot of the cross, and there may they be found clothed and in their right mind. Oh God visit them not in wrath, leave them not to themselves as thou might in justice do, thou has been very Merciful unto them." Shortly thereafter, Leland noted the reverence for both faith and family that her children exhibited, giving Leland reason to believe that they would soon join the "fold of Christ." Although she wanted each child dutifully to serve God while on earth, her chief concern was that they be prepared "for his kingdom, where we may all meet an unbroken family."[66]

Parents did not restrict their expressions of concern regarding their children's conversions solely to the privacy of diaries but pressed for evidence of conversion. Ann Thomas wrote to her daughter, Anna, "I hope you are brought to think seriously on the all important subject of religion, though I have no doubt but your judgment has been informed, long since, all that is wanting is to yield to terms of the Gospel." During an 1858 trip to New York City, Kentuckian Richard Collins told his wife, Mary, that he had witnessed the moving scene of a boy's conversion: "If he, but 9, could thus experience the grace of God, may we not pray *in faith* for our dear little girls." When his daughter, Mary Ellen, retained lingering doubts about the authenticity of her conversion, Collins reassured her, "I am not without hope that you have experienced that change of heart which is necessary to salvation—for very often, to children of the church and covenant as you are, that change is gentle and gradual and imperceptible, like the softest summer breezes that scarcely stir the air." The conversion process often enveloped the entire family circle. When Richard and Mary Collins's oldest daughter, Annie, questioned the authenticity of her conversion at the age of thirteen, Mary's sister, Lizzie Cox, came to Annie's aid: "The *world* may think you too young to have taken such solemn vows, but there are very few devoted *Christians* but would approve of your conduct." After Annie

Collins converted, she became her parents' accomplice in the great effort to get her younger sister to discuss her faith and ultimately to convert: "I pray every day that, if it is His will, Sister may become a child of God, before the meetings close, and if not now, before many weeks. Has she ever spoken on the subject—I know she must have thoughts about religion, even though she does not express them."[67] Given that evangelical parents devoted so much paper to their concerns about their children's conversions, evangelical children likely received considerable daily nurture and pressure on the subject.

The sons of ministers too faced familial pressure from far and near. As Anne and Joseph Davis's sons, Robert and Jonathan, approached conversion, George and Anna Andrews counseled their nephews on the conversion experience. Anticipating Robert's argument that he remained intellectually unprepared for such a transformation, George Andrews reminded the boy that conversion required a change of heart, not of mind:

> Do you want to know what I mean by "a new heart"? I mean being born again of the spirit of God. The renewal of the Holy Ghost. Then and not until then you will have eyes to see and a heart to love. Thus you see, that we ought to love God and feel grateful to our saviour and walk faithfully in his commandments, we are incapacitated by the fall to do so. But then there is help. The Lord Jesus. Remember, always remember his words. "Without me ye can do nothing"?

Although he used the familiar vocabulary of Christian conversion, Andrews asked his nephew to divulge his thoughts on faith in his own "language," "ideas," and "writing" because Andrews wanted "to see if you are not mature enough to begin to receive the light of Gods word, and be so affected by this light as to fear that you are depraved and must be made holy." When George Andrews's ministerial labors diverted him from providing spiritual advice, his wife picked up the slack. Less theologically driven than George, Anna nonetheless emphasized that Robert should convert soon: "No my dear Robert, dont procrastinate, but seek the favor of the good Lord now in your youth, it will smooth the path of life, and make it even, and open in your heart a little heaven." Describing religion as the "sweetest comfort" of life, she implored him to answer her letter and "write freely." Evangelical youth of the antebellum era confronted the difficult task of creating a conversion narrative that spoke of genuineness through its unique and individualized components while addressing the issue of orthodoxy by including all the essential components of the ritual.[68]

The promise of conversion spread across the generations within southern families too. Encouraged by the news that one child in their family circle had "obtained a hope" of conversion at a recent protracted meeting, Sarah Fountain recalled the duty she shared with distant kin to instill faith in the next generation: "O my sister how can we be thankful enough to our Heavenly Parent for what He will continue doing until our own dear little children shall be brought to a knowledge of truth." Word of conversion sent relief and thanksgiving reverberating throughout the family. When his daughter converted to Methodism, Samuel Henderson Jr. reaffirmed his trust in her devotion to her faith and family, praying, "May God protect her." On the occasion of her son's fourteenth birthday, Eugenia Leland wrote, "My prayers have been answered in behalf of my dear Aaron in his coming out boldly on the Lord's side and how that he has united himself with the church on earth, I earnstly pray that his name may be written in the Lamb's Book of Life." Eliza Leland thanked God when her granddaughter was admitted to church membership and prayed that the event might be a harbinger of future conversions in the family.[69]

Because faith increasingly needed to be shared with one's family and not just the community of believers, evangelicals faced a great challenge when members of their households spurned their faith. In spite of their parents' best efforts, many evangelical children failed to yield to the conversion process that remained the hallmark of southern evangelicalism. No matter how well parents educated their children about their faith or how badly parents wanted to transmit their faith to their children, faith would not necessarily pass on to the next generation. According to the Reverend Sidney Bumpass, many members of the Methodist Church's Hillsborough, North Carolina, circuit had adult children who had not yet converted and joined the church. One of Bumpass's prominent colleagues, the Reverend William Winans of Mississippi, gained painful firsthand knowledge of such an outcome when his son, Wesley, entered adulthood without a conversion experience, causing his mother, Martha, great distress: "I heard from Wesley. . . . [H]is letters are in every respect highly interesting and satisfactory except on the subject of religion. On this he is silent. On this ground I feel great fear and anxiety. If I could only see him a Christian, all my fondest hopes would be fulfilled in Him but I can only pray for his conversion." Young men such as Wesley Winans may have struggled to reconcile manly independence with the conversion experience, an emotional outpouring that hinged on a sense of personal unworthiness. Not content to leave the matter between son and God, Martha Winans insisted on blaming herself: "I often reflect on myself that I was not more faithful by example and precept while he was yet with me, to strive to win his tender heart to ways of piety & virtue."[70]

When all else failed in the way of religious instruction, parents of unconverted souls held out hope that God might aid their proselytizing efforts by demonstrating the fragility of human existence and the dependence of all humans on God. When dysentery struck Mary Bethell's household in 1853, all of the white residents survived, but four slave children died, and Bethell claimed that she saw God's logic in such events: "The Lord has been good to us, those that died were children, he spared the grown ones, who were not prepared. That shows plainly the goodness of God." Bethell's grown (and unconverted) children had been spared, allowing them one more opportunity to absorb the lesson of God's authority, while the young slave children died before they could be held accountable for their failure to convert. Bethell followed the same line of reasoning several years later when her son was captured at the Battle of Gettysburg. She prayed not only for his survival but also that his trial might finally underscore his dependence on God and lead him to convert: "My dear son George was taken prisoner. I thank my Saviour that it is no worse, I pray that God may save his life and grant that this trial may be the means of making him a christian. Man's extremity is God's opportunity, 'tis my daily prayer that God may convert his soul." George nevertheless remained unconverted, and his mother continued to pray that he would see the light.[71] George's return home was but a brief taste of divine mercy. Unless he converted, her broader vision of an uninterrupted chain of faith within the family circle and ultimately in heaven would go unfulfilled.

White women struggled to convey their faith not only to their own children but also to their slaves. Although they never discussed their slaves' faith with as much frequency or detail as the faith of their children, slaveholding women clearly gauged their success as mistresses on their ability to proselytize among slaves. Frances Bumpass prayed in her diary for "grace to enable me to govern my family aright," lumping together the misbehavior of her daughter and that of a slave and concluding, "Our servant is willful, & obstinate. May I manage her & our child properly." Similarly, giving birth to a healthy daughter, Mary Bethell reflected on the dual burdens of raising pious children and pious slaves: "It is my daily prayer that all my children should become Christians, my servants also." Scholars have often noted that white family members commonly included greetings to family slaves in correspondence, but at least in one case, Richard Wills added an evangelical twist when he acknowledged the family's converted slaves in a letter to his mother: "Tell Wash[ington] & Leah to be faithful in all things and I want their prayers too."[72] Particularly with his father's frequent absences on behalf of the Methodist Protestant Church, this eldest son hoped that piety and loyalty would go hand in hand.

In most cases, white slaveholders used spare language to describe the piety of their slaves, typically in informal eulogies for slaves included in diaries or letters. Occasionally on smaller holdings, however, the conversion of a slave marked a dramatic moment in the master-slave relationship. Frances Douglass reported to her husband that one of their slaves showed the telltale signs of the first steps toward conversion, an emotionalism laced with apparent introspection: "I have been talking seriously with Nelly about her salvation. She wept profusely whilst I endeavoured in my poor way, to set before her the wonderful forbearance of God towards sinners, & his great goodness & mercy in providing a saviour. She never showed any feeling before. She has been less boisterous for the last two days. I dont mean that she is serious. But let us not despise the day of small things." But if Douglass hoped that a pious slave would be an obedient slave, she was surely disappointed a month later when she sent Nelly to market in the morning and she had still not returned home at nine that evening. Nelly's recent pious turn also had not caused her to solemnize a monogamous relationship with a slave man.[73]

Mary Bethell enjoyed swifter success with her slave, Betty. While riding home from a camp meeting and discussing the sermons they had heard and singing Methodist hymns, Betty "broke out to saying Oh! Miss Mary I believe God will have mercy on *me*. I was astonished and told her yes that God would bless her if she would believe after she got home, she professed religion. I felt very thankful, I hope God will convert all of my negroes." Elizabeth Early enthusiastically reported that her slave, Til, "was powerfully converted in my room" after she "discovered that her disease was as much of the mind as the body." Early continued,

> I left her in my room after dinner. . . . I heard her groaning & making a noise, and thought she was sick. Was about to go to her, when I heard

her coming down the steps. & turned & said—"Til what is the matter,["]—The words were scarcely spoken when she fell on her knees at my feet—threw her arms around me & exclaimed—"O Mrs. Early, I am so happy! O I love God & every body—Praise the Lord for what he has done for me.["] & many other expressions of joy. . . . She wept & rejoiced full one hour without cessation in the most rational manner. Nothing boisterous but one of the *clearest*, & most *satisfactory* conversions I have ever seen. Once she exclaimed—"Well, I reckon I'll get well now—Bless the Lord! I've nothing to trouble me now. O I never was happy before in all my life." "I thought I was seeking the Lord for the last 6 weeks, but I never before in earnest until Saturday." . . . Perhaps poor Margaret, & the rest of our careless ones might be influenced to reflect & prepare to meet God. . . . Til says, . . . "Tell them all, I *know* I am converted now. My soul is full of love, Love to God & all—yes every body" . . . O is not the God we serve a *great God*? No respecter of person—but in every time & place, & in all nations. They that call upon him shall be saved.

Although Til had clearly struggled with some minor physical illness—a common precursor to conversion—and had struggled with the state of her soul for over a month, the clarity of her salvation and her eagerness to voice that change with others stands in contrast to many of the adolescent children of white evangelicals who struggled to convince themselves that they had indeed experienced conversion. And as a bishop's wife, Elizabeth Early presumably knew a model conversion when she saw it. But perhaps most importantly, Early could celebrate not only the passage of "another soul . . . from death unto life" but also confirmation of her skill and benevolence as a slave mistress.[74]

While parents celebrated the conversion of children and slaves alike, they showed much greater concern and held much higher expectations for their children's piety. Converted children testified to a mother's spiritual triumph, but women increasingly found little comfort in such accomplishments. Thanks to their success at ushering their children through the conversion process early in life, evangelical mothers continued to fear that their hard-won gains would be erased by children's missteps amid the myriad snares that confronted antebellum adolescents. Maternal nature seemingly had little hope in the face of the world's seductions.[75] These deep-seated fears of a treacherous outside world hid women's concerns regarding the erosion of their authority within the home. For women who discovered both moral authority and self-importance in their exercise of maternal duties, each child's departure represented a sudden diminution of domestic authority. Fathers, conversely, encouraged their sons in particular to embark on spiritual and personal journeys. Seeking to instill greater assertiveness and competitiveness in their sons, fathers showed much greater trust in their children's judgment and tended to show much greater tolerance for missteps than mothers did. For women, every child's misdeed, every threat posed by a new temptation, only confirmed the ongoing need for maternal oversight.

After Anne Davis established the sanctity of motherhood and projected those responsibilities onto the pupils at the Wesleyan Female College, she began to question the depth of her children's postconversion piety, writing, "It is true that all of them have made a profession of the religion of Jesus except one but this is of no avail, unless they live up to this profession, I see them so much of the worldly mind, and so little of the mind of Christ that I am often so discouraged that I am almost constrained to give up my despair." The nagging fear that her children were Christians in name only plagued Davis throughout their adolescence. Dispensing with the self-effacing language she used to explain the events surrounding the revival at Wesleyan Female College, Davis implored her sons, Robert, Wilbur, and John, to police their souls lest they drift away from the path of eternal salvation. When they failed to govern their thoughts and behavior, she did everything in her power to reassert her control, making up for what she saw as her husband's failure to provide adequate guidance for their sons as a result of his attention to the girls at the Wesleyan Female College. The boys, she believed, were "exposed to vice & temptation almost every hour," "necessarily away," as they were, "from under the paternal roof" while attending college.[76]

Anne Davis used every means of moral suasion she could muster on her sons. In a typical letter to Wilbur, she harped on the absolute depravity of college students: "Oh! my son, how anxious I am about you? A thousand fears crowd upon me, concerning you, I know what R[andolph]. M[acon]. C[ollege]. used to be; and I shudder when I think of the many temptations and snares to which you are exposed." Anne Davis had reason to believe that her sons' immature piety would be outmatched by the forces of peer pressure. From their inception, southern colleges and universities served as the proving grounds for young men's autonomy and sociability, leading to ribald behavior that administrators and faculty could not rein in. Consequently, Anne continued to insert herself directly into her sons' devotional lives after they left home: "Whenever inclined to do any thing of doubtful propriety, ask yourself: 'Will this be pleasing in the sight of my Father in Heaven'? Will this meet with the expectations or wishes of my dear father & mother at home?" When her eldest son spent his first Christmas away from home, Davis plainly stated that she considered herself the primary guardian of his eternal soul: "God knows I pray ardently for you, but unless you will unite in prayer with me, you can never successfully resist the many snares & vices which bestrew your pathway."[77] In Davis's eyes, maturation into Christian manhood still required dependence on one's mother.

When evidence of her sons' moral failures reached home, Davis let them know that she had not relinquished her authority. In 1858, Anne learned that her third son, John, had missed prayer forty-seven times during four months at college. Such a blatant disregard for routine devotion deeply offended both mother and God. She wrote unsparingly, "This slight in a means of grace . . . is a crime in my eyes and much more so in the sight of God for you my own precious boy, who has been nursed in the cradle of piety, and who has taught to be up in time to bend the infant knee at our family altar, ere you could articulate your mother tongue. If tears, bitter tears could obliterate from your report those hateful 47 absences, they would ere this have been blotted out!" When the Davis sons failed to meet the high devotional standards their mother had set, the language of devotion became the language of damnation. Repeated failures on the part of her sons to prove their moral and pious perfection gave Anne Davis many opportunities to continue to intercede on their spiritual behalf well into their early twenties.[78]

In stark contrast to Anne Davis's emphasis on the need for her sons to exercise vigilant circumspection and caution in dealing with the world, Joseph Davis instead emphasized the need for young men to exhibit strength and resolve in their quest for wisdom. Like his wife, he drew on the Bible for precept and direction. But unlike Anne, who urged their son to seek refuge in God from a sinful world, Joseph suggested that Robert work in tandem with God to enhance his will power, wisdom, and discipline: "*Will it*, and yourself for it, and, in humble reliance upon your Almighty and ever present friend[—]spring to it. Make Israel's covenant, consecrate all to God. Let usefulness be your motto, to do good in the name, and for the sake of your Master. Such a resolution will be to you a tower of strength."

Joseph Davis's favorite role model for his sons was the young Solomon, "who asked wisdom in preference to riches and honors, and God was so pleased as to grant his desire and add the rest." When his son bemoaned his academic skills, his father shot back that God had blessed Robert with "numerous and invaluable gifts"; he merely needed to use those skills to better effect. Unlike his wife, who saw every academic and moral failure as evidence of impiety, Rev. Davis remained optimistic that his son's academic success hinged on the application of his piety. When one of his sons faltered, Joseph was more likely than Anne to stress the possibility of forgiveness over the inveterate nature of sin. "When you from any cause fall away from the path of duty," he wrote, his son should recall the words of Saint John: "If any man sin he has an advocate with the Father, let this encourage you when you from any cause fall away from the path of duty, and delay not to confess your sin and obtain forgiveness."[79] While Joseph Davis viewed mistakes as an unfortunate but inevitable part of growing up, Anne Davis viewed them as unmistakable proof that her sons could not adequately defend their morality and piety without her aid.

Taking a markedly different approach from his wife's fire-and-brimstone letters, Rev. Davis expressed his confidence in his son's piety, imploring him to apply himself fully to the attainment of godliness. Joseph Davis confidently observed that Robert had set "a high standard of excellency" for all his pursuits in life and avoided the company of those "persons of questionable principles." Like most parents of the era, Joseph emphasized the paramount role of environment in shaping personal piety and morality: "Under the restraining and renewing influence of the grace of God," he believed, Robert's character had just started to flourish. For all of this emphasis on the need to seek divine influence in daily life, however, Rev. Davis appealed time and again to his son's independence, free will, and individual accountability:

> I write . . . to encourage you, and remind you that you are to be the maker of your own destiny, both as to this life, and that which is to come. God has endowed you with the ability, he has appointed the means and to the faithful the application of these means he has promised his blessings. Upon yourself alone rests the responsibility. How impressive Davids language to Solomon! "And thou Solomon, my son, know thou the God of thy Father and serve him with a perfect heart and with a willing mind; for the Lord searcheth all hearts, & understandeth all the imagination of the thoughts;

if thou seek him he will be found of thee; but if thou forsake him he will cast thee off forever."[80]

No longer able directly to supervise his son, Rev. Davis transferred some of his most important paternal duties to the "God of thy father," encouraging Robert to seek both support and assessment from God while referencing the punishment meted out to those who drifted from the Gospel. Where Anne Davis employed fear and threats, Joseph Davis employed trust and accountability. While Anne Davis worried that her sons' behavior might tarnish her reputation as a moral steward, Joseph Davis hoped to instill devotional independence in his sons.

Much like Anne Davis, Frances Douglass attempted to exercise strict moral oversight of her son, Henry Taylor, as he came of age. As her only child and a stepson of the Reverend James Walter Douglass, however, Taylor faced challenges different from those of the Davis sons. Frances Douglass expected her son to demonstrate sterling piety, devotional discipline, and sparkling intellect so that he could enter the Presbyterian ministry. The tension between mother and son emerged when she remarried and attempted to foster a relationship between her son and her new husband. Finding a stellar evangelical role model for her son thrilled Frances Douglass as much as the companionship of her husband, and she worked to forge a relationship between the husband she adored and the son who carried the burden of her expectations. On one occasion, she wrote to her son, "I long to see you confide in Mr. D. as you do me. I know you w[oul]d find him a kind & sympathising friend." She also encouraged Rev. Douglass to interact meaningfully with Taylor.[81]

Despite Frances Douglass's efforts, the two men remained cool toward one another, and Taylor refused to call Rev. Douglass "father" despite his mother's requests that he do so. When Taylor posed spiritual queries to his stepfather, the responses bore the formal, condescending tone of a prominent minister rather than the intimacy of a father. Rev. Douglass "grudge[d] the time" consumed by letter writing, preferring to write sermons: unlike letters, which were read once and thrown into a fireplace, sermons required erudition and contributed to a permanent ministerial legacy. Even when Douglass offered advice on education for the ministry, he remained distant and terse.[82] Frances Douglass clearly failed to fit her marriage to James Douglass into the ideal of the seamless evangelical family. In addition, although Taylor was admitted to Princeton and began to study for the ministry, Rev. Douglass died before the young man could finish, effectively ending all financial support for his education.

James Douglass's death in the fall of 1837 caused his widow to redouble her attention on her son. She had frequently criticized Taylor's lack of focus and discipline, but she had often tempered her criticism with references to the limitations imposed by his poor health. In 1834, for example, Frances sought advice from James, explaining that Taylor's "constitution seems so delicate that I know not how to urge him to greater diligence least his health should be permanently injured, & yet he is not living, as I think, one preparing for the christian ministry should live." After her husband's death, however, Frances criticized those same weaknesses as evidence of moral and spiritual rather than physical frailty, freely informing Taylor that he greatly disappointed her. The earlier skirmishes over Taylor's work habits and career escalated into a full-pitched battle. Three years after Rev. Douglass's death, Taylor had bounced among several potential careers—the ministry, medicine, and silk farming—and his mother made no more excuses for what she saw as his "langour & seeming indolence": "None of us love labour. It is only the experience that employment brings peace & comfort & profit that makes us give ourselves to work. You know this is the time to work. Our rest remaineth." And, if physical, moral, and spiritual discomfort accompanied that struggle, Frances Douglass encouraged her son to embrace the feeling as a necessary precondition to improvement: "My dear Henry I believe there must be first a thorough humiliation. I believe you must be made to say thy will be done, even though I thus suffer through life. If this humiliating fall, & these humiliating consequences are necessary to my sanctification, I would say Lord sanctify me by all means. May the Lord preserve you from making the consequences of sin the occasion of other sins."[83]

As she reproved her son's character, Frances Douglass reaffirmed his need to look to his faith for renewal and his mother for approval. Since his birth, she had hoped that Taylor would become a minister, and "since that time, I have been led to entertain higher desires. I have felt risings of ambition, earthly honour!" Rev. Douglass had encouraged her to believe that her son "would be a vessel of honour." Despite his meager accomplishments thus far in life, she wrote, "I still hope & pray that you may be made Holy & Useful & happy. Still I offer you to God through Christ, in whom is Wisdom & righteousness & sanctification & redemption. My hopes have been cast down but not destroyed." Although she encouraged her son to look to God to "put a new song in your mouth," Douglass put Taylor on notice that she would be the first in line to judge the legitimacy of his reforms: "I still hope that with the blessing of God you may be made a comfort & blessing to your mother to the church & the world."[84] Appealing to God and maternal solicitude, Frances Douglass made one last attempt to goad her son into the ministry as a validation of her and her child rearing.

Though less critical than Anne Davis or Frances Douglass, Baptist Lucy Ann Gwathmey of Virginia similarly sought both to inspire and frighten her son and daughter as they came of age. When writing to her son, Edward, at the University of Virginia, she noted his gloominess and instructed him that only God could provide a salve for soul: "Then don't I beg you longer resist the spirit of his grace, but just yield yourself a poor sinner as you are to Him the saviour of sinners feeling that you can do nothing to recommend yourself to him but trust humbly yet firmly in his all sufficient righteousness. Don't look to yourself, but look away to Christ. The more you look into your own heart the more deceitful and depraved you will find it to be, and you must give up all hope of saving yourself." Too much dependence on himself—the typical course for young southern men coming of age—would only reveal his innate depravity. Rather than independence among men, true peace and progress would come from Christian dependence among fellow evangelicals. She thrilled at the news that preaching had stimulated Edward's spirituality but reminded him to pay close attention to personal devotion as well, particularly Bible reading, if he had any hope of "removing all the difficulties from your mind, which have so long obstructed your spiritual vision, and prevented a free communication of the grace of God into your soul, and hindered your usefulness as a Christian." At the request of her daughter, Nelly, Lucy Gwathmey sent a Bible to the girl so that she could participate in a Bible study class at her academy. In spite of Nelly's advances along the path to salvation, however, her mother still feared the worst: "I do trust, my dear, that your present favorable opportunities for improvement will not be neglected by you; and that you may not only obtain the wisdom needful for this life, but, be also, made wise unto salvation. Remember, my child, you will be accountable to God if you do not improve the talents committed to you."[85] No matter how much evidence of personal piety the Gwathmey children showed, their mother believed that they still needed maternal guidance.

When evangelical children reached adulthood, they often discovered that their mothers doggedly clung to the moral authority that they had exercised over their children's entire lives. Like their nonevangelical counterparts, evangelical women acknowledged the unique influences of mothers and environment on young children. Early conversions thus reflected on both maternal and filial piety. According to evangelical mothers, however, a world of temptation and sin lurked beyond the household, requiring them to police their children's souls even after conversion. Thus, women such as Anne Davis, Frances Douglass, and Lucy Gwathmey took pride in their spiritual and moral preparation of their children while simultaneously warning that they could not thrive spiritually or morally beyond the household. Mothers found a renewed sense of self-importance when their children demonstrated moral and spiritual weakness beyond the home. These youthful missteps validated maternal fears about the dangers the world posed to untested piety while justifying ongoing maternal intervention. Each youthful error, however minor, not only jeopardized children's character but called into the question their mothers' piety and jeopardized the family's heavenly reunification. Evangelical fathers, by contrast, agreed on the need for maternal stewardship at an early age but often sided with their sons, seeing fewer risks in the world outside of the home and demonstrating a greater tolerance for adolescent miscues. Seeking to add assertiveness and social acumen to earlier evangelical traits such as obedience, virtue, and piety, young evangelical men could expect their fathers to be more tolerant of failure than their mothers.

Childbirth and child rearing thus formed the cornerstone of women's moral and spiritual authority within and beyond the southern home. Women claimed that the physical and spiritual trials of childbirth enriched their devotion to God, and if they survived, they simultaneously gave thanks to God and pledged their children to the ranks of the disciples. Men—both lay and clergy—ceded so much authority in early child rearing that women readily shifted their religious education of children to public arenas such as Sunday schools and academies. Women's ability to expand their use of skills honed in nurturing piety at home echoes the conversion process and even the claims of evangelical clergymen in the early national era.[86] These women were most concerned with their own children, however. Women scrutinized their children's conduct as young adults to ensure that hard-won gains would not be erased. Evangelical women occasionally spoke of their stewardship of children and slaves in the same breath, feeling that conversion reflected positively on mistresses' personal piety in both instances and hoping that white and black converts alike would more readily accept mistresses' authority. But mistresses distanced themselves from their slaves' piety: unconverted children indicted women's moral authority and stewardship, but unconverted slaves reflected only individual choice.

Women often found their domestic authority all too brief and qualified. When children died, women often blamed themselves for demonstrating too much affection, and women feared tempting God by loving their children too much. Even when children became pious converts, their mothers were so insecure about their domestic authority that they took little solace from these accomplishments, reminding their children of the snares and pitfalls that awaited them outside the home and thereby reinforcing the need for maternal oversight. When fathers urged sons to apply their young faith to the challenges of the world, evangelical mothers cringed. And youthful stumbles resulted in ringing denunciations in a rhetoric that easily interwove religious and moral values. Errant sons did not merely fail themselves, they failed their families, their God, and most importantly their mothers.

CHAPTER 5

Authoring the Good Death
Illness, Deathbed Narratives, and Women's Authority

In 1844, Methodist Ann Sexton stole a moment away from nursing her dying mother in Alabama to write an update for her aunt in North Carolina. Like other white southern evangelicals, Sexton struggled to align her neat expectations of the Good Death with the messy realities of the deathbed. The Good Death involved three core principles, the first two of which were interconnected. The faithful believed that death froze an individual's religious and moral status, serving as an indicator of the life led and the fate to come. To that end, antebellum Americans hoped that dying persons would retain control of their faculties so that they could relay their thoughts and feelings during this moment of utmost clarity and piety. Sexton observed, however, that her mother's "mind seems to decay faster than her body" and that "she takes very little notice of any thing that's going on." Yet Sexton found a way to make her narrative coincide with evangelical expectation: her mother's silences, she argued, stemmed not from physical exhaustion but rather from spiritual fortitude. "She does not say much about *dying*," Sexton wrote, "but I think she reflects a great deal, appearing perfectly reconciled to the will of *God*, and apparently waiting His summons, to call her to her *long resting place*." Having established her mother's awareness and Christian comportment in spite of her silences, Sexton stressed the domestic orientation of death, the third fundamental principle of the Good Death. Death was no longer a community affair, and Americans believed that its lessons and purpose originated within the family: death required observation and assessment by kin, who sought assurances that their family would be unified in heaven. Sexton believed that she would find the ultimate reward for her labors when her mother's "*spirit reaches its* Heavenly Mansion, there to meet her beloved *Husband & Children . . . to unite her voice* with *theirs & myriads* of other redeemed spirits in *singing songs of praises* to *God* & to *the Lamb*."[1] A deathbed scene was but one episode in a larger, familial drama, but each episode required careful management to close the gap between ideal and reality.

Because antebellum Americans never tired of discussing death, historians have frequently used the deathbed as a window on the era's culture, often suggesting that these rituals shed light on an increasingly divergent North and South. Using records as varied as prescriptive literature, fiction, and local associational records, scholars of dying in the antebellum North have stressed the twin influences of an emerging market economy and the feminization of American Protestantism. Some scholars have taken a dim view of this nexus, arguing that middle-class women's embrace of mourning rituals and etiquette, for example, stripped American Protestantism of its theological rigor, leaving these women trapped in a culture where the line between genuine grief and artifice blurred.[2] Other scholars have stressed how women mobilized their concerns regarding domestic piety into associations that gave them a new public voice as well as an opportunity to cope with the reality of increasing child mortality rates.[3] In sharp contrast, historians of the antebellum South have used death and dying to stress the reinvigoration of patriarchal authority in a slave society. In addition to underlining southern men's quest for mastery over everything, including death, most scholars have been inclined to point to women's intellectual and spiritual isolation.[4] In the absence of an associational network on par with the North and scattered across the southern countryside, women most often struggled privately with their grief.[5] Indeed, if grieving served any public role for southern white women, it was seemingly to allow clergymen to prey on women's fear of death as a means to frighten them into joining congregations, where parishioners reaffirmed the moral and religious authority of southern patriarchs.[6] Gone were the days of the early nineteenth century when blacks, women, and a youthful corps of clergymen seized evangelicalism's egalitarian rhetoric to question the South's hierarchies of race, class, and gender.[7]

But the nexus of slavery, patriarchy, and evangelicalism in the antebellum South raises a pivotal question: How did women, who continued to numerically dominate the mainline evangelical denominations, shape religious experience in this era? An analysis of southern white women's work at the deathbed illustrates how they could operate as religious stewards in a culture that sacralized patriarchal authority and consequently permits the untangling of prescriptive rhetoric from deed while exposing the tensions bound up in death and dying. Women feared illness because it might take the life of an unprepared Christian, yet they embraced illness and its attendant suffering as a means to purify and rededicate themselves to their faith. Evangelical women spoke resolutely about an individual's accountability to God for deeds and misdeeds over a lifetime yet worked frantically to prepare loved ones for Christian deaths. After a loved one's passing, women spoke of resignation to God's will yet worked endlessly to align and realign death's realities with their vision. While southern white women worshipped in congregations that celebrated the secular and religious underpinnings of patriarchy, these women operated with nominal aid from clergymen or physicians in managing this increasingly important ritual. As evangelicals of all denominational stripes and all ages realized, getting to heaven in the antebellum South more often than not required the labors of devoted women. That work, however, was never without peril for the deathbed attendant.

Illness: Redirecting Wayward Pilgrims

Illness pervaded the lives of all antebellum southerners, but it held uniquely religious meaning for evangelicals. Because they viewed illness as God's most potent corrective for wayward pilgrims, evangelicals set out to humble themselves before God, improve their piety, and seek relief from their physical misery. In evangelical rhetoric, theirs was a quest to sanctify suffering, literally transforming it from a curse into a blessing. In A. Gregory Schneider's words, even "passive suffering" could lead to "a sense of active triumph" in evangelical thought and practice. The God who inflicted physical pain also provided physical and spiritual healing. Jane Lide informed David Lide that his sickbed allowed him "to look for the Hills from which our help must come, that only rock on which we should, build, my blessed Saviour has supported me in the furnace of affliction &

in deep waters he has held me up." Many evangelicals—men and women, lay and clergy—thus embraced illness as an opportunity to reinvigorate piety. The persistent threat of death—uncertainty about whether a symptom such as a fever represented a minor or grave illness—made illness appear arbitrary and mysterious, making it alive to God's purposes. Evangelicals wanted to position themselves squarely in the middle of that uncertainty, hoping that they might more clearly discover God's purpose for their family. When evangelicals emerged from an illness with their health restored, they thanked God for his merciful action and proclaimed a rejuvenation of their piety.[8]

Illness affected antebellum males and females of all ages and classes with alarming frequency and often severity. Passing references reveal that most antebellum southerners viewed severe pain as an integral part of everyday life. To merit sustained attention in personal writing, illnesses had to be either severe or widespread, as when Maggie Whitaker added a postscript to a letter home from the Chowan Female Institute in Murfreesboro, North Carolina, reporting that all instruction had ceased while the entire faculty recuperated from an unnamed illness. Mary Bethell justified a four-month hiatus from writing in her diary by explaining that measles had overrun her household: "I have been confined to the house two months by sickness, measles, all of the children and several of the negroes have been sick." Because Anne Davis managed the boardinghouse at her husband's academy while rearing her own children, she felt she had little time to nurse herself back to health. Although "excruciating ... Rheumatism" in her right arm caused her to cry when she brushed her teeth or combed her hair, she still wrote to her son at college. She feared not only that he would be disappointed if he did not receive a note from her but also that his immortal soul would become imperiled without regular parental guidance on morality and spirituality.[9]

When friends and family failed to correspond regularly, loved ones jumped to the conclusion that a serious illness rather than neglect or an unreliable postal system had prevented the exchange of correspondence. Frances Douglass tried hard to understand what kept her son, Henry Taylor, from writing to her: "Little did I anticipate the painful state of suspense in which we have been held for two weeks; I have thought you were with relations, & if you should be unable to write from sickness, or any other cause, they would write for you, but now I know not what to think."

The exception to discussions and inferences of sickness were affirmations of a household's health: James Whitaker opened a letter to his cousin, George Whitaker, with the words, "In the first place I am happy to inform you that we are all in the enjoyment of a reasonable degree of health at this time for which great blessing I desire to feel thankful to the Giver of all good."[10] Even such a qualified report served as a welcome change from monotonous reports of illness.

Given their familiarity with sickness and the physical isolation typical of the rural South, most southerners diagnosed routine ailments without guidance from doctors. With her husband, William Wills, away at the Methodist General Conference, Anna Wills wrote to him that one of their slaves had a headache and a green tongue—"something of the bilious," she concluded. Many other southerners remained wary of doctors, typically relying on medical professionals only as a last resort for severe illnesses. At the Wesleyan Female College, Anne Davis and her husband, Joseph Davis, diagnosed several of the girls at the academy with "eruptive fever." Most of the girls recovered quickly, but one girl had a more severe case; she "acted wisely," Anne Davis thought, in choosing to have Rev. Davis rather than a doctor attend to her. According to Presbyterian Hu Brown of eastern Tennessee, his wife's chronic illness had only been aggravated by treatments from beyond the family circle: "I shall always begrudge the money I paid for your crucifixion here and shall always regret that we had a little spirit as not to dismiss one, who I seriously believe has been the cause of your sufferings." Brown wondered whether the heroic measures such as bleeding and purgatives favored by medical doctors did little more than add unnecessary suffering, and she compared such trials to those suffered by Jesus. Many southerners, nonevangelical and evangelical alike, of course credited doctors with providing relief from illness. But as Steven M. Stowe points out, because nineteenth-century southern physicians often were not consulted until a patient's health had deteriorated to the point where family members were no longer familiar with the symptoms—that is, until the patient was beyond hope of recovery—country doctors often relied on their evangelical faith to interpret and explain events.[11]

Southerners not only self-diagnosed their ailments but individually reflected on the religious meaning behind their physical maladies. Evangelicals commonly viewed physical illness as a manifestation of a spiritual impurity. Devout evangelicals understood sickness as one of God's most important tools for renewing and reinvigorating piety among the faithful. Reflecting on a recent recovery, Sarah Fountain wrote to her cousin, Hannah Coker, in 1838, "I think, I have seen, & felt, that 'afflictions spring not from the dust,' nor 'troubles rise by chance,' but that they are sent for some wise purpose, and a great mercy that I am one of its subjects, for I know I should go much farther astray, were it not for my various afflictions." In the evangelical cosmology, God administered sickness to awaken the spiritually drowsy and then keep the faithful on the narrow path to redemption.[12]

Devout evangelicals claimed that illness allowed them to see more clearly God's mysterious designs. Women such as South Carolinian Mary Brown sought to place themselves squarely in the middle of that mystery to locate God's purposes for them. Writing in her journal in 1855, Brown reflected on a recent spate of illnesses: "We have had two months of wonderful sickness.... We bless the[e] that thou hast heard our prayers and commanded delliverance to those that has been under thyne afflictive hand.... [M]ay we ever remember that a recovery is only a reprieve."[13] Debilitating illness thus reaffirmed God's sovereignty over all living creatures, but despite her self-abnegation, Brown located her place in this divine mystery, thereby confirming that she played a role in God's awesome designs. Only God definitively knew the purpose of an affliction, but evangelicals relentlessly set out to try to read his mind.

Many evangelical women took even greater license than Brown, incorporating explanations and understandings of God's purpose into their narratives of illness and recovery. Looking back at a protracted illness, Anne Davis connected divine agency to personal and family piety, recasting her hardship into a narrative redolent of a biblical drama. Although she opened her analysis by proclaiming, "How inscrutable are the ways of Providence," she forged ahead with her attempts to understand:

> I was busily preparing to leave our last appointment ... in good health, and spirits, expecting to start on the 12th of october; when lo! a good and gracious God, saw fit to hedge up our way, but suddenly laying His afflicting hand upon me, on the 10th of that month, for some weeks I was ill, and not at all able to travel until six weeks after our first appointed time to move; Through all this disappointment, and deep affliction and suffering, the Lord was with me, enabling me to look far beyond this vale of tears to a permanent place of rest, reserved in Heaven for me.... Oh! I ought to

bless the Lord, whilst life lasts for what I enjoyed of His presence during that illness. In His goodness, and care, (probably on account of my little ones, so dependent upon me), I was restored to health.[14]

Undoubtedly under stress as she and her family prepared to move to a new Methodist circuit, Davis took comfort in rediscovering heaven as "a permanent place of rest." Amid life's tumult, God remained her compass; however, much like Mary Brown, Davis needed an illness to reorient her faith in a way that simultaneously diminished and highlighted her as a Christian. Even as suffering effaced her pride and opened up new religious vistas, Davis underscored her sense of religious authority and importance. The preservation of her health and life, she theorized, stemmed from God's awareness of her irreplaceable role in the lives of her children.

Resignation to illness was not the exclusive domain of women; southern men also searched their souls to come to terms with the afflictions they or those in their immediate family circle suffered. Joseph Davis rejoiced over the news of his son's return to health but paused in the midst of his celebration to inform Robert of the higher purpose of sickness: "Every such visitation my son is intended to remind us that the body is made subject to vanity, while the soul is immortal, and to point us to the unending future for which we should shape our moral character. While you give diligence to study and improve the mind try to keep the body healthy and the heart pure." Physical afflictions invariably interfered with manly pursuits of public importance. The Reverend James Douglass surely hoped for more steely determination than his stepson, Henry Taylor, showed when he wrote that illness had led him to contemplate leaving Princeton without taking final exams. Douglass informed Taylor of the stakes involved and provided guidelines for his decision making: unless Taylor was "absolutely sick, unable to study, & likely to continue so," Douglass advised, he should persevere, because it would be "very dishonorable to you as a man, & especially as a christian & a candidate for the ministry, to fly from the examination." Leaving the final decision to Taylor's "light" and "conscience," Douglass surely feared for his reputation among his Presbyterian peers as well as his stepson's future. In another instance, when Douglass learned that his daughter had just lost another child to scarlet fever, he pleaded in his diary that she might accept God's plans for her and rest easier knowing that her children now resided in heaven: "God works in a misterious way his wonders to perform.—Thanks be to the Almighty dispenser of events.

He knows what is best for his children and does not willingly afflict under such circumstances. we ought to be still—and aquesce in all the dispensations of a wise God and merciful father. I would pray for the bereaved family—O! Lord give them what they need a calm resigned spirit—that their dear little ones are now in Heaven." It is the "believers hope," he concluded, that his daughter's family would know and enjoy "God better hereafter" and that God would "calm all our troubled hearts under every severe dispensation."[15]

On occasion, evangelicals acknowledged that an illness exceeded their interpretive ability or failed to profit them spiritually. Mary Gray reported to her sister-in-law, Frances Douglass, that her overall health was better but held out hope that her chronically poor eyesight might yet improve: "'Not my will but thine.' I think this short prayer has often been repeated by me without taking in its full meaning. His will, to break off the very purposes of my heart, break up all my schemes of comfort, take friends & health away still I must say, 'Thy will be done.'" After experiencing crippling arthritis for the better part of nine months, Mary Craddock confided in her diary that she had not reaped the desired spiritual fruits from her suffering: "I was submissive to the will of him that afflicts when and in what way he sees fit: but did not feel the presence of God with me as I desired. I felt my suferings were not sanctified to me[.] I thought I was indeed a rebellious child that did not greatly advance in knowledge and will of my Father in heaven." Craddock finally experienced the spiritual renewal she craved later in the month, in part because she attended a protracted meeting and in part because her arthritis subsided enough to allow her to kneel during her domestic devotions.[16]

Evangelicals more commonly credited God for sparing them from far worse fates. Writing to her sister about her complete recovery from a serious fall that resulted in torn muscles and tendons, Charlotte Verstille imagined that the situation could have been much more serious had her faith not shielded her: "Much as I have suffered, it might have been worse. I might have been made a cripple for life. And being somewhat of a practical believer in the doctrine of special Providence, I do trust the occurrence will be over ruled for good in some way, even if I see it not." Merely sharing one's illness with fellow evangelicals might temporarily relieve the physical suffering and psychological isolation. Sarah Fountain wrote that receiving a letter from her cousin, Hannah Coker, "accompanied with one from Maria [Lide], acted as a balm to me, at least for a short time, for I was suffering great pain at the time, but it was almost entirely relieved until I had finished reading them, when it all returned as usual."[17]

Amid their prayers of thanksgiving, some evangelical women flatly stated that their petitions to God had been granted, directly altering the outcome of events on earth. When her husband, William, abandoned plans to move their family from North Carolina to Arkansas, Mary Bethell celebrated God's intervention. Like most women in the antebellum South, Bethell opposed migration westward because it would have entailed permanent separation from family and friends as well as the physical hardships associated with an arduous move and life on the frontier. "I don't think we could have health in that sickly country," she wrote in her diary. She then questioned the frontier's suitability for her family's piety. William Bethell returned from an extended trip to Arkansas with title to a piece of land and a grave fever that "made him reflect, and I think he has abandoned all idea of moving for the present." Mary Bethell believed that her prayers had been answered, even though her husband's illness threatened his life:

> I think it is the will of Providence for us to remain here, I hope and believe the Lord has directed my husband to remain here, thanks to his holy name. I do believe he is a prayer hearing and prayer answering God, every time I prayed that prayer (That my husband would be directed by God) it seemed to go right up to a throne of grace, and I've had faith, strong faith in God. . . . I have been in trouble many times, but the Lord has always delivered me, and in every extremity I shall trust in him. Oh what a privilege to be a child of God, and to have our names written in Heaven.

This providential deliverance continued to shape Bethell's relationship with God: she recounted the event and its accompanying feelings of joy more than two years later in her diary. Deliverance from illness or other undesirable outcomes nourished spirituality. But even more ambiguous outcomes caused evangelicals to continue to search for God's designs in their daily lives as they sought to use their personal pain to enhance their intimacy with God.[18]

Authoring the Good Death

When ill southerners lost all hope of recovery, the resulting deathbed symbolized the family's hope for the dying family member's salvation, the collective hope of family reunification in heaven, and the reality of sacrifice to an all-powerful and all-wise God. Women stood at the center of these evangelical wishes, constantly attempting to link the living and the dead through the deathbed and experiencing the stark fear of failure and the unbounded thrill of success. Southern evangelicals professed confidence in differentiating Christian deathbeds from a non-Christian deathbeds, but in practice, many complicating variables threatened to muddy those neat distinctions. In the process, evangelical women in particular sought to steer their kin toward the Good Death even as they loudly professed resignation to God's will.

While evangelicals eagerly anticipated the Good Death, they never tired of warning the unrepentant of their immortal danger. Evangelicals saw these lessons almost daily as they interpreted God's actions in their midst. Laity used deathbeds palpably to contrast the benefits of piety with the punishments awaiting the wicked. After announcing that a woman "died quite happy" shortly after her baptism at a Baptist meeting, Elizabeth Fountain noted the death of a "very wicked" individual who "made a practice of going to all the [Baptist] meetings about to do mischief," including physically threatening ministers on the Alabama frontier. When taken sick, the man became "deranged," and "he died a miserable death." The "great contrast between the two" deaths reinforced the evangelical supposition that the faithful experienced calm resignation at death's precipice while the dying impenitent writhed in uncertainty and unsanctified suffering. The women who married evangelical clergymen often visited ailing parishioners as an extension of their informal public duties. After visiting two women nearing death, Frances Bumpass assessed their comportment and their piety much in the same way as Fountain did: "Have visited at Mrs. Pritchets' & Mrs Dossey, both near death—one fearing to meet it, the other rejoicing in prospect of a blissful immortality—Felt the importance of being constantly prepared."[19] Heaven and hell thus remained very much alive in the minds of antebellum southern evangelicals, and laypeople self-assuredly judged their neighbors' ultimate resting places.

Evangelicals' confidence in distinguishing the saved from the damned stemmed in large part from the promise of the conversion experience. As Mary Bethell elaborated in 1858, death made individuals transparent in the face of their final judgment: "The secret of the Lord is with them that fear him. The way to heaven is the only way of safety. The wicked prosper in this world and deceive a good many, but the day is coming when *all* of *their* conduct, and *actions* will be *exposed* at the great judgement day." Bethell recalled that she might have suffered just such a fate had she not renewed her quest for a full conversion as a young girl: "If I had died [unconverted] I would have gone to everlasting punishment, but the Lord did not cut me off as I deserved, he sent his spirit to my heart once more to invite me to Christ." While Bethell looked backward, Hu Brown proclaimed that the fear of a sudden death spurred him toward conversion: "The cowardliness of postponing repentance to a death bed and the danger that such a repentance would not be effectual, were among the motives that stimulated me to take up the cross and not be ashamed to make a profession, as I felt conscious I would ardently desire peace with God when I came to die." Conversion served both men and women as a hedge against uncertainty in a world where believers professed to know the saved from the damned in their midst.[20]

When death struck evangelical households, men's and women's deathbed reports differed markedly in tone, detail, and perspective. Women, who wrote the majority of informal deathbed accounts, wrote with a zealous voice, a flair for detail, and an emphasis on family reunification in the afterlife. Men wrote in a more dispassionate tone that required readers—typically male friends or family members—to infer the sense of drama. Men captured the essential elements of the Good Death—the profundity of the deathbed, the need for the dying to communicate final thoughts and beliefs, and the centrality of family—but did so in a cursory manner. Writing to Cary Whitaker regarding the death of a cousin, Martha Pope, James Whitaker strung together a few popular pronouncements on pious deaths and left the rest to the imagination: "Yes she is gone from whence no traveler has ever yet returned, But she has gone to her reward. It is enough to say that she died as she had lived a devoted *Christian*." Her piety spoke for itself. Similarly, when the Reverend James Walter Douglass's mother-in-law died, he acknowledged her piety in his diary but did not embellish his recollection with details: "We her relatives & friends have more reason to rejoice than mourn! for she is relieved from a life of sin & much sorrow! *Hers was a life of affliction!* but of devoted piety. she lived devoted to her God, and died—the death of the righteous." Men who wrote deathbed reports for family members thus typically affirmed the Christian plot line but allowed readers to surmise the details or insert their own knowledge of the character and habits of the deceased.[21]

Evangelical women not only devoted greater attention to the dying but also placed greater emphasis on the caregiver's role. Even more than illness did, death evoked divine mystery, a moment saturated with God's presence that demanded scrutiny from fellow believers. The intensity of women's spiritual intimacy with God at the deathbed rivaled that at times of spiritual triumph, such as conversion. In spite of the obvious pain, women told and retold deathbed narratives, seeking to confirm their faith, validate their work at the deathbed, and use spiritual intimacy to narrow their geographic isolation. Women offering condolences also asked to hear deathbed details. Julia Gilchrist, for example, reluctantly obliged Margaret Van Wyck's request for more information about the dying moments of Gilchrist's sister, Carrie: only for Van Wyck could Gilchrist "again open the wound that is so slowly closing." For individual evangelicals, these hallowed tales reinforced evangelical identity and rewards; for faithful families, they confirmed the possibility of heavenly reunification.[22]

Never merely storytellers from the deathbed, women found their piety enriched through cooperative work with God. In the throes of nursing several ill members of her household, including her dying husband, Frances Douglass found her work physically therapeutic. Although she felt "so exhausted in mind and body as scarcely to think at all," she wrote to her son, "I am not sick . . . I have been unusually free from those distressing headaches which constitute my principal sickness." Unable to nurse a man back to health, Mary Craddock of Louisville, Kentucky, labored to save his soul. After private prayer in which the Cumberland Presbyterian observed the "near approach I was permitted to make to my heavenly father this morning," she returned to the deathbed with greater confidence in her salvation and her role in ministering to the dying individual: "O how good my heavenly father is to me: to grant me the assurance I have of my acceptance in him. . . . I look to him not only as my spiritual but my true moral guide for he is my best friend."[23] Working the deathbed provided women with a sense of spiritual exhilaration and confidence as well as unparalleled intimacy with God. For many women, that intimacy transformed the language of resignation into resolve, inspiring them to make every effort to square the events unfolding before them with evangelical notions of the Good Death.

The fear of failure combined with a sense of spiritual empowerment at the deathbed enabled many women to author original readings of the scene. Adding and subtracting to deathbed narratives most often occurred in one of three circumstances: when a family member died in a questionable state of salvation, thereby jeopardizing the hope for family reunification in the afterlife; when individual evangelicals died without the full use of their faculties, thereby interfering with their profession of faith to loved ones; and when sudden death occurred, thereby preventing the unfolding of the deathbed ritual. Moments in which expectation did not match experience most clearly delineate women's spiritual authority. Retaining a focus on the dying person, women worked diligently to guarantee that the collective promise of family unification in heaven would be fulfilled one soul at a time.

Fearing that Alfred Cox's lapsed Presbyterian faith jeopardized his salvation and the family's collective hope of heavenly reunion, his sisters mobilized to "prepare" him for heaven. "*We don't know* that he is prepared to die," wrote Fanny Brodrick to Mary Collins, "it is so difficult to get him to speak of himself that we don't know what his views are upon the subject of religion." Ever anxious and often indecisive, Brodrick nonetheless initiated a two-pronged offensive to move Alfred's deathbed from uncertainty toward certainty, beseeching her sister to press their brother for a statement of faith and asking a church elder to visit the dying man. As Alfred lingered near death for nearly a year, he frequently sang hymns and repeated Scripture, actions that Lizzie Cox interpreted as signs that "God is preparing him for a better world." But the real measure of his faith, his ability quietly to endure his suffering, revealed his total submission to God's will. Ellen Blatterman, Alfred's sister-in-law and an eyewitness to his death, rendered the family's final verdict on his fate in a letter to Mary Collins: "We feel assured of your brothers final preparation for death, he felt no fear at its approach and so calmly did he enter its cold embrace that those around did not know he was gone for some seconds." The family's Presbyterian pastor confirmed this assessment based on his last meeting with Alfred, providing Brodrick with enough "comfort" to declare, "I feel assured that he fell asleep in Jesus."[24]

In 1864, another of the Cox siblings, George, suddenly became ill, and neither he nor his family had substantial time to prepare for his death. Other kin believed that George was the least prepared for death of the family's members, and his brother-in-law, Richard Collins, voiced their concerns: "I am anxious to know something of the experience of his dying hours. While I am not without hope, I dread to hear—lest he may have sunk too rapidly for preparation.... Oh! the danger of delay in 'setting our houses in order' for the Destroyers' summoning!" Ultimately, according to Blatterman, a visiting church elder named Coons "was very much gratified with his conversation with [George]. He gave evidence of that

Authoring the Good Death 195

acceptance of our Saviour which we feel to be so necessary to an inheritance and entrance into the better land. [George's] mother seems resigned, she feels very much consoled about him since hearing of his conversations with Mr. Coons and of some ejaculatory prayers uttered in his rational moments showing the burthen of his thoughts." The favorable verdict on George Cox's salvation gave Collins "a thrill of joy. Oh, the blessedness of a re-union with our loved ones in heaven, tongues cannot describe it! God grant that not one link in [the] household chain may be missing from before the great white throne and Him that sitteth therein."[25]

Many evangelicals had even quicker deaths, forcing laywomen to improvise in collecting deathbed testimonials. Anne Beale attended the deathbed of a woman whose condition left her aware but unable to speak, so Anne improvised to ensure that her narrative captured the central element of the Good Death, the dying individual's profession of faith: "I frequently interogated her as to her prospects beyond the grave, and would say to her, that if she could not speak, and felt that she could answer in the afirmative to my questions, to raise her hand which she did repeatedly in holy triumph, and would no doubt have often clapped her hands in prospect of a final release from all earth's sorrows, but for a paralasis of her left arm, which rendered it perfectly useless for several days." In her waning hours, the woman's voice returned, enabling her to verbalize her confidence in God, a miracle that Beale vowed never to forget: "You must know I never saw a christian, in full possession of their mental faculties in their last moment before, and long, long may I remember, the comforting, the encouraging expressions, which from time to time fell from her lips ere her departure." Beale gave herself high marks for her novice work at the deathbed, for she could confidently render the verdict that the woman "has since entered into that rest prepared for all God's children who are faithful until death."[26]

Evangelical parents also struggled mightily to make their family tragedy fit the model of the Good Death, particularly when the child's age prevented a deathbed confession. With repeated emphasis on her nephew's mental acuity, love of family, and obedience as an indicator of resignation on his deathbed, Charlotte Verstille drew parallels between the baby's death and that of an adult evangelical:

> A few hours before he left us, as his father was sitting on the bed at his left hand, I on his right, and Rebecca at his foot, he turned his little head

entirely around to look at me with an expression I shall never forget and at the same time took his little hand from under the clothes and gave it to me; he then turned his head to his father in the same manner and gave him his other hand then he turned his eyes directly upon his mother, with the same expression. We kissed his dear hands and he then returned them calmly into the bed again. Words could not have uttered a more expressive farewell.

Her infant nephew's deathbed quite literally and figuratively aligned with the Good Death, showcasing his Christian resignation as the scene of gathering family members evoked the image of the crucifix. Verstille thus claimed victory: "His weeping parents have the consolation of feeling that they have been the favoured instruments of adding one more to the heavenly throne."[27]

Although women crafted the bulk of deathbed narratives for family members, they drew on the experiences and style of published works. Some of those accounts reveal that clergymen and their families confronted similar crises when their loved ones were dying and called on those attending to knit together their observations, statements from the dying, and the survivors' hunches about God's plans. Methodist bishop Henry B. Bascom was struck with cholera in Louisville, Kentucky, in August 1850 after attending the St. Louis Conference's meeting in Independence, Missouri. Although he lingered for several days, he could no longer vigorously pronounce his faith. The recorder of his final moments observed Bascom's "solemn majesty in his sufferings, which no human language can adequately describe" and his *"silent submissive endurance!"* Just as the attending physician declared that the bishop would soon expire, those attending him asked if his faith in God remained firm, to which he "promptly replied, with great earnestness and self-possession, 'Yes! Yes! YES!' This was enough." His attendants, including his wife, who had been summoned, were disappointed when his failing strength prevented him from speaking "yet once more of 'Jesus and the resurrection.'" In one of his final death throes, however, "he gave us a last, intelligible parting *look*—and such a *look*!—a look that spoke a final adieu to earth, and proclaimed the readiness of a soul immortal to take its upward flight."[28] Bascom's attendants read each diminished stage of communication as a manifestation of his steadfast faith.

Dying after childbirth in 1842, Ann Amelia Andrew, the wife of Bishop

James O. Andrew, suffered mightily. Dropsy (fluid in her lungs) inflicted acute pain and rendered her unable to speak or even to breathe for extended intervals, causing her husband to declare his powerlessness at the sight of her anguish: "I scarcely knew how to preach moderation to her or how to comfort her, except by exhorting her to trust God in this dark and stormy night. . . . [I]t was no ordinary trial: nor can its heart-rending character be understood, except by those who were with us from day to day." In the midst of her physical battle, Ann Andrew anticipated an even greater spiritual struggle, not merely with personal doubt or anxiety but with Satan: according to her husband, she announced, "'I feel as if I shall have a very sore conflict with Satan to-day'; and so it turned out. During the whole day, her great adversary assailed her with the utmost violence. She was tempted to doubt her conversion—her sincerity in her motives in all she had done and suffered—the reality of the blessings she had received during her sickness." Despite his professed confidence in her salvation, Bishop Andrew found "the thought of her dying in this state of mind" quite distressing. She ultimately died in peace, however, allowing her widower to proclaim, "This . . . has been a hard struggle: but the grace of God has triumphed." Although she could no longer speak in her waning moments, she nodded vigorously in the affirmative when asked if God was good and "her way bright and glorious."[29] Even as she lost her ability to communicate, her closeness to death's threshold and God's designs meant that any response, however limited, took on increasing importance. Ann Andrew's epic physical and spiritual struggle provided the surest confirmation that she had indeed lived and died a Christian.

Both unpublished and published deathbed accounts were often inventive, as attendants parsed out complications or filled in silences with Christian introspection. On some occasions—most notably, the death of a loved one outside of the family circle—events exceeded female attendants' ability to weave together successful narratives. Although Charlotte Verstille ably worked her way through the death of her nephew, the death of her brother "amongst strangers" left her outraged: "I feel as if I dont care whether I live or die," she wrote to her sister, "when I give up my mind to the contemplation of the subject.—I know it is wicked—but my heart almost murmurs against the decrees of that Being, of whome we are told that mercy is his darling attribute, and judgment and justice his strange work.—But let me forbear—I feel it is impiety." Similarly, Cary Whitaker anxiously notified his son-in-law that a mutual acquaintance would not live long enough to die among his kin: "How glad I should be if Mr Smith was with his family, to be nursed and tended by them, to live with, or die among them; it would be gratifying to them." And at one burial, thirteen-year-old Frances Bestor commented that it was the first time she had attended a funeral at which the deceased had no family: "The congregation followed the corps[e] to the grave, I never was at the grave of one before this, who had not a relation near, to see, him intered. Every one who was near seemed to feel for his situation."[30] Evangelicals struggled to grasp why God would have allowed death to occur without the succor and most importantly witness of family members.

Ten years later, Bestor found herself unprepared to move her mother, Eliza, through the Good Death. Early in the illness, Frances found that she could give her mother "no comfort when I go to her, & I fear she thinks I do not appreciate her situation, but it is not that, it is that I feel so deeply I cannot talk with her about her leaving us." Six months later, Frances desperately sought to have that conversation with her mother, but Eliza's condition now left her speechless. Attempting to resign herself to the impending loss, Frances found little comfort: "For the last three years I have looked forward to this day as the most melancholy one during my life, and yet it is more grievous, heartbreaking, and wretched than I ever imagined." The heartache of seeing her dying mother, compounded by her mounting domestic responsibilities, eventually cracked the facade of Christian duty and resignation maintained by Frances and her four siblings: "Poor Julia, gave way to a burst of grief & stood in the floor and wrung her hands & prayed, Frank kneeled by my side, I told [him] to pray for his Mother, he said he did not know what to say, I then told him to ask God to take his Mother to Heaven & he did so. John kneeled in silence, but the tears flowed & his lips moved. Daniel was near & cried aloud, Mary Ann, kneeled by & prayed aloud all was distress and anguish. May I never spend such another day." As they prepared the body for burial, family and friends did their best to efface any signs of the physical trials Eliza Bestor had endured. "She was layed in the coffin, by Miss Anne Chapman, Brother, an old nurse of hers & several other persons. I felt as tho' I wished to go too. Father kissed her hands & forehead then the children followed his example. The lid was then put on & she who looked so beautiful, her form so perfect, her hands so graceful & natural, was for ever shut from the eyes of her children." Frances neglected her diary for several weeks thereafter, and when she finally returned, she offered a forthright explanation: "We have spent a gloomy month[.] I have not written, because I felt so miserable."[31]

Partly because they used the sudden deaths of the impious to moralize on the dangers of procrastinating one's salvation and partly because they hoped to experience the full sequence of the Good Death, evangelicals shuddered at the thought of death with little or no warning. Unlike lingering deaths of the impious or the partially incapacitated, quick deaths provided few opportunities to read an individual's thoughts and beliefs. The unexpected death of Mary Bethell's sister, Cornelia Thornton, took an immense emotional and physical toll on Bethell. Because of the illness's sudden onset and accompanying pain, Thornton said little on her deathbed except, "I'm most gone." Bethell attempted to console herself about Thornton's eternal fate, writing, "I trust our loss is her gain, she died in the faith," but also voiced tremendous unease. In another instance, Eliza Heiskell shuddered as she relayed word of a death in the community to her sister, Nancy Lincoln: the woman "died out of her senses & never said any thing about dying oh! what a sense of mourning is here."[32]

The combined fear of a sudden death and the pressure properly to perform the role of the dying evangelical led many evangelicals, especially women, to spend much of their lives anticipating death. Confronting the possibility of death with the birth of each child and spending much of their lives preparing others for their deathbeds, women wrote more frequently of their individual preparation for death. Even while enjoying good health, Anne Davis marked the tenuousness of her mortal journey: "My good and gracious Master in mercy, has lengthened out the brittle thread of my earthly existence unto the present time."[33] This relentless emphasis on the need to prepare for death left many southerners preoccupied with matters of death and dying.

White evangelicals' vigilance and passion toward death in their households changed noticeably when the dying person was a slave. Slaveholders still freely judged the piety of their dying chattel and in some cases witnessed deaths with interest. But slave deaths offered little insight into slaveholders' individual or familial piety and usually bore witness only to the individual slave's piety. Even when masters noted the deaths of favorite slaves, the emphasis remained slaveholder benevolence and Christian stewardship, not the familial implications. Whites were much more likely to recall the deaths of favorite Christian slaves than those of non-Christian or relatively unknown slaves. When one of Tennessean Samuel Henderson

Jr.'s favorite slaves died at the age of seventy-three, Henderson noted that Tom had been a member of the Methodist Church for most of his life and that "a better man seldom ever died. He lived like a Christian and died like he lived." Although such a death represented a triumph for Tom, it had little bearing on Henderson's life or afterlife. Henderson saw an ensuing spate of slave illnesses and deaths less as related to their piety or individual circumstances and more as indicative of Henderson's relationship with God: "It appears like I am under the frowns of Providence for I am loosing all my Negroes and becoming poor[.] Lord help me to bear the misfortune without a murmur." Henderson assumed that God was directing a message to the master, not his slaves. Similarly, Mary Craddock demonstrated responsibility when her slaves died without religion: "O Lord may their blood not be required at my hands." Still, Craddock remained at a psychological distance, worrying less about the feelings of her slaves or their kin than about how God might judge her: "Give me strength to go forth in discharge of all my numerous duties. . . . so that I maybe at last accounted a just and wise steward."[34] White evangelicals may have worried about the salvation of individual slaves and perhaps even used their deaths to testify to masterly benevolence, but feelings of ultimate accountability and hopes for eternal rewards were reserved for white family members.

Indeed, white slaveholders often recorded slaves' illnesses and deaths as just another vexation, a trial of patience and pocketbook. Managing a plantation in her husband's absence, Mary Bethell dealt with a slave woman who scalded her child, the illness of Bethell's daughter, and serious injuries Bethell's son suffered when he was kicked by a horse. These trials nearly proved too much to bear: "I was very much cast down as my husband was not at home to help bear the burden, but the Lord was with me to comfort and support me in these trying times. I was sorely tempted nearly all last week, my soul was surrounded by darkness, doubts and gloomy fears." When an elderly slave named Dick died in 1860, Bethell philosophically concluded that his fate was out of her hands: he had "made no profession of religion but he is in the hands of a merciful God." At the death of her servant, Sucky, Bethell merely shrugged, "Poor women I hope she was saved." In a stark contrast to the active role she assumed at the deathbeds of members of her white family, Bethell merely served as a passive reporter of slave misfortunes. When Bethell did insert herself into the drama, she simply enumerated slave illnesses and deaths as God's test of her faith. When Sarah Fountain learned that one of her father's most trusted slaves, Ned, had become gravely ill, she worried much more about the state of slave discipline than about Ned's soul: "If he should not recover it will be a great loss to pa, not only for his work, but example among the other negros, they all have great respect for him, & he has all the charge of pa's keys."[35] In spite of their incessant efforts to demonstrate their mastery over their slaves, white slaveholders readily stepped aside when it came to an individual slave's eternal fate.

That slaves' piety did not raise greater concern among evangelical women foregrounds the amounts of energy these women expended to connect living and dead white family members through deathbed attendance and accounts. Women knew how to usher the dying through the proper stages of death to ensure family reunification in the afterlife. Moreover, these women seemed to have antidotes for the deathbed's most vexing circumstances, contrasting the awareness, peacefulness, and optimism of believers' deathbeds with the purported obliviousness and wretchedness present at nonbelievers' deathbeds. These narratives traveled throughout the network of family and friends, collectively reaffirming individual and family piety while further distancing the religious from the irreligious.

Moral Authority at the Deathbed

Evangelical believers faced their greatest challenges after loved ones died, as surviving kin sought to square the pain of loss with God's designs. On one hand, they wanted to celebrate God's sovereignty and pronounce their submission to providential wisdom; on the other hand, the firm conviction that God controlled all events, from the mundane to the sublime, caused them endlessly to reinterpret God's purpose. Women, accustomed to acting as stewards and narrators at the deathbed, found this need to divine God's logic an enormous strain. First, the death of any family member, even under the best of circumstances, complicated the sacralization of the evangelical family. For evangelicals who had spent lifetimes constructing their households—and their inhabitants—into shrines of domestic worship, the loss of a single family member represented a direct and immediate diminution in the everyday practice of piety. Second, a loved one's death, particularly under difficult circumstances, often led to outright self-recrimination for anything within the family circle that might have displeased God. In a culture that celebrated mourning, some women accepted blame for events far outside their control; others welcomed the thought of death as the only means to family restoration or to reclaim an idyllic past.

Third, many southern women used their grief to search and cleanse their souls, reconciling their experiences with God's plans.

For clergymen in particular, death offered a blunt instrument for conversion, but men more often than not proved the target for the clergy's harangues. Because of women's predominance in evangelical congregations and thus in the Good Death, clergymen extolled female church members' lives and deaths as models for unconverted kin. When the Methodist Protestant Church lost faithful members who had been living among irreligious kin, the Reverend William Wills penned obituaries that celebrated the deceased and rebuked the living: "Notice of the dead benefit them not.... If the dead were vicious here, the living should be warned by their example, if virtuous, encouraged by their precepts to go and do like wise." Wills's obituary for Fanny Pitts Vinson, for example, eulogized her Christian character and then used it to condemn her husband's piety: "Mr. Vinson is not a member of the Church. He ought to be. On the 10 of May I preached the funeral of his wife. 5 weeks before precisely I was in the same house to bury his aged mother. These dispensations and these calls I hope will not be unimproved by him. He feels the stroke, he bows his head in humble submission. God grant that they may avail in his behalf." Wills's family members were not exempt from his public critiques of impious survivors. He concluded a lengthy published obituary for his father-in-law, Cary Whitaker, with a direct call to the unconverted members of his wife's family: "May his children strive to emulate him.... My Dear C. & M. I know your fathers anxiety; nothing on earth would have gratified him more than to have witnessed your reception into the bosom of the church. This was denied him, but if his pure spirit is more cognizant of the affairs of man. do I entreat you, hasten to perform this hitherto neglected duty and let him witness a consummation we all so devoutly wish." Wills not only published such obituaries in the *Methodist Protestant*, the denomination's national newspaper, but also instructed the editor to deliver complimentary copies to surviving kin, a heavy-handed tactic targeted toward the most intransigent of potential converts.[36]

Published funeral sermons established women's deathbed piety as the cornerstone of southern evangelicalism. When Thomas Earle, a student at the University of Mississippi, died in 1856, the presiding Presbyterian clergyman launched into a diatribe against alcohol consumption, novel reading, and card playing and then stressed the unpredictability of God's designs: "Who next of our number will be called by death to follow

James T. Earle? Is it I? Is it you? Or You? or You? Ponder the question well." Where should the anxious college student turn for guidance and solace? "Young man! Have you not a Bible? Do you not remember the parting gift of that tender mother, when she bade you farewell with tearful eyes, as you were about to go beyond the reach of her kindly offices, though not beyond the influence of her prayers?" Baptist Jane Draughon Edwards of Society Hill, South Carolina, who represented the ideals of restrained Christian womanhood, was "filled . . . with an ecstacy of joy" when her son converted at her deathbed, fulfilling the "very sum of all her desires in his behalf." As Bishop Andrew witnessed his wife's slow and painful death, his role shifted from teacher to pupil. On her deathbed in 1842, Ann Andrew told her husband,

> When you first addressed me, I scarcely knew how to act. I was poor, and you were poor. I carried the matter to God in prayer; and these words were powerfully impressed upon my mind, "seek first the kingdom of God, and all those things shall be added." I became yours, and we have journeyed together for almost twenty-six years; yet God's promise has never failed us. We have never lacked. Continue to trust in him to the end: he will never fail you. And now . . . I solemnly charge you never to falter in your Master's work.

His wife's shattering illness reinforced his personal and professional piety while permitting him to attribute the success of his ministry to her: "From the time of our union, she sought not only my comfort but my improvement: and to her sensible and pious counsels I am more indebted for whatever of ministerial usefulness and respectability I may have attained, than to those of any other human being."[37] Hindsight, combined with his position as the sole author of the narrative of his wife's death, enabled James Andrew to offer a complicated account that ended happily for all involved.

Evangelicals generally had little trouble interpreting God's message in the death of an unconverted adult. When death struck the impeccably pious, however, condolence letters both sympathized and scrutinized. Letters that simultaneously extolled the Christian virtues of the deceased and attempted to explain God's logic often worked at cross-purposes. Unlike northern middle-class women, who often put form over function in the mourning process, southern evangelical women's letters and diaries suggest a torturous intellectual and spiritual struggle over the meaning of a death in their midst.[38]

When the irreproachably pious Reverend James Douglass died, his widow, Frances, received an unusually broad range of support—a result of her roles as individual believer, mother, congregant, and leading light of her community—but nevertheless struggled to understand God's purpose in creating such a void in her life. She had difficulty interpreting the nature and timing of Rev. Douglass's death because he had not fully anticipated events and died speechless, thereby failing to accomplish the Good Death—that is, to communicate his love for his family, reaffirm his faith, and celebrate his family's heavenly prospects. Moreover, he was deeply in debt. Rev. Douglass's mother interpreted this combination of circumstances as part of God's plan, even though it deviated from evangelical expectation, arguing that God had rendered the pastor mute because he would have been hysterical about leaving his wife in such dire financial straits. Frances Douglass still wondered about the timing: "His delight whilst on earth was to do the will of him that sent him & to finish his work there. I look a round I see many things which he begun that are incomplete but the Lord did not design that he should procede farther with them. He has called him home in the midst of his labours."[39]

As she sought to make sense of her husband's death, Frances Douglass received words of consolation that are typical of sympathy letters written by grieving evangelicals. The surest source of consolation rested on the reaffirmation that the deceased had lived a Christian life and died a Christian death. H. Potter, the clerk of session of the Presbyterian Church of Fayetteville, North Carolina, wrote, "'Sorrow not as others who have not hope,' for we trust [that the deceased] have a hope of full immortality, and the relievement . . . from the suffering & confines of this lower world, is but a passport to the liberty and glories of the upper world." E. G. Plumer, one of the pastor's friends, saw his death as creating a great loss for the "Church of God . . . but oh how great his gain. Everlasting rest. Joy unspeakable, a crown of glory." The Reverend Drury Lacy not only reiterated much of the same language but also stressed the familial rewards awaiting the Christian family: "Remember," he told Frances Douglass, "that the separation is but for a season; our dear friend is not lost. . . . [H]e is awaiting our arrival." Such plaudits restated the obvious assumption: God's servants went to heaven to await the arrival of faithful family members and friends. While Frances Douglass clearly agreed with this verdict, she still remembered her husband's search for a more disciplined piety. His peers might eulogize James Douglass as nearly perfect, but she knew better.[40]

Turning from a celebration of the deceased to lessons for the living, clergymen inevitably offered advice to Frances Douglass. Some of it pertained to her exceptionally public profile, but most of it echoed throughout evangelical condolences more broadly. The Reverend W. M. Atkinson hoped that she would remain stoic despite her loss, thus using her public profile as a minister's widow to convince the religiously indifferent of evangelicalism's confidence and optimism: "Prove especially to those who will look on with eager curiosity, that the religion you profess is a glorious reality, not an empty name; and that it can console and strengthen, when all earth born comforts would be vain and worthless! May the Lord enable you to do this? May He be your strength and your comfort your portion, your God!" While Atkinson worried more about appearances than genuine comfort, women who wrote to Frances acknowledged crying as an inevitable part of the grieving process. Though other clergymen showed more sensitivity than did Atkinson, their letters nevertheless reminded her that the grief-stricken could find true solace and resolution only by turning to God: "It is my earnest prayer," Lacy wrote, "that the God who reveals himself as the Father of the fatherless, & the husband of the widow, may take you under his especial protection, and supply you with those rich and ineffable consolations which are neither few nor small." This scriptural paraphrase became one of the most often-repeated phrases in condolence letters because it captured the centrality of the familial metaphor to antebellum evangelicalism. God may have sundered the earthly family, but God would also fill the void and create links between families on earth and in heaven. Potter's formal condolence letter captured that tension: "We are admonished to humble ourselves before the mighty hand of God, & to return unto Him: for he 'hath torn, & he will heal us; he hath smitten & he will bind us up.'"[41] Thus, even as evangelical condolences celebrated the deceased's virtue and faith, they unsettled the survivors' faith, asking them to probe it anew.

While clergymen anticipated that the bereaved would and should look to God for succor and resolution, at least one laywoman went a step farther, attempting to explain God's logic to Frances Douglass. Ann Reid, a member of Rev. Douglass's previous congregation in Lexington, Virginia, sought to console Frances but also suggested that she had tempted a jealous God to reclaim her husband. According to Reid, God had mandated that Douglass leave his Lexington church when his parishioners became too fond of him, and "perhaps dear friend, you have done the same, &

even in this world you may... feel it was necessary." Frances Douglass agreed with this explanation, writing to her son, Henry Taylor, "I fear we all regarded my beloved husband almost idolitrously.... I did not know until he was taken away how much he was associated with all I did & thought."[42]

This pattern of womanly accountability to God in all familial relations (that is, as wives, sisters, and mothers) confirms that southern women believed they had an especially close relationship with God when it came to matters of domestic devotion. Men almost never saw any causal link between a family member's death and excessive affection for that individual. While several historians have noted the burden of this spiritual accountability, they have focused on the mother-child relationship, which is uniquely dependent and nurturing. But that sense of godly stewardship extended to husbands, grown children, and even grown siblings. When Elizabeth Harewell, for example, wrote to thank the Reverend William Wills for his kindness in the aftermath of her brother's 1834 murder, she blamed herself for his violent death:

> Sometimes, I feel I bestowed too much love on my dear brother and not enough to my God that blessed me with such a kind affectionate Brother, not knowing the intent of my affection and love towards him until the cruel hand of assassination forced me to give him up. When I reflect on it[,] it causes my heart to mourn to know that I loved him as much as I did and perhaps God in mercy to me has suffered us to be separated for a short time to show me the evil of setting my affection too closely on the transitory things of this world.

Piety may have allowed evangelical women to speak with a strong voice in all manner of domestic concerns, but such an expansive sense of religious self-importance carried negative consequences, too. Women often shouldered the blame for their entire families' shortcomings and sins.[43]

Frances Douglass somehow reconciled her doubts about the means and timing of her husband's death, proclaiming the benefits of her trials and suggesting to her son, Henry Taylor, that he too use the tragedy to seek spiritual renewal and purpose: "Oh God teach me patience & submission, let my son live to glorify thee on the earth, & if pain & suffering is necessary to make him holy far be it from me to say withhold the stroke. I believe this affliction was needful for me. I was too happy for earth, & now I am made to know that this is not my rest."[44] Death had forced Frances

Douglass to reassess all of her relationships as she moved from emotional crisis to spiritual epiphany, but as moral and religious steward, she also sought to shore up individual piety within the family circle and thus guarantee its sanctity.

The death of James Douglass required much more than soul-searching for his widow. Frances Douglass's immediate concerns included the question of where she would live and how she would satisfy her husband's creditors: "Where shall I go! This is a homeless world to me & were it not for my dear Henry I could pray to be taken away from the evil to come." Paying the creditors would require Douglass to sell nearly all of her worldly possessions, including her house and its furnishings. Her husband's congregation rallied to her side, however. She was relieved when church officials vowed to pay his salary for the remaining three months of the year but found much greater comfort in individual donations of a dollar or two, often from female congregants who had little money to spare. Frances marveled at the generosity of these "tenderest brothers & sisters": "It seems as if the Lord had come & looked over Fayetteville & called to himself the choice spirit of the peace. A thrill is felt through the community. All sympathize."[45]

The aura of Christian goodwill that surrounded James Douglass's death vanished in the wake of internecine battles over his intellectual legacy. Only six months after his death, rival denominational newspapers vied over the rights to publish his sermons, part of the acrimonious New School/Old School debate that wracked the Presbyterian Church. William Plumer, an old Virginia colleague of Douglass's, stood by the Old School and announced his intention to publish Douglass's sermons in the *Watchman of the South*. Simeon Colton, a Fayetteville clergyman and supporter of New School Presbyterianism and its publication, the *Telegraph*, attempted to dissuade Frances Douglass from donating James Douglass's papers to Plumer and the *Watchman* by claiming that the majority of North Carolina's clergy supported the *Telegraph*. Colton reported that many in Fayetteville viewed the *Watchman*'s promotion of the publication "as a mere attempt to introduce the paper, & thereby instill its peculiar notions into the people under the color of Mr Douglass' papers." Not only was Plumer duping Frances Douglass, Colton continued, but she was also taking a course of action her late husband would not have approved. Pulling back only momentarily from his condescension, Colton also argued that Frances Douglass could gain financially (and avoid alienating anyone) if she published Rev.

Douglass's sermons as a book. Colton even falsely claimed to have initial pledges for sixty copies of such an anthology.[46]

Rather than ceding control of her husband's legacy to Colton, however, Frances Douglass remained an active participant. She did not shy away from the high-stakes clerical struggle, entering freely and confidently into the acrimonious politics of the Presbyterian Church by having Plumer publish her husband's sermons in the *Watchman* and soliciting subscriptions to the journal. She also mobilized the allies she and her husband had gained as they worked together to build his Fayetteville congregation. In addition, to solve her financial problems, she began teaching.

Similarly, the death of her husband, Sidney, prompted Frances Bumpass to begin an assessment of her piousness, and she came close to blaming herself for his death: "O! that I had lived better—been less worldly—more spiritual. Then might I not have been spared such afflictions." Bumpass ultimately pulled back from the precipice of self-incrimination, leaving the final answer to God: "But why he who was as dear as life was taken I know not. The Lord gives & the Lord has taken away blessed be his holy name." That dose of resignation soon enabled her to move on with her life as she redirected her attention to improving and focusing her Christian character: "May I learn the lesson which I should, & not suffer so much in vain." With the proper attitude toward mourning, particularly incessant prayer, she hoped that her "trials may yield the peaceable fruits of righteousness." Amid the confusion and anguish of her loss, she prayed for clarity of conviction: "May the Lord condescend to direct me in all things, & to make every path of duty strait & plain."[47]

Frances Bumpass found her answer: "Through encouragements from above and discouragements from below the Lord hath greatly led me and cleared my way, enabling me to glorify his name by attending to my beloved employment left to me by my dear husband.... My spiritual sky is clear, & by trusting in the Lord to work in me to will & to do that which is well-pleasing in his sight, I enjoy that love which casts out fear, that peace which flows."[48] From the depths of her despair—and from the need to support her family—Bumpass formulated a plan: she acquired her husband's denominational newspaper, the *Greensboro (North Carolina) Weekly Message*. Doing so enabled Bumpass to carry on her husband's legacy, generate revenue, and stimulate her faith.

But her elation quickly turned to doubts and consternation: "I fear I must give [the *Weekly Message*] up." Not only did she encounter resistance from other clergymen, many of whom resented a woman in such a prominent public role, but she found that she was losing money. Bumpass again turned to her faith for guidance: "May the Lord direct me in this matter, & my mind turns to what I shall do for a support. O! for heavenly direction in all things."[49]

Having resigned herself to God's will, Bumpass experienced a renewed desire to hold onto the newspaper at all costs. Amid the language of dependency on God emerged a Frances Bumpass who held a stronger sense of herself and her purpose. When doubts cropped up over her ongoing management of the newspaper, she blamed the devil: "Satan sometimes tempts me to think the Lord is about to forsake me in my attempts to do good, by carrying on my paper." But after she prayed, "the tempter fled & I was left with my soul calmly staid on the Lord who will keep those in perfect peace whose minds are staid on him." Her resolve stiffened once again: "I should fear I might do wrong to give [the newspaper] up. I believe [God] will succeed my efforts." When the paper was doing well, Bumpass read the events as vindicating her faith: "Friends have arisen to vindicate the Message at the time needed. The Lord is good & whatever opposers may say, may faith mount cheering above all, & rejoice in the will of the Lord, whether prosperous or adverse." With such steadfast belief in the righteousness of her editorship of the *Weekly Message*, Frances Bumpass retained the position for twenty years, maintaining control of her husband's legacy.[50] More than a religious duty or even an obligation to preserve her husband's memory, Bumpass's editorship became a testament to her faith. Surrendering the newspaper would have conceded defeat to God's adversary.

While the experiences of Frances Douglass and Frances Bumpass might suggest exceptionalism among clerical families, many other evangelical women followed a similar profile when grieving. Mary Bethell, for example, lost multiple children at young ages but was most disturbed by the horrific death of her three-year-old daughter, Phereba. In the midst of the Civil War, as two of her sons fought for the Confederacy, Bethell marked the twelve-year anniversary of Phereba's death and recalled the awful events: "She was burnt on Saturday, died Sunday night at 8 oclock and Jesus took her to his bosom." Despite her anguish, Bethell took solace in the fact that Phereba had been able to communicate with her family on her deathbed, allowing Bethell to declare that her child now resided in heaven. Bethell's reflections on her daughter's death centered more on Bethell than the girl, prompting endless reexaminations of her ordeal to identify God's logic in afflicting her. Bethell used the anniversary to reawaken her piety and renew her devotion to God: "I now consecrate myself to God, I beg him to direct me in all things. . . . All my trials are permitted to cut loose my affections from this world. I will thank God for them. I go to God as a weak and dependent child to its Father, he knows our wants, he is able and will help us at the right time. I long and pray to be filled with the Holy Ghost, I shall expect it, for I will fast and pray for it." Though she shrouded her words in the language of dependency, Bethell still made demands of God, anticipating rich rewards for her faithfulness amid the sacrifice of her children. In expecting "to be filled with the Holy Ghost," Bethell anticipated spiritual nourishment. On one level, this commingling of conversion and death points to the shared vocabulary ("mourners") and physical responses (crying, lifelessness) of these two evangelical processes. On another level, Bethell's annual resurrection of her grief also suggests her ties to early American evangelicalism's reliance on affliction and self-denial as a means to "spiritual clarity" and ultimately, to borrow from Lynn Lyerly, "complete self-dominion, . . . fully sublimat[ing] the flesh to the spirit."[51] Much like illness, grief demonstrated the believer's willingness to suffer with an eye toward spiritual enrichment in the here and eternal rewards in the hereafter.

From the deathbed to the grieving process, southern evangelical women experienced events that tested the boundaries of their interpretive reach. Mary Gray illustrates this process taken to extremes. She became so absorbed with the death of her brother, James Douglass, and the anticipation of her mother's death that she focused all of her energy on death and dying. With her elderly mother "*quiet waiting* for the coming of our Lord to summon her away from earth to a permanent home," Gray began to prepare for her own death:

> Gone, forever gone, my days of gayity, too often those of sadness are around me. I keep a trunk under the foot of my bed, read old letters, sermons & little scraps I love better than history, recall past scenes & departed friends these papers have a tongue in every character—A language in their very silentness, that speaks to my heart like a voice from the grave, warms & encourages me to get ready for the exchange of worlds, which may soon come.

After Rev. Douglass's death, Gray took perverse delight in the hope that his widow would now understand and partake of her sister-in-law's morbid fascination: "You used to wonder at my sadness," Gray wrote to Frances Douglass, but "there has since been a chord in your own heart that is strung" for a "far more melancholy tune."[52] Gray allowed death to overwhelm her imagination, stripping her of any joy. Far away from much of her family, she dwelled on the idea that death would re-create her past.

Grieving among evangelical women fell along a spectrum, with those mired in the past at one extreme and those with newfound zeal for public pursuits at the other. Most women fell somewhere in the middle, revisiting the anniversaries of the deceased not only to resurrect memories but also to renew piety. As their families' religious and moral stewards, southern women embraced grieving and its language of self-abnegation, sorrow, and even uncertainty as an opportunity to test their faith and ultimately to enhance their piety. The mourning process thus underscores women's struggle to assess their relationship with God. Though women ran the risk of finding incongruity between their expectations and the outcomes they confronted at the deathbed, most worked through a process of grieving that included sorrow, self-recrimination, introspection, and ultimately religious renewal whose trajectory and tone resemble the stages of evangelical conversion.

Constructing a Heavenly Family

Most southern evangelicals described heaven as an eternal and happy home where a perfected family reunion would occur. Southern evangelicals described heaven using other metaphors as well—a city crowded with the sainted deceased or a great throne around which the redeemed worshipped God—but all of these visions pointed to the ingathering of family. All of these projections featured rejection of the earthly world and embraced domesticity and affection free from the irreligious and worldly cares. In these respects and others—the immediacy of heaven to earth, heaven as an extension of life on earth, heaven seen not as a site of rest but of action among the sainted, and the love of family as a focal point—the heaven of antebellum southerners seems remarkably similar to what Colleen McDannell and Bernhard Lang label a "modern" version of heaven that emerged in the mid-eighteenth century and gained widespread popularity in the nineteenth century among European and American Christians.[53] In their visions of heavenly families, evangelicals eliminated many of the uncertainties, disappointments, and conflicts that routinely shaped their lives on earth but also clung tenaciously to their faith in individual final judgment by God and the existence of hell. That perception made heaven all the greater reward for the faithful but created perilous stakes for those family members who remained unconverted.

Evangelical women often imagined angels as a direct link to the deceased. Angels entered letters most often as "ministering spirits" to ease the emotional pain and spiritual crises of moral stewardship and self-recrimination. Angels provided the morbid Mary Gray with a necessary respite from her dreary view of life and maintained her focus on the afterlife: "I believe in the guardianship of good Angels. 'tis often a delightful thought when alone & depressed by the sorrows of life to feel I am surrounded by these pure & happy spirits 'Sent forth by the God of Angels, to minister to the tempted, tossed & bereaved wanderer thro this sorrowing world.['] Our Father is good, infinite in kindness, else we had been forever lost." Indeed, Gray believed so strongly in angels that she found a small piece of common ground between her Presbyterianism and her neighbors' Catholicism, which she otherwise strongly abhorred: "If there is any one thing for which I can find in my heart to excuse the absurdities of the Roman C[atholic].'s it is the prayers to Saints." Ann Thomas, Frances Bumpass, and other Methodist women also invoked angels as guardians in their own lives or the lives of loved ones, forging ever stronger ties between the living and the dead. Thomas told her daughter, Anna Fuller, "O that wing of Heaven may overshadow you; May the angel of the Lord tent around your bed by night and guide and direct your footsteps by day." Similarly, Bumpass wrote in her diary, "Have been much cheered for some days by thinking & writing of the ministering care of angels—& as, 'saints are as the angels in heaven' of their messages of consolation, & have felt that the best of all is, God is present to bless."[54]

Heaven itself so absorbed the evangelical imagination that discussions about its familial essence reconnected the faith of family members scattered across the South. As she waited to hear of her sister's safe return, Ann Thomas soothed her loneliness with memories of their shared worship experiences and the promise of a heavenly reunion: "My dear Sister I think of our siting around the Communion Table for the last time but not hopeless—may we not anticipate the time when we all Drink it anew in our Fathers Kingdom. And enjoy the blessings that are in reserve for his cross bearing followers here below." With many members of the Gaston and Crawford families scattered between South Carolina and Alabama, visits were few and far between, but letters focusing on spiritual intimacy and heavenly reunions were common. As both women mourned recent family deaths, Martha Gamble commented on the nature and promise of her lifelong correspondence with her cousin, Jane Crawford:

> It would afford me great pleasure, if you were so nigh that I could step over and see you any time. I wished, but that privelege is denied me[.] [A]ll the entercourse, we now have is by the pen, we have coresponded with each other nearly forty years: that is but a short time to the eternity, we hope to spend together. There we shall meet loved ones that have crossed the stream before us[.] [A]ll the blood washed throng shall meet together in that happy shore, and sing the song of triumph, unto him that loved us and washed us in his own blood, and made us kings and priests unto our God[.] [W]hen we get to that happy world, there will be no more death among us no vacant seats.

When forced to move, evangelical women tempered their unease with the belief that they would experience eternal reunion with fellow evangelicals. As she prepared to depart from eastern Tennessee, Eliza Haskell waxed sentimental about the relationships she had formed during her years there, writing that she viewed the move as a mere rehearsal for death's separation and heavenly bliss: "I will not indulge in unavailing regrets. . . . I think all these removes ought only to make [us] more engaged to prepare for that great remove to our final home. If we are only ready[.] If we only have the wedding garment on and are cloathed with the robe of Christs righteousness it will be a great matter." Evangelical women sought to transform their painful separations, like life's other hardships, into Christian purpose. Never content merely to bear their crosses alone, they created intense intimacy through religious ritual and imagery, placed their individual pilgrimages in sacred time, and imagined the eternal rewards they (and their kin) would receive. Separations from female relations undoubtedly generated sadness and tension among southern evangelical families, but women sought ways to transform these afflictions into blessings and short-term losses into eternal gains. The rich language that united faith, family, and female kin may have thus blunted some of the psychological devastation that physical separation generated as families relocated across the South.[55]

Evangelicals commonly defined the character of life in heaven in negative rather than positive terms and in relation to life on earth. To paraphrase the most common saying, heaven would be free from sin, sorrow, and suffering. Even the family would now be "unbroken." Simply put, heaven was stable and certain, a far cry from life on earth for these weary pilgrims, as evangelicals often referred to themselves. An earthly life filled with agonizing uncertainties about God's designs would be erased by heaven's certain joys. Some evangelicals positioned God and Jesus at the center of these perfected family relationships: wrote Mary Brown, "When summoned away from earth I will enter a pure life where theire shall be no troubling years and changeful seasens but an unceasing round of worship and joy in the presence of God and the Lamb." Cary Whitaker, a doctor in Florida, echoed Brown's sentiments when he recalled the first anniversary of his wife's death: "Oh! that I may, when my time of dissolution comes, be filled and prepared for reception into heaven with the welcome approbation of well done good and faithful servant enter into the joy of thy Lord, there to be united, [with] my dear and sainted wife, and spend a blissful eternity, in the presence of our Father and God." But most evangelicals paid less attention than Brown and Whitaker did to casting God or Jesus in a starring role in heaven. That role was reserved for family, as Mary Bethell stated simply: "Oh 'tis a good thought to think of our home in Heaven, where we shall meet with those we love, to part no more." For evangelicals in general and especially for women, who labored so diligently to deliver to God the souls under their charge, heaven represented proof of their stewardship. Unable to idealize their homes on earth, with their numerous physical, spiritual, and familial challenges, women chose to idealize their home in heaven.[56]

Cemeteries thus became more than memorials to the deceased, providing physical evidence of the direct links among the living, deceased family members, and heaven. Southern evangelicals often commented on the religious inspiration they received when they visited graveyards. Anne Davis, for example, recalled that the first stirrings of her conversion experience occurred while she prayed in a graveyard, while Mary Gray wrote, "I often feel as if it would be a privelege to live near the graves of buried love, 'tis a good & proper place for meditation. 'To kneel, to sit beside the sacred place & think, O that the once loved now sainted yet still loved, Was there.'" Visits to family grave sites could shift from unmitigated grief to intimacy over time. Frances Bestor, who initially found her mother's grave site unbearable, found spiritual solace there two years after her mother's death. "'Tis a very sad place to visit—yet it always makes me feel so very near to Mother, I feel when I leave it as tho' I had seen her." Reflecting on her mother's life and death, Bestor exorcised her lingering regrets over her inability to freely discuss her feelings and piety with her mother prior to her loss of speech on her deathbed: "Her life was such a beautiful example of Christian fortitude that her death presented no horror at all, for I feel so secure that she is in Heaven, that when I go to her grave I feel as tho' a spirit was near me from Heaven." That her sister's child rested next to her mother further reified her belief that they together enjoyed the bounties of heaven and may have helped absolve Bestor of any lingering guilt resulting from the child's death while under Bestor's care.[57]

As they anticipated a perfected family in heaven, southern evangelicals sought to forget many undesirable elements of their lives and relationships on earth. As Ted Ownby persuasively argues, Confederate soldiers typically made no mention of patriarchal or paternalistic authority over family and slaves in their domesticated visions of heaven. Pointing to widespread spousal separation during the war and to Confederate soldiers' fears of Yankee depredations on the Confederate home front, Ownby suggests that Confederate men started to idealize home and family in ways unlikely prior to the war.[58] But even before the Civil War, southern evangelicals' romantic notions of heaven had little space for power relationships.

Close attention to the personal, familial, and social context of individual southern evangelicals permits a glimpse into the appeal of such a construction of heaven. For someone like Richard Collins, who had repeatedly bankrupted himself and his family, a domesticated heaven had obvious appeal. By uncoupling his failures as a businessman from his self-proclaimed success as a father, Collins hoped to evade his wife's criticisms that his risky investments had jeopardized their family's economic and emotional welfare. Finally confronting the scope of his business failures in 1864, Collins turned to his wife and family for solace: "You have proved the true & loving & willing wife & help-meet that I planned & reckoned on; but I!—how disappointed all your proud hopes of position, usefulness, fame, influence, independence, connected with your husband & his success in life! In the main, a kind, good, loving husband—sharer of your trials & your joys; how much of care, & troubles, anxiety and disappointment, poverty & self-denial you have undergone & borne, all cheerfully, for *his* sake!"[59] Amid his praise for his wife's forbearance, Collins accepted blame for his public failings but even then downplayed any knowledge of the financial hardship he had created for his family, instead stressing his failure to win the influence of other men. In reality, the earlier criticisms of Richard by his wife, Mary, had centered on his domestic failings—that is, on his frequent absences from home and his inability to provide a stable income—making her home and family a far cry from the sentimentalized household to which he clung. She had asked him to stop seeking fame and fortune through risky investments, preferring instead that he practice law, an occupation that would have kept him at home and the family afloat financially. Now seeking to efface the entire history of their conflicts over money, migration, and child rearing responsibilities, Richard Collins eagerly retreated to his own version of a domesticated heaven:

> And don't I think of my home, & my wife, & our little ones—everywhere & all the time. . . . [T]he sight of a pleasant-looking, good-tempered-looking woman—or of a happy-faced school-girl with books under her arm—or of *little ones* at play, with their merry ringing voices—the sight of any of these dashes business & care from my mind, & away bound my thoughts, quick as lightning to my happy cottage-home; and with a smile on my face, and a smile on my heart, and a thrill all over that *can't* transfer to paper. I clasp you in my arms and am *happy*, for a moment. Oh, these are happy moments in *this* life, my Mary—sweet foretastes of happier moments in angel-life hereafter! God grant us many more of such moments and use us for His glory![60]

An absentee father for much of the late 1850s and the Civil War, Collins nevertheless maintained the ideal of the sanctified home. In so doing he again transformed himself into the victim of his absences (the businessman cut off from the blessing of domestic piety) and his wife into the beneficiary (the domestic mistress surrounded by adoring and pious children). By narrowing the gap between a sentimentalized vision of heaven and their Kentucky home, Richard Collins hoped to remove from discussion his abilities as a father and as a husband.

While heaven in some cases brought closure to thorny domestic issues, the issue of slavery was not one of those subjects. White southerners often spoke inclusively of whites and blacks as members of one household but consistently pushed slaves to the margins of family-oriented faith. Many evangelicals worried about converting their slaves, often hoping to achieve even greater control over them. But a heaven free of work and free of conflict had little need for slaves, converted or otherwise, who had been such a challenge on earth.

The death of Methodist Protestant clergyman William Wills's son during the Civil War underscores both southern white evangelicals' struggle to reconcile their notions of heaven with war's realities and their ambivalence toward slaves. Like many slaveholding southerners, the Wills family made little mention of their slaves in ordinary correspondence. William Wills's concerns regarding his ministry and his white family crowded out any need to inquire extensively about his slaves. But when his son, George, died in combat near Winchester, Virginia, in 1864, William Wills struggled to piece together his son's heavenly prospects. Several letters from the young man's comrades echoed the optimistic summary offered by E. W. Thompson, the regiment's chaplain: George Wills's "amiable and gentle disposition—his zeal in his country's cause—his fidelity in the discharge of his duties as an officer; together with his well ordered life as a Church member all united to make me love him, and to impress me with his same excellence as a gentleman, his fidelity as a patriot, his superior qualities as a soldier and more than all his genuine piety as a Christian." In spite of such reassurances and the family's intimate knowledge of George's piety (William Wills had made periodic visits to his son's encampments to check on his health and deliver food and supplies from home), surviving family members could never fully allay their concerns about George's piety. After George's death, William Wills wrote, "George was a noble youth and I think a Christian. No more letters from him! O God! Help me to be resigned to thy will, and may I meet him in thy Kingdom." Rev. Wills thus equivocated regarding his son's piety: he thought George had been saved but nevertheless felt uneasy in the immediate wake of his death.[61] Wills, the same man who had used obituaries to urge the impious immediately to seek God, now felt the sting of his own logic as he pondered his son's fate.

Seeking to firm up their knowledge of George's death and perhaps clarify George's fate, members of the Wills family took a deposition from someone who had witnessed George's everyday bearing, his personal slave, Washington. A slave with little previous presence in the family's correspondence suddenly provided invaluable testimony about George's countenance just prior to the battle that claimed his life. Washington noted George Wills's well-kept appearance (he had shaved and his uniform was crisp); his settlement of all debts within his regiment; his fearlessness (his ability literally to laugh in the face of death on the battlefield); his fondness for his family and praise for his upbringing; and above all else his deep piety. Washington "hope[d] and trust[ed] [that George] is saved[.] I have reason to believe so by the light which he gave me." Washington also pointed to the copy of the New Testament George kept in his breast pocket, a recent spate of revivals in the Confederate Army, discussions about religion that led the two men to agree that they had "to give up all to religion," and finally George's resignation to "the hands of Providence" on the battlefield. In other words, Washington, with the assistance of the family member who transcribed the letter, provided the best-case scenario for George Wills's experience of the Good Death. And while Washington professed his own piety, his reference to heaven included no mention of the Wills family: "I desire to be a better Christian I want to get to heaven. I hope I have your prayers for me to do right. I will try to do right: my earnest desire is to be at rest after this life." Washington clearly hoped that his piety would see him through the war's trials, but he did not perceive his ultimate rest coming alongside his white masters. The war removed George Wills's death from the home and thus put the men of his family and of his regiment in charge of bearing witness to the dying man's piety. Despite the certainty expressed by George's comrades and family regarding his piety and fate, William Wills's lingering doubts and Washington's silences illustrate that heaven, in spite of its construction as a domestic sanctuary, continued to create challenges for the southern evangelical imagination.[62]

In contrast to southerners' static construction of a domesticated heaven, their quest for that hallowed destination involved ongoing emotional, intellectual, and spiritual struggle. Diverse personal and family contexts illustrate the range of responses that emerged from that struggle. Some evangelicals embraced death as an escape from a lifetime of disappointments and sufferings. Other familial constructions of heaven transformed relationships on earth and offered the fulfillment of lifelong wishes, viewing heaven's intimacy as a means to express their eternal love and fellowship. Still others scrutinized loved ones' deaths to discover God's intentions for survivors. As they struggled to better understand God's forceful lessons for both roles, women often redoubled their demands on family members to refine their piety and therefore ensure heavenly reunions. Finally, some believers struggled to reconcile fully their faith in heaven with their experiences on earth—for example, family members' refusal to convert.

White women in the antebellum South could no longer claim the kind of public religious authority possessed by their early national forbears but nevertheless used domesticity to shape religious experience. Death particularly underscores the family orientation of antebellum evangelicalism because the ultimate reward—reunification in heaven—required family members to share and shape each other's piety on earth. However, southern whites conceived of their eternal household as segregated. Slaveholders applauded faithful servants on their deathbeds and spoke of the heavenly reward that awaited them, but this vision did not place master and slave together. Evangelical women not only cared for the sick but also constructed deathbed narratives that distinguished the saved from the damned. By offering rich details regarding the final thoughts and actions of the dying, women downplayed their roles as interpreters and managers of what emerged as the most important evangelical ritual of the era. But making dying persons conform to the Good Death formula was no easy task. While women shepherded many relatives through the evangelical Good Death, any failure along the way created tremendous emotional and spiritual disquiet by jeopardizing the family's collective hope of eternal reunion in heaven. Consequently, many southern women took full responsibility for events over which they had little or no control.

Death and dying thus underscore the persistent tension in evangelical thought between resignation and examination, particularly after the Second Great Awakening. Evangelicals wanted to take comfort in their belief that God controlled everyday events in their lives that somehow contributed to their ultimate salvation, either positively reinforcing or testing faith so that it might align more closely with God's will. Yet that fundamental faith in God's presence in daily life forced evangelicals to decode the religious meaning of events, challenging their wish for resignation. While both southern and northern evangelical women stressed the links between heaven and family, evangelical southern women's toil within the household combined with the abiding fear of sudden death and their certainty of God's judgment left little room for the sentimental evangelicalism that scholars have identified with the women of the North's emerging middle class.

EPILOGUE

"We Walk by Faith and Not by Sight"
Evangelicals and the Civil War–Era South

Southern evangelicals welcomed introspection and suffering as a means to forge spiritual intimacy with God and family. Such, after all, had been their introduction to evangelical Christianity during the conversion process. During the antebellum era, those dramas increasingly played out domestically, permitting women to interpret God's profound and often mysterious ways within their households—conversions, courtship, marriage, childbirth, and sickness and death. Even if the clergy called for manly dominion and female submission, the female majority in the pews also heard the clergy's evocations of womanly piety and morality. Indeed, clergymen readily depended on their wives to assist in managing their households and their congregations. And authority once ceded was often difficult to reclaim. Whether denouncing the behavior of grown children, spurning a lover in God's name, or editing a denominational newspaper in the name of Christian resignation, antebellum white evangelical women showed considerable resolve in spite of the South's rural landscape and celebration of manly authority.

These claims to authority both at home and in public, however tenuous and vexing, reveal persistent discussion and debate about how to construct

221

godly homes, congregations, and communities in the evangelical South. As a consequence of custom and law, men retained the privileges of power at home and in the church; however, evangelical men's professions of mutuality and love in the name of piety opened them up to womanly critiques of their work as fathers and husbands. And complaints could yield change: Methodist clergyman Joseph Davis heeded his wife's call to spend more time at home by sharing with her his operational duties at the Wesleyan Female College; Presbyterian clergyman James Douglass continued to travel regularly but insisted that his wife accompany him at all times. But evangelical men, women, and children alike proclaimed domestic piety as integral to their devotional experiences and practices. Indeed, southern evangelicals considered domestic devotion indispensable to personal happiness and salvation, as is demonstrated by Richard Wills's lament regarding the incompleteness of a Sabbath spent without family and by William McCampbell and Sue Heiskell's discussions of how their marriage would enrich their piety.

But women also confronted daunting psychological challenges as they increasingly assumed accountability for events they could neither control nor interpret. Not only the family's happiness but also its salvation increasingly depended on a pious mother and wife who could assure the salvation of all kin. Women's calling to redeem their families ran headlong into many challenges: the perception of an irreligious South eager to undo faith learned at home; anxiety of second- and third-generation evangelicals regarding the authenticity of their conversions; the hard-edged language of damnation that left no margin for error; the relatively large size of families; and especially the unpredictability of illness and death. Evangelical women never resigned themselves to these realities, no matter how much they spoke of resignation to God's will. Indeed, faith was kept alive by precisely the factors that daily complicated women's claims to religious stewardship of their families. Even when life's events proceeded smoothly, women praised God and braced for the next test. They never stopped struggling to locate their place in God's designs for them as individuals and families. Although that process could destabilize individual women and stir doubts and despair, such responses were the exception, not the rule. For every Mary Gray who wallowed in morose self-pity with one eye on the afterlife, there existed a Mary Bethell, who returned to her daughter's death to re-create intimacy with God; a Mary Craddock, who ultimately dropped all claims of religious stewardship for her impious family and took solace in her individual salvation; and a Frances Douglass and a Frances Bumpass, who used the loss of their spouses to rally their faith and pursue ambitious agendas that placed them at odds with clergymen. This quest to redeem their families thus illuminates why women continued to form the majority of most congregations even as their clergymen turned up the rhetoric of patriarchal authority in the antebellum era.

The Civil War and its aftermath presented dramatic interpretive challenges for all southern white evangelicals. The sanctity of the household was suddenly called into question, as the husbands, brothers, and sons who had formed such an integral part of women's domestic evangelism left for the battlefield, many of them never to return.[1] Slaveholders also experienced a redefinition of the southern household as their slaves gained freedom. Although women pressed against the most limiting aspects of patriarchy in the name of family and faith, white southerners clung tenaciously to their paternalistic attitudes toward their former slaves. Southern slaveholders who had kept their slaves' piety at arm's length before the war—embracing opportunities to spread evangelical piety to their slaves but always doing so with a bit of wariness and less than complete inclusiveness in the southern white household—now watched as their slaves formed their own households and congregations. Slaveholders sought to understand why the slaves had left and what such dramatic changes might signal about God's designs for the South as a whole and for individual slaveholders. Although the Poulton family of Loudoun County, Virginia, dodged much of the war's physical devastation, they faced a commonplace but wrenching loss, the death of Rose Poulton as a result of complications from childbirth shortly after the war ended. Her death underscores evangelical women's continuing centrality as family religious steward. In her absence, her mother pressed claims of authority on her former son-in-law. The experiences of the Collins family of Kentucky reveal just how divisive the war could be on the border and how southerners sympathetic to the Confederacy immediately began to use their faith to explain military defeat and destruction. White southerners set out to construct the prewar southern household as a nostalgic, trouble-free site where piety and peace reigned.

The Civil War opened up a new sort of crisis for slaveholders as slaves departed for Union lines. The loss of slaves called into question owners' fundamental belief in both their mastery and their benevolence. The demise of the long-standing Christian defenses of slavery and the Confederacy forced white evangelicals to grapple with their piety in entirely new ways in an effort to discern God's logic. As was often the case, male and female evangelicals from the slaveholding classes looked at this crisis as yet one more affliction that they hoped their faith could withstand. White evangelicals' ambivalence toward their slaves' piety before the war—shifting uncomfortably between praise for slave preachers and recently converted slaves and criticism of the ways in which slaves interfered with domestic piety—persisted in an ambivalence toward the perceived effects of freedom. On one hand, whites wished to proclaim their liberation from the everyday trials of slaveholding. Without the inherent strife of slave management, some whites envisioned a more tranquil domestic sanctuary. On the other hand, slavery's demise struck at the heart of the slaveholder's mastery and sense of self. Consequently, evangelical white responses to slavery's demise ranged from disbelief to deep satisfaction. But whites' ruminations only tangentially considered former slaves' moral, religious, and physical plight, instead examining slavery's eclipse for God's purpose for the South.

Slaves' flight to Union lines often constituted only the first of many jarring transitions for slaveholding evangelicals. Living just south of Nashville, Tennessee, Samuel Henderson Jr. watched helplessly as his slaves left one by one for the Union-occupied city in the fall of 1862. Soon thereafter, when Union troops cleaned out his storehouse of livestock and food and he heard rumors that nearby slaves had poisoned their masters, Henderson made no mention of his faith, writing merely, "My health is very bad—I will certainly go crazy." North Carolina's Mary Bethell and other slaveholding evangelicals expressed a mix of condescension and persistent paternalism as the slaves left: "14 of ours have left," she wrote, "but all of them left with our consent except 2 who ran away. I hope they will get homes and become Christians. I hope they are on the road to Heaven. I do pity them and pray for them." After learning that some of his slaves wanted to remain and work for wages, the Reverend William Wills, also in North Carolina, wrote, "I am of the opinion that it will be better that there shall be a general breaking up, believing that we can get along better with other negroes than our own. But to me that future is dark, dark, dark. Whether I consider it, socially, politically, or in any way, it is so." He concluded by returning to his faith: "I never felt the force of the Apostles declaration so much as now: 'We walk by faith and not by sight.'" Not even worship offered South Carolinian Eugenia Leland relief from the social transformation wrought by slavery's demise. With newly freed slaves worshipping ecstatically under the direction of a black clergyman in the woods near her church, Leland observed that in her church, "the windows had to be closed back of the pulpit to enable the ministers to preach." With biting condescension, she echoed Bethell's thoughts: "Poor creatures, they may not find freedom (such as they will have) to be so sweet a thing as they imagine."[2]

Even with their disquiet over the loss of their slaves, slaveholding whites looked to piety at the personal, familial, and congregational level to gauge God's work in their midst. What they found compounded the disheartening loss of their slaves. According to Wills, "This year we have had no spiritual prosperity on the C[ircui]t's and I think I have at no time seen less interest manifested. The world is largely influencing the Church." Writing from a lay perspective, Bethell also found little to celebrate in her congregation: "I feel sad when I look at the church, almost desolate, some of the members have died, and some have backslidden, nearly all of the rest worldly minded, prayer meetings, class meetings, Sunday school are all broken up because iniquity abounds. The love of many has waxed cold, all are selfish and seeking their own."[3] Evangelicals still looked to their communities to gauge the prospects for God's work in their midst, but the effort took on greater anxiety in the wake of the war's destruction.

Yet amid their crises, following a pattern familiar to more peaceful times, white evangelicals continued to evince faith in God's will. In response to the boisterous slave meeting nearby, Leland concluded, "Neither black nor white know what is in store for them. There is one comfort, and that is—God reigns." As he weighed his prospects for work in the Methodist Protestant Church, the amnesty oath required of former Confederates, and his indebtedness, Wills concluded, "As it is however, my faith has not failed me yet, and I will endeavor to look with full confidence to our kind Father in Heaven. . . . I desire that my trust may be unwavering in Him who rules the Heavens above and in the earth beneath. God grant that it may be so!" Amid the desolation, Bethell reminded herself to look only to God for direction: "Oh Lord pity and save us from eternal death, there is none good, no not one, none but God, he alone is perfect."[4] The war generally and emancipation in particular provided a test like no other, but it did not change white evangelicals' prewar mingling of anxiety and action with resignation and serenity. Where southern evangelicals and women in particular had so often inserted themselves directly into God's unfolding narrative in their daily lives, however, they now watched passively as slavery unraveled.

White southerners' prewar willingness to omit their slaves from their collective vision of their household foreshadowed the postwar racial segregation of worship. Evangelical churches embarked on a new era of expansion after the war as they sought to address the prevailing spiritual, educational, and social chaos. Shifting away from the radically egalitarian and individualistic values and practices of the early nineteenth century as well as from the family-dominant values and practices of midcentury, postwar evangelical denominations focused on institutional growth. As white and black southerners turned to evangelical churches to provide economic welfare and literacy education along with religious education, women of both races readily and publicly embraced the call to sustain the institutional life of their churches.[5]

The Poultons were luckier than most Virginians during the Civil War. The Loudoun County couple experienced separations, but only once a year, during the Methodist Church's November annual meeting. And while so many Virginians experienced economic hardship when the battlefront and the home front merged, the Reverend John Poulton's career allowed him to continue making his livelihood in spite of the war's chaos. Indeed, compared to the ups and downs geographic separation caused the couple during their courtship in 1857–58, their marriage seemed remarkably stable during the Civil War. During their separations, John Poulton celebrated his marriage, family, and faith in warm tones that echo the attitudes of southern evangelical men in this era: "I feel almost lost without you," he wrote to his wife during one of his absences, "yet how sweet the thought that I have a dear, devoted and happy wife at home waiting for my return." After the birth of their first child, Eddy, in 1859, John offered parenting advice even when he was not at home. In keeping with the notion that God might reclaim infants who received excessive affection from doting mothers, he reminded Rose, "God will take care of you. Bless his dear life—he is the light and joy of our hearts. And yet I hope *you* do not think too much of him. I am sure *I* do not." Like other evangelical men, he relied on God's superintendence to relieve his wife's burdens and cares. He professed his longing for home yet demanded that Rose keep up with her housekeeping and parenting during his absences: "I want to see you badly. I hope you are well and happy. I hope you manage Eddy without difficulty. Don't forget my request—be prompt—be careful of little matters—little matters make up great matters—*be severe* if necessary—manage *him yourself.* Bless our darling, promising boy. You know now how anxious I am about his early training. One misstep may spoil all we have done. But I confide in your judgment."⁶ John Poulton's seemingly unbounded expectations for his wife's influence highlight the tremendous challenge southern mothers faced: they exercised the greatest, seemingly indelible influence over their children yet should refrain from excessive attention and affection.

John Poulton's absences, though infrequent, forced Rose to reconcile the physical risks of travel with the higher calling of his profession. Like many other evangelical women periodically separated from their husbands, as she weighed her interest in his preservation against his selflessness on behalf of the Methodist Church, she sought to transform his absences into spiritual renewal. Nonetheless, Rose could not help but contemplate the worst-case scenario: "I could feel resigned (I think) to the death of my children; but oh how could I ever give you up. You upon whom is lavished the whole wealth of my love? Oh never, never. And yet this is not right. I think of it sometimes and almost shudder. I know I should not care for life if you were taken from me. But this is a point I dare not trust myself upon."⁷ She pondered whether she had the spiritual mettle for such a heavy affliction.

Rose Poulton never confronted the scenario she feared most because she died from complications due to childbirth in 1869. In one obituary, J. Davenport Blackwell reminded the community that Rose's "meekness, patience, unselfishness, devotion, conscientiousness, united to illustrate in her the excellence of wife and mother." Less than ten months later, rumors began to spread that John was seeing and was perhaps even engaged to the daughter of another Methodist clergyman, opening old wounds between Poulton and his in-laws. Elizabeth Davisson's correspondence with her son-in-law shifted quickly from consolation to condemnation. At first she dismissed the gossip altogether, believing that it perhaps had resulted from a harmless visit by Poulton to a female parishioner that had been misperceived by an outsider as something more; Davisson then posited that the rumor might be explained by John's "excessive grief" over Rose's death. In any case, Davisson demanded a full explanation of his behavior, particularly if he expected his wife's family to continue to defend his name against such "slander." Elizabeth Davisson resurrected from John and

Rose's courtship Poulton's doubts regarding her family's approval of him: "I have fought some hard battles for you before you married my child," she wrote him, "but I am unable to do it now, if it becomes necessary, because I cannot think you will do right to get married under two years anyhow." Her tersely worded letter, written out of a sense of maternal duty because she believed herself the only adult woman from whom he might seek counsel, failed to dissuade Poulton from marrying Eva Watson fourteen months after Rose's death. Davisson freely criticized the choice, arguing that Poulton had married a "young wife but not a *mother* for your orphan children." Davisson's candor ultimately mingled with outrage when she wrote, "Believe me I am sincere when I hope you may be happy in the future while candidly I fear you will not."[8]

Two years later, Poulton still opened his letters to Davisson with "My dear Ma," and he still contended that enough time had elapsed between Rose's death and his second marriage. He argued that he had remarried out of necessity—particularly the need for child care. He then offered a "painful confession": "My present wife has many lovely qualities. She seems to love the children and I believe so—the best she can—but I will say to you what I have said to no other mortal. I never expect to be as happy as I was with my darling Rose. It does seem to me I love her more and more every day of my life." Poulton hoped that some combination of his undying love for Rose and the knowledge that he had remarried for the sake of his children would induce his mother-in-law to call a truce in the gossip war she and others were waging, conflict that Poulton claimed "frets and chafes my soul every day."[9]

Poulton endured other assaults on his character during this period. On October 21, 1871, another Methodist clergyman, William Pattie, charged that Poulton had collaborated to smear the name of another pastor. Moreover, Poulton was reportedly seen at both the circus and Baptist church services. The Methodist Conference dropped all of these charges in early 1872, but the damage to Poulton's reputation may already have been done.[10] But Rose Poulton retained an unsullied Christian reputation, a fact that undoubtedly offered quite a bit of consolation to her mother.

John and Rose Poulton's relationship illustrates the rich dynamics of authority, emotion, and faith that coursed through the family life of southern white evangelicals—Rose's persistent struggle to find words to evoke her feelings for John during their courtship in spite of her articulate writing on every other matter; a wealthy family's uncertainty regarding their daughter's choice of a mate, which created long-simmering resentment and tension; a wife who voiced conflict between her self-interest and her sense of Christian duty; a husband who celebrated domesticity as a unique site of spiritual clarity and communion; and a mother, Elizabeth Davisson, willing to stake claims to her grandchildren in the name of her deceased daughter's virtue and piety. After the Civil War, piety continued to shape conflict as well as consensus within the evangelical family, and women continued to lay claim to moral and religious authority based in a Christian framework.

Just as in earlier years when he had scoured the Midwest for a get-rich-quick investment scheme, Kentuckian Richard Collins patrolled the South during the Civil War in search of investment opportunities. His travels brought him face to face with the ravages of war. Writing in 1864 from aboard a steamship just above Natchez, Mississippi, Collins let loose his Confederate sympathies. Along the riverbank he saw countless charred homes with only chimneys left standing, and he lamented, "This is *war*; war on women and children; and the men who drove these women and children from their homes and then burnt down their homes . . . are called brave men; and shouted and hallooed, when they saw the flames bursting out of the windows and through the roofs." He further decried the takeover of southern Presbyterian churches by Union troops and northern philanthropic groups, alternately mocking their orthodoxy and their efforts to educate former slaves. In Memphis, however, Collins reported, it was possible to hear "the gospel unadulterated" at the First Presbyterian Church, where the congregation's lead pastor had not preached for nearly three months because he refused to take a loyalty oath to the United States. By vilifying Union destruction of civilian homes, the seat of domestic piety, as well as northern clergymen and philanthropists, who sullied the surviving pulpits and classrooms of his beloved Presbyterian Church, Collins had begun to forge a link between faith, family, and the Confederacy.[11]

At home, his wife, Mary, and her sisters lamented that the war had interrupted the familiar summertime pattern of family visits among kin scattered up and down the Ohio River. In 1861, one sister, Fanny Brodrick, invited Mary Collins and her children to leave Covington, Kentucky, and stay with Brodrick in Maysville should the Confederacy take nearby Cincinnati. Brodrick, a Unionist, scoffed at the Confederacy's ability to accomplish such an audacious goal but nonetheless welcomed the opportunity to spend more time with her sister and her family. The sisters, who had previously feared that Richard Collins's financial missteps might force his family to relocate even farther away, took relief in the notion that war might bring them closer together. Two years later, when Confederate raiders visited Maysville in the summer of 1863, female kin reported widely divergent stories to Mary Collins in Covington, underscoring just how divided their loyalties were. According to Lizzie Cox, the two hundred or so raiders "were very orderly and quiet after they first entered" and spent the bulk of their time and attention on the local population of single women. Ellen Blatterman, however, reported that the Confederates "stole a great many horses, clothing, boots, and shoes and hardware &c. to the amount of from 20 to 25 thousand dollars," and she hoped that "they will be well thrashed before they get out of the state. . . . [E]nough of rebels I pray God I may never see another."[12] Mostly, however, the women of the Cox and Collins families distanced themselves from political and military concerns even at the height of the war, focusing instead on maintaining their faith at home and at the meetinghouse.

Sustaining Maysville's Presbyterian Church proved difficult, not only because of the war but also because the pastorate was vacant. Church members questioned the political loyalties of potential pastors and became more financially cautious than ever, creating distrust and distress within the congregation. Mary Collins's sister, Lizzie Cox, viewed the internecine wars of the congregation and nation in nothing short of apocalyptic terms: "It seems to me that this must be the close of the 'thousand years' when Satan should be let loose upon the earth and these are his last dying throes, his struggles for victory." Yet over time, her youthful exuberance gave way to a message from one of her favorite pastors, Rev. R. L. Breck: "The true Christian cannot escape or shun suffering if he would, but with it all there is strength and grace given to bear it." Lizzie Cox was not the only member of the congregation who liked Breck: Fanny Brodrick reported the formation of a committee of three men and two women to collect pledges sufficient to entice Breck to take the pastorate permanently and put an end to the wartime parade of interim pastors. Although the committee's efforts failed and the church continued to languish without strong leadership, the fact that the delegation included women shows the importance of female participation in any attempt to save the congregation. The women of the Cox and Collins families had long played an integral role in the operations of the Maysville Presbyterian Church (see chap. 1). In the fall of 1863, when yet another clergyman, Dr. Breckenridge, was being considered for the pulpit, Brodrick was eager to have the candidate for dinner so that she could evaluate him closely. Tentatively at least, she was "delighted with him as a preacher and he is pleasant in the social circle." Brodrick continued to voice her anguish over her congregation's political and religious divisions yet found a way to make sense of the seeming chaos: "This *rending* of our churches in our land, I verily believe this is *man's* work, but Christ can make all things work for the good of *His* church, in this is my trust."[13] Discerning between the work of man and God in a time of civil war would have seemed daunting had southern women not had extensive experience routinely performing such tasks before the war.

Keeping their political differences in check, the women of the Cox and Collins families set out to preserve their faith, their families, and their congregation. They took solace in God's control of events and pledged one another to God's safekeeping as they professed resignation to God's will. Yet they also worked actively to interpret God's plans in the midst of the chaos and fought to protect the things they cherished—their family and their congregation—from the war's harsh realities.

Although white southerners' wartime attitudes toward their slaves demonstrate an unwillingness to question racism, southern women increasingly questioned prevailing attitudes toward gender. Oriented toward white women's public work in benevolent movements and paid work as well as women's increasing self-reliance within the household economy, recent studies stress that women who came of age in the Civil War era challenged the most limiting aspects of the antebellum South's patriarchal society even if they did not focus their efforts on politics. Women's postwar participation in new roles within and beyond their families frequently stemmed from an inclination to save southern souls.[14] As the examples from the Poulton and Collins/Cox families suggest, that inclination may have originated in the antebellum era, when southern evangelical women exercised considerable authority over domestic devotion, even occasionally calling into question male prerogative when matters of faith and family intersected. Elizabeth Davisson's quest to retain her family's honor in spite of John Poulton's second marriage and other missteps and Mary Collins's female relatives' quest to reassure her that they understood her anguish may seem limited because of their domestic emphasis, but they illustrate the extension of womanly authority within the family. John Poulton's plea that the members of the Davisson family cease their private and public attacks on him suggests that his in-laws had considerable success in impugning his reputation and thereby vindicating Rose Davisson's name and the legacy of her children. And as Mary Collins's sisters and sisters-in-law offered her their support, they clearly called into question her husband's decision making. That chorus of criticism isolated Richard Collins within his family and increased his reliance on his wife for moral and financial support of his business operations. Fanny Brodrick continued the long tradition of laywomen's scrutiny of clergymen. In the name of Christian resignation and often with the approval of their male kin, evangelical white women in the antebellum South routinely shifted between claiming and renouncing authority in the name of personal and familial piety. Although white women's postwar efforts received greater official sanction and became bureaucratically organized, women had always been central to the institutional life of southern evangelical churches. Their prewar work and calling may have been oriented around the family, but evangelical women used their faith to transform their communities, their families, and themselves. Little remained static on any of these fronts. Indeed, evangelicals began searching their souls at conversion and never let up. Since they envisioned God's judgment and providence in their everyday lives, they could not distance themselves from self-reflection. Consequently, their postconversion pilgrimages to salvation were neither effortless nor steady and increasingly occurred in the context of the family, where kin more than clergy judged the authenticity of everyday piety and counseled loved ones. In the process, the southern clergy's declaration of women's superior piety, even if only in the household, provided women with unlikely latitude both domestically and beyond. With growing responsibility over domestic piety in particular, women confronted the potential for a spiritual catastrophe, where the failure to control outcomes jeopardized a family's hope of eternal reunification and the female steward bore the burden of discerning the reasons behind God's seeming disfavor. And as in the antebellum era, white women played an integral role in maintaining racial segregation after the Civil War. Women's persistent struggle to minister to their families and their congregations underscores Donald Mathews's point that "women made southern Evangelicalism possible."[15]

APPENDIX

Principal Families

Mary Jeffreys Bethell (1821–?) and William D. Bethell (1815?–?)
Mary Jeffreys Bethell Diary, Southern Historical Collection, Wilson Library, University of North Carolina, Chapel Hill

Mary and William were a wealthy Methodist couple from Rockingham County, North Carolina, who had five children in the 1850 U.S. Census and twenty-five slaves in their household. The Census lists William's occupation as farmer, and he considered relocating his household to Arkansas. Mary Bethell's diary records her devotional struggles and the challenges of rearing devout children, including seven of her own and four orphans. (William D. Bethell, Manuscript Population Schedules, Rockingham, North Carolina, Seventh Census, 1850, p. 5)

Mary Davis Brown (1822–1903) and Robert Brown (?–1855)
Mary Davis Brown Journal, in Jane Dupree Begos, comp., *American Women's Diaries*, segment 2, *Southern Women* (microfilm, 34 reels, Readex, 1988–90), reel 3

Mary Davis was a Presbyterian who married clergyman Robert Jackson Brown, her first cousin and the pastor of Beersheba Church. The couple lived in York County, South Carolina, and had eleven children.

Frances Bumpass (1819–98) and Sidney Bumpass (1808–51)
Bumpass Family Papers, Southern Historical Collection, Wilson Library, University of North Carolina, Chapel Hill

Sidney Bumpass was a Methodist clergyman in North Carolina and editor of the *Greensboro Weekly Message*. His diary captures his conversion and early work for the Methodist Church. In addition to illuminating the experiences and expectations placed on a minister's wife, her diary captures her struggles to sustain her family after her husband's death. In spite of her reservations and of resistance from Methodist clergymen, Frances clung tenaciously to editorship of her husband's newspaper for twenty years.

Mary Cox Collins (1823–?) and Richard Collins (1824–88)
Richard Collins Journal and Collins Family Letters, 1808–1895, 51M13, Special Collections and Digital Programs, University of Kentucky Libraries, Lexington

Mary Cox and Richard Collins belonged to the First Presbyterian Church of Maysville, Kentucky, where his father, Lewis Collins, served as a church elder.

After their marriage, Richard Collins set out to equal his father's success, working as an attorney, editor of the Maysville Eagle, land speculator, and author (most importantly of the History of Kentucky [1874], which relied heavily on his father's earlier Historical Sketches of Kentucky [1848]). Richard's business ventures repeatedly failed, and he filed for bankruptcy more than once, although the 1850 U.S. Census records him as owning $13,000 in property. His temporary absences from home on business, which often lasted several weeks, and the relocation of his family from Maysville to Covington, Kentucky, created friction with both his wife and his extended family. Mary received many letters of support from her sisters, Fanny and Lizzie, and sisters-in-law, Ellen and Kate. The couple had six children, five of whom survived childhood. While the 1830 Census shows Richard's father owning two slaves, Richard and Mary typically had one foreign-born young woman living with them, presumably working as a servant. (Richard Henry Collins, Manuscript Population Schedules, Maysville, Kentucky, Seventh Census, 1850, p. 56; Lewis Collins, Manuscript Population Schedules, Maysville, Kentucky, Fifth Census, 1830, p. 177)

Mary Kelly Craddock (1802–46) and Pascal Craddock (1791–1856)
Mary K. Craddock Diary and Craddock Family Papers, Filson Historical Society, Louisville, Kentucky

Married to Pascal in 1820 and a member of the Cumberland Presbyterian Church in Louisville, Kentucky, Mary continually lamented the failure of her family, including her children, to convert. Undeterred, she declared in her journal that she would continue to seek their conversion along with that of her neighbors and slaves. Records from the family Bible suggest that Mary and Pascal Craddock had seven children and owned many slaves. A lawyer, Pascal speculated heavily in land and slaves in the Bashford Manor area of Louisville, leading him to frequent court battles with business rivals and neighbors. He was murdered in August 1856, only six months after his neighbors publicly demanded that he and several of his associates leave Kentucky. (Pangburn, Pascal Craddock Mystery)

Anne Beale Davis (1809–94) and Joseph Hoomes Davis (1809–79)
Beale and Davis Family Papers, Southern Historical Collection, Wilson Library, University of North Carolina, Chapel Hill

After the death of her sister, Martha (Nannie) in 1835, Anne Beale first cared for her sister's surviving infant, Robert, and later married her sister's widower, Joseph Davis, a Methodist clergyman. Anne and Joseph went on to have four children of their own. Joseph Davis received appointments in both Virginia and North Carolina (the 1850 Census records them living in Fredericksburg, Virginia), and the couple worked together to start and maintain the Wesleyan Female College in Murfreesboro, North Carolina, in the 1850s. Their sons attended Randolph-

Macon College and the University of Virginia. (Joseph H. Davis, Manuscript Population Schedules, Fredericksburg, Virginia, Seventh Census, 1850, p. 368)

James Walter Douglass (1797–1837) and Frances Ann Richardson Taylor Douglass
James Walter Douglass Correspondence, 1800–1897, Rare Book, Manuscript, and Special Collections Library, Duke University, Durham, North Carolina

James Walter Douglass served as a Presbyterian minister in Virginia and North Carolina until his unexpected death in Fayetteville, North Carolina. Frances Douglass corresponded with her son from her previous marriage, Henry Taylor, and their letters highlight the often contentious relationship between evangelical mothers and their children as they approached adulthood. Frances also corresponded with two rival Presbyterian clergymen, William Plumer and Simeon Colton, regarding access to James Douglass's sermons for posthumous publication in rival New School and Old School Presbyterian newspapers. These letters reveal Frances's central role in shaping her husband's ministerial legacy, efforts that went well beyond serving as executrix of her husband's will. After James's death, Frances also maintained regular correspondence on death, family, and faith with a woman addressed only as "sister Mary"—most likely, James's sister, Mary Douglass Gray, who resided in Virginia and later St. Charles, Missouri.

Elizabeth Brown Rives Early (1805–57) and John Early (1786–1873)
Early Family Papers, Virginia Historical Society, Richmond

John Early served as a Methodist minister and then bishop of the Methodist Episcopal Church, South, while living in Lynchburg, Virginia. His wife, Elizabeth, corresponded regularly with their daughter, Mary Virginia Early, who attended boarding school at the Female Collegiate Institute in Buckingham County, Virginia, and then married and started a family. Elizabeth Early provided unusually vivid insight into the 1839 conversion of one of the family's slaves. According to the 1840 Census, the family owned eight slaves, including five women. (Jonathan Early, Manuscript Population Schedules, Campbell County, Virginia, Sixth Census, 1840, p. 27)

Fountain, Coker, and Lide Families
Lide-Coker Family Papers, 1827–94, and Papers of the Lide, Coker, and Stout Families, 1828–1914, South Caroliniana Library, University of South Carolina, Columbia

Sarah Lide Fountain (c. 1798?–?) and her family, natives of Darlington County, South Carolina, migrated to Alabama in 1835. Sarah corresponded regularly with her cousin, Hannah Lide Coker (1812–1900), who remained in South Carolina, about life as a Baptist in antebellum Alabama, near Carlowville and Mount Pleasant. The Fountains offered keen observations about denominational competition on the Alabama frontier and helped transplant their Baptist faith by hosting Rev. Jesse Hartwell while his home was being constructed in 1837. Other women from the Lide and Fountain families in Alabama—including Maria Lide and Sarah's daughter, Lizzie Fountain—corresponded with their Coker kin in Society Hill, South Carolina, throughout the antebellum era. The women often leaned on their piety to close the distance between South Carolina and the Alabama frontier.

Anna Thomas Fuller (1825?–?) and Jones Fuller (1808–70)
Fuller-Thomas Papers, Rare Book, Manuscript, and Special Collections Library, Duke University, Durham, North Carolina

Originally from Louisburg, North Carolina, Jones Fuller migrated to Mobile, Alabama, where he worked principally as a cotton broker. From Alabama he continued to court Anna Thomas, who remained in North Carolina. As their courtship neared engagement in 1846–47, Jones Fuller found himself in the middle of a strenuous debate over his fitness as a suitor and whether Anna's filial duties required her to remain in North Carolina to care for her mother, Ann Thomas. By the time of the 1860 U.S. Census, Anna and Jones Fuller had returned to Franklin County, North Carolina, where the couple had two children, eight slaves, $7,000 in real estate, and more than $130,000 in personal estate. (Jones Fuller, Manuscript Population Schedules, Mobile, Alabama, Seventh Census, 1850, p. 322; Jones Fuller, Manuscript Population Schedules, Franklin, North Carolina, Eighth Census, 1860, p. 508)

Gaston, Boyd, and Crawford Families
Gaston-Crawford Family Papers, South Caroliniana Library, University of South Carolina, Columbia

Presbyterians with roots in South Carolina, these women, like the Baptist Lide and Coker families, sought to maintain spiritual intimacy even as their families migrated westward to Alabama. Martha Gaston and Mary Boyd provided regular updates from Dallas and Wilcox Counties, Alabama, to their cousin, Jane Gaston, who resided in the vicinity of Chester, South Carolina.

Lucy Ann Garlick Gwathmey (1806–91) and Richard Gwathmey (1789–1866)
Gwathmey Family Papers, Virginia Historical Society, Richmond

This Baptist couple lived in Hanover County, Virginia, and offer insight into child-rearing patterns among elite lay evangelicals. The couple often exhorted their children—including their daughter, Eleanor (Nelly, 1842–1931), who attended a female academy, and their son, Edward (1839–1931), who attended the University of Virginia in the 1850s—to guard their faith. The 1850 Census records Richard Gwathmey as owning twelve thousand dollars worth of real estate and twenty-eight slaves. (Richard Gwathmey, Manuscript Population Schedules, Hanover, Virginia, Seventh Census, 1850, p. 363)

Samuel Haycraft (1795–1878)
Samuel Haycraft Journal, 1849–78, Filson Historical Society, Louisville, Kentucky

Haycraft was a Baptist layman from Elizabethtown, Kentucky, who recorded his daily activities and religious reading in his journal. According to the 1850 Census, he worked as a county clerk, was married, had three children, and owned real estate valued at $19,460. In 1857, he was elected to the Kentucky State Senate. (Samuel Haycraft, Manuscript Population Schedules, Northern District, Hardin, Kentucky, Seventh Census, 1850, p. 306)

Samuel Henderson Jr. (1804–76?)
Samuel Henderson Jr. Diary, Microfilm #148, Tennessee State Library and Archives, Nashville

A wealthy planter, physician, and lay Methodist, Henderson lived in Franklin, Tennessee. Early in the Civil War, his slaves ran away to nearby Union-occupied Nashville. Samuel married Rachael Jane Henderson in 1844; she died of typhoid fever in 1858. The couple had six children. (Samuel Henderson Jr., Manuscript Population Schedules, Williamson County, Tennessee, Seventh Census, 1850, p. 260)

Mary Hort (1796–1872?)
Mary Hort Papers, 1830–68, South Caroliniana Library, University of South Carolina, Columbia

Originally from Britain, Hort was an unmarried woman who lived in Sumter, South Carolina, where she worked as a schoolteacher. She reported on her frequent attendance at evangelical services, including Baptist, Methodist, and Presbyterian churches. According to the 1850 Census, she owned two slaves. (Mary Hort, Manuscript Population Schedules, Sumterville, South Carolina, Seventh Census, 1850, p. 428)

Eliza Hibben Leland (1796–1856), Aaron Leland (1787–1881), and Eugenia Rebecca Griffin Leland (1824–96)
Eliza Hibben Leland Journal, 1850 Dec.–1856 Dec. 26, Eugenia Rebecca Griffin Leland Journal, 1865–68, South Caroliniana Library, University of South Carolina, Columbia

Aaron Leland was a Presbyterian clergyman and professor at Columbia Theological Seminary. He and his wife, Eliza, lived in Columbia, South Carolina, where Eliza kept a revealing journal about the clergymen she heard speak, including such luminaries as James H. Thornwell. The couple's son, Horace Leland (1820–85), married Eugenia Rebecca Griffin, who maintained a journal detailing the intersection of her Presbyterian faith and her growing family amid slavery's end in their hometown of Ninety Six, South Carolina.

Susan Heiskell McCampbell (1834–1917) and William McCampbell (1830–64)
Collection of Heiskell, McCampbell, Wilkes, and Steel Family Materials, Southern Historical Collection, Wilson Library, University of North Carolina, Chapel Hill

William McCampbell was an attorney and the son of a clergyman from Dandridge, Tennessee, just outside Knoxville, while Susan Heiskell lived with her family at the nearby Fruit Hill Plantation. Their correspondence illustrates an evangelical man's coming of age, the shift from courtship to marriage, and William's concerns for his two children and his wife during his service with the Confederate Army.

Rosannah Davisson Poulton (1835–69) and John Poulton (1831–1901)
Poulton Family Papers, 1852–86, Virginia Historical Society, Richmond

John Poulton served as a dentist and Methodist clergyman in several Virginia cities, including Warrenton and Petersburg. After their courtship in 1857–58, the couple married and had several children. Rose died of complications during childbirth. Her widowed mother, Elizabeth Davisson (1812–81) challenged John's care for her grandchildren and attempted to delay his remarriage to Eva Watson, the daughter of a local Methodist clergyman.

Frances Jane Bestor Robertson (1829–?) and J. G. Robertson (1819?–74)
Frances Jane Bestor Robertson Journal, in Jane Dupree Begos, comp., American Women's Diaries, segment 2, Southern Women [microfilm, 34 reels, Readex, 1988–90], reel 2

Frances Jane Bestor was the daughter of a noted Baptist clergyman, Daniel Perrin Bestor, and lived in Alabama. According to the 1850 U.S. Census, Frances's father was forty-six and mother forty-four, and she had four siblings, though she was eleven years older than her next oldest sibling. Her father owned forty-six slaves. Frances married widower J. G. Robertson in November 1854 and relocated to Clarke County, Mississippi. According to the 1860 U.S. Census, Robertson was a merchant with $400 in real estate and $17,100 in personal estate. He had two children from his earlier marriage, a situation that heightened Frances's anxiety regarding their courtship. The couple eventually had three children together. (Daniel P. Bestor, Manuscript Population Schedules, Gainesville, Sumter, Alabama, Seventh Census, 1850, p. 320; J. G. Robertson, Manuscript Population Schedules, Eighth Census, 1860, Clarke County, Mississippi, p. 121)

Tristram, Rebecca, and Charlotte Verstille
Tristram Verstille Papers, 1811–1960, South Caroliniana Library, University of South Carolina, Columbia

Tristram and Rebecca married in 1812 and settled in Robertville, South Carolina. Charlotte, Tristram's sister, lived with the couple for some time, relaying this Presbyterian family's concerns to kin in Connecticut and Massachusetts in the 1820s and 1830s.

Anna Whitaker Wills (1817–93) and William Wills (1809–89)
William Henry Wills Papers, 1712–1921, Southern Historical Collection, Wilson Library, University of North Carolina, Chapel Hill

William Wills was a successful businessman, cotton planter, and Methodist Protestant clergyman who rose quickly to leadership positions within his denomination. The couple resided in Halifax County, North Carolina, where the 1860 Census records them as having eight children ranging in age from two to twenty-three. They also enjoyed considerable wealth. According to the 1850 Census, they possessed twenty-one slaves; ten years later, they claimed more than $15,000 in real estate and nearly $30,000 in personal property. Their oldest son, Richard, joined his father in the clergy, while a younger son, George, died in Civil War combat. The Wills correspondence delves deeply into personal, family, and professional concerns. (William H. Wills, Manuscript Population Schedules, Seventh Census, 1850, Halifax, North Carolina, p. 85; W[illiam]. H. Wills, Manuscript Population Schedules, Western District, Halifax, North Carolina, Eighth Census, 1860, p. 456)

NOTES

Introduction. From Cane Ridge to the Bible Belt

1. Mary K. Craddock Diary, May 23, 1842. Unless a full citation is provided in the notes, consult the appendix for locations of all unpublished works cited.

2. According to Heyrman, the percentage of white southerners over the age of sixteen who held membership in the Methodist, Baptist, and Presbyterian churches jumped from 14.9 percent in 1790 to 25.6 percent in 1835. When adding church "adherents," or nonmembers who often attended worship services, to the membership numbers, Heyrman estimates that among adult white southerners, 38.8 percent in 1790 and 65.8 percent in 1835 had "regular contact with evangelical preaching." See Heyrman, *Southern Cross*, appendix, tables 5, 6, and 7, pp. 264–65. For an enumeration of Baptist, Presbyterian, and Methodist churches, see Gaustad and Barlow, *New Historical Atlas*, 78–83, 131–33, 219–21. On the broader influence of evangelical thought and evangelical institutions in the Old South, see, for example, Fox-Genovese, "Religion," 209; McCurry, *Masters of Small Worlds*, 158–60; Mathews, *Religion in the Old South*, 47–48. For local studies that demonstrate that white women routinely outnumbered white men in the pews of evangelical churches in this era, see, for example, Bode, "Transformation," 723; Gregory Wills, *Democratic Religion*, 54; Sparks, *On Jordan's Stormy Banks*, 44, 49; Friedman, *Enclosed Garden*, 4; Kierner, *Beyond the Household*, 184–85. As Sparks points out in his study of Mississippi's evangelical churches, the dominance of women is all the more impressive where they comprised a minority of the population, as they did in Mississippi.

3. Mary K. Craddock Diary, November 12, 1849.

4. For studies that demonstrate how women used conservative language to advance their interests, see Bode, "Common Sphere"; Kierner, "Women's Piety within Patriarchy."

5. William McCampbell to Susan Heiskell, March 22, 1858, Collection of Heiskell, McCampbell, Wilkes, and Steel Family Materials; Heyrman, *Southern Cross*, 158–59.

6. Kierner, *Beyond the Household*, 199.

7. Lewis also notes the ways in which early nineteenth-century evangelicalism created profound distress among believers, arguing that as "evangelical religion increased doubt and heightened pain, it also reassured that those feelings were marks of grace," ultimately creating "a suit of armor and a fortress, a means to protect and isolate the individual from the cruelty of others and of life itself" (*Pursuit of Happiness*, 62, 67).

8. See Kierner, *Beyond the Household*, 212–18, esp. 216.

9. Even with "an excellent practical sermon," "good singing *by the choir*," Bible reading, and meditation, Richard lamented that he "could not so confine [his] attention but that *home* would come up before [him]" (Richard Collins to Mary Cox Collins, April 19, 1857, Collins Family Letters). For additional examples of men who craved domestic devotion, see chaps. 1, 4.

10. Schweiger, "Max Weber on Mount Airy," 48.

11. Mathews, *Religion in the Old South*, xvi–xvii; Mathews, "'Christianizing the South,'" 87. Mathews also expands his definition of evangelicalism: "Essential was the personal experience of being convicted of sin after a period of self-examination followed by a further experience of being declared righteous, that is, justified by faith in the efficacious death of Christ Jesus. This experience would be accompanied (or followed) by a further inner assurance that this new found righteousness was authentic (that saints would persevere), that one had indeed been born of the spirit (born again—John 3:3–8) and was committed to living a life guided by study of the Bible, and discipline by fellow believers" ("'Christianizing the South,'" 86). Orsi defines cosmology as "the people's religion defined as the totality of their ultimate values, their most deeply held ethical convictions, their efforts to order their reality. . . . This could be called their 'ground of being,' but only if this is understood in a very concrete, social-historical way, not as a reality beyond their lives, but as the *reason* that, consciously and unconsciously, structured and was expressed in their actions and reflections. More simply stated, *religion* here means 'what matters'" (*Madonna of 115th Street*, xvii). For definitions that stress the core values that spanned evangelical denominations, see, for example, Owen, *Sacred Flame of Love*, 16; Sparks, *On Jordan's Stormy Banks*, 1–2; Sweet, *Health and Medicine*, 3–5; Lyerly, *Methodism and the Southern Mind*, 17; Payne, *Self and the Sacred*, 3–4.

12. Hall, *Lived Religion in America*, vii; Orsi, "Everyday Miracles," 7, 15. Orsi argues that "four things are necessary to understand religious practice" in this approach: "(1) a sense of the range of idiomatic possibility and limitation in a culture—the limits of what can be desired, fantasized, imagined, and felt; (2) an understanding of the knowledges of the body in the culture, a clear sense of what has been embodied in the corporeality of the people who participate in religious practices, what their tongues, skin, ears, 'know'; (3) an understanding of the structures of social experience—marriage and kinship patterns, moral and juridical responsibilities and expectations, the allocation of valued resources, and so on; and (4) a sense of what sorts of characteristic tensions erupt within these particular structures" ("Everyday Miracles," 7).

13. As scholars have recently noted, gender probably merits at least equal scholarly attention to class as a category of analysis. While the vicissitudes of the antebellum economy might quickly shift a family's class standing, constructions

of gender remained fairly stable and even permitted relationships across class boundaries. See Cashin, *Our Common Affairs*, 10; Kierner, *Beyond the Household*, 4.

14. On the need to appreciate the theological rigor of southern clergymen in this era, see, for example, Holifield, *Gentlemen Theologians*, 3–4; Farmer, *Metaphysical Confederacy*, 2–6.

15. Lewis, *Pursuit of Happiness*, 221. On the intersection of evangelical values and the South's emerging middle class, see Wells, *Origins*, 76–85.

16. Lewis, *Pursuit of Happiness*, 228

17. Schneider, *Way of the Cross*, 50–51.

18. On the advantages of this approach, see Bingham, "Thou Knowest Not," 68–69.

19. Fox-Genovese, *Within the Plantation Household*, 251.

20. Anne Beale Davis Diary, December 1838, Beale and Davis Family Papers.

21. Scott notes this stark contrast in the attitudes of Davis's diary and correspondence: "It may be that one way to manage fears and anxieties is to write them down, after which one can then go on to live a reasonably normal life. Some hint of this is contained in a huge collection preserved at the University of North Carolina, wherein a woman's religious diary is as perfervid as any to be found, while her daily letters to sons away at school are matter-of-fact and down to earth, with only the normal amount of reference to salvation, church attendance, and the like." Ultimately, however, Scott believes that evangelical women's overriding concern for salvation kept them obsessed with themselves and the slightest sins they might commit, causing them "to apologize abjectly for the very qualities which make a woman (or a man for that matter) an interesting and rich personality—for spirit, for a roving mind, for pride to think well of themselves" (*Making the Invisible Woman Visible*, 196–97). Additional references to the Davis diary appear in the works of Friedman (*Enclosed Garden*, 4, 5, 18 n.80), who employed Davis's journal to illustrate the electric power of conversion and the lifetime of struggle needed to remain on the path toward salvation. The contrast between Davis's diary and her correspondence also emerges in publications that profile Davis's activities as a boarding school matron. Unlike treatments that use her diary to underscore her sense of failure as a Christian, these works rely heavily on her correspondence to underscore a woman who confidently executes her role as an "assistant principal in charge of student life." See Farnham, *Education*, 132, 139; Stephenson, "Davises," 269, 273.

22. I owe an obvious debt to all of the scholars who have already worked with these documents. In addition, Cashin's outstanding collection of primary source materials, *Our Common Affairs*, led me to several useful families.

23. Frances Douglass to James Walter Douglass, May 31, 1837, James Walter Douglass Correspondence.

24. On the relationship between slave mistresses and slaves, see, for example, Weiner, *Mistresses and Slaves*, chap. 4; Fox-Genovese, *Within the Plantation Household*, 328–30; Cole, "Servants and Slaves."

25. On slaveholders' surprising paucity of references to slaves, see Stowe, *Intimacy and Power*, xvi–xvii; Lewis, *Pursuit of Happiness*, 141. Similarly, on the gap in affection evidenced in planters' discussions of their offspring and those of their slaves, see Censer, *North Carolina Planters*, 139–40. On how white evangelicals constructed a heaven free of blacks, see the epilogue; Ownby, "Patriarchy."

26. Lyerly, "Women and Southern Religion," 249.

27. For a critique of the ways in which individualism and concerns regarding the South's political economy have overshadowed the field of gender in southern religious history, see Schweiger, "Max Weber on Mount Airy." On the need to "put aside both the standard of a reform-oriented culture on the Northern model and a radical counterculture on the order of the 1960s" in analyzing southern women's history, see Cashin, *Our Common Affairs*, 7.

28. These works on southern evangelicalism define many core issues of the field—revivalism, individualism, racism, and the shift from sects to denominations—but often privilege moral assessments over analysis and make hasty leaps between individual believers and southern culture writ large. Later writings by some of these scholars criticize their earlier efforts. Mathews, for example, recently described his early work, along with that of Hill, as "possibly too moral, certainly too ironic, and probably too densely crafted in fusing history and ethics" ("'We Have Left Undone,'" 311). Hill's recent reprise to *Southern Churches in Crisis* sums up these weaknesses: an inattention to the role of gender and the homogenization of evangelicalism at the expense of denominational, regional, and class variations (xxiii–xxiv).

29. Boles, *Great Revival*, 183.

30. See, for example, Klein, *Unification of a Slave State*; Aron, *How the West Was Lost*, chap. 8.

31. Heyrman, *Southern Cross*, esp. chap. 5; Lyerly, *Methodism and the Southern Mind*, 176–86.

32. Snay, *Gospel of Disunion*; Daly, *When Slavery Was Called Freedom*; Farmer, *Metaphysical Confederacy*; Goen, *Broken Churches, Broken Nation*.

33. Kuykendall, *Southern Enterprize*.

34. Scott, *Southern Lady*, 14, 17.

35. Fox-Genovese, *Within the Plantation Household*, 40, 38. For Clinton's development and definition of the term *New Englandization* of women's studies, see *Plantation Mistress*, xv. For additional efforts at synthesizing the literature on women and family in the Old South, see, for example, Cashin, *Our Common Affairs*, 1–41; Edwards, *Scarlett Doesn't Live Here Anymore*, chaps. 1–3. For analysis of the ways in which northern middle-class women transformed their growing

moral authority over the domestic sphere into expanded authority in the public sphere, see, for example, Cott, *Bonds of Womanhood*; Ryan, *Cradle of the Middle Class*.

36. Clinton, *Plantation Mistress*, 95–96. Clinton concludes, "Myth and manipulation combined to keep females subordinated. The cult of the lady may have been in part a collaboration: southern gentlemen enshrined and adorned their females, while women were willing to exhibit these 'ladylike' virtues. Oppression thus was exercised not only through sanctions against rebellion but internally, as women's compliance with the silencing stereotypes determined their own self-censuring behavior" (97).

37. Friedman, *Enclosed Garden*, 37; Scott, *Southern Lady*, chap. 3. In a reprise to *Southern Lady*, Scott identifies miscegenation as "the fatal flaw in the patriarchal doctrine." But in a separate essay, she argues, "The southern women who left a record . . . were expected to be meek, mild, quiet, outside their homes, self-abnegating, kind to all, and to accept their husbands as lord and master" (*Making the Invisible Woman Visible*, 180, 191–92). On the differences between Friedman's and Fox-Genovese's interpretations of patriarchy's impact on the lives of white southern women, see Fox-Genovese, *Within the Plantation Household*, 44.

38. Fox-Genovese, "Religion," 219. See also Genovese and Fox-Genovese, "Religious Ideals."

39. "If men were encouraged to assume responsibility for others whom they were also obliged to govern and discipline, women were encouraged to accept governance" (Genovese and Fox-Genovese, "Religious Ideals," 15). According to Fox-Genovese, "Slaveholding women fully understood that, from the perspective of their society and, especially, their clergy, the arguments for slavery depended on and were grounded in the prior argument for woman's subordination to man" ("Religion," 208).

40. McCurry, *Masters of Small Worlds*, 185, 196, 197.

41. Several studies certainly challenge this consensus position on the relationship between gender and evangelicalism. For a historiographical synthesis that captures the consensus view, see Cashin, *Our Common Affairs*, esp. 18–19, 22–24. For examples of works that challenge aspects of that viewpoint, see, for example, Lebsock, *Free Women of Petersburg*; Sparks, *On Jordan's Stormy Banks*, chap. 3; Pogue, "'I Cannot Believe.'" For illuminating studies of evangelicalism's dynamics within the southern household, see, for example, Bode, "Common Sphere"; Kierner, "Women's Piety within Patriarchy."

42. Heyrman, *Southern Cross*; Lyerly, *Methodism and the Southern Mind*; Wigger, *Taking Heaven by Storm*; Andrews, *Methodists and Revolutionary America*; Lindman, "Acting the Manly Christian." On the application of the democratization thesis to the entire nation, see Hatch, *Democratization of American Christianity*. Rankin, *Ambivalent Churchmen and Evangelical Churchwomen*, also

shows how elite white women in particular gravitated toward the Methodist Church in the early national South.

43. Gregory Wills, *Democratic Religion*, chap. 4, esp. 51–53; Sparks, *On Jordan's Stormy Banks*, chap. 3, esp. 50–51; Bode, "Common Sphere," 783–85.

44. Quist, *Restless Visionaries*.

45. Schweiger, *Gospel Working Up*.

46. Mathews, *Religion in the Old South*, 97–124. More recent studies that also note that tension include Sparks, *On Jordan's Stormy Banks*, 41–59, esp. 58–59; McCurry, *Masters of Small Worlds*, 130–70; Bode, "Common Sphere."

Chapter 1. Taming the Second Great Awakening

1. Lyerly, *Methodism and the Southern Mind*, 184. Although the Methodists retained greater faith in the efficacy of camp meetings and the anxious bench, its use cut across denomination, particularly in the earliest years of the Second Great Awakening. For a variety of perspectives on camp meetings, emotional conversions, and the anxious bench, see Heyrman, *Southern Cross*, 33–41; Cross, *Burned-Over District*, 173–84; Hambrick-Stowe, *Charles G. Finney*, 108–9; Richey, *Early American Methodism*, 21–32; Eslinger, *Citizens of Zion*, 218–41; Wigger, *Taking Heaven by Storm*; Bruce, *And They All Sang Hallelujah*, 61–95; Boles, *Great Revival*; Gregory Wills, *Democratic Religion*, 34; Hatch, *Democratization of American Christianity*, 49–56.

2. See Heyrman, *Southern Cross*, 33–41. For other treatments of conversion that suggest this point, see, for example, Schweiger, "Max Weber on Mount Airy," 49–51; Payne, *Self and the Sacred*; Schneider, *Way of the Cross*, 42–77; Mathews, *Religion in the Old South*, 59; Bruce, *And They All Sang Hallelujah*, 77–79; Boles, *Great Revival*, 131–35.

3. Douglass, *Work to Do*, 15. In his study of the conversion experience, Rambo echoes many of Douglass's points: "Conversion is precarious; it must be defended, nurtured, supported, affirmed. It needs community, confirmation, and concurrence" (*Understanding Religious Conversion*, 170).

4. To counter the perception of antebellum southern evangelicalism as anti-intellectual and static, several scholars use church and clergy records to demonstrate the intellectual rigor of southern clergymen. See, for example, Holifield, *Gentlemen Theologians*; Farmer, *Metaphysical Confederacy*; O'Brien, *Conjectures of Order*, 1067–1157.

5. For an insightful look into how Baptist and Methodist clergymen in antebellum Virginia constructed expansive organizations—meetinghouses, seminaries, publishing enterprises, and the like—yet accounted for the informal power of their congregations, see Schweiger, *Gospel Working Up*, 77–89. On the broader debate over the sources of evangelicalism's institutional success during the early national era, see Hatch, *Democratization of American Christianity*

(pointing to evangelicalism's populist ethos); Butler, *Awash*, 225–88 (highlighting evangelicalism's coercive, institutional thrust). For an insightful critical essay that suggests ways to incorporate both perspectives into the patterns of nineteenth-century American religious history, see Stein, "Radical Protestantism and Religious Populism."

6. McDannell, *Christian Home*, 49.

7. Schneider, *Way of the Cross*, 42–58. Although Schneider focuses on Methodism, he adds that "the psychological pattern of self-denial leading to joy, peace, and spiritual labor was not, of course, the sole property of Methodism. Baptist and Presbyterian documents of the period display similar sorts of emotional patterning" (*Way of the Cross*, 56). Lewis also articulates the emotional perils of domestic piety for southern women (*Pursuit of Happiness*, 59–68).

8. Bruce, *And They All Sang Hallelujah*, 126. Loveland, *Southern Evangelicals*, 91–129, advances a similar argument using clerical sources.

9. Loveland argues that antebellum southern evangelicals "set themselves against popular opinion and were sharply critical of the actions of 'public men.' On other issues, such as slavery, evangelicals were more in line with the dominant ideology, yet they never went so far as to defend slavery as a 'positive good,' and their demands for religious instruction of the Negroes often contained an implicit criticism of the Old South's 'peculiar institution'" (*Southern Evangelicals*, ix–x). McCurry, conversely, sees no vestiges of evangelicalism's early national antislavery attitudes in her study of antebellum South Carolina's Low Country (*Masters of Small Worlds*, chap. 4, esp. 147 n.36).

10. Eliza Hibben Leland Journal, November 6, 1853.

11. James Walter Douglass to Frances Douglass, June 9, 1836, Douglass Correspondence.

12. Frances Douglass to Henry Taylor, September 1, 1837, Douglass Correspondence; William McCampbell to Susan Heiskell, March 14, 1857, Collection of Heiskell, McCampbell, Wilkes, and Steel Family Materials. For Taylor's similar disgust at the drunkenness present at a militia muster, see Henry Taylor to Frances Douglass, July 6, 1835, Douglass Correspondence. On the militia muster as the proving ground for southern manhood, see Laver, "Refuge of Manhood."

13. Charlotte Verstille to Nancy O. Verstille, March 2, 1821, Verstille Papers; Anne Beale Davis Diary, January 6, 1839, Beale and Davis Family Papers; S. Jane Boyd to Jane Crawford, October 8, 1852, Gaston-Crawford Family Papers. On evangelicalism's critique of the self-indulgence of the planter class and their wealth in late eighteenth-century Virginia, see Isaac, *Transformation of Virginia*, 161–80. On the clergy's critique of materialism in the antebellum South, see Startup, *Root of All Evil*.

14. Mary [Douglass Gray] to Mr. and Mrs. William Plumer, April 13, 1839,

Douglass Correspondence. She continued her lament with a passage from Psalm 84:10: "'I have rather be a door keeper' &c."

15. Wyatt-Brown, *Shaping of Southern Culture*, 83–105.

16. Maria E. Lide to Hannah Coker, March 1, 1841, Lide-Coker Family Papers. On alcohol consumption and temperance in the South, see, for example, Quist, *Restless Visionaries*, 155–234. In his focused study of Tuscaloosa County, Alabama, Quist finds that many slaveholders and the upwardly mobile tended to back temperance movements that variously promoted moral suasion and legalized Prohibition. The interests of these groups thus overlapped with the career interests of the clergy, presenting new professional avenues of advancement for many men in the antebellum South (Schweiger, *Gospel Working Up*, 35–54). Ownby nicely captures the gendered tension between evangelical ideals and alcohol consumption in the South (*Subduing Satan*, 168–73).

17. Anne Beale to Joseph Davis, May 25, 1837, Beale and Davis Family Papers.

18. Anne Beale Davis to Joseph Davis, November 9, 1837, Beale and Davis Family Papers. For the evangelical critique of dueling and southern evangelicals' efforts to establish reform societies aimed at ending dueling, see Loveland, *Southern Evangelicals*, 180–85. On dueling and its relationship to the code of honor among elite southerners, see, for example, Wyatt-Brown, *Southern Honor*, 166, 350–61; Stowe, *Intimacy and Power*, 5–45.

19. James Walter Douglass to George P. [Shannon], December 4, 1816, Douglass Correspondence; William McCampbell to Susan Heiskell, September 13, 1856, Collection of Heiskell, McCampbell, Wilkes, and Steel Family Materials; Mary Jeffreys Bethell Diary, February 14, 1857; Mallary, *Social Visits*, 27. On the importance of dancing to courtship among elite southerners, see Stowe, *Intimacy and Power*, 71–73.

20. Jones Fuller to Anna Thomas, January 28, 1846, Fuller-Thomas Papers; [Sarah Fountain] to Hannah Coker, May 1, 1842, Lide-Coker Family Papers.

21. Margaret Wallace to Susan Heiskell, August 19, 1856, William McCampbell to Susan Heiskell, November 1, 1856, both in Collection of Heiskell, McCampbell, Wilkes, and Steel Family Materials.

22. Frances Moore Webb Bumpass Diary, February 14, 1843, Bumpas Family Papers. For overviews of this process, see, for example, Mathews, *Slavery and Methodism*; Genovese, *Consuming Fire*, 1–34; Cornelius, *Slave Missions*; Snay, *Gospel of Disunion*, 53–112. For specific cases, see, for example, Sparks, *On Jordan's Stormy Banks*, 115–31; Owen, *Sacred Flame of Love*, 28–56.

23. Martha Gaston to Jane Gaston, November 22, 1824, Gaston-Crawford Family Papers. In the same letter, Martha Gaston noted that Cunningham mentioned similar dangers in his missionary activity among the slaves: "It was in addressing these poor creatures, and he determined to persevere in it, though it should cost him his blood."

24. Joseph Davis to Robert Davis, April 17, 1855, Beale and Davis Family Papers; Sarah Fountain to Hannah Coker, October 21, 1839, Lide-Coker Family Papers.

25. Richard Wills to Anna Wills, December 1860, Richard Wills to William Wills, March 11, 1861, both in Wills Papers.

26. Joseph Davis to Robert Davis, April 17, 1855, Beale and Davis Family Papers. For excellent historical accounts of these early missionary efforts, see Snay, *Gospel of Disunion*, 88–109; Mathews, *Religion in the Old South*, 138–40.

27. Snay, *Gospel of Disunion*, 126–34; Mathews, *Slavery and Methodism*, 246–83.

28. Mary Davis Brown Journal, June 3, 1855.

29. Mary [Douglass Gray] to James Walter and Frances Douglass, March 25, 1835, Douglass Correspondence. For state-based studies that capture both community and conflict among evangelical congregations, see Sparks, *On Jordan's Stormy Banks*; Schweiger, *Gospel Working Up*, esp. 27–33.

30. H. Edwards to Charlotte Verstille, February 9, 1821, Verstille Papers; John 4:35.

31. Mary Jeffreys Bethell Diary, July 23, 1860; Martha Gaston to Jane Gaston, April 17, 1822, Gaston-Crawford Family Papers; E[liza]. H[eiskell]. to Nancy Lincoln, October 3, 1836, Collection of Heiskell, McCampbell, Wilkes, and Steel Family Materials.

32. Mary Boyd to Jane Crawford, October 1, 1844, J. M. C. Boyd to Jane Crawford, June 15, 1848, both in Gaston-Crawford Family Papers. For further evidence of congregations that rapidly declined in membership during pastoral vacancies, see unknown to Frances Douglass, June 11, 1842, Douglass Correspondence; S. Jane Boyd to Jane Crawford, October 8, 1852, Gaston-Crawford Family Papers. While all branches of evangelicalism struggled at one point or another to furnish adequate numbers of clergy for the faithful, Presbyterians felt this challenge more keenly than Methodists and Baptists because of the Presbyterian requirement that clergy possess college educations. As Methodists and Baptists professionalized their clergy in the antebellum era, they increasingly had college-educated clergy in their ranks, but as Schweiger points out, only about one-third of Virginia pastors ordained prior to 1850 had "attended college for at least a time" (*Gospel Working Up*, 21–22). On the growing divide between college-educated clergy and their non-college-educated peers, see Holifield, *Gentlemen Theologians*, 24–49. On Presbyterianism's institutional weaknesses that prevented it from competing effectively with the Methodists and Baptists, including more stringent educational demands, see Hatch, *Democratization of American Christianity*, 21, 60–61, 195–201.

33. J. M. C. Boyd to Jane Crawford, June 15, 1848, Gaston-Crawford Family Papers; Mary Jeffreys Bethell Diary, September 16, 1858, June 6, 1860; Mary Hort Journal, September 2, 1843, Hort Papers.

34. William McCampbell to Susan Heiskell, November 1, 1856, Collection of Heiskell, McCampbell, Wilkes, and Steel Family Materials; Frances Moore Webb Bumpass Diary, October 20, [1854?], Bumpas Family Papers; Anne Beale Davis Diary, December 7, 1838, Beale and Davis Family Papers. After partaking of the Lord's Supper, Davis wrote, "To die would be great gain." Although she often pondered death, she likely dwelled on it even more during this period because she was four to five months pregnant. For insight into the theological splits—typically centered on eligibility for participation—among southern evangelicals regarding the Lord's Supper, see Holifield, *Gentlemen Theologians*, 175–85.

35. Anne Beale Davis Diary, October 28, 1838, Beale and Davis Family Papers; Elizabeth Fountain to Hannah Coker, October 19, 1837, Lide-Coker Family Papers. On camp meeting revivalism, see, for example, Bruce, *And They All Sang Hallelujah*; Boles, *Great Revival*; Eslinger, *Citizens of Zion*, 236–38. On the migration of Baptists and Presbyterians away from outdoor camp meetings, particularly because of their seeming disorder, see Boles, *Great Revival*, 89–102. While mid-nineteenth-century Methodist clergy continued to embrace the camp meeting, many older clergy lamented that the turn toward orderly camp meetings muted genuine religious enthusiasm (Wigger, *Taking Heaven by Storm*, 173–96).

36. James Walter Douglass to unknown, February 19, 1834, Douglass Correspondence. Although part of the Douglass Correspondence, this particular piece lacks the earmarks of a letter (e.g., salutation), suggesting that this may have been a diary scrap hashed out in the field during a revival.

37. Anne Beale Davis Diary, September 11, 1838, Beale and Davis Family Papers. Antebellum revivals often failed to live up to evangelicals' grand expectations. Fountain admitted that she and her family "were quite disappointed in our protracted meetings." Only two ministers appeared at the event, and only four people were baptized in spite of large crowds (Sarah Fountain to Hannah Coker, October 21, 1839, Lide-Coker Family Papers).

38. Frances Moore Webb Bumpass Diary, December 12, 1846, Bumpas Family Papers; George Whitaker to Cary Whitaker, September 1, 1845, Wills Papers; Maria [Lide] to Jane Lide Coker, September 21, 1846, Lide-Coker Family Papers. On the nature of protracted meetings among Baptists, see Gregory Wills, *Democratic Religion*, 34–35. On the connection between camp meetings and their importance to the formation of religious communities in the early nineteenth-century South, see Eslinger, *Citizens of Zion*, 238–41.

39. Mary E. Lide to Hannah Coker, March 9, 1836, Lide-Coker Family Papers; Samuel Haycraft Journal, March 27, 1864; Sidney D. Bumpass Autobiography and Diary, January 31, 1842, Bumpas Family Papers.

40. See S[arah]. J. Fountain to Hannah Coker, November 11, 1836, Lide-Coker

Family Papers; William McCampbell to Susan Heiskell, January 23, 1858, Collection of Heiskell, McCampbell, Wilkes, and Steel Family Materials; Maria Lide to Jane Coker, May 11, 1846, Lide-Coker Family Papers; Charlotte Verstille to Nancy Verstille, June 4, 1835, Verstille Papers.

41. Mary E. Lide to Hannah Coker, March 9, 1836, Lide-Coker Family Papers; Frances Moore Webb Bumpass Diary, May 15, 1842, Bumpas Family Papers. For additional treatments that note how white evangelicals drew inspiration from black piety and the nature of antebellum biracial fellowship, see, for example, Sparks, *On Jordan's Stormy Banks*, 64–68; Mathews, *Religion in the Old South*, 201–3; Boles, *Masters and Slaves*.

42. Charlotte Verstille to Nancy O. Verstille, March 2, 1821, Verstille Papers; Eliza Hibben Leland Journal, April 3, 1853.

43. Sidney D. Bumpass Autobiography and Diary, April 29, 1842, May 19, 1842, Bumpas Family Papers.

44. Frances Moore Webb Bumpass Diary, August 5, 1844, Bumpas Family Papers.

45. William Wills to editor of the *Methodist Protestant*, August 24, 1855, Wills Papers. Wills often retained copies of letters he sent to the editor of the *Methodist Protestant*. As Wigger shows, older Methodist clergy of all stripes often lamented the drift from "primitive Methodism's" class meetings, love feasts, and camp meetings in the antebellum era (*Taking Heaven by Storm*, 173–96). On the larger Methodist quest for respectability, see Lyerly, *Methodism and the Southern Mind*, 176–86.

46. Richard Wills to William Wills, March 14, 1864, Wills Papers; William McCampbell to Susan Heiskell McCampbell, May 1, 1858, August 8, 1858, Collection of Heiskell, McCampbell, Wilkes, and Steel Family Materials.

47. Mary [Douglass Gray] to Frances Douglass, October 7, 1840, Douglass Correspondence; G[eorge]. A. T. W[hitaker]. to Anna Wills, June 28, 1842, Wills Papers.

48. Between January 10, 1838, and October 25, 1841, Bumpass recorded delivery of 565 sermons (and 145 individuals who "professed religion" whom he took credit for bringing into the Methodist fold). See Sidney D. Bumpass Autobiography and Diary, January 10, 1838, January 1, 1839, January 17, 1840, January 1, 1841, October 25, 1841.

49. Frances Jane Bestor Robertson Journal, October 26, 1851; for a report of another unsuccessful missionary sermon, see October 19, 1851.

50. Phebe Brodrick to Mary Cox Collins, April 23, 1859, Maria Collins to Mary Cox Collins, May 29, 1859, Fanny Cox Brodrick to Mary Cox Collins, June 6, 1859, all in Collins Family Letters.

51. Maria F. Lide to Hannah Coker, September 21, 1842, Lide-Coker Family Papers.

52. Sarah Lowry Pollard to John McGill, June 12, 1851, John McGill Papers, Virginia Historical Society, Richmond; Frances Douglass to James Walter Douglass, April 7, 1835, Douglass Correspondence.

53. Mary [Douglass Gray] to Frances Douglass, May 11, 1839, Douglass Correspondence. On female benevolent activities in the antebellum South, see Quist, *Restless Visionaries*, 19–102; Lebsock, *Free Women of Petersburg*, 195–236. On the Presbyterian schism and its underlying theological and sectional tensions, see, for example, Hambrick-Stowe, *Charles G. Finney*, 24–45; Snay, *Gospel of Disunion*, 115–26; Farmer, *Metaphysical Confederacy*, 125–36.

54. Ann Thomas to Anna Jones, May 24, 1849, Fuller-Thomas Papers; E. H. Lide to Hannah Lide, April 6, 1830, Lide-Coker Family Papers; Mary Hort Journal, August 14, 1844, Hort Papers; Hu Brown to Mary Ann Susan Brown, April 29, 1834, Collection of Heiskell, McCampbell, Wilkes, and Steel Family Materials. On the ministerial need to inspire and the variety of paths to the pastorate among Baptists, Methodists, and Presbyterians, see Mathews, *Religion in the Old South*, 84–85.

55. Frances Jane Bestor Robertson Journal, October 23, 1851. On the Baptists' quest for more educated and polished clergy, see Holifield, *Gentlemen Theologians*, 17–18.

56. Hu Brown to Mary Ann Susan Brown, April 19, 1834, Collection of Heiskell, McCampbell, Wilkes, and Steel Family Materials; Frances Douglass to Henry Taylor, June 15, 1836, Douglass Correspondence. On the debate among Old School and New School Presbyterians that Finney inspired and how that debate shaped Presbyterianism in the antebellum South, see Snay, *Gospel of Disunion*, 112–26.

57. Lizzie Cox to Mary Cox Collins, April 8, 1861, Collins Family Letters.

58. Ibid.

59. Fanny Cox Brodrick to Mary Cox Collins, April 12, 1861, Collins Family Letters.

60. According to the church's published history, McElroy "was a strict disciplinarian," but "not much is known of his pastorate which was just 16 months in duration" (Mary L. Wilson and Wilson, *History*, 46). On women's informal but powerful influence on clergymen in the antebellum North, see Gedge, *Without Benefit of Clergy*, chap. 6.

61. Andrew, *Family Government*, 7–8, 26–27.

62. James Walter Douglass to Frances Douglass, May 17, 1835, Douglass Correspondence.

63. Frances Douglass to Henry Taylor, August 13, 1837, Douglass Correspondence.

64. Richard Wills to Anna Wills, October 3, 1861, Wills Papers.

65. Mary K. Craddock Diary, November 12, 1849.

66. Mary Jeffreys Bethell Diary, n.d.; B. E. V[erstille]. to Ann Verstille, July 12, 1820, Verstille Papers; Mary Hort Journal, November 1842, Hort Papers; Hebrews 12:6. For a similar passage, see Anne Beale Davis Diary, December 1838, Beale and Davis Family Papers.

67. Mary Davis Brown Journal, January 1, 1858.

68. Mary Jeffreys Bethell Diary, August 2, 1855, November 11, 1864; Luke 18:7.

69. Schneider, *Way of the Cross*, 50–51.

70. E. B. Early to Mary Virginia Early, August 30, 1841, Early Family Papers.

71. Mary Jeffreys Bethell Diary, February 10, 1861; Eugenia Rebecca Griffin Leland Journal, April 20, 1865; Lucy Gwathmey to Maria Watts Gwathmey, August 25, 1844, Gwathmey Family Papers. For a detailed description of domestic devotions outlined in advice literature in this period, see McDannell, *Christian Home*, 77–85.

72. Samuel Haycraft Journal, 1851, February 13, 1859, August 4, 1861, March 5, 1853, July 1, 1860.

73. Mary [Douglass Gray] to Frances Douglass, May 11, 1839, Douglass Correspondence; Frances Moore Webb Bumpass Diary, August 30, [1854?], February 4, 1845, Bumpas Family Papers; Mary Jeffreys Bethell Diary, February 5, 1861; see also January 3, 1863.

74. Richard Collins Diary, December 2, 1840.

75. Eugenia Rebecca Griffin Leland Journal, April 10, 1865. Even the deaths of her children "call[ed] forth gratitude and love from our hearts to God for all his loving kindness to us" during her passage "through the deep waters of affliction."

76. Richard Collins Diary, November 11, 1840.

77. William McCampbell to Susan Heiskell McCampbell, October 15, 1857, Collection of Heiskell, McCampbell, Wilkes, and Steel Family Materials.

78. Mary Jeffreys Bethell Diary, January 1, 1864.

79. Samuel Haycraft Journal, August 14, 1853; Mary Davis Brown Journal, December 31, 1855.

Chapter 2. Courting Women, Courting God

1. According to Jabour, in the early nineteenth century, "companionate marriage permitted individual choice in marriage based on personal affection and sexual attraction and encouraging loving, rather than authoritarian, relationships betweens husbands, wives, and children" (*Marriage in the Early Republic*, 9).

2. Stowe, *Intimacy and Power*, 50–121, esp. 78. Stowe, Wyatt-Brown, and Glover caution against taking at face value southerners' rhetoric of mutuality and companionate love in courtship and marriage, instead stressing the primacy of traditional concerns of economic and social stability among the South's elite. See Stowe, *Intimacy and Power*, esp. 95–100; Wyatt-Brown, *Southern Honor*,

199–225; Glover, *Southern Sons*, 132–34. For his profile of a blacksmith's son futile efforts to mimic the gentry and marry into that class, which substantiates this perspective, see Friend, "Belles, Benefactors, and the Blacksmith's Son." For the argument that elite southerners emphasized companionship rather than conflict, see Censer, *North Carolina Planters*, 65–95; Lewis, *Pursuit of Happiness*, 169–208. Jabour connects the two perspectives, arguing that a competitive courtship offered women their only assurance of a companionate marriage (*Scarlett's Sisters*, 113–80). Studies of courtship in the South remain largely silent on what impact, if any, evangelicalism might have had in shaping courtship patterns, instead stressing the roles of class, gender, and family. Stevenson acknowledges the importance of faith in limiting potential matches among Virginia Quakers and suggests that church social events provided one of the principal meeting sites for the opposite sexes (*Life in Black and White*, chap. 2, esp. 46–47, 56). Jabour also notes piety among many other characteristics in the courtship calculus of one couple (*Marriage in the Early Republic*, 16). In her broader study, southern women coming of age often viewed courtship rituals as a threat to expressions of piety rather than as a tool for screening suitors (Jabour, *Scarlett's Sisters*, 113–50, esp. 126). On northern courtships in the antebellum era, see, for example, Rothman, *Hands and Hearts*; Lystra, *Searching the Heart*. While both books trace general courtship patterns, the authors acknowledge that their primary sources center on the North, Midwest, and West, with much less attention to the South.

3. Lystra, *Searching the Heart*, 8.

4. Maria Lide to Hannah Lide Coker, August 17, 1846, Lide-Coker Family Papers. As chap. 3 discusses, some evangelical women married nonevangelical men in spite of the preference for the already converted. Most scholars of courtship in the antebellum South suggest that elite families formally or informally placed considerable pressure on their children to marry within their social class. See, for example, Wyatt-Brown, *Southern Honor*, 199–225; Fox-Genovese, *Within the Plantation Household*, 207; Stowe, *Intimacy and Power*, 104–6; Edwards, *Scarlett Doesn't Live Here Anymore*, 20.

5. According to Stowe, one southern evangelical man's vision of "domestic happiness [was] rather subversive in its southern context," a view "from inside the woman's sphere" (*Intimacy and Power*, 121). The evangelical clergy possessed deep-seated fears that members of their congregations would marry primarily for wealth. Ironically, the man who issued one of the strongest warnings on this front, Bishop James O. Andrew, accelerated the North-South split of the Methodist Episcopal Church when his marriage to a wealthy widow made him a slaveholder. For Andrew's admonitions against material interests in the calculus of courtship, see *Family Government*, 12–15.

6. For a similar finding on women's reluctance to concede to marriage, par-

ticularly in the final days of courtship, see Rothman, *Hands and Hearts*, 56–59; Jabour, *Scarlett's Sisters*, 151–80. On male attitudes toward marriage, see esp. Glover, *Southern Sons*, 133–46.

7. Clinton, *Plantation Mistress*, 60; Cashin, *Our Common Affairs*, 14.

8. In analyzing antebellum courtships in the North and South, Clinton (*Plantation Mistress*, 59–86) and Cashin (*Our Common Affairs*, 14) stress demographic and cultural differences rather than similarities. On men's advantages in courtship as a consequence of their age, see Jabour, *Scarlett's Sisters*, 167; Glover, *Southern Sons*, 137.

9. Andrew, *Family Government*, 35, 20–21, 23.

10. C. A. Hill to Sarah Thomas, September 16, 1817, Fuller-Thomas Papers. On sexual double standards among white men and women in the antebellum South, see, for example, Jabour, *Scarlett's Sisters*, 140; Glover, *Southern Sons*, 126–31. On honor and family pride in courtship, see, for example, Wyatt-Brown, *Southern Honor*, 233–34; Stowe, *Intimacy and Power*, 50–121.

11. C. A. Hill to Sarah Thomas, September 16, 1817, Fuller-Thomas Papers. See also Ephesians 6:11–18, where Paul outlines the power of faith to withstand evil. On the use of this passage in Christian advice literature, see Demers, *Heaven upon Earth*, 123.

12. C. A. Hill to Sarah Thomas, September 16, 1817, Fuller-Thomas Papers.

13. William Wills to Spencer Cotten, June 18, 1833, Wills Papers.

14. Spencer Cotten to William Wills, July 11, 1833, Wills Papers.

15. Glover, *Southern Sons*, 134.

16. Stowe, *Intimacy and Power*, 65.

17. Andrew, *Family Government*, 127–39, esp. 135.

18. On the frequency with which daughters cared for ill or elderly parents, see Carter, *Southern Single Blessedness*, 73–77.

19. On the frequency of men marrying their deceased wives' sisters, see Wyatt-Brown, *Southern Honor*, 219. Several scholars note that cousins married more frequently in the antebellum South than in the antebellum North. Jabour contends that the relative freedom cousins experienced may have facilitated courtship in a society where formality and reserve between the sexes dominated (*Scarlett's Sisters*, 145).

20. Anne Beale Davis Diary, September 11, 1853, Anne Beale to Joseph Davis, October 11, 1836, both in Beale and Davis Family Papers.

21. Anne Beale to Joseph Davis, August 11, 1836, January 25, 1838, both in Beale and Davis Family Papers.

22. Ibid., February 22, 1838.

23. Ibid.

24. Ibid., April 7, 1838.

25. William Fulton to John Poulton, February 4, 1857, Poulton Family Papers.

26. Rosannah Davisson to John Poulton, March 2, 1857, February 18, 1857, July 17, 1857, November 2, 1857, Poulton Family Papers. As scholars note, women frequently regretted their inability to discuss their affection, See Jabour, *Marriage in the Early Republic*, 21.

27. Rosannah Davisson to John Poulton, July 1, 1857, March 20, 1857, Poulton Family Papers. On the frequency with which southern women turned to "innocent" and "impersonal" topics to sidestep discussions of their feelings, see Jabour, *Scarlett's Sisters*, 141. For further evidence of women referring to marriage in the language of loss (even denouement) as well as their fears about marriage, see Stowe, *Intimacy and Power*, 104, 107; Edwards, *Scarlett Doesn't Live Here Anymore*, 21–23; Friedman, *Enclosed Garden*, 33; Weiner, *Mistresses and Slaves*, 26–30; Jabour, *Scarlett's Sisters*, 151–214.

28. Rosannah Davisson to John Poulton, June 22, 1857, Elizabeth Davisson to John Poulton, February 18, 1857, both in Poulton Family Papers. For additional examples of Davisson's critical analysis of the clergy at her church, see Rosannah Davisson to John Poulton, July 1, 1857, September 17, 1857, March 15, 1858, Poulton Family Papers.

29. Rosannah Davisson to John Poulton, May 22, 1857, Poulton Family Papers.

30. Ibid., October 2, 1857, November 27, 1857. In her research on courtship patterns in the antebellum North, Rothman notes, "Women generally made the decision to marry with far less conflict than the decision of *when* to marry." Knowing that marriage often entailed motherhood shortly after their nuptials, many women showed considerable ambivalence about delays in their wedding date (*Hands and Hearts*, 70–71). On the broader phenomenon of women participating in courtship gossip when it affected others but lamenting such gossip when it concerned their own relationships, see Stowe, "Rhetoric of Authority," 929–30; Jabour, *Scarlett's Sisters*, 127–31. For evidence of Lee's persistent curiosity, see Rosannah Davisson to John Poulton, September 17, 1857, October 2, 1857, Poulton Family Papers. On Rose's efforts to reassure John that her father still regarded him affectionately, see Rosannah Davisson to John Poulton, October 15, 1857, Poulton Family Papers. This example reaffirms Stowe's point that the involvement of the entire family in courtship process allowed a suitor to try his luck with various kin when one individual showed resistance (*Intimacy and Power*, 99). As the epilogue discusses, letters between Elizabeth Davisson, Rose's mother, and John Poulton after Rose's death in 1869 suggest that John may have had good reason to fear Frederick Davisson's feelings.

31. Rosannah Davisson to John Poulton, September 17, 1857, October 9, 1857, September 18, 1857, May 15, 1847, May 21, 1858, Poulton Family Papers.

32. Frances Jane Bestor Robertson Journal, September 25, 1854, September 8, 1854; for Bestor's strong critiques of men other than Robertson, see October 23, 1851, October 27, 1851.

33. Ibid., September 25, 1854, September 8, 1854. On the difficulties widowers with children faced in finding mates, see Jabour, *Scarlett's Sisters*, 131.

34. Frances Jane Bestor Robertson Journal, September 8, 1854.

35. Ibid., August 26, 1854, October 27, 1854, September 8, 1854.

36. Gabriel Thomas to Anna Thomas, November 1, 1845, Fuller-Thomas Papers. For the financial risks of Fuller's work as a cotton factor, see Ann Thomas to Anna Thomas Fuller, December 26, 1846, Fuller-Thomas Papers.

37. W. George Thomas to Anna Thomas, January 4, 1845, Fuller-Thomas Papers.

38. Anna Thomas to Jones Fuller, December 22, 1845, Jones Fuller to Anna Thomas, January 1, 1846, both in Fuller-Thomas Papers.

39. Anna Thomas to Jones Fuller, [1846?], December 22, 1845, Fuller-Thomas Papers.

40. Anna Thomas to Jones Fuller, February 3, 1846, Jones Fuller to Anna Thomas, January 28, 1846, both in Fuller-Thomas Papers.

41. Jones Fuller to Anna Thomas, March 14, 1846, April 8, 1846, Anna Thomas to Jones Fuller, March 27, 1846, all in Fuller-Thomas Papers.

42. Ann Thomas to Jones Fuller, March 27, 1846, Fuller-Thomas Papers; Matthew 10:30; Luke 12:7.

43. Ann Thomas to Jones Fuller, March 27, 1846, Fuller-Thomas Papers.

44. Jones Fuller to Ann Thomas, April 7, 1846, Fuller-Thomas Papers. Fuller thought Ann Thomas's letter "a mark of peculiar regard" and vowed that George Thomas would approve of him and of the marriage when the two men finally met (Jones Fuller to Anna Thomas, April 8, 1846, Fuller-Thomas Papers). Despite Fuller's promises, Ann Thomas soon perceived herself as having lost her maternal authority, writing less than a year after the marriage that Fuller "ought to recollect that a word spoken in season, 'is like apples of gold in pictures of silver.' One consoling word from him would induce me to believe I was not forgotten by him, I am very sure I am not—yet we dont object to frequent declarations of these things. I amagine myself sometimes, like a weaned child, somewhat forsaken—a little notice from the mother will receive and cheer its drooping spirits in a moment. I look for this from my dear children; and I have cause to return a thousand thanks & do not look in vain—a kind and gracious God,' has implanted in their bosoms all that filial love and affection that I could ask of them, perhaps, more than due me" (Ann Thomas to Anna Thomas Fuller, January 27, 1847, Fuller-Thomas Papers; Proverbs 25:11).

45. Wyatt-Brown, for example, writes, "Men feared domestication, not simply because it inhibited their business and pleasure but also because of male ribbing about a too-uxurious manner" (*Southern Honor*, 273–74). On antebellum southern men's general inability of to speak openly about their emotions, see Faust, *Mothers of Invention*, chap. 5, esp. 117–20.

46. See William McCampbell to Susan Heiskell, February 2, 1857, November 3, 1857, November 17, 1857, Collection of Heiskell, McCampbell, Wilkes, and Steel Family Materials.
47. Susan Heiskell to William McCampbell, July 22, 1856, Collection of Heiskell, McCampbell, Wilkes, and Steel Family Materials.
48. William McCampbell to Susan Heiskell, November 17, 1857, Collection of Heiskell, McCampbell, Wilkes, and Steel Family Materials.
49. Ibid., February 19, 1857, March 1857.
50. Ibid., November 3, 1857.
51. Ibid., February 2, 1857.
52. Ibid.
53. Ibid., [1857?].
54. William McCampbell to T. H. Heiskell, December 18, 1857, Collection of Heiskell, McCampbell, Wilkes, and Steel Family Materials.
55. William McCampbell to Susan Heiskell, March 10, 1858, Collection of Heiskell, McCampbell, Wilkes, and Steel Family Materials. The verse is from Sir Thomas Moore, *Lalla Rookh: An Oriental Romance* (1817), chap. 19.
56. William Wills to Anna Whitaker, January 1, 1835, Wills Papers.
57. Ibid., March 23, 1835.
58. Richard Wills to George Wills, April 18, 1861, Wills Papers.
59. Richard Wills to William Wills, July 10, 1861, Wills Papers.
60. Ibid., September 5, 1861.
61. William Wills to Richard Wills, September 19, 1861, Wills Papers. For additional advice from a Presbyterian clergyman to his stepson that courtship should be delayed until his ministerial training was completed, see James Walter Douglass to Henry Taylor, January 18, 1836, Douglass Correspondence. For the concern by a clergyman's wife that marriage among young clergyman was creating a "monstrous thinning in the ranks of the single preachers" in the Methodist Episcopal Church, South and threatened to leave posts in certain circuits unfilled, see Anne Beale to Joseph Davis, January 25, 1838, Beale and Davis Family Papers.
62. William Wills to Richard Wills, September 19, 1861, Wills Papers. For a brief description of Richard's wife, Anna Louisa Norman, and her ties to the planter elite of eastern North Carolina, see "Biographical Note," Inventory, Wills Papers, which estimates the year of Richard and Anna's marriage at 1864.
63. For a similar model for understanding elite southerners' courtship correspondence, see Stowe, *Intimacy and Power*, 88.

Chapter 3. Improvising on the Ideal
1. Susan Heiskell McCampbell to William McCampbell, August 14, 1858, August 16, 1858, June 9, 1858, all in Collection of Heiskell, McCampbell, Wilkes,

and Steel Family Materials. For evidence on the frequency with which men's fanciful expectations for marriage outstripped those of their brides and on couples' shared fears of a disappointing union, see Lystra, *Searching the Heart*, 192–226.

2. Scholars of southern evangelicalism's institutional history have spent considerable time scouring disciplinary records from across the South in an attempt to chart this transformation in areas where judicial proceedings centered on members' accusations of sexual impropriety (e.g., adultery, bigamy, desertion). Thus far, they have returned a mixed verdict. Both Friedman (*Enclosed Garden*, 11–18) and McCurry (*Masters of Small Worlds*, 176–81, 201–7) find that antebellum church courts nearly always sided with men in sexual and marital disputes, thereby erasing the ambiguity in evangelicalism's prescriptive literature. In contrast, Sparks finds that church courts in Mississippi sided with women as often as with men in domestic disputes, leading him to describe these tribunals as representing a broader attempt by evangelicals "to revise the patriarchal marriage to include companionship, love, and mutual respect" (*On Jordan's Stormy Banks*, 127). In Twiggs County, Georgia, according to Bode, men much more frequently ran afoul of church tribunals than did women because men's most common sins, such as drunkenness, took place in the public eye. And while he found a handful of women who appeared before the church courts for sexual offenses, he argues that "one cannot suppose that most women were uncomfortable with the evangelical ideal of female purity and chastity. There was little reason for them to oppose a standard of church discipline that provided even limited sanctions against male violence and disorder" ("Transformation," 736–37).

3. Lyerly, "Women and Southern Religion," 264.

4. See Heyrman, *Southern Cross*, 117–60, 206–52. See also Lyerly, *Methodism and the Southern Mind*, 94–118, 154–56; Lyerly, "Women and Southern Religion," 263.

5. By the 1830s, as evangelicals dropped their earlier egalitarian rhetoric to court favor among the South's elite, they co-opted and then sanctified the secular South's language of patriarchal privilege. Now referring to their faith as "family religion," the evangelical clergy elided many of their demands that questioned male authority within the home, decreasing the frequency with which male members faced disciplinary proceedings within the church; constructing the image of the "warrior" clergyman who stoutly defended his personal honor (and ultimately the honor of the South through the defense of slavery); and promoting marriage, even among Methodist clergyman, who were now expected to wed, have children, and live with some modicum of comfort. See Heyrman, *Southern Cross*, 206–52.

6. Historians of the antebellum southern family have traditionally downplayed domestic strife, with the exception of church tribunals, though evan-

gelicalism as a discrete variable has received relatively little attention compared to class and gender. Some scholars have minimized substantive differences in the marital relationships of southerners and northerners, arguing that in both sections, in Censer's words, husbands and wives alike believed they "should be linked by mutual attraction and should provide affectionate support for each other while rearing a family" (*North Carolina Planters*, 72). In other words, elite southern couples had made the transition from traditional, patriarchal models of marriage to a more modern, companionate model that more or less mirrored transformations occurring in the North. For a more recent analysis that observes the mutual dependence of elite men and women in the antebellum South, see Berry, *All that Makes a Man*. For an excellent synthesis of northern courtship and marriage patterns as they shifted from a patriarchal model to a companionate model, see, for example, Lystra, *Searching the Heart*, 237. In sharp contrast, Wyatt-Brown, for example, argues that "companionate marriage would have to await changes in women's property rights, prospects of decent employment for wives and mothers, and a culture devoted to egalitarian principles generally. Until then, the feminine ethic had to encourage submission to reality" (*Southern Honor*, 234–35). Some scholars, such as Fox-Genovese, seek something of a middle path in the debate: elite white southerners often found true love and emotional fulfillment in their marriages while remaining well aware that final authority rested with the patriarch. Fox-Genovese also contends that southerners espoused many emerging bourgeois values, ranging from separate spheres to domesticity, but that any use of those notions must be interpreted against southerners' more fundamental faith in paternalism, or the "legitimate" and "protective domination of the father over his family" (*Within the Plantation Household*, 63–64). On the passion of elite, southern marriages, see Fox-Genovese, *Within the Plantation Household*, 240–41. Most recently, Jabour offers a much less sanguine interpretation, arguing that the frequency with which elite men relocated and devoted themselves to their professional labors "increased women's need for their husbands' affection at the same time that men's careers limited husbands' availability to their wives. As a result, the power of love, rather than drawing husbands and wives together, reinforced men's dominance over women—and undermined women's resistance" (*Scarlett's Sisters*, 211). Although marital satisfaction was not foreclosed, Jabour contends that most women resigned themselves to their subordinate role in their marriage and turned their attention to fulfilling their duties as mothers and housekeepers.

7. Although more inclined to see conflict in marital relations than either Fox-Genovese or Wyatt-Brown, Stowe similarly emphasizes the emotional distance that often emerged in elite southerners' marriages as women sought to manage the home and men eagerly sought confirmation of their mastery in the public sphere. Thus elite southerners often wrote of their domestic work as a "joint

effort" even as they "emphasized its striking dissimilarities" (*Intimacy and Power*, 127). For a similar conclusion by a lay Presbyterian couple, Elizabeth and William Wirt, see Jabour, *Marriage in the Early Republic*, 100–139.

8. For other scholarly examinations of prescriptive literature that highlight this divide in marital ideals, see Mathews, *Religion in the Old South*, 97–124; Sparks, *On Jordan's Stormy Banks*, 158–59; McCurry, *Masters of Small Worlds*, 171–72; Clarke, *Dwelling Place*, 213–15; Bode, "Common Sphere," 797.

9. Andrew, *Family Government*, 31; Proverbs, 10–31. For an example of this reference appearing in southern evangelical correspondence, see Ann Thomas to Anna Thomas Fuller, May 27, 1846, Fuller-Thomas Papers.

10. Bailey, *Family Preacher*, 36, 44–45; Andrew, *Family Government*, 28, 30.

11. Bailey, *Family Preacher*, 26; Rogers, *Obligations and Duties*, 5. For an insightful look at how antebellum Americans' attention to maternal influence "offered a way of holding onto the ideal of civic virtue in an increasingly ambition-driven culture [that] helped to create a male self appropriate for a modern democratic society, one that seized and subordinated mother's love," see Lewis, "Motherhood," 156.

12. Rogers, *Obligations and Duties*, 13–15.

13. Bailey, *Family Preacher*, 31–38.

14. Ibid., 42–43, 52.

15. Andrew, *Family Government*, 33; Bailey, *Family Preacher*, 54.

16. Andrew, *Family Government*, 31–32.

17. On the South's reliance on patriarchal rather than judicial authority to settle marital disputes even as the North eased restrictions on divorce, see, for example, Bardaglio, *Reconstructing the Household*, 32–36; Jabour, *Scarlett's Sisters*, 91, 165.

18. The cycle of doubt, anxiety, and confidence in leadership among this class of southern women parallels the doubts that many early nineteenth-century clergymen voiced about their abilities. See Schneider, *Way of the Cross*, 63. Although focused on the Ohio River Valley, Schneider's study also examines the vital role of clergymen's wives in their ministerial fortunes (*Way of the Cross*, 12). See also Jeffrey, "Ministry through Marriage"; Schweiger, *Gospel Working Up*, 21–23.

19. Frances Douglass to James Walter Douglass, May 4, 1834, Douglass Correspondence.

20. Ibid., May 27, 1835.

21. Frances Moore Webb Bumpass Diary, December 30, 1842, April 19, 1842, Bumpas Family Papers.

22. Ibid., December 4, 1842, April 19, 1842. For examples of the Bumpasses' relocations, see Frances Moore Webb Bumpass Diary, October 15, 1842, October 16, 1842, November 2, 1842, November 9, 1842, December 7, 1844, Bumpas Family Papers. For an excellent description of early American Methodist love feasts,

see Lyerly, *Methodism and the Southern Mind*, 14. On the frequency of such age discrepancies at marriage, particularly older men marrying teenage women, in the antebellum South, see Wyatt-Brown, *Southern Honor*, 203–6. Bishop Francis Asbury moved Methodist clergymen to new appointments every two years to avoid parochialism and foster collegiality in the ranks, especially among the early circuit riders. See Wigger, *Taking Heaven by Storm*, 34–36.

23. Frances Douglass to James Walter Douglass, May 20, 1835, Douglass Correspondence.

24. Ibid., April 9, 1835, May 4, 1834.

25. Sidney D. Bumpass Autobiography and Diary, December 11, 1842, Frances Moore Webb Bumpass Diary, December 12, 1842, both in Bumpas Family Papers.

26. James Walter Douglass to Frances Douglass, August 4, 1834, Douglass Correspondence.

27. Frances Douglass to James Walter Douglass, August 2, 1834, James Walter Douglass to Frances Douglass, August 9, 1834, both in Douglass Correspondence.

28. For a detailed analysis of the ways in which physical distance in southern elite marriages often precipitated emotional distance, see Stowe, *Intimacy and Power*, 127–28.

29. William Wills to Anna Wills, September 2, 1835, September 10, 1835, Wills Papers. On her pregnancy interfering with her travel plans, see Anna Wills to William Wills, September 22, 1835, Wills Papers.

30. Matthew 11:29; Joseph Davis to Anne Beale Davis, April 29, 1847, April 19, 1849, Beale and Davis Papers.

31. Joseph Davis to [Robert?] Davis, July 27, 1855, Beale and Davis Papers.

32. William Wills to Anna Wills, September 2, 1850, May 11, 1854, April 10, 1850, August 3, 1849. At the 1854 Methodist Protestant annual meeting, held in Steubenville, Ohio, Wills reported optimistically, "We have had as a matter of course some abolition speeches and some abolition resolutions," but "there is decidedly . . . a greater desire to harmonize the Conference than I have heretofore seen. Indeed I feel assured if the Southern members can be kept quiet, we have nothing to fear. There are, I fear, a few from the South as indiscreet as some in the West" (William Wills to Anna Wills, May 11, 1854, Wills Papers). Four years later, however, Wills reported that virtually no northern counterparts attended a conference meeting in Lynchburg, Virginia, signaling the denomination's rupture along sectional lines (William Wills to Anna Wills, May 5, 1858, Wills Papers).

33. Joseph Davis to Anne Beale Davis, April 29, 1847, Beale and Davis Papers.

34. Anne Beale Davis Diary, December 24, 1843, Beale and Davis Papers.

35. Ibid., January 1, 1843, April 14, 1850.

36. Ibid., January 20, 1850.

37. Ibid., June 2, 1850.

38. Frances Douglass to James Walter Douglass, January 9, 1834, June 9, 1836. Frances wrote, "Once before I had similar forebodings, which were fatally realized, this increases my apprehension" (Frances Douglass to James Walter Douglass, April 7, 1835, Douglass Correspondence).

39. James Walter Douglass to Frances Douglass, May 17, 1835, Douglass Correspondence.

40. Anna Wills to William Wills, August 21, 1850, William Wills to Anna Wills, September 2, 1850, both in Wills Papers. When their four-year-old son became seriously ill while William was away from home, he received a taste of what Anna endured in worrying about him, and he did not like it, writing, "My mind is on the rack." He second-guessed his decision not to return home but also used writing to his wife as a way to reassure both of them that all would be well (William Wills to Anna Wills, July 16, 1850, Wills Papers).

41. Anna Wills to William Wills, May 16, 1850, August 15, 1850, Lawrence Whitaker to Anna Wills, November 29, 1850, Cary Whitaker to William and Anna Wills, April 4, 1838, all in Wills Papers. For similar complaints, see Cary Whitaker to Anna Wills, February 2, 1838, Wills Papers. Most treatments of plantation mistresses stress the gendered dichotomy of white labor on the plantation, with much less attention given to women like Anna Wills who managed slaves, children, and crops during the plantation patriarch's absences. For excellent discussions of the gender and racial division of labor on southern plantations, see, for example, Fox-Genovese, *Within the Plantation Household*, 100–145; Weiner, *Mistresses and Slaves*, chap. 4. For a unique analysis of how widowed women managed slaves with minimal or no assistance from men, see Wood, *Masterful Women*, 35–60.

42. William Wills to Anna Wills, May 21, 1837, April 11, 1837, March 27, 1836, Wills Papers.

43. Joseph Davis to Anne Beale Davis, April 29, 1847, March 4, 1850, Beale and Davis Papers. Historians who emphasize the public face of masculine honor in the Old South contend that relationships with immediate family often competed for attention and primacy with relationships involving other honorable men. See, for example, Wyatt-Brown, *Southern Honor*, chaps. 8, 9; Stowe, *Intimacy and Power*, 122–60.

44. James Walter Douglass to Frances Douglass, May 31, 1835, Douglass Correspondence.

45. Ibid.

46. Ibid.

47. Nancy Lincoln to "My Dear Niece," December 2, 1852, Collection of Heiskell, McCampbell, Wilkes, and Steel Family Materials.

48. Mary K. Craddock Diary, December 14, 1825.

49. Ibid., May 23, 1842, March 16, 1843, February 23, 1844; see also September 14, 1854. For a similar event in which hiring out a slave created tremendous distress for a woman, though she claimed that God had resolved the issue in response to her prayers, see Mary Jeffreys Bethell Diary, January 5, 1855.

50. Mary K. Craddock Diary, May 23, 1842.

51. Ibid., January 22, 1846, October 7, 1854, July 8, 1856; for additional evidence of Craddock's sustained efforts to convert her irreligious family, see March 2, 1846, November 12, 1849, September 14, 1854.

52. Ibid., July 8, 1856.

53. For more on the frequency of antebellum bankruptcy and its meaning, particularly for men, see Balleisen, *Navigating Failure*; Sandage, *Born Losers*.

54. Richard Collins to Mary Cox Collins, May 31, 1857, May 22, 1856, June 30, 1850, Collins Family Letters.

55. Ibid., April 19, 1857, May 10, 1857.

56. Mary Cox Collins to Richard Collins, May 19, 1850, Collins Family Letters.

57. Richard Collins to Mary Cox Collins, May 26, 1850, August 30, 1850, Collins Family Letters.

58. Mary Cox Collins to Richard Collins, May 24, 1850, [ca. late 1850, early 1851], Collins Family Letters.

59. Richard Collins to Mary Cox Collins, October 6, 1857, October 13, 1857, Collins Family Papers. For evidence of Richard's increasing dependency on Mary's support for his financial schemes, see Richard Collins to Mary Cox Collins, May 22, 1856, April 13, 1857, September 18, 1857, May 10, 1857, Collins Family Letters.

60. Richard Collins to Mary Cox Collins, October 13, 1857, Collins Family Letters.

61. Ibid., January 18, 1855, June 1, 1864.

62. Ibid., April 14, 1864, August 20, 1859. On penmanship and letter writing as symbols of personal character among young southerners, see Glover, *Southern Sons*, 93; Jabour, *Scarlett's Sisters*, 144.

63. Richard Collins to Mary Cox Collins, May 9, 1864, Collins Family Letters.

64. Ibid., May 10, 1857; Ellen Collins Blatterman to Mary Cox Collins, March 1860, Kate Collins to Mary Cox Collins, February 1860, both in Collins Family Letters.

65. Fanny Cox Brodrick to Mary Cox Collins, February 17, 1860, February 20, 1860, March 2, 1860, Collins Family Letters.

Chapter 4. "Unto Whom Much Is Given"

1. Luke 12:48; Anne Beale Davis to Robert Davis, December 25, 1854, November 22, 1855, Beale and Davis Family Papers; Lucy Gwathmey to Nelly Gwathmey, February 12, 1860, Gwathmey Family Papers; see also Lucy Gwathmey to Edward Garlick Gwathmey, October 6, 1858.

2. As Lewis suggests, "Since the home was a woman's place, the burden of everyone's happiness, including her own, fell to a woman" (*Pursuit of Happiness*, 203). Even historians who chart the appeal of evangelicalism to groups such as women and blacks on the fringes of southern society in the late eighteenth century have found that the "world of southern evangelicals converged with that of southern masters" in the antebellum era (Heyrman, *Southern Cross*, 248). See also Lyerly, *Methodism and the Southern Mind*, 176–86.

3. Weiner, *Mistresses and Slaves*, 57. For the classic formulation of separate spheres, see Welter, "Cult of True Womanhood." For syntheses of how this formulation has evolved in different times and regions, see, for example, Cott, *Bonds of Womanhood*, esp. 197–204; Kerber, "Separate Spheres." For a study on how northern women transferred these ideals into benevolent work and on some of the limits of that work, see Ginzberg, *Women and the Work of Benevolence*; Boylan, *Origins of Women's Activism*. On the limitations of this conceptualization in the South, see, for example, Fox-Genovese, *Within the Plantation Household*, chap. 1; Cashin, *Our Common Affairs*, 2–6; Edwards, *Scarlett Doesn't Live Here Anymore*, 27.

4. Kierner, *Beyond the Household*, 218. See also Weiner, *Mistresses and Slaves*, 68–71.

5. See McMillen, *Motherhood in the Old South*, 1–6, 170. For the classic study of the northern middle-class mother as moral steward and exemplar who turned her household into a virtual sanctuary, see Kuhn, *Mother's Role*, esp. 99–174.

6. See, for example, Kierner, *Beyond the Household*, 174; Censer, *North Carolina Planters*, 24–28; Pease and Pease, *Ladies, Women, and Wenches*, 10–14.

7. Glover persuasively argues that "this intense—and racialized—zeal for independence was rooted in slaveholding. . . . Whites compelled submissiveness from their slaves and defined slaves as dependent and therefore debased" (*Southern Sons*, 23).

8. William Wills to Anna Wills, March 27, 1836, Wills Papers. Evangelical men did not always share Wills's optimism about the blessings of fatherhood. See, for example, Richard Beale to Anne Beale Davis, August 22, 1842, Beale and Davis Family Papers.

9. McMillen, Censer, and Jabour argue that fertility rates remained higher among southern women than northern women in the antebellum period, even as national fertility rates declined "from an average of 7.04 children per woman of childbearing age in 1800 to 5.4 in 1850." See McMillen, *Motherhood in the Old*

South, 32–33; Censer, *North Carolina Planters*, 26–28; Jabour, *Scarlett's Sisters*, 217–25. McMillen also argues that southern women had twice the maternal mortality rate of New England women: "At least one out of twenty-five white women in the South who died in 1850 died in childbirth" (*Motherhood in the Old South*, 81, appendix 1, table 3).

10. Frances Moore Webb Bumpass Diary, February 6, 1843, 18, Bumpass Family Papers; Anne Beale Davis Diary, April 7, 1839, Beale and Davis Family Papers; 2 Corinthians 12:9–10.

11. Anne Beale Davis Diary, February 18, 1843, Beale and Davis Family Papers; Mary Davis Brown Journal, October 28, 1857. For additional examples of women dedicating their infant children to God's service, see Penelope Eliza Howard Alderman Diary, February 20, 1855, Southern Historical Collection, Wilson Library, University of North Carolina, Chapel Hill; Anne Beale Davis Diary, November 20, 1842, Beale and Davis Family Papers.

12. Mary Davis Brown Journal, October 28, 1857; Mary Jeffreys Bethell Diary, December 9, 1857.

13. Diary Excerpt, July 21, 1834, Douglass Correspondence; Mary Jeffreys Bethell Diary, November 18, 1860. For additional examples of how women incorporated additional kin within a spiritual framework when childbirth narratives moved beyond the mother-child-God relationship, see Mary Jeffreys Bethell Diary, n.d. Naming practices also underscore women's deep-seated desire to have piety transfer across the generations. When Eliza Heiskell heard that her sister had named her newborn son in honor of their grandfather, she hoped "he will inherit his grandfather[']s sound sense & sterling piety" (E[liza]. H[eiskell]. to Nancy Lincoln, October 3, 1836, Collection of Heiskell, McCampbell, Wilkes, and Steel Family Materials).

14. Sarah Fountain to Hannah Coker, January 18, 1837, Lide-Coker Family Papers; Mary Jeffreys Bethell Diary, March 3, 1862, May 17, 1862. See also, for example, Jabour, *Scarlett's Sisters*, 223–29; Stowe, *Doctoring the South*, 170–71; Leavitt, *Brought to Bed*, 13–63.

15. Anne Beale Davis Diary, January 7, 1844, February 18, 1843, April 4, 1841; Sarah Fountain to Hannah Coker, January 18, 1837, Lide-Coker Family Papers; Mary Jeffreys Bethell Diary, March 3, 1862, May 17, 1862. The idea that faith could reshape the southern religious landscape contrasts with Lewis's notion of the restrictive influence of maternal piety beyond the antebellum household ("Motherhood," 152–53).

16. Anne Beale Davis Diary, November 5, 1843, Anne Beale to Joseph Davis, August 11, 1836, both in Beale and Davis Family Papers; Anna Thomas Fuller to Jones Fuller, March 14, 1848, Fuller-Thomas Papers. For similar claims to helplessness in child rearing and dependency on God for guidance, see Anne Beale to Joseph Davis, November 9, 1837, Beale and Davis Family Papers.

17. Anne Beale Davis Diary, October 15, 1840, Beale and Davis Family Papers.

18. Elizabeth Early to Mary Virginia Early, July 3, 1854, Early Family Papers; Mary Jeffreys Bethell Diary, September 21, 1860.

19. Ruby Gillett to Sarah Gillett, August 2, 1830, Fuller-Thomas Papers; Cary Harrison to Mary Cox Collins, February 2, 1849, Collins Family Letters.

20. A[nn]. R. Sexton to Ann Thomas, September 21, 1845, Fuller-Thomas Papers. See also Ann Thomas to Anna Thomas Fuller, April 15, 1846, Fuller-Thomas Papers; Mary K. Craddock Diary, August 20, 1849.

21. Anne Beale Davis Diary, February 8, 1843, February 18, 1843, Beale and Davis Family Papers; 1 Corinthians 6:20; for additional evidence of Davis envisioning her children as cherubs, see January 22, 1843.

22. Rebecca Verstille to Nancy Verstille, December 2, 1827, Verstille Papers; Priscilla Taylor to Mary Cox Collins, August 20, 1854, Collins Family Letters. In her study of northern motherhood, Kuhn points to the eagerness of mothers to see their children convert in case they should perish in childhood, but she offers no evidence of maternal accountability for a child's death (*Mother's Role*, 74–75).

23. Juliette Dorland to Mary Cox Collins, April 7, 1860, Collins Family Letters.

24. Lizzie Cox to Mary Cox Collins, January 5, 1861, Collins Family Letters; Hebrews 12:11. See chap. 5 for Mary Bethell's frequent references to the death and angelic fate of her daughter, often occasioned by the anniversary of the child's birth or death.

25. Eugenia Rebecca Griffin Leland Journal, April 20, 1865. For an excellent discussion of evangelical parents' deep-seated concern for the perils that faced children in particular, see Greven, *Protestant Temperament*, 110–16.

26. For discussions of republican motherhood, see, for example, Kerber, "Republican Mother"; Lewis, "Motherhood"; Boylan, "Growing Up Female."

27. Baker, *Affectionate Address to Fathers*, 15; Moore, *Discourse*, 4, 5, 6–7; Manly, *Sunday School*, 32.

28. Moore, *Discourse*, 8–11; Baker, *Affectionate Address to Fathers*, 35–36.

29. Frances Jane Bestor Robertson Journal, January 1, 1852; Proverbs 22:6; William McCampbell to Susan Heiskell, March 22, 1858, Collection of Heiskell, McCampbell, Wilkes, and Steel Family Materials. Mary Bethell recalled how her stepmother, whom she described as "pious and sensible," introduced her father to evangelical religion, and he and his children subsequently converted. But her stepmother's piety transcended the boundaries of the family, for Bethell's father joined the clergy and brought many converts into the Methodist fold (Mary Jeffreys Bethell Diary, n.d.).

30. Anne Beale Davis Diary, January 4, 1846, Joseph Davis to Anne Beale Davis, January 21, 1850, both in Beale and Davis Family Papers; Richard Collins

to Mary Cox Collins, May 3, 1857, Collins Family Letters. For an excellent discussion of Methodist class meetings, see Lyerly, *Methodism and the Southern Mind*, 14.

31. Anne Beale Davis Diary, January 4, 1846, March 24, 1849, Joseph Davis to Anne Beale Davis, November 22, 1851, all in Beale and Davis Family Papers.

32. Baker, *Daniel Baker's Talk*, 8–11, 41–42, 18–19. For useful overviews of this genre of children's literature as well as antebellum religious publishing, see MacLeod, *American Childhood*, esp. 95; MacLeod, *Moral Tale*; Murray, "Rational Thought and Republican Virtues"; Nord, *Faith in Reading*; Demers, *Heaven upon Earth*, esp. 154.

33. Mallary, *Social Visits*, iv, 20, 32–33; see also 109–23.

34. Anne Beale to Joseph Davis, October 12, 1837, Beale and Davis Family Papers; Frances Moore Webb Bumpass Diary, May 8, 1845, April 9, 1845, Bumpas Family Papers. Greven points out that evangelicals sought to make a "child's obedience, habitual and 'natural' from infancy, so that physical punishments . . . would be rarely necessary" (*Protestant Temperament*, 50). MacLeod and Wishy, conversely, stress that the call for self-restraint, conscience, and cooperation in antebellum children's literature stemmed from Americans' anxiety over unchecked individualism in the nation's economic and political institutions. See MacLeod, *American Childhood*; MacLeod, *Moral Tale*; Wishy, *Child and the Republic*. On "evil passions" among both parents and children, see, for example, Baker, *Affectionate Address to Fathers*, 15–19. Elsewhere, Baker wrote, "The kindling of passion is like the kindling of fire; you don't know what it may lead to" (*Daniel Baker's Talk*, 22).

35. Frances Moore Webb Bumpass Diary, June 11, 1845. Greven argues that "what ultimately guaranteed [children's] obedience was their inability to exist comfortably on their own. Conscience therefore provided them with internalized rules, which mirrored their parents' wishes and wills more faithfully than even parents might have thought possible" (*Protestant Temperament*, 55). On the model of Protestant self-restraint in child rearing, see Kuhn, *Mother's Role*, 149–74.

36. Richard Collins to "My Dear Wife and Children," December 26, 1863, Richard Collins to Mary Cox Collins, April 10, 1859, May 7, 1858, all in Collins Family Letters.

37. Jabour, *Scarlett's Sisters*, 36. See also, for example, Glover, *Southern Sons*; Stowe, *Intimacy and Power*; Wyatt-Brown, *Southern Honor*.

38. Sidney D. Bumpass Autobiography and Diary, January 1, 1842, Bumpas Family Papers; Anne Beale to Joseph Davis, October 12, 1837, Beale and Davis Family Papers.

39. Richard Collins to "My Dear Wife and Children," December 26, 1863, Collins Family Letters.

40. Richard Collins to Mary Cox Collins, May 3, 1857, Collins Family Letters. For scholars who see the autonomy of sons and lax parental oversight as distinctively southern, see esp., Wyatt-Brown, *Southern Honor*, 117–74, esp. 143; Glover, *Southern Sons*, 9–36. For an overview of the debate on whether the sons of the South were raised to prize thrift and industry like their northern counterparts or to prize leisure and consumption, see Censer, *North Carolina Planters*, 53–55.

41. Richard Collins to Mary Cox Collins, May 10, 1857, Collins Family Letters. Richard's emphasis on piety and family as the conduit to manly confidence and independence rather than the means for probing self-assessment, humiliation, and emotion illustrates Heyrman's suggestion (*Southern Cross*, chap. 5) that evangelicals sought to attract more men into the antebellum fold by closing the gap between secular and sacred norms of masculinity.

42. Samuel Haycraft Journal, November 11, 1863.

43. Cary Whitaker to Anna M. B. Whitaker, August 1, 1831, Richard Wills to Mary Wills, June 10, 1861, both in Wills Papers.

44. Richard Collins to Mary Cox Collins, May 21, 1857, Collins Family Letters; Richard Wills to Mary Wills, June 10, 1861, Wills Papers.

45. Frances Douglass to Henry Taylor, August 19, 1836, Douglass Correspondence.

46. Mary Jeffreys Bethell Diary, September 21, 1860, November 20, 1862.

47. Maria [Lide] to Hannah Coker, June 9, 1845, Lide-Coker Family Papers; E. Heiskell to Nancy Lincoln, [1846?], Collection of Heiskell, McCampbell, Wilkes, and Steel Family Materials; Mary K. Craddock Diary, August 20, 1849; Eugenia Rebecca Griffin Leland Journal, [November 1865]. For a general survey of the growth of Sunday schools in the antebellum era, see Boylan, *Sunday School*. For the southern context of the Sunday school movement, see Sparks, *On Jordan's Stormy Banks*, 53, 95, 107; Schweiger, *Gospel Working Up*, 73–75; Bode, "Common Sphere," 794; Bode, "Transformation," 724–27.

48. Heyrman, *Southern Cross*, chap. 4, esp. 161–77; Andrew, *Miscellanies*, 382.

49. Anne Beale Davis to Wilbur Davis, September 13, 1855, Beale and Davis Family Papers; Stephenson, "Davises," 261. As evangelical clergymen tabulated their achievements at revivals, they used the label "convert" to denote an individual who had obtained acceptance from God. They used "mourners" to denote individuals who had been "awakened" and who voiced (and often showed) distress over the state of their souls but who could not yet proclaim reconciliation with God. Individuals might spend minutes, hours, days, or weeks as mourners before experiencing conversion, but this precondition allowed clergymen to expand the claims of their revival work since most mourners ultimately converted. On the conversion process in the South and the place of mourners in that process, see Mathews, *Religion in the Old South*, 59; Bruce, *And They All*

Sang Hallelujah, 77–79; Heyrman, *Southern Cross*, 33–41. On the curriculum and nature of female academies in the South, see, for example, Farnham, *Education*, 68–93; Stowe, "Rhetoric of Authority," 922.

50. Anne Beale Davis to Joseph Davis, December 10, 1855, Beale and Davis Family Papers.

51. While both Stephenson and Farnham report on the revival, they emphasize the event's significance for female education in the South rather than Anne Davis's personal and familial piety (Stephenson, "Davises," 266; Farnham, *Education*, 172). For additional examples of the ways in which evangelical women employed the language of Christian resignation and duty as they enhanced their roles beyond their homes, see, Bode, "Common Sphere," 784–87; Junk, "'Ladies, Arise!'" introduction.

52. Anne Beale Davis Diary, January 11, 1857, Joseph Davis to Anne Beale Davis, December 17, 1855, both in Beale and Davis Family Papers. Because Farnham and Stephenson privilege Anne Davis's correspondence in their examinations, they provide a dramatically different profile of her than do historians who rely on her diary. Rather than the highly self-critical Christian profiled by Scott and Fox-Genovese, Davis appears as a woman who stirred conflict when she allowed an unmarried male instructor at the academy to date one of the female students (against the wishes of some in the young lady's family) (Farnham, *Education*, 132, 139). Stephenson notes that episode as well, adding a case where Davis intercepted a letter between her son and one of the pupils because she refused to allow him to court the girl as long as she remained at the Wesleyan Female College ("Davises," 271–73).

53. Anne Beale Davis to Robert Davis, December 5, 1855, Beale and Davis Family Papers; see also December 3, [1855].

54. Anne Beale Davis to Robert Davis, December 3, 1855, December 5, 1855, Anne Beale Davis to Joseph Davis, December 3, [1855], all in Beale and Davis Family Papers. The active exhortations by fellow female pupils within the academy parallel the public role that women often played in camp meetings as exhorters in the early national era (Heyrman, *Southern Cross*, esp. 164–67; Bruce, *And They All Sang Hallelujah*, 75–77). Among antebellum evangelicals, conviction signaled intense introspection and often emotional anguish because an individual "mourned" his or her sinfulness but had not yet discovered the convert's assurance of God's acceptance.

55. Anne Beale Davis to Joseph Davis, December 10, 1855, Beale and Davis Family Papers; for virtually the same wording on her humble role in the events, see Anne Beale Davis to Robert Davis, December 5, 1855, Beale and Davis Family Papers.

56. Clergymen would also have downplayed their agency in the process of any revival, though they regularly tallied their converts at the conclusion of a meet-

ing or revival season as a means of measuring personal and professional success. These tallies not only were celebrated locally but also were often reported to local and regional religious publications. For an example of a more typical female academy revival under the watchful supervision of men, see Thomas's account of a revival at the Wesleyan Female College in Macon, Georgia, in 1849 (*Secret Eye*, chap. 1, esp. 83, 86). Although a first-generation evangelical herself, Anne Davis had experience proselytizing among her siblings after her mother's early death. However, at least two of her siblings failed to convert. See Anne Beale Davis Diary, November 20, 1842, Beale and Davis Family Papers.

57. Anne Beale Davis to Robert Davis, December 5, 1855, Beale and Davis Family Papers. Bode observes how white women used a religiously informed language of deference in other contexts "to subvert notions of their inferiority" ("Common Sphere," 786).

58. Anne Beale Davis to Robert Davis, December 5, 1855, Wilbur Davis to Anne Beale Davis, January 2, 1856, both in Beale and Davis Family Papers.

59. Anne Beale Davis to Robert Davis, December 5, 1855, Beale and Davis Family Papers.

60. Boles observes how evangelical clergy during the Great Revival used evidence of social, religious, and moral decline as a springboard to success (*Great Revival*, 42–43). On the southern social context of revivalism and individual conversion, see Mathews, *Religion in the Old South*, 48–52, 11–14; Bruce, *And They All Sang Hallelujah*, 61–95. For detailed information on enrollment at Wesleyan and Chowan, see Stephenson, "Davises," 260–61.

61. In his community study of Twiggs County, Georgia, Bode observed a steady decline in the age of converts in the Baptist church there. While the median age for the conversion of white men stood at 30.5 years of age in the period 1830–40, it dropped to 17 for the period 1854–61. Similarly, for white women, the age of conversion dropped from a median of 26 years during the 1830s to 19 between 1854 and 1861 ("Transformation," 722–23).

62. On the conversion process in the South, see Mathews, *Religion in the Old South*, 59; Bruce, *And They All Sang Hallelujah*, 77–79; Heyrman, *Southern Cross*, 33–41; Boles, *Great Revival*, 131–35. For a useful synthesis of the conversion process among Methodists in the Ohio River Valley, see Schneider, *Way of the Cross*, 43–44. On individual improvisation within the conversion narrative formula, see Payne, *Self and the Sacred*, 33–49, esp. 33–34. In her study of post–Civil War southern Sunday schools, McMillen observes how conversions, previously deemed spontaneous and individual events, had become "crafted lessons that encouraged pupils to make this decision in a controlled group setting and as a collective—and directed—experience," ultimately leading to "Decision Day, when groups of children from various schools all underwent conversion simultaneously" (*To Raise Up the South*, 12–13).

63. Mary Jeffreys Bethell Diary, n.d.; Anne Beale Davis Diary, February 9, 1851, Beale and Davis Family Papers; Frances Moore Webb Bumpass Diary, May 12, 1851, Bumpas Family Papers.

64. Samuel Henderson Jr. Diary, n.d.; Sidney D. Bumpass Autobiography and Diary, January 1, 1842, chap. 2, Bumpas Family Papers; William Wills to W. W. Hill, May 23, 1830, Wills Papers.

65. Frances Moore Webb Bumpass Diary, May 12, 1851, Bumpas Family Papers; William Wills to W. W. Hill, May 23, 1830, W. W. Hill to William Wills, June 7, 1830, both in Wills Papers.

66. Anne Beale Davis Diary, October 8, 1848, Beale and Davis Family Papers; Eliza Hibben Leland Journal, August 14, 1853, September 24, 1853.

67. Ann Thomas to Anna [Thomas], February 1842, Fuller-Thomas Papers; Richard Collins to Mary Cox Collins, May 10, 1858, December 26, 1863, Lizzie Cox to Annie Collins, June 7, 1860, Annie Collins to Richard Collins, February 6, 1863, all in Collins Family Letters. For further examples of attempts to persuade relatives to convert, see Ann Richmond Hill Inge to Sarah Thomas, July 30, 1824, Fuller-Thomas Papers; Lizzie Fountain to Hannah Coker, October 30, 1841, Lide-Coker Family Papers.

68. George Andrews to Jonathan Davis, April 5, 1850, Anna Andrews to Robert Davis, October 3, 1850, Beale and Davis Family Papers. On nineteenth-century evangelicals' struggle to strike a balance in their conversion narratives between the familiar components of the conversion experience and the individualized qualities of a personal conversion, see Payne, *Self and the Sacred*; Brereton, *From Sin to Salvation*.

69. Sarah Fountain to Hannah Coker, August 22, 1835, Lide-Coker Family Papers; Samuel Henderson Jr. Diary, November 15, 1863. See also Samuel Haycraft Journal, May 22, 1861; Eugenia Rebecca Griffin Leland Journal, April 23, 1865; Eliza Hibben Leland Journal, 1853.

70. Sidney D. Bumpass Autobiography and Diary, December 1, 1841, Bumpas Family Papers; Holder, "My Dear Husband," 321–22 (Martha Winans to William Winans, April 25, 1844). On the risks to male mastery posed by the conversion process, see Heyrman, *Southern Cross*, 206–52; Greven, *Protestant Temperament*, 100–102.

71. Mary Jeffreys Bethell Diary, December 12, 1853, July 29, 1863, March 7, 1865, August 7, 1865; for additional evidence that Bethell thought the hardships of military service might benefit her son's spirituality, see May 18, 1861.

72. Frances Moore Webb Bumpass Diary, April, 24, 1845, Bumpas Family Papers; Mary Jeffreys Bethell Diary, December 9, 1857; Richard Wills to Anna Wills, December 2, 1859, Wills Papers. For detailed discussions of white women's central role in the dissemination of religious values within the southern

home, see, for example, Weiner, *Mistresses and Slaves*, 72–88, esp. 80–83; Fox-Genovese, *Within the Plantation Household*, 140–45.

73. Frances Douglass to James Walter Douglass, April 9, 1835, May 15, 1835, May 27, 1835, Douglass Correspondence.

74. Mary Jeffreys Bethell Diary, November 3, 1856; Elizabeth B. Early to Mary Virginia Brown, n.d., Early Family Papers.

75. Greven, *Protestant Temperament*, 110.

76. Anne Beale Davis Diary, January 1857, August 23, 1857, Anne Beale Davis to [Robert?] Davis, November 22, 1855, all in Beale and Davis Family Papers.

77. Anne Beale Davis to Wilbur Davis, October 23, 1855, Anne Beale Davis to Robert Davis, December 25, 1854, both in Beale and Davis Family Papers; Glover, *Southern Sons*, 37–96. For further evidence of Anne Davis's simultaneous confidence in her sons' piety and distrust of his decision making, see her directions to her brother when she left one of her sons with him (Anne Beale Davis to R[ichard]. L. T. Beale, August 9, 1853, Beale and Davis Family Papers).

78. Anne Beale Davis to John Davis, March 15, 1858, Joseph Davis to Robert Davis, February 1, 1856, both in Beale and Davis Family Papers. For additional references to young Solomon as a worthy model, see Joseph Davis to [Robert?] Davis, July 27, 1855, Beale and Davis Family Papers.

79. Joseph Davis to Robert Davis, February 1, 1856, August 21, 1855, August 30, 1855, Beale and Davis Family Papers; see also July 27, 1855. Judging from Robert Davis's report card at Randolph-Macon, his parents had good reason for their anxiety and advice. After he failed a course on Virgil and received only fair grades for the rest of his coursework, the faculty at Randolph-Macon allowed Davis to remain at the school only on the condition that he reside with his uncle in town. Rev. Davis's brother, W. J. Davis, offered to take in his nephew but warned of the recent misbehavior of students at the college and sought advance permission from his brother to use the switch "if the faculty complain to me of him as they have during the past session" (W. J. Davis to Joseph Davis, December 20, 1848, Beale and Davis Family Papers).

80. Joseph Davis to [Robert] Davis, August 30, 1855, Beale and Davis Family Papers; 1 Chronicles 28:9.

81. Frances Douglass to William Henry Taylor, May 2, 1834, Frances Douglass to James Walter Douglass, May 8, 1834, both in Douglass Correspondence.

82. James Walter Douglass to William Henry Taylor, January 18, 1836, Douglass Correspondence. For an example of Rev. Douglass's pontificating style to his stepson, see James Walter Douglass to William Henry Taylor, April 4, 1836, Douglass Correspondence.

83. Frances Douglass to Henry Taylor, July 4, 1836, March 14, 1836, May 15, 1840, Frances Douglass to James Walter Douglass, May 8, 1834, James and

Frances Douglass to Henry Taylor, February 21, 1836, all in Douglass Correspondence. Glover notes in her study of college-aged southern men that many students used poor health as a justification for underperformance in the classroom (*Southern Sons*, 66).

84. Frances Douglass to Henry Taylor, May 15, 1840, Douglass Correspondence.

85. L[ucy]. A[nn]. Gwathmey to Edward Garlick Gwathmey, n.d. [fragment], October 17, 1860, L[ucy]. A[nn]. Gwathmey to Nelly Gwathmey, February 12, 1860, all in Gwathmey Family Papers.

86. As Schneider observes, even Methodist clergymen in the early nineteenth century professed their inadequacy for leadership over others (*Way of the Cross*, 63–64).

Chapter 5. Authoring the Good Death

1. A[nn]. R. Sexton to Ann Thomas, November 20, 1844, Fuller-Thomas Papers. The classic formulation for understanding death and dying remains Ariès, *Hour of Our Death*. For summaries of death and dying in the antebellum North, see esp. Laderman, *Sacred Remains*; Saum, "Death." For excellent summaries of the Good Death in its southern context, which in its broadest terms parallels the patterns identified by Laderman and others, see Faust, "Civil War Soldier," esp. 6–16; Greenberg, *Honor and Slavery*, 92–93; Sparks, "Southern Way of Death."

2. For critiques of the "domestication of death" and mourning rituals among northern middle-class women, see, for example, Douglas, *Feminization of American Culture*, 200–226; Halttunen, *Confidence Men and Painted Women*, chap. 5.

3. See, for example, Ryan, *Cradle of the Middle Class*, esp. 83–104; Marshall, "'In the Midst of Life.'"

4. For starkly contrasting views of how southern slaveholding men responded to death and dying, see Greenberg, *Honor and Slavery*, chap. 4, which stresses the ways in which slaveholding men used the secular ethic of honor to demonstrate mastery over death, and Oakes, *Ruling Race*, chap. 4, esp. 112–17, which argues that slaveholders' guilt over slavery emerged most forcefully at their slaves' deathbeds, even prompting slaveholders to fear eternal damnation for their reliance on human bondage.

5. Studies of how slaveholding women understood the deathbed illustrate a range of responses, but they share an emphasis on the individualized nature of death and grieving among southern women. For studies that stress the psychological burdens of death within the family—particularly the loss of children—on southern women, see, for example, Friedman, *Enclosed Garden*, 5; McMillen, *Motherhood in the Old South*, chap. 7; Censer, *North Carolina Planters*; Fox-Genovese, *Within the Plantation Household*, 16–18.

6. McCurry, *Masters of Small Worlds*, 172–77.

7. Historians continue to debate whether the Second Great Awakening substantively challenged inegalitarianism in the early national South. Historians who see little if any change resulting from the event include, among others, McCurry, *Masters of Small Worlds*, 136–47; Spangler, "Becoming Baptists," 243–86. Historians who note a marked contrast between evangelical and nonevangelical beliefs and standards in the early national period include, among others, Isaac, *Transformation of Virginia*; Heyrman, *Southern Cross*.

8. Schneider, *Way of the Cross*, 119; Jane Lide to David Lide, June 3, 1844, Papers of the Lide, Coker, and Stout Families.

9. Maggie Whitaker to Cary Whitaker, May 26, 1853, Wills Papers; Mary Jeffreys Bethell Diary, June 5, 1855; Anne Beale Davis to John Davis, October 20, 1858, Beale and Davis Family Papers.

10. Frances Douglass to Henry Taylor, August 1, 1835, Douglass Correspondence; James Whitaker to George Whitaker, November 13, 1848, Wills Papers. See also James Walter Douglass to Frances Douglass, June 23, 1834, May 11, 1835, Douglass Correspondence.

11. Anna Wills to William Wills, May 16, 1850, Wills Papers; Anne Beale Davis to John Davis, March 15, 1858, Beale and Davis Family Papers; Hu Brown to Mary Ann Susan Brown, May 18, 1838, Collection of Heiskell, McCampbell, Wilkes, and Steel Family Materials; Stowe, *Doctoring the South*, 151–53, 224–27. For a patient's praise of a doctor, see, for example, Anne Beale to Joseph Davis, May 25, 1837, Beale and Davis Family Papers.

12. S[arah]. J. F[ountain]. to Hannah Coker, February 15, 1838, Lide-Coker Family Papers. Anne Beale reported to Joseph Davis that severe illness drove her sister, Emily, to convert and then proselytize among family members and slaves (Anne Beale to Joseph Davis, October 12, 1837, Beale and Davis Family Papers).

13. Mary Davis Brown Journal, April 26, 1855.

14. Anne Beale Davis Diary, March 24, 1849, Beale and Davis Family Papers.

15. Joseph Davis to Robert Davis, March 26, 1855, Beale and Davis Family Papers; James Walter Douglass to Henry Taylor, July 26, 1837, Douglass Correspondence; James Walter Douglass Diary Excerpt, July 31, 1834, Douglass Correspondence; William Cowper, "Olney Hymn 63: Light Shining out of Darkness."

16. Mary [Douglass Gray] to Frances Douglass, August 5, 1841, Douglass Correspondence; Mary K. Craddock Diary, January 6, 1845.

17. C[harlotte]. L. S. V[erstille]. to Nancy Verstille, September 1, 1837, Verstille Papers; S[arah]. J. F[ountain]. to Hannah Coker, February 15, 1838, Lide-Coker Family Papers.

18. Mary Jeffreys Bethell Diary, July 23, 1860, February 12, 1863. For more on southern families, westward migration, and the anxiety of women, see Cashin, *Family Venture*, esp. 85–91, 108–12; Censer, "Southwestern Migration." In this

instance, Bethell was unusually sanguine in her spiritual vindication; see also, for example, Mary Jeffreys Bethell Diary, May 2, 1865. Of course men also observed the ways in which God answered prayers. When his son-in-law converted, Kentucky Baptist Samuel Haycraft recorded in his diary, "My daughter wrote to me the welcome intelligence that her husband the Col. had professed religion, to that end my prayers had been offered twice a day for months" (Samuel Haycraft Journal, May 22, 1861).

19. E[lizabeth]. Fountain to Hannah Coker, September 14, 1835, Lide-Coker Family Papers; Frances Moore Webb Bumpass Diary, April 2, 1852, Bumpas Family Papers.

20. Mary Jeffreys Bethell Diary, January 1, 1858, n.d.; Psalms 25:14; Hu Brown to Mary Ann Susan Brown, April 1835, Collection of Heiskell, McCampbell, Wilkes, and Steel Family Materials. See also Mary [Douglass Gray] to Frances Douglass, September 5, 1839, Frances Douglass to Henry Taylor, August 27, 1843, July 4, 1836, August 1, 1835, August 19, 1836, all in Douglass Correspondence; Jones Fuller to Anna Thomas, February 14, 1846, Fuller-Thomas Papers. The clergy also pronounced that those without faith would shrink in the face of illness and the possibility of judgment; see, for example, M'Iver, *Virginia and North Carolina Presbyterian Preacher*, 58.

21. James Whitaker to Cary Whitaker, April 7, 1846, Wills Papers; James Walter Douglass Diary Excerpt, December 6, 1834, Douglass Correspondence.

22. Julia A. Gilchrist to S. M[argaret]. Van Wyck, June 22, 1855, Papers of the Maverick and Van Wyck Family, 1772–1972, South Caroliniana Library, University of South Carolina, Columbia; E. G. Plumer to Frances Douglass, September 12, 1837, Douglass Correspondence.

23. Frances Douglass to Henry Taylor, September 1, 1837, Douglass Correspondence; Mary K. Craddock Diary, May 29, 1842.

24. Fanny Cox Brodrick to Mary Cox Collins, September 20, 1860, n.d., November 1, 1860, Lizzie Cox to Mary Cox Collins, June 3, 1861, Kate Collins to Mary Cox Collins, November 6, 1861, Ellen Collins Blatterman to Mary Cox Collins, November 2, 1861, all in Collins Family Letters.

25. Richard Collins to Mary Cox Collins, March 23, 1864, March 28, 1864, Ellen Collins Blatterman to Mary Cox Collins, March 18, 1864, all in Collins Family Letters.

26. Anne Beale to Joseph Davis, January 25, 1838, Beale and Davis Family Papers.

27. Charlotte Verstille to Nancy Verstille, December 2, 1827, Verstille Papers. I thank Ann Kirschner for her insight regarding this piece of evidence.

28. Andrew, *Cross of Christ*, 74–77.

29. Andrew, *Miscellanies*, 382–93.

30. Charlotte Verstille to Nancy Verstille, October 29, 1821, Verstille Papers;

Cary Whitaker to William Wills, February 2, 1838, Wills Papers; Frances Jane Bestor Robertson Journal, January 17, 1842.

31. Frances Jane Bestor Robertson Journal, January 4, 1852, June 25, 1852, June 26, 1852, August 10, 1852, September 17, 1854.

32. Mary Jeffreys Bethell Diary, September 7, 1858; E[liza]. H[eiskell]. to Nancy Lincoln, December 1827, Collection of Heiskell, McCampbell, Wilkes, and Steel Family Materials.

33. Anne Beale Davis Diary, April 14, 1850, Beale and Davis Family Papers.

34. Samuel Henderson Jr. Diary, May 7, 1857, September 19, 1857; Mary K. Craddock Diary, March 16, 1843.

35. Mary Jeffreys Bethell Diary, April 2, 1861, June 6, 1860, n.d.; Sarah Fountain to Hannah Coker, December 9, 1839, Lide-Coker Family Papers.

36. McCurry, *Masters of Small Worlds*, 172–75; William Wills, obituary for Fanny Pitts Vinson, July 8, 1852, obituary for Cary Whitaker, July 1, 1858, both in Wills Papers. For an example of a clergyman using an impious man's deathbed to warn unconverted men about their eternal risks, see James Walter Douglass to Henry Taylor, May 1, 1836, Douglass Correspondence.

37. Waddel, *Sermon*, 24, 21; Furman, *Sermon*, 15–16; Andrew, *Miscellanies*, 392–93, 381.

38. Halttunen, *Confidence Men and Painted Women*, chap. 5.

39. Frances Douglass to Sally Richardson, September 12, 1837, Frances Douglass to Henry Taylor, September 15, 1837, both in Douglass Correspondence.

40. H. Potter to Frances Douglass, September 9, 1837, E. G. Plumer to Frances Douglass, September 12, 1837, Drury Lacy to Frances Douglass, October 26, 1837, all in Douglass Correspondence; 1 Thessalonians 4:13. On James Douglass's quest for improved piety through greater reliance on his wife and domestic devotion, see chap. 3.

41. W. M. Atkinson to Frances Douglass, September 13, 1837, E. G. Plumer to Frances Douglass, September 12, 1837, Ann A. Reid to Frances Douglass, December 16, 1837, Drury Lacy to Frances Douglass, October 26, 1837, H. Potter to Frances Douglass, September 9, 1837, all in Douglass Correspondence; Hosea 6:1. Much like Lacy, Frances Devereux wrote, "May it be your consolation my dear christian friend, to know by sweet experience the promises of the widows God, & in all your trials find His arm a sure support" (Frances Devereux to Frances Douglass, October 26, 1837, Douglass Correspondence).

42. Ann A. Reid to Frances Douglass, December 16, 1837, Frances Douglass to Henry Taylor, September 15, 1837, both in Douglass Correspondence. As chap. 4 discusses, Frances Douglass also attempted to use her husband's death to stir discomfort and drive in her son.

43. Elizabeth S. Harewell to William Wills, December 10, 1834, Wills Papers. For studies that detail women's sense of accountability for their children's

deaths, see McMillen, *Motherhood in the Old South*, 173–75; Censer, *North Carolina Planters*, 29–30.

44. Frances Douglass to Henry Taylor, September 15, 1837, Douglass Correspondence.

45. Frances Douglass to Sally Richardson, September 12, 1837, Douglass Correspondence.

46. Simeon Colton to Frances Douglass, March 24, 1839, May 14, 1838, Douglass Correspondence. On the debate between Old and New School Presbyterians in the South, including the situation in North Carolina, see Snay, *Gospel of Disunion*, 112–26.

47. Frances Moore Webb Bumpass Diary, February 2, 1852, Bumpass Family Papers.

48. Ibid., August [1852?].

49. Ibid., April 2, 1852. For more on Frances Bumpass's editorship of the *Weekly Message*, see Junk, "'Ladies, Arise!'"

50. Frances Moore Webb Bumpass Diary, March 17, 1852, November 16, [1854?], January 29, [1854?], Bumpas Family Papers.

51. Mary Jeffreys Bethell Diary, October 24, 1864, January 1, 1853, n.d., October 24, 1864; Lyerly, *Methodism and the Southern Mind*, 41–46, esp. 43. According to Sparks, late-antebellum evangelicals increasingly used the metaphor of death rather than birth to refer to the conversion process ("Southern Way of Death," 34).

52. Mary [Douglass Gray] to Frances Douglass, May 11, 1839, April 17, 1839, December 25, 1837, Douglass Correspondence.

53. McDannell and Lang, *Heaven*, 183. For heaven as a "celestial city," see Frances Douglass to Sally Richardson, September 12, 1837, Douglass Correspondence; for the heavenly throne, see William Wills to Anna Wills, March 27, 1836, Wills Papers; Mary [Douglass Gray] to Frances Douglass, September 5, 1839, Douglass Correspondence. McDannell and Lang demonstrate how these core notions of heaven mark a sharp departure from earlier versions of heaven, which stressed "purgatory or sleeping in the grave until the general resurrection": in the "modern" vision of heaven, "delighting the senses, once perceived as a frivolous pastime, becomes a major aspect of eternal life," the "journey to God does not end with admittance to heaven but continues eternally," and "God is loved not only directly but also through the love and charity shown to others in heaven" (McDannell and Lang, *Heaven*, 183).

54. Mary [Douglass Gray] to Frances Douglass, October 7, 1840, Douglass Correspondence; see also September 5, 1839, August 5, 1841; Ann Thomas to Anna Thomas Fuller, November 10, 1846, Fuller-Thomas Papers; Frances Moore Webb Bumpass Diary, February 10, 1852, Bumpas Family Papers. For more on spirits and angels, see McDannell and Lang, *Heaven*, 188–93.

55. Ann Thomas to "very dear Sister," November 1840, Fuller-Thomas Papers; Martha Gamble to Jane [Crawford], March 9, 1860, Gaston-Crawford Family Papers; E[liza]. Heiskell to Nancy Lincoln, September 21, 1835, Collection of Heiskell, McCampbell, Wilkes, and Steel Family Materials. For similar examples from the Gaston-Crawford family, see Mary Boyd to Jane Crawford, October 1, 1844, Martha Gamble to "dear cousin," September 10, 1857, Gaston-Crawford Family Papers. Women's work on the deathbeds of dying kin reinforced the religious and familial bonds that spanned the South and reached into heaven. These bonds did more than foster sympathy; they also renewed a collective sense of pilgrimage. Even though Ruby Gillett had never met her sister-in-law, Sarah Gillett, in person, the death of Ruby's brother (Sarah's husband) inspired Ruby to offer religious consolation: "There is one who is able to grant consolation even this bereavement one who has promised to be the widows husband and Father to the fatherless. how consoling are these expressions and may we even be enabled to trust the promise of a Saviour and find comfort in them in all times of trial" (Ruby Gillett to Sarah A. Gillett, April 15, 1828, Fuller-Thomas Papers). For studies that emphasize the emotional and psychological stress created by rural isolation, particularly among women, see Friedman, *Enclosed Garden*; Cashin, *Family Venture*.

56. Mary Davis Brown Journal, October 7, 1855, December 31, 1856; Eliza Hibben Leland Journal, October 2, 1853; Cary Whitaker to Anna Wills, March 14, 1837, Wills Papers; Mary Jeffreys Bethell Diary, June 9, 1863; Kierner, *Beyond the Household*, 140–41. See also Cary Whitaker to Anna Wills, February 2, 1838, Wills Papers.

57. Anne Beale Davis Diary, February 9, 1858, Beale and Davis Family Papers; Mary [Douglass Gray] to Frances Douglass, October 7, 1840, Douglass Correspondence; Frances Jane Bestor Robertson Journal, September 17, 1854. Although Frances Bestor continued to feel discomfort at her mother's grave, it paled in comparison to her feelings at her mother's burial: "When I reached the grave I could not realize it was my Mother's. Oh may I never spend another hour of such unuterable anguish as I did over her grave" (Frances Jane Bestor Robertson Journal, June 26, 1852). For more on the cemetery movement as both a liminal site for the grieving and a growing business venture across the nation, see, for example, Laderman, *Sacred Remains*, chap. 3, esp. 44–45; Gary Wills, *Lincoln at Gettysburg*, chap. 2.

58. Ownby, "Patriarchy," 237–38. On how wartime hardships and separation caused Confederate men to discuss their feelings and emotions in novel ways, see Faust, *Mothers of Invention*, 114–38.

59. Richard Collins to Mary Cox Collins, February 7, 1864, Collins Family Letters. For more details on these circumstances and the Collins family, see chap. 3.

60. Ibid.

61. E. W. Thompson to William Wills, November 7, 1864, George Wills to Richard Wills, September 14, 1864, Wills Papers. According to a family member fighting alongside George, he died instantly from the explosion of a shell (I. R. Whitaker to William Wills, September 20, 1864, Wills Papers). George's instantaneous death on the battlefield away from home only added to the uncertainty, causing the family to try to re-create his demeanor before and during battle for evidence of his foreknowledge and preparation for death. For more on how conditions in the Civil War complicated evangelical notions of the Good Death, see Faust, "Civil War Soldier."

62. Washington to Richard Wills, October 30, 1864, Wills Papers. The letter was transcribed by a Wills family member (most likely Edwin Wills, based on handwriting style and references). On the often tense relationships between masters and slaves during the Civil War, see, for example, Faust, *Mothers of Invention*, 53–79. On the nexus of piety and Confederate troops, see Faust, "Civil War Soldier"; Berends, "Confederate Sacrifice." On wartime revivals among Confederate troops, see, for example, Woodworth, *While God Is Marching On*; Faust, "Christian Soldiers."

Epilogue. "We Walk by Faith and Not by Sight"

1. Faust nicely captures how the war transformed southern white women's relationship to their families, necessitating "significant alterations, even perversions, of this system of meaning; women's self-sacrifice for personally significant others—husbands, brothers, sons, family—was transformed into sacrifice of those individuals to an abstract and intangible 'Cause'" ("Altars of Sacrifice," 1209).

2. Samuel Henderson Jr. Diary, September 26, 1862, November 14, 1862, February 10, 1863, March 31, 1863, April 13, 1863; Mary Jeffreys Bethell Diary, August 7, 1865; William Wills to Richard Wills, October 4, 1865, Wills Papers; 2 Corinthians 5:7; Eugenia Rebecca Griffin Leland Journal, June 4, 1865.

3. William Wills to Richard Wills, October 4, 1865, Wills Papers; Mary Jeffreys Bethell Diary, August 7, 1865.

4. Eugenia Rebecca Griffin Leland Journal, June 4, 1865; William Wills to Richard Wills, October 4, 1865, Wills Papers; Mary Jeffreys Bethell Diary, August 7, 1865.

5. On the racial segregation of evangelical congregations after the Civil War, see, for example, Walker, *Rock*; Harvey, *Redeeming the South*; Stowell, *Rebuilding Zion*. On the dramatic surge in institution building among white and black evangelicals, see, for example, Higginbotham, *Righteous Discontent*; Schweiger, *Gospel Working Up*; McMillen, *To Raise Up the South*; Censer, *Reconstruction of White Southern Womanhood*, 153–206.

6. John Poulton to Rosannah Davisson, November 18, 1859, John Poulton to Rosannah Davisson Poulton, February 4, 1860, November 22, 1860, Poulton Family Papers.

7. Rosannah Davisson to John Poulton, April 5, 1858, March 1, 1858, Rosannah Davisson Poulton to John Poulton, July 9, 1862, all in Poulton Family Papers.

8. Obituary for Rosannah Davisson Poulton, December 29, 1869, Elizabeth Davisson to John Poulton, September 16, 1870, October 19, 1870, all in Poulton Family Papers.

9. John Poulton to Elizabeth Davisson, December 31, 1872, Poulton Family Papers.

10. For the charges of Poulton's professional misconduct, see William Pattie to J. H. Davis, October 21, 1871, Poulton Family Papers.

11. Richard Collins to Lewis Collins Jr., Sue Peers Collins, and Valen Peers Collins, April 17, 1864, Richard Collins to Mary Cox Collins, April 10, 1864, both in Collins Family Letters. On the powerful intersection of evangelicalism and the Lost Cause mythology, see, for example, Charles Reagan Wilson, *Baptized in Blood*; Poole, *Never Surrender*, 37–56.

12. Fanny Cox Brodrick to Mary Cox Collins, April 25, 1861, Lizzie Cox to Mary Cox Collins, June 15, 1863, Ellen Collins Blatterman to Mary Cox Collins, June 17, 1863, all in Collins Family Letters.

13. Lizzie Cox to Mary Cox Collins, June 3, 1861, September 8, 1861, Fanny Cox Brodrick to Mary Cox Collins, October 2, 1863, November 9, 1863, May 18, 1868, all in Collins Family Letters.

14. For scholars who argue that women experienced limited social change because of the war, see, for example, Whites, *Civil War*; Faust, *Mothers of Invention*. For scholars who see limited but significant changes in white women's roles in the postwar South, see, for example, Censer, *Reconstruction of White Southern Womanhood*; Jabour, *Scarlett's Sisters*, 239–84. For the classic statement of women's transformation in the wake of Civil War, see Scott, *Southern Lady*.

15. Mathews, *Religion in the Old South*, 102.

BIBLIOGRAPHY

Published Primary Sources

Andrew, James O. *The Cross of Christ; Being a Sermon Preached by the Late H. B. Bascom, D.D., LL.D., before the General Conference of the Methodist Episcopal Church, South, in St. Louis, Missouri, May 12th, 1850; to Which Is Added a Brief Sketch of His Illness and Death; Together with the Funeral Discourse, Delivered on the Occasion, before the Louisville Conference, at Greensburg, Kentucky, September 21st, 1850.* Louisville, Ky.: Morton and Griswold, 1851.

———. *Family Government: A Treatise on Conjugal, Parental, and Filial Duties.* Charleston, S.C.: Jenkins, 1847.

———. *Miscellanies: Comprising Letters, Essays, and the Addresses to Which Is Added a Biographical Sketch of Mrs. Ann Amelia Andrew.* Louisville, Ky.: Morton and Griswold, 1854.

Bailey, Rufus William. *The Family Preacher; or, Domestic Duties Illustrated and Enforced in Eight Discourses.* New York: Taylor, 1837.

Baker, Daniel D. *An Affectionate Address to Fathers.* Philadelphia: Presbyterian Board of Education, 1852.

———. *Daniel Baker's Talk to Little Children.* Philadelphia: Presbyterian Board of Education, 1856.

Douglass, James W. *A Work to Do: The Substance of a Discourse, Delivered November 26, 1836, at the Funeral of Mrs. Winifred Miller, Relict of the Late Colonel Stephen Miller, and of Her Daughter, Mrs. Rachel Winifred McIver, Wife of Rev. Alexander McIver, All of Duplin County, N.C.* Richmond, Va.: White, 1837.

Furman, James C. *A Sermon Occasioned by the Death of Mrs. Jane Draughon Edwards, Preached at Society Hill, S.C., Oct. 18th, 1835.* Cheraw, S.C.: Gazette, 1836.

Holder, Ray, ed. "My Dear Husband: Letters of a Plantation Mistress: Martha Dubose Winans to William Winans, 1834–1844." *Journal of Mississippi History* 49 (November 1987): 301–24.

Mallary, Charles. *Social Visits; or, A Few Chestnuts for the Children, and a Dinner for the Old Folks.* Charleston, S.C.: Southern Baptist Publication Society, 1854.

Manly, Basil. *A Sunday School in Every Baptist Church.* Charleston, S.C.: Southern Baptist Publication Society, 1858.

M'Iver, Colin, ed. *The Virginia and North Carolina Presbyterian Preacher; or, Monthly Sermons, from the Manuscripts of Presbyterian Ministers, Who Either Now Reside, or Have Formerly Resided in Virginia and North Carolina.* Fayetteville, N.C.: Evangelical Printing Office, 1829.

Moore, T. V. *A Discourse to Young Ladies, Delivered in the First Presbyterian Church, Richmond, Virginia, Feb. 29th, 1852.* Richmond: Ellyson, 1852.

Plumer, William S. *Thoughts on Religious Education and Early Piety.* New York: Taylor, 1836.

Rogers, E. P. *The Obligations and Duties of the Female Sex to Christianity: An Address, Delivered at the Annual Examination of the Washington Female Seminary, Thursday, June 14th.* Augusta, Ga.: McCafferty, 1849.

Thomas, Ella Gertrude Clanton. *The Secret Eye: The Journal of Ella Gertrude Clanton Thomas, 1848–1889.* Edited by Virginia Ingraham Burr. Chapel Hill: University of North Carolina Press, 1990.

Waddel, John N. *A Sermon on Occasion of the Death of Thomas Jas. Earle of Aberdeen, a Member of the Sophomore Class in the University of Mississippi, Preached in the Presbyterian Church, of Oxford, Miss., Dec. 7th, 1856.* Memphis: Morning Bulletin, 1857.

Secondary Sources

Andrews, Dee. *The Methodists and Revolutionary America, 1770–1800: The Shaping of an Evangelical Culture.* Princeton: Princeton University Press, 2000.

Ariès, Philippe. *The Hour of Our Death.* New York: Knopf, 1981.

Aron, Stephen. *How the West Was Lost: The Transformation of Kentucky from Daniel Boone to Henry Clay.* Baltimore: Johns Hopkins University Press, 1996.

Balleisen, Edward J. *Navigating Failure: Bankruptcy and Commercial Society in Antebellum American.* Chapel Hill: University of North Carolina Press, 2001.

Bardaglio, Peter. *Reconstructing the Household: Families, Sex, and the Law in the Nineteenth-Century South.* Chapel Hill: University of North Carolina Press, 1995.

Berends, Kurt O. "Confederate Sacrifice and the 'Redemption of the South.'" In *Religion in the American South: Protestants and Others in History and Culture*, edited by Beth Barton Schweiger and Donald G. Mathews, 99–124. Chapel Hill: University of North Carolina Press, 2004.

Berry, Stephen W., II. *All That Makes a Man: Love and Ambition in the Civil War South.* New York. Oxford University Press, 2003.

Bingham, Emily. "Thou Knowest Not What a Day May Bring Forth: Intellect, Power, Conversion, and Apostasy in the Life of Rachel Mordecai Lazarus (1788–1838)." In *Religion in the American South: Protestants and Others in History and Culture*, edited by Beth Barton Schweiger and Donald Mathews, 67–98. Chapel Hill: University of North Carolina Press, 2004.

Blassingame, John. *The Slave Community: Plantation Life in the Antebellum South.* New York: Oxford University Press, 1991.

Bode, Frederick A. "A Common Sphere: White Evangelicals and Gender in Antebellum Georgia." *Georgia Historical Quarterly* 79 (Winter 1995): 775–809.

———. "The Transformation of Evangelical Communities in Middle Georgia: Twiggs County, 1820–1861." *Journal of Southern History* 60 (November 1994): 711–48.

Boles, John B. *The Great Revival: Beginnings of the Bible Belt*. Rev. ed. 1972; Lexington: University Press of Kentucky, 1996.

———, ed. *Masters and Slaves in the House of the Lord*. Lexington: University Press of Kentucky, 1988.

Boylan, Anne. "Growing Up Female in Early America, 1800–1860." In *American Childhood: A Research Guide and Historical Handbook*, edited by Joseph M. Hawes and N. Ray Hiner, 153–84. Westport, Conn.: Greenwood, 1985.

———. *The Origins of Women's Activism: New York and Boston, 1797–1840*. Chapel Hill: University of North Carolina Press, 2002.

———. *Sunday School: The Formation of an American Institution, 1790–1880*. New Haven: Yale University Press, 1988.

Brereton, Virginia Lieson. *From Sin to Salvation: Stories of Women's Conversion*. Bloomington: Indiana University Press, 1991.

Bruce, Dickson D., Jr. *And They All Sang Hallelujah: Plain-Folk Camp-Meeting Religion, 1800–1845*. Knoxville: University of Tennessee Press, 1974.

Butler, Jon. *Awash in a Sea of Faith: Christianizing the American People*. Cambridge: Harvard University Press, 1990.

Carter, Christine Jacobson. *Southern Single Blessedness: Unmarried Women in the Urban South, 1800–1865*. Urbana: University of Illinois Press, 2006.

Cashin, Joan E. *A Family Venture: Men and Women on the Southern Frontier*. New York: Oxford University Press, 1991.

———, ed. *Our Common Affairs: Texts from Women in the Old South, 1800–1860*. Baltimore: Johns Hopkins University Press, 1996.

Censer, Jane Turner. *North Carolina Planters and Their Children, 1800–1860*. Baton Rouge: Louisiana State University Press, 1984.

———. *The Reconstruction of White Southern Womanhood, 1865–1895*. Baton Rouge: Louisiana State University Press, 2003.

———. "Southwestern Migration among North Carolina Planter Families: 'The Disposition to Emigrate.'" *Journal of Southern History* 57 (August 1991): 407–26.

Clarke, Erskine. *Dwelling Place: A Plantation Epic*. New Haven: Yale University Press, 2005.

Clinton, Catherine. *The Plantation Mistress: Woman's World in the Old South*. New York: Pantheon, 1982.

Cole, Stephanie. "Servants and Slaves: Domestic Service in the Border Cities, 1800–1850." Ph.D. diss., University of Florida, 1994.

Cornelius, Justin Duitsman. *Slave Missions and the Black Church in the Antebellum South*. Columbia: University of South Carolina Press, 1993.

Cott, Nancy F. *The Bonds of Womanhood: "Woman's Sphere" in New England, 1785–1835*. New Haven: Yale University Press, 1977.
———. *Public Vows: A History of Marriage and the Nation*. Cambridge: Harvard University Press, 2000.
Cross, Whitney R. *The Burned-Over District: The Social and Intellectual History of Enthusiastic Religion in Western New York, 1800–1850*. Ithaca: Cornell University Press, 1950.
Daly, John Patrick. *When Slavery Was Called Freedom: Evangelicalism, Proslavery, and the Causes of the Civil War*. Lexington: University Press of Kentucky, 2002.
Degler, Carl. *At Odds: Women and the Family in America from the Revolution to the Present*. New York: Oxford University Press, 1980.
Demers, Patricia. *Heaven upon Earth: The Form of Moral and Religious Children's Literature to 1850*. Knoxville: University of Tennessee Press, 1993.
Douglas, Ann. *The Feminization of American Culture*. New York: Knopf, 1977.
Edwards, Laura F. *Gendered Strife and Confusion: The Political Culture of Reconstruction*. Urbana: University of Illinois Press, 1997.
———. *Scarlett Doesn't Live Here Anymore: Southern Women in the Civil War Era*. Urbana: University of Illinois Press, 2000.
Eslinger, Ellen. *Citizens of Zion: The Social Origins of Camp Meeting Revivalism*. Knoxville: University of Tennessee Press, 1999.
Farmer, James O. *The Metaphysical Confederacy: James Henley Thornwell and the Synthesis of Southern Values*. Macon, Ga.: Mercer University Press, 1986.
Farnham, Christie Anne. *The Education of the Southern Belle: Higher Education and the Student Socialization in the Antebellum South*. New York: New York University Press, 1994.
Faust, Drew Gilpin. "Altars of Sacrifice: Confederate Women and the Narratives of War." *Journal of American History* 76 (March 1990): 1200–1228.
———. "Christian Soldiers: The Meaning of Revivalism in the Confederate Army." *Journal of Southern History* 53 (February 1987): 63–90.
———. "The Civil War Soldier and the Art of Dying." *Journal of Southern History* 67 (February 2001): 3–39.
———. *Mothers of Invention: Women of the Slaveholding South in the American Civil War*. Chapel Hill: University of North Carolina Press, 1996.
Fox-Genovese, Elizabeth. "Religion in the Lives of Slaveholding Women of the Antebellum South." In *That Gentle Strength: Historical Perspectives on Women in Christianity*, edited by Lynda L. Coon, Katherine J. Haldane, and Elisabeth W. Sommer, 207–29. Charlottesville: University Press of Virginia, 1990.
———. *To Be Worthy of God's Favor: Southern Women's Defense and Critique of Slavery*. Gettysburg, Pa.: Gettysburg College, 1993.
———. *Within the Plantation Household: Black and White Women of the Old South*. Chapel Hill: University of North Carolina Press, 1989.

Friedman, Jean E. *The Enclosed Garden: Women and Community in the Evangelical South, 1830–1900*. Chapel Hill: University of North Carolina Press, 1985.

Friend, Craig Thompson. "Belles, Benefactors, and the Blacksmith's Son: Cyrus Stuart and the Enigma of Southern Gentlemanliness." In *Southern Manhood: Perspectives on Masculinity in the Old South*, ed. Craig Thompson Friend and Lorri Glover, 92–112. Athens: University of Georgia Press, 2004.

Gaustad, Edwin Scott, and Philip L. Barlow. *New Historical Atlas of Religion in North America*. New York: Oxford University Press, 2001.

Gedge, Karen E. *Without Benefit of Clergy: Women and the Pastoral Relationship in Nineteenth-Century American Culture*. New York: Oxford University Press, 2003.

Genovese, Eugene. *A Consuming Fire: The Fall of the Confederacy in the Mind of the White Christian South*. Athens: University of Georgia Press, 1998.

Genovese, Eugene, and Elizabeth Fox-Genovese. "The Religious Ideals of Southern Slave Society." *Georgia Historical Quarterly* 70 (Spring 1986): 1–16.

Ginzberg, Lori D. *Women and the Work of Benevolence: Morality, Politics, and Class in the Nineteenth-Century United States*. New Haven: Yale University Press, 1990.

Glover, Lorri. *All Our Relations: Blood Ties and Emotional Bonds among the Early South Carolina Gentry*. Baltimore: Johns Hopkins University Press, 2000.

———. *Southern Sons: Becoming Men in the New Nation*. Baltimore: Johns Hopkins University Press, 2007.

Goen, C. C. *Broken Churches, Broken Nation: Denominational Schisms and the Coming of the American Civil War*. Macon, Ga.: Mercer University Press, 1985.

Greenberg, Kenneth S. *Honor and Slavery: Lies, Duels, Noses, Masks, Dressing as a Woman, Gifts, Strangers, Humanitarianism, Death, Slave Rebellions, the Proslavery Argument, Baseball, Hunting, and Gambling in the Old South*. Princeton: Princeton University Press, 1996.

Greven, Philip. *The Protestant Temperament: Patterns of Child-Rearing, Religious Experience, and the Self in Early America*. New York: Knopf, 1977.

Hall, David, ed. *Lived Religion in America: Toward a History of Practice*. Princeton: Princeton University Press, 1997.

Halttunen, Karen. *Confidence Men and Painted Women: A Study of Middle-Class Culture in America, 1830–1870*. New Haven: Yale University Press, 1982.

Hambrick-Stowe, Charles E. *Charles G. Finney and the Spirit of American Evangelicalism*. Grand Rapids, Mich.: Eerdmans, 1996.

Harvey, Paul. *Redeeming the South: Religious Cultures and Racial Identities among Southern Baptists, 1865–1925*. Chapel Hill: University of North Carolina Press, 1997.

Hatch, Nathan O. *The Democratization of American Christianity*. New Haven: Yale University Press, 1989.

Heyrman, Christine Leigh. *Southern Cross: The Beginnings of the Bible Belt*. New York: Knopf, 1997.

Higginbotham, Evelyn Brooks. *Righteous Discontent: The Women's Movement in the Black Baptist Church, 1880–1920*. Cambridge: Harvard University Press, 1993.

Hill, Samuel S. *Southern Churches in Crisis Revisited*. Tuscaloosa: University of Alabama Press, 1999.

Holifield, E. Brooks. *The Gentlemen Theologians: American Theology in Southern Culture, 1795–1860*. Durham, N.C.: Duke University Press, 1978.

Isaac, Rhys. *The Transformation of Virginia, 1740–1790*. Chapel Hill: University of North Carolina Press, 1982.

Jabour, Anya. *Marriage in the Early Republic: Elizabeth and William Wirt and the Companionate Ideal*. Baltimore: Johns Hopkins University Press, 1998.

———. *Scarlett's Sisters: Young Women in the Old South*. Chapel Hill: University of North Carolina Press, 2007.

Jeffrey, Julie Roy. "Ministry through Marriage: Methodist Clergy Wives on the Trans-Mississippi Frontier." In *Women in New Worlds: Historical Perspectives on the Wesleyan Tradition*, edited by Hilah F. Thomas and Rosemary Skinner Keller, 143–60. Nashville, Tenn.: Abingdon, 1981.

Junk, Cheryl Fradette. "'Ladies, Arise! The World Has Need of You': Frances Bumpass, Religion, and the Power of the Press, 1851–1860." Ph.D. diss, University of North Carolina at Chapel Hill, 2005.

Kerber, Linda K. "The Republican Mother: Women and the Enlightenment—An American Perspective." *American Quarterly* 28 (Summer 1976): 187–205.

———."Separate Spheres, Female Worlds, Woman's Place: The Rhetoric of Women's History." *Journal of American History* 75 (June 1988): 9–39.

Kett, Joseph F. *Rites of Passage: Adolescence in America, 1790 to the Present*. New York: Basic Books, 1977.

Kierner, Cynthia A. *Beyond the Household: Women's Place in the Early South, 1700–1835*. Ithaca: Cornell University Press, 1998.

———. "Woman's Piety within Patriarchy: The Religious Life of Martha Hancock Wheat of Bedford County." *Virginia Magazine of History and Biography* 100 (1992): 79–98.

Klein, Rachel. *Unification of a Slave State: The Rise of the Planter Class in the South Carolina Backcountry, 1760–1808*. Chapel Hill: University of North Carolina Press, 1990.

Kuhn, Anne L. *The Mother's Role in Childhood Education: New England Concepts, 1830–1860*. New Haven: Yale University Press, 1947.

Kuykendall, John W. *Southern Enterprize: The Work of National Evangelical Societies in the Antebellum South*. Westport, Conn.: Greenwood, 1982.

Laderman, Gary. *Sacred Remains: American Attitudes toward Death, 1799–1883.* New Haven: Yale University Press, 1996.

Laver, Harry S. "Refuge of Manhood: Masculinity and the Militia Experience in Kentucky." In *Southern Manhood: Perspectives on Masculinity in the Old South*, edited by Craig Thompson Friend and Lorri Glover, 1–21. Athens: University of Georgia Press, 2004.

Leavitt, Judith Walzer. *Brought to Bed: Childbearing in America, 1750–1950.* New York: Oxford University Press, 1986.

Lebsock, Suzanne. *The Free Women of Petersburg: Status and Culture in a Southern Town, 1784–1860.* New York: Norton, 1984.

Lewis, Jan. "Motherhood and the Construction of the Male Citizen in the United States, 1750–1850. In *Constructions of the Self*, edited by George Levine, 143–63. New Brunswick, N.J.: Rutgers University Press, 1992.

———. *The Pursuit of Happiness: Family and Values in Jefferson's Virginia.* New York: Cambridge University Press, 1983.

Lindman, Janet Moore. "Acting the Manly Christian: White Evangelical Masculinity in Revolutionary Virginia." *William and Mary Quarterly*, 3rd ser., 57 (April 2000): 393–416.

Loveland, Anne. *Southern Evangelicals and the Social Order, 1800–1860.* Baton Rouge: Louisiana State University Press, 1980.

Lyerly, Cynthia Lynn. *Methodism and the Southern Mind, 1770–1810.* New York: Oxford University Press, 1998.

———. "Women and Southern Religion." In *Religion in the American South: Protestants and Others in History and Culture*, edited by Beth Barton Schweiger and Donald G. Mathews, 247–82. Chapel Hill: University of North Carolina Press, 2004.

Lystra, Karen. *Searching the Heart: Women, Men, and Romantic Love in Nineteenth-Century America.* New York: Oxford University Press, 1989.

MacLeod, Anne Scott. *American Childhood: Essays on Children's Literature of the Nineteenth and Twentieth Centuries.* Athens: University of Georgia Press, 1994.

———. *Moral Tale: Children's Fiction and American Culture, 1820–1860.* Hamden, Conn.: Archon, 1975.

Marshall, Nicholas. "'In the Midst of Life We Are in Death': Affliction and Religion in Antebellum New York." In *Mortal Remains: Death in Early America*, edited by Nancy Isenberg and Andrew Burstein, 176–86. Philadelphia: University of Pennsylvania Press, 2003.

Mathews, Donald G. "'Christianizing the South'—Sketching a Synthesis." In *New Directions in American Religious History*, edited by Harry S. Stout and D. G. Hart, 84–115. New York: Oxford University Press, 1997.

———. *Religion in the Old South*. Chicago: University of Chicago Press, 1977.
———. *Slavery and Methodism: A Chapter in American Morality, 1780–1845*. Princeton: Princeton University Press, 1965.
———. "'We Have Left Undone Those Things Which We Ought to Have Done': Southern Religious History in Retrospect and Prospect." *Church History* 67 (June 1998): 305–25.
McCurry, Stephanie. *Masters of Small Worlds: Yeoman Households, Gender Relations, and the Political Culture of the Antebellum South Carolina Low Country*. New York: Oxford University Press, 1995.
McDannell, Colleen. *The Christian Home in Victorian America, 1840–1900*. Bloomington: Indiana University Press, 1986.
McDannell, Colleen, and Bernhard Lang. *Heaven: A History*. New Haven: Yale University Press, 1988.
McMillen, Sally G. *Motherhood in the Old South: Pregnancy, Childbirth, and Infant Rearing*. Baton Rouge: Louisiana State University Press, 1990.
———. *To Raise Up the South: Sunday Schools in Black and White Churches, 1865–1915*. Baton Rouge: Louisiana State University Press, 2001.
Murray, Gail S. "Rational Thought and Republican Virtues: Children's Literature, 1789–1820." *Journal of the Early Republic* 8 (Summer 1988): 159–77.
Nord, David Paul. *Faith in Reading: Religious Publishing and the Birth of Mass Media in America*. New York: Oxford University Press, 2004.
Oakes, James. *The Ruling Race: A History of American Slaveholders*. New York: Knopf, 1982.
O'Brien, Michael. *Conjectures of Order: Intellectual Life and the American South, 1810–1860*. Chapel Hill: University of North Carolina Press, 2004.
———, ed. *An Evening When Alone: Four Journals of Single Women in the South, 1827–1867*. Charlottesville: University Press of Virginia, 1993.
Orsi, Robert. "Everyday Miracles: The Study of Lived Religion." In *Lived Religion in America: Toward a History of Practice*, edited by David Hall, 3–21. Princeton: Princeton University Press, 1997.
———. *The Madonna of 115th Street: Faith and Community in Italian Harlem, 1880–1950*. New Haven: Yale University Press, 1985.
Owen, Christopher H. *The Sacred Flame of Love: Methodism and Society in Nineteenth-Century Georgia*. Athens: University of Georgia Press, 1998.
Ownby, Ted. "Patriarchy in the World Where There Is No Parting? Power Relations in the Confederate Heaven." In *Southern Families at War: Loyalty and Conflict in the Civil War South*, edited by Catherine Clinton, 229–44. New York: Oxford University Press, 2000.
———. *Subduing Satan: Religion, Recreation, and Manhood in the Rural South, 1865–1920*. Chapel Hill: University of North Carolina Press, 1990.
Pangburn, Richard L. *The Pascal Craddock Mystery*. N.p., 1985.

Payne, Rodger M. *The Self and the Sacred: Conversion and Autobiography in Early American Protestantism*. Knoxville: University of Tennessee Press, 1998.

Pease, Jane H., and William H. Pease. *Ladies, Women, and Wenches: Choice and Constraints in Antebellum Charleston and Boston*. Chapel Hill: University of North Carolina Press, 1990.

Pogue, Blair. "'I Cannot Believe the Gospel That Is So Much Preached': Gender, Belief, and Discipline in Baptist Religious Culture." In *The Buzzel about Kentuck: Settling the Promised Land*, edited by Craig Thompson Friend, 217–42. Lexington: University Press of Kentucky, 1999.

Poole, W. Scott. *Never Surrender: Confederate Memory and Conservatism in the South Carolina Upcountry*. Athens: University of Georgia Press, 2004.

Quist, John W. *Restless Visionaries: The Social Roots of Antebellum Reform in Alabama and Michigan*. Baton Rouge: Louisiana State University Press, 1998.

Rable, George C. *Civil Wars: Women and the Crisis of Southern Nationalism*. Urbana: University of Illinois Press, 1989.

Rambo, Lewis R. *Understanding Religious Conversion*. New Haven: Yale University Press, 1993.

Rankin, Richard. *Ambivalent Churchmen and Evangelical Churchwomen: The Religion of the Episcopal Elite in North Carolina, 1800–1861*. Columbia: University of South Carolina Press, 1993.

Richey, Russell E. *Early American Methodism*. Bloomington: Indiana University Press, 1991.

Rothman, Ellen K. *Hands and Hearts: A History of Courtship in America*. New York: Basic Books, 1984.

Ryan, Mary P. *Cradle of the Middle Class: The Family in Oneida County, New York, 1790–1865*. New York: Cambridge University Press, 1981.

Sandage, Scott. *Born Losers: A History of Failure in America*. Cambridge: Harvard University Press, 2006.

Saum, Lewis O. "Death in the Popular Mind of Pre–Civil War America." In *Death in America*, edited by David Stannard, 30–48. Philadelphia: University of Pennsylvania Press, 1975.

Schneider, A. Gregory. *The Way of the Cross Leads Home: The Domestication of American Methodism*. Bloomington: Indiana University Press, 1993.

Schweiger, Beth Barton. *The Gospel Working Up: Progress and the Pulpit in Nineteenth-Century Virginia*. New York: Oxford University Press, 2000.

———. "Max Weber on Mount Airy; or, Revivals and Social Theory in the Early South." In *Religion in the American South: Protestants and Others in History and Culture*, edited by Beth Barton Schweiger and Donald G. Mathews, 31–66. Chapel Hill: University of North Carolina Press, 2004.

Scott, Anne Firor. *Making the Invisible Woman Visible*. Urbana: University of Illinois Press, 1984.

———. *The Southern Lady: From Pedestal to Politics, 1830–1890.* Chicago: University of Chicago Press, 1970.
Snay, Mitchell. *Gospel of Disunion: Religion and Separation in the Antebellum South.* New York: Cambridge University Press, 1993.
Spangler, Jewell L. "Becoming Baptists: Conversion in Colonial and Early National Virginia." *Journal of Southern History* 67 (May 2001): 243–86.
Sparks, Randy J. *On Jordan's Stormy Banks: Evangelicalism in Mississippi, 1773–1876.* Athens: University of Georgia Press, 1994.
———. "The Southern Way of Death: The Meaning of Death in Antebellum White Evangelical Culture." *Southern Quarterly* 44 (Fall 2006): 32–50.
Startup, Kenneth Moore. *The Root of All Evil: The Protestant Clergy and the Economic Mind of the Old South.* Athens: University of Georgia Press, 1997.
Stein, Stephen J. "Radical Protestantism and Religious Populism." *American Quarterly* 44 (June 1992): 262–70.
Stephenson, William E. "The Davises, the Southalls, and the Founding of Wesleyan College, 1854–1859." *North Carolina Historical Review* 57 (July 1980): 257–79.
Stevenson, Brenda E. *Life in Black and White: Family and Community in the Slave South.* New York: Oxford University Press, 1996.
Stowe, Steven M. *Doctoring the South: Southern Physicians and Everyday Medicine in the Mid–Nineteenth Century.* Chapel Hill: University of North Carolina Press, 2004.
———. *Intimacy and Power in the Old South: Ritual in the Lives of the Planters.* Baltimore: Johns Hopkins University Press, 1987.
———. "The Rhetoric of Authority: The Making of Social Values in Planter Family Correspondence." *Journal of American History* 73 (March 1987): 916–33.
Stowell, Daniel. *Rebuilding Zion: The Religious Reconstruction of the South, 1863–1877.* New York: Oxford University Press, 1998.
Sweet, Leonard I. *Health and Medicine in the Evangelical Tradition: "Not by Might nor Power."* Valley Forge, Pa.: Trinity, 1994.
Walker, Clarence E. *A Rock in a Weary Land: The African Methodist Episcopal Church during the Civil War and Reconstruction.* Baton Rouge: Louisiana State University Press, 1982.
Weiner, Marli F. *Mistresses and Slaves: Plantation Women in South Carolina, 1830–1880.* Urbana: University of Illinois Press, 1997.
Wells, Jonathan Daniel. *The Origins of the Southern Middle Class, 1800–1861.* Chapel Hill: University of North Carolina Press, 2004.
Welter, Barbara. "The Cult of True Womanhood, 1820–1860." *American Quarterly* 18 (Summer 1966): 151–74.
Whites, LeeAnn. *The Civil War as a Crisis in Gender: Augusta, Georgia, 1860–1890.* Athens: University of Georgia Press, 1995.

Wigger, John H. *Taking Heaven by Storm: Methodism and the Rise of Popular Christianity in America*. New York: Oxford University Press, 1998.

Wills, Gary. *Lincoln at Gettysburg: The Words That Remade America*. New York: Touchstone, 1992.

Wills, Gregory A. *Democratic Religion: Freedom, Authority, and Church Discipline in the Baptist South*. New York: Oxford University Press, 1997.

Wilson, Charles Reagan. *Baptized in Blood: The Religion of the Lost Cause, 1865–1920*. Athens: University of Georgia Press, 1980.

Wilson, Mary L., and Florence Wilson. *A History of the First Presbyterian Church, Maysville, Kentucky*. Maysville, Ky.: Session of the First Presbyterian Church, 1950.

Wishy, Bernard. *The Child and the Republic: The Dawn of Modern American Child Nurture*. Philadelphia: University of Pennsylvania Press, 1968.

Wood, Kristin E. *Masterful Women: Slaveholding Widows from the American Revolution through the Civil War*. Chapel Hill: University of North Carolina Press, 2004.

Woodworth, Steven. *While God Is Marching On: The Religious World of Civil War Soldiers*. Lawrence: University Press of Kansas, 2001.

Wyatt-Brown, Bertram. *The Shaping of Southern Culture: Honor, Grace, and War, 1760s–1890s*. Chapel Hill: University of North Carolina Press, 2001.

———. *Southern Honor: Ethics and Behavior in the Old South*. New York: Oxford University Press, 1982.

Young, Jeffrey Robert. *Domesticating Slavery: The Master Class in Georgia and South Carolina, 1670–1837*. Chapel Hill: University of North Carolina Press, 1999.

INDEX

advice literature: child rearing, 149–50, 152–53; courtship, 63–64, 68; death, 203–4; domestic devotion, 49–50; marriage, 99–104

Alabama, 17; Bestor, Eliza, 199–200; Boyd, Mary, 35, 236; Fountain, Lizzie, 236; Fuller, Jones, 31, 77–83, 236; Gaston, Martha, 32, 35, 236; Robertson, J. G., 74–77, 238; Sexton, Ann R., 144–45, 183–84. *See also* Fountain, Sarah Lide; Lide, Maria; Robertson, Frances Bestor

alcohol, 27, 28–29

Andrew, Ann Amelia, 160, 197–98, 204

Andrew, James O.: courtship advice literature, 63–64, 68; death of wife, 204; 1844 schism of Methodist Church, 33; importance of domestic devotion, 49–50; marriage advice literature, 99, 100, 102–3; women's role in church, 160

Andrews, Anna, 170

Andrews, George, 170

angels, 100, 119, 127, 213, 217, 267n21

Arkansas, 35, 55, 191. *See also* Bethell, Mary Jeffreys

Arminianism, 44

Asbury, Francis, 107

Atkinson, W. M., 206

Bailey, Rufus, 49, 99–100, 101–2, 103

Baker, Daniel, 149, 152–53

balls, and dancing, 30–31, 45, 150

bankruptcy, 124, 126, 129, 130, 208, 216

baptism, 35, 41, 192

Baptists: Bestor, Daniel, 150, 238; Bestor, Eliza, 199–200; Coker, Hannah Lide, 188, 190, 235; Edwards, Jane Draughon, 204; Fountain, Lizzie, 236; Gwathmey, Edward, 180, 236; Gwathmey, Eleanor, 180, 236; Lide, David, 185; Lide, Jane, 185; Lide, Mary, 39, 40; Mallary, Charles, 153; Manly, Basil, 149; Robertson, J. G., 74–77, 278. *See also* Fountain, Sarah Lide; Gwathmey, Lucy Ann; Haycraft, Samuel; Lide, Maria; Robertson, Frances Bestor

Bascom, Henry B., 197

Beale, Anne. *See* Davis, Anne Beale

Bestor, Daniel, 150, 238

Bestor, Eliza, 199–200

Bethell, Mary Jeffreys: Bible reading, 55; childbirth, 51, 140, 141; child rearing, 158–59; clergy, critique of, 36; conversion, 167, 172; dancing and novel reading, 30–31; death, 192–93, 200, 201, 210–11, 222; family profile, 233; heaven, 215; illness, 191; journal keeping and religious life, 52, 57; possible relocation from North Carolina to Arkansas, 35, 191; slaves, 172, 173, 201, 225

Bible: reading, 31, 53–55, 127
—references: 1 Chronicles, 273n80; Colossians, 100, 101; 1 Corinthians, 267n21; 2 Corinthians, 266n10, 280n2; Ephesians, 65, 255n11; Hebrews, 253n66, 267n24; Hosea, 277n41; Job, 45; John, 36, 242n11, 249n30; Luke, 122, 253n68, 257n42; Matthew, 111, 257n42, 262n30; Proverbs, 99, 257n44, 261n9, 267n29;

Bible (*continued*)
    Psalms, 54, 276n20; 1 Thessalonians, 277n40
Blackwell, J. Davenport, 227
Blatterman, Ellen Collins, 129–30, 195
Boles, John, 14
Boyd, Jane, 27
Boyd, J. M. C., 35–36
Boyd, Mary, 35, 236
Breck, R. L., 230
Brodrick, Fanny: controversy over Rev. McElroy, 46–48; death of Alfred Cox, 195; Maysville during Civil War, 229, 230; support of Mary Collins, 130
Brown, Hu, 45, 46, 187, 193
Brown, Mary, 139–40; domestic devotion, 52, 57; family profile, 233; heaven, 215; illness, 188; Sabbath, 34
Bumpass, Frances: Bible reading, 54–55; black clergymen, 32, 40; camp meetings, 38; childbirth, 139; child rearing, 153–54; conversion, 167; death, 192, 223; family profile, 233; Lord's Supper, 36; marriage, 106–7; slave management, 172–73; teaching, 109
Bumpass, Sidney: childhood, 155; child rearing, 154, 171; conversion, 39, 167, 168, 171; family profile, 233; marriage, 106–7, 109; piety of blacks, 40–41; preaching, 251n48

Calvinism, 8, 44, 106
camp meetings. *See* revivals
Cane Ridge, 14
Capers, William, 33
Cashin, Joan, 243n22
Catholicism, 213
celibacy, 66, 93
cemeteries, 215–16, 279n57

Centre College, 56
childbirth: dedication of newborn sons to ministry, 141; dedication of newborns to God, 139–40; pregnancy rates for southern women, 110, 135, 138; religious trial, 51, 138–39; women's moral authority, 140–42. *See also* child rearing
child rearing: advice literature, 149–50, 152–53; daughters, 157–59, 180–81; domestic religious training, 151–52; environment, 135–36; expectations of parents, 137–38, 141–42; fathers, 151, 154, 174–75, 226–27; infant mortality, 142–47, 184, 196–97, 266n9; mothers' diminishing authority, 174–81; mothers' influence, reflections on, 150–51; mothers' spiritual accountability, 151–52, 154, 168–70, 171–72, 226; punishment, 153–54, 227; sons, 155–57, 174–80, 226–27, 269n40. *See also* childbirth
Chowan Baptist Female Institute, 161, 166, 186
Christ. *See* Jesus Christ, invocations of
Christmas, 113
church: collections and fund-raisers, 26–27, 43–44; courts, 228, 259n2; membership, 2–3, 241n2; minister's wife's role, 107–9, 261n18; worship, 34–49 passim. *See also* clergy; clergymen; revivals
circus, 45
Civil War: childbirth, 141; Confederate Army, 217–19, 229–30; courtship, 91; Maysville Presbyterian Church, 230–31; piety and family separation, 50, 141, 172, 216; piety and slavery's demise, 223–26; wartime destruction of South, 229
class meetings, 41–42, 151

clergy: congregations during Civil War, 229–30; discipline, 228; ecumenical efforts, 39; emancipation of slaves, 225–26; female fund-raising, 43–44; marital stress, 110–20, 227; personal piety, 119–20; preaching, 35–40, 42; Presbyterian schism, 208–10; professionalization, 249n32, 259n5; publishing efforts, 127, 203, 208–10; relationship with laity, 34–49 passim, 107–9; work, 18, 45, 112–18, 114–15, 225, 227. *See also* advice literature; preaching; revivals; slavery, and conflict between southern and northern clergymen

clergymen: Asbury, Francis, 107; Atkinson, W. M., 206; Baker, Daniel, 149, 152–53; Bascom, Henry B., 197; Breck, R. L., 230; Capers, William, 33; Colton, Simeon, 208–9; Early, John, 53, 235; Lacy, Drury, 205, 206; Mallary, Charles, 153; Manly, Basil, 149; Moore, T. V. 149–50; Plumer, William, 208–9; Terry, 32; Winans, William, 171–72. *See also* Bailey, Rufus; Bumpass, Sidney; Davis, Joseph; Douglass, James Walter; Poulton, John; Wills, Richard; Wills, William

Clinton, Catherine, 15–16, 245n36

Coker, Hannah Lide, 188, 190, 235

Collins, Kate, 129, 156

Collins, Lewis: church elder, 47–48; family profile, 234; parenting, 156

Collins, Mary Cox: child rearing, 144, 146–47, 154, 229–30; family profile, 233–34; marriage, 124–31, 229–30, 231, 232

Collins, Peers, 156–57

Collins, Richard: child rearing, 151, 154, 155–56, 158; controversy with Rev. McElroy, 47–48; conversion, 169–70; death, 195; domestic devotion, 56, 216–17; family profile, 233–34; marriage, 124–31, 216–17, 223

colonization of African Americans, 108

Colton, Simeon, 208–9

coming of age: conversion, 147, 168–72, 270–71n56; courtship, 62–67; parenting, 174–81. *See also* child rearing

communion, 36, 213

condolence. *See* correspondence

conversion: coming of age, 147, 168–72, 270–71n56; deathbed, 193, 195–96, 203–4; demographics, 271n61; evangelical identity, 7–8, 21–25; first-generation evangelicals, 167–68; lifelong process, 10, 23, 38, 96, 211; marriage, 120–23; revivals, 21–22, 37–39; stages, 166, 269n49, 271n62. *See also* Wesleyan Female College

correspondence: children, 128–29; condolence, 205–8; courtship, 69, 71–74, 79–81, 83–87, 89–90; deathbed attendants, 183–84, 191–202; heaven, 213–14; marriage, 110–20, 124–25, 216–17; primary source, 11, 242n21, 270n52; Sabbath, 31–32, 124–25

cosmology, 7, 188

Cotten, Spencer, 66–67

cotton, 78, 117

courtship: alienation between sexes, 62–67, 71–73, 76–77, 79–81; class, 254n4; clergy, 68–70, 72–73, 91–93, 228; doubts and melancholy, 72, 76–77, 81, 87; family approval, 69–70, 73, 75–76, 77–79, 81–82, 88; gossip, 256n30; in-laws, 68–70; marital expectations, 83–87, 89–90; masculinity, 66–67, 83–84, 254n5, 257n45; prayer, 70, 75–76, 80; professional concerns, 72–73, 78, 91–93;

courtship (*continued*)
  widowers, 68–70, 75. See also coming of age; honor
Cox, Alfred, 195
Cox, George, 195–96
Cox, Lizzie: child rearing, 146–47; controversy with Rev. McElroy, 47–48; conversion, 169–70; death of Alfred Cox, 195; Maysville Presbyterian Church during war, 230
Cox, Mary. *See* Collins, Mary Cox
Craddock, Mary: deathbed work, 194, 222; death of slaves, 201; domestic devotion, 1–2, 18–19, 51, 121–23; family profile, 234; illness, 190; Sunday school, 160
Crawford, Jane, 214
cult of domesticity, 134. *See also* courtship; marriage; spheres, separate
Cumberland Presbyterians. *See* Craddock, Mary
Cumming, John, 162

dancing, 30–31, 45, 150
Davis, Anne Beale: camp meetings, 37, 38; childbirth, 139, 141; child rearing, 133–34, 141, 142, 151–52, 153, 155, 175–78; conversion, 167, 169, 170; courtship, 69–70; deathbed work, 196; diary and correspondence, purposes of, 12, 243n12; family profile, 234–35; illness, 145, 186, 187, 188; Lord's Supper, 36; marriage, 111–15, 222; nonevangelicals, critique of, 27, 29–30; Wesleyan Female College, 108–9, 160–65, 175, 270n52
Davis, Joseph: child rearing, 151, 152, 155, 176–78, 189; conversion, 170; courtship, 69–70; family profile, 234–35; illness, 187, 189; marriage, 111–15, 222; Methodist mission to slaves, 33; Wesleyan Female College, 109, 161–62, 163, 165–66
Davis, Robert, 69–70, 133, 155, 163, 176–78
Davisson, Elizabeth, 72, 227–29, 231, 238
Davisson, Frederick, 73
Davisson, Rosannah. *See* Poulton, Rosannah Davisson
death: of children, 142–47, 153, 210–11; and conversion, 195–96, 203–4; fear of sudden, 192–93; of impious, 29, 192, 195–96; mourning, 205–12; and obituaries, 203, 227; of slaves, 200–202; of spouse, 205–10, 227–28. *See also* deathbed; Good Death
deathbed: female caregivers' improvisation, 194–98; men's correspondence, 193; women's correspondence, 184–85, 191–202. *See* also death; Good Death
Delaware, 30
devil, 40, 53, 198, 210, 230; hell, 123, 213
domestic worship, 49–58 passim; courtship, 90; illness, 190; marriage, 124–25; Sabbath, 6, 50–57. *See also* Bible; child rearing; prayer, occasions for
Dorland, Juliette, 146–47
Douglass, Frances: child rearing, 158, 178–80; deathbed work, 194; domestic devotion, 50; family profile, 235; Finney, Charles G., views on, 46; husband's death, 205–9, 223; husband's ministry, 107–8, 205–7; husband's sermons, 208–9; illness, 186, 190; marriage, 105–6, 109, 119–20, 178, 222; slaves, 13, 173; son's piety, 26–27
Douglass, James Walter: birth of granddaughter, 140; conversion

298 Index

process, 23; death, 193, 205–9; domestic devotion, 50; family profile, 235; illness, 189–90; marriage, 105–6, 109, 119–20, 222; proselytizing, 26, 37–38; relationship with stepson, 178–80, 189–90; slaves, 13
Douglass, Mary. *See* Gray, Mary Douglass
dreams, 69–70, 74, 143, 155
dueling, 29–30

Earle, Thomas, 203–4
Early, Elizabeth Brown: child rearing, 142–43; domestic devotion, 53; family profile, 235; slaves, 173–74
Early, John: domestic devotion, 53; family profile, 235
Early, Mary Virginia: child rearing, 142–43; domestic devotion, 53; family profile, 235
Edwards, Jane Draughon, 204
emancipation. *See* slaves
Eslinger, Ellen, 37
evangelical: definition, 7–8, 241n2, 242n11; estimates of members and adherents, 2–3; identity versus non-evangelical southerners, 25–34. *See also individual denominations*

family, separation of, 110–11, 113–14, 115–16, 126–28, 190–91, 213–14, 217. *See also* child rearing; courtship; death; marriage
Finney, Charles G., 44, 46
Florida, 117, 215. *See also* Whitaker, Cary
Fountain, Lizzie, 236
Fountain, Sarah Lide: camp meetings, 37; child rearing, 171; cross-denominational church attendance, 39; dancing, views on, 31; family profile, 235; illness, 188, 190–91; slaves, 201–2
Fox-Genovese, Elizabeth, 12, 15–16, 245n39
Friedman, Jean E., 16
Fuller, Anna Thomas: childbirth, 142; conversion, 169; courtship, 77–83; death, 213; family profile, 236
Fuller, Jones: courtship, 77–83; dancing, views on, 31; family profile, 236
fund-raising, 26–27, 43–44, 208

Gaston, Martha, 32, 35, 236
gender: child rearing, 134–35; coming of age, 174–81; courtship, 62–67, 83–84; death, 193–94; southern household, 14–18, 24–25. *See also* honor; spheres, separate
Georgia, 40, 100–101
Gilchrist, Julia, 194
Gillett, Ruby, 144
Good Death: deathbed, 191–202 passim; definition, 183–84, 192–93; failure, 192, 198–200. *See also* correspondence; death
Gray, Mary Douglass: angels, 212; Bible reading, 54; cemeteries, 215; death, 211–12, 222; evangelical identity, 28; family profile, 235; fund-raising, 44; illness, 190; preaching, critique of, 43
Gwathmey, Edward, 180, 236
Gwathmey, Eleanor (Nelly), 180, 236
Gwathmey, Lucy Ann: Bible reading, 54; child rearing, 134, 180–81; family profile, 236

Harewell, Elizabeth, 207
Harrison, Cary, 144
Haycraft, Samuel, 39, 54, 57, 157, 237

heaven: family reunification, 169, 213–14; judgment, 101, 123; Lord's Supper, 36; materialism, 27; notions, 214–15, 278n53; reward for faithful, 159, 160; slaves, 216, 217–19
Heiskell, Eliza, 35, 159, 200, 214
Heiskell, Susan. *See* McCampbell, Susan Heiskell
Heiskell, T. H., 88
hell, 123, 213. *See also* devil
Henderson, Samuel, Jr., 167, 171, 200–201, 224, 237
Heyrman, Christine Leigh, 4, 17, 160
Hill, C. A., 64–66
Hill, Sam, 14
Hill, W. W., 168
Holy Ghost. *See* Holy Spirit
Holy Spirit: conversion, 35, 38, 147, 163, 170; domestic devotion, 55, 211; evangelical identity, 7; Lord's Supper, 36
honor: coming of age, 269nn40–41; courtship, 61–62, 84; marriage, 110, 118, 263n43; profession, 127–28
Hort, Mary, 36, 45, 237

illness: children, 142, 145, 172, 159–60; clergy, 115, 116;; minister's wife, 106; religious purpose, 185–91; slaves, 121–22, 172, 187, 201–2
—specific ailments: bilious fever, 142, 187; cholera, 115, 197; dropsy, 198; scarlet fever, 145, 189

Jesus Christ, invocations of: death, 195, 197, 210, 215; faith in God, 113, 145, 146, 170; justice, 122; model for personal piety, 23, 52, 159; sin, 30, 36
journals, and religious purpose, 11, 56–57

Kentucky: Blatterman, Ellen Collins, 129–30, 195; Collins, Kate, 129, 156; Collins, Lewis, 47–48, 156, 234; Cox, Alfred, 195; Cox, George, 195–96. *See also* Brodrick, Fanny; Collins, Mary Cox; Collins, Richard; Cox, Lizzie; Craddock, Mary; Haycraft, Samuel

Lacy, Drury, 205, 206
laity. *See* clergy
Lanco (black clergyman), 40
Lang, Bernhard, 212
Leland, Eliza, 25, 40, 53–54, 169, 171, 237–38
Leland, Eugenia, 55, 147, 160, 225, 238
Lewis, Jan, 10
Lide, David, 185
Lide, Jane, 185
Lide, Maria: alcohol consumption, views on, 28; camp meetings, 38–39; church fund-raisers, 44; correspondence, 190; family profile, 236; marriage, 61; preaching, reaction to, 40; Sunday school teaching, 159
Lide, Mary, 39, 40
Lincoln, Nancy, 35, 200
literature, advice. *See* advice literature
lived religion, 8–9, 242n12
Lord's Supper, 36, 213
love feast, 107
Loveland, Anne, 247n9
Lyerly, Cynthia Lynn, 14, 17, 21–22, 97, 211
Lystra, Karen, 60

Mallary, Charles, 153
Manly, Basil, 149
marriage: advice literature, 99–104; clergymen, 91–93, 104–20, 226–27; companionate notions, 253nn1–2;

conflict over separation, 109–20, 125–31; correspondence, 110–20, 126–31, 226–27; evangelical expectations, 86–89, 90, 92–93, 104–7, 110–14, 120, 121, 124–25; impious husbands, 120–23; widowers, 68, 74–77, 227–29; widows, 82–83, 115. *See also* death

materialism, evangelical critique of, 27–28, 127–28

Mathews, Donald, 7, 232, 244n28

Maysville Eagle, 47

Maysville Presbyterian Church, 46–48, 230–31

McCampbell, Susan Heiskell, 30, 84–87, 95–96, 222, 238

McCampbell, William: alcohol, views on, 27; courtship, 84–87, 96–97; dancing, views on, 30; domestic devotion, 56, 222; family profile, 238; letter writing on Sabbath, 31–32; Lord's Supper, 36; mother's influence on piety, 150–51; preaching, reaction to, 39–40, 42–43

McCurry, Stephanie, 16

McDannell, Colleen, 24, 212

McElroy, William T., 46–48

McMillen, Sally, 135

Men. *See* child rearing; clergy; coming of age; death; gender; honor; marriage

Methodist Protestants: Harewell, Elizabeth, 207; Hill, W. W., 168; Wills, George, 217–19, 239; Wills, Mary, 157, 158. *See also* Wills, Anna Whitaker; Wills, Richard; Wills, William

Methodists: Andrew, Ann Amelia, 160, 197–98, 204; Andrews, Anna, 170; Andrews, George, 170; Bascom, Henry, B., 197; Early, John, 53, 235; Fuller, Jones, 31, 77–83, 236; Gillett,

Ruby, 144; Sexton, Ann R., 144–45, 183–84; Winans, William, 171–72. *See also* Andrew, James O.; Bethell, Mary Jeffreys; Bumpass, Frances; Bumpass, Sidney; Davis, Anne Beale; Davis, Joseph; Early, Elizabeth Brown; Fuller, Anna Thomas; Henderson, Samuel, Jr.; Poulton, John; Poulton, Rosannah Davisson; Thomas, Ann

missions: fund-raising for, 27, 43, 44, 152; to slaves, 32–33; to Texas, 153

Mississippi, 229; Earle, Thomas, 203–4; Winans, William, 171–72

Missouri, 115, 127. *See also* Gray, Mary Douglass

Moore, T. V., 149–50

More, Sir Thomas, 89

motherhood. *See* child rearing

mourning, 205–12. *See also* death; heaven

North Carolina: Harewell, Elizabeth, 207; Hill, W. W., 168; Thomas, George, 77, 78–79, 82; Wills, Mary, 157, 158. *See also* Bethell, Mary Jeffreys; Bumpass, Frances; Bumpass, Sidney; Davis, Anne Beale; Davis, Joseph; Douglass, Frances; Douglass, James Walter; Fuller, Anna Thomas; Thomas, Ann; Wills, Anna Whitaker; Wills, Richard; Wills, William

novels, 31

obituaries. *See* death

Orsi, Robert, 9, 242nn11–12

Ownby, Ted, 216

parenting. *See* child rearing

Pattie, William, 228

Payne, Rodger M., 166

Index 301

physicians, 140–41, 187, 215
Plumer, E. G., 205
Plumer, William 208–9
Potter, H., 205, 206
Poulton, John: child rearing, 226–27; church tribunals, 13; courtship, 70–74; family profile, 38; marriage, 223, 226–27, 231–32
Poulton, Rosannah Davisson: child rearing, 226–27; courtship, 70–74; death, 227–29; family profile, 238; marriage, 226–27, 231–32
prayer, occasions for: affliction, 52–53, 126, 190, 191, 206, 209; conversion, 38, 121, 172, 173; courtship, 70, 75–76, 80; deathbed, 194; domestic devotion, 31, 34, 55–57, 102, 124, 204; parenting, 176; separation of loved ones, 50, 124, 276n18; thanksgiving, 141, 191
preaching: clergy, 32, 37–39, 41–42, 43; community piety gauge, 34–36, 41–42; laity's views, 39–40, 42–46, 47–48, 72, 114, 116, 180, 225
pregnancy, rates of, for southern women, 110, 135, 138. *See also* child rearing
Presbyterians: Baker, Daniel, 149, 152–53; Blatterman, Ellen Collins, 129–30, 195; Boyd, Jane, 27; Boyd, J. M. C., 35–36; Boyd, Mary, 35, 236; Collins, Kate, 129, 156; Cox, Alfred, 195; Cox, George, 195–96; Crawford, Jane, 214; Dorland, Juliette, 146–47; Earle, Thomas, 203–4; Gaston, Martha, 32, 35, 236; Moore, T. V., 89; Plumer, E. G., 205; Plumer, William, 208–9; Reid, Ann, 206–7; Rogers, E. P., 100–101. *See also* Bailey, Rufus; Brodrick, Fanny; Brown, Hu; Brown, Mary; Collins, Mary Cox; Collins, Richard; Cox, Lizzie; Douglass, Frances; Douglass, James Walter; Finney, Charles G.; Gray, Mary Douglass; McCampbell, Susan Heiskell; Verstille, Charlotte
Princeton, 179, 189
proselytizing, 26
protracted meetings. *See* revivals

Quist, John W., 17

Randolph-Macon College, 175, 235
reform movements: alcohol, 28–29; dancing, 30–31, 44–45, 150; dueling, 29–30; northern, 22; Sabbath keeping, 25–27, 31–32, 124–25; southern, 15, 17–18
Reid, Ann, 206–7
revivals: camp meetings, 21–22, 36–39, 167–68; clerical dissatisfaction with turnout, 41–42; conversion, 21–22, 37–38, 116, 173; protracted meetings, 22, 250nn37–38; spiritual renewal for laity, 38–39; Wesleyan Female College, 160–66
Robertson, Frances Bestor: cemetery, 215–16; courtship, 74–77; funeral, 199; mother's deathbed, 199; mother's influence on piety, 150; preaching, reaction to, 43
Robertson, J. G., 74–77, 238
Rogers, E. P., 100–101

Sabbath: community piety gauge, 25–27; letter writing, 31–32, 124–25; Sunday school, 149, 159–60
saints, 213
Sanitary Fair, 129

Satan. *See* devil
Schneider, A. Gregory, 10, 24, 185, 247n7
Schweiger, Beth Barton 6, 18
Scott, Anne Firor, 15, 243n21, 245n37
Scripture. *See* Bible
separate spheres. *See* spheres, separate
separation, family. *See* family, separation of
sermons. *See* preaching
Sexton, Ann R., 144–45, 183–84
sickness. *See* illness
sins: alcohol, 27, 28–29; dancing, 30–31, 44–45, 150; dueling, 29–30; Sabbath breaking, 25–27, 31–32, 124–25
slavery, and conflict between southern and northern clergymen, 14, 18, 22, 33, 44, 46, 112. *See also* slaves
slaves: Civil War, 223–26; clergy, 32, 40; conversion, 167, 173–74; death, 200–202; emancipation, 223–26, 280n5; heaven, 216, 218–19; illness, 121–22, 172, 187, 201–2; infrequency in white letters and diaries, 13; insurrection, rumored, 41; management by white women, 117, 121–22, 173–74; missionary work, 32–33; religious obligations of masters, 121–22, 172–74, 200–202. *See also* slavery, and conflict between southern and northern clergymen
South Carolina, 40, 117, 145; Boyd, Jane, 27; Coker, Hannah Lide, 188, 190, 235; Crawford, Jane, 214; Edwards, Jane Draughon, 204; Gilchrist, Julia, 194; Hort, Mary, 36, 45, 237. *See also* Brown, Mary; Leland, Eliza; Leland, Eugenia; Verstille, Charlotte

spheres, separate: child rearing, 149–50; northern and southern notions, 4, 96–99, 134–35; southern clergy's definition, 99–103
Stowe, Steven, 98, 187
Sunday. *See* Sabbath
Sunday school, 149, 159–60

Taylor, Henry, 26, 178–80, 186, 189–90, 207, 235
temperance, 27
Tennessee: Heiskell, T. H., 88; Lincoln, Nancy, 35, 200. *See also* Brown, Hu; Heiskell, Eliza; Henderson, Samuel, Jr.; McCampbell, Susan Heiskell; McCampbell, William
Terry (black preacher), 32
Texas, 27, 153
Thomas, Ann: child rearing, 144–45; conversion, 169; courtship of daughter, 77–83; family profile, 236; heaven, 213; preaching, reaction to, 44
Thomas, Anna. *See* Fuller, Anna Thomas
Thomas, Gabriel, 77–78
Thomas, George, 77, 78–79, 82
Turner, Nat, 32, 41

Uncle Charles (Mallary), 153
Union Army, 224
University of Virginia, 180

Verstille, Charlotte, 27, 40, 190, 198–99, 239
Vesey, Denmark, 32
Virginia: Davisson, Frederick, 73; Early, John, 53, 235; Gwathmey, Edward, 180, 236; Gwathmey, Eleanor, 180, 236; Moore, T. V., 149–50; Plumer, E. G., 205; Reid, Ann,

Virginia (*continued*) 206–7; Thomas, Gabriel, 77–78. *See also* Davisson, Elizabeth; Early, Elizabeth Brown; Gwathmey, Lucy Ann; Poulton, John; Poulton, Rosannah Davisson

Voices of the Dead (Cumming), 162

Washington (slave), 173, 218–19
Washington, D.C., 29
Watchman of the South, 208–9
Wesleyan Female College, 108–9, 160–66, 175, 222, 235
Whitaker, Anna. *See* Wills, Anna Whitaker
Whitaker, Cary, 117, 157, 193, 198–99, 203, 215
Whitaker, George, 38, 43, 187
widowers, 68, 74–77, 227–29
widows, 82–83, 115
Wills, Anna Whitaker: coming of age, 157; family profile, 239; management of slaves, 116–17; marriage, 110–11, 112; parenting, 137–38

Wills, George, 217–29, 239
Wills, Mary, 157, 158
Wills, Richard: child rearing, 157, 158; family profile, 239; prayer and family separation, 50, 222; preaching, 42; slaves, 173
Wills, William: conversion, 167–68; courtship: 66–67; death, 203, 207, 217–19; family profile, 239; marriage, 110–11, 112; *Methodist Protestant* newspaper, 203; obituaries, 203; parenting, 137–38, 217–19; prayer and family separation, 50; revivals, 41; slavery, 225
Winans, William, and family, 171–72
women: academy training, 100, 160–66; fertility rates, 265–66n9; fund-raising for churches and clergy, 26–27, 43–44, 208; Sunday school, 149, 159–60. *See also* child rearing; marriage; spheres, separate
Wyatt-Brown, Bertram, 28

www.ingramcontent.com/pod-product-compliance
Lightning Source LLC
Chambersburg PA
CBHW011754220426
43672CB00018B/2962